WITHDRAWN

The Writings of Pilgram Marpeck

CLASSICS OF THE RADICAL REFORMATION is an English language series of Anabaptist and Free Church documents translated and annotated under the direction of the Institute of Mennonite Studies, which is the research agency of the Associated Mennonite Biblical Seminaries, 3003 Benham Avenue, Elkhart, Indiana 46514, and published by the Mennonite Publishing House, Scottdale, Pennsylvania 15683.

1. *The Legacy of Michael Sattler.* Translated and edited by John H. Yoder, 1973.

2. *The Writings of Pilgram Marpeck.* Translated and edited by William Klassen and Walter Klaassen, 1978.

The Writings of Pilgram Marpeck

Translated and edited by

William Klassen

and

Walter Klaassen

1978

herald press kitchener, ont.
scottdale, pa.

Canadian Cataloguing in Publication Data
Marbeck, Pilgram, d. 1556.
   The writings of Pilgram Marpeck

(Classics of the radical Reformation; 2)

Bibliography: p.
Includes indexes.
ISBN 0-8361-1205-9

1. Anabaptist-Collected works. 2. Theology-
Collected works-16th century. I. Klassen,
William, 1930-   II. Klaassen, Walter, 1926-
III. Title. IV. Series.

BX4946.M313 1978   284'.3   C77-001640-5

Photos by Jan Gleysteen, from the Anabaptist Heritage Collection, Scottdale, Pennsylvania.

THE WRITINGS OF PILGRAM MARPECK
Copyright © 1978 by Herald Press, Kitchener, Ont. N2G 4M5
   Published simultaneously in the United States by
   Herald Press, Scottdale, Pa. 15683
Library of Congress Catalog Card Number: 77-87419
International Standard Book Number: 0-8361-1205-9
Printed in the United States of America
Book designed by Jan Gleysteen

10 9 8 7 6 5 4 3 2 1

To

Jarold Tyler Klassen
Kirsten Leigh Klassen
Karis Lynee Klassen

Frank Frederick Klaassen
Michael Walter Klaassen
Philip John Klaassen

General Editors' Preface

For many years a committee of European and North American historians known as the *Täuferaktenkommission* has published source materials of the sixteenth-century Anabaptist movement under the title *Quellen zur Geschichte der Täufer*. Published in the original languages, these sources continue to be the indispensable tool of the specialist. However, except for the available translations of the writings of Menno Simons, Dirk Philips, and Peter Riedemann, the collection prepared by Professor George H. Williams of Harvard University for the *Library of Christian Classics*, Volume 25, the century-old version of the *Martyrs Mirror*, and a handful of other documents, these materials remain largely inaccessible to the growing number of students, churchmen, and lay readers who do not read German or Dutch. The recent initiation of the *Documents in Free Church History* paperback series, edited by Franklin H. Littell and George H. Williams, adds significantly to the primary literature available in the English language.

The intention of the *Classics of the Radical Reformation* series is to make available in the English language a scholarly and critical edition of the primary works of major Anabaptist and Free Church writers of the sixteenth and seventeenth centuries. It has not been considered essential to the purposes of the series to include every known document of the writers under translation and, unless some contribution can be made to a fuller understanding of the substance of the text, it is not deemed essential to pursue at length critical textual issues. Those scholars interested in the details will, in any case, turn to the original language text. Where a choice had to be made between clarity and awkward literalism, the translators were encouraged to favor readability but without compromising the text.

The first volume in this series, *The Legacy of Michael Sattler* by John H. Yoder, appeared in 1973. Translators and editors are at work on subsequent volumes in the series. The next volume will likely be the letters of Conrad Grebel, prepared by Leland Harder. Additional books will include the writings of Andreas Karlstadt, Dirk Philips, Balthasar Hubmaier, and the Czech Reformation.

It is appropriate to express appreciation to the translators-editors who so willingly volunteered their services. Both the counsel of the North American Committee for the Documentation of Free Church Origins (NACDFCO), of which Professor George H. Williams serves as chairman, Professor Walter Klaassen as secretary, and Professor Franklin H. Littell as treasurer, and the help and encouragement of the late Professor Carl S. Meyer, director of the Foundation for Reformation Research, St. Louis, Missouri, are gratefully acknowledged. Finally, without the commitment to the work of the church on the part of Mennonite Publishing House and its willingness to include the series in its responsibility to society and the church, this venture could not have been undertaken.

The Institute of Mennonite Studies
Cornelius J. Dyck, Director
Walter Klaassen, Associate Editor

Preface

The important place which Pilgram Marpeck occupies in the development of South European Anabaptism has long been recognized. During the past two decades, new manuscripts have been discovered and various monographs and books published. At the same time, Marpeck's two earliest books were located, and the opinion was often expressed that these materials should be made available in English not only for scholars but also for other readers.

Both of the principal translators of these writings initially worked independently on issues which led us to explore more fully Marpeck's thought. After having completed one phase of our research, we agreed that the major writings of Marpeck deserved translation. This interest was communicated to the directors of the Institute of Mennonite Studies whose support and encouragement enabled us to embark on the project. Over the past few years, while our translation was in progress, it became evident that others were working along similar lines. Two such endeavors, one by Henry Klaassen and the other by Claude Foster, were translations of one of Marpeck's works of 1531. However, although they were available to us, neither one of these translations was used in this edition. The Confession of 1532, together with Bucer's reply to it, has appeared in a modern edition prepared by Manfred Krebs and Hans Georg Rott. It was felt best to present Marpeck's text without Bucer's answer for the English readers. The translation of the letters owes much to Heinold Fast's willingness to provide us with a typescript of the text which he is preparing in German.

It was decided not to incorporate the longest work of Marpeck: the Reply of 1544. Many of the issues dealt with in that work are covered in the shorter treatises and, since the present volume is already quite extensive, it was felt wise to leave the translation of the longer work to others. From the *Testamentserleutterung*, we have provided only the Preface, since the other materials in it consist primarily of scriptural quotations which would lose much of their point through translation. The verse designations have been added to most of the biblical chapter references without special notation in each instance.

We wish to acknowledge our gratitude to the two students who gave assistance in the final phases of the project, Victor Kliewer and Garry Enns. We are also grateful to Jeannine Watson, Pauline Bauman, and Lorena Reimer who typed the final draft. Richard Bailey prepared the indices. Without the financial assistance provided by the Canada Council, the Research Board of the University of Manitoba, and the Institute of Mennonite Studies, this work could never have been completed. The personal interest and encouragement given to the project by John Howard Yoder and Cornelius J. Dyck are also gratefully acknowledged. Anne Boeckx gave much time to make the whole more readable by painstaking editing.

We dedicate this book to our children for, like many others, they will most likely never read Marpeck in German. May they, as they read him in English, come to their own conclusions about whether the faith for which he lived also has meaning for them in their lives.

William Klassen
Department of Religion, University of Manitoba

Walter Klaassen
Conrad Grebel College, University of Waterloo
April, 1977

10

Abbreviations

ARG	*Archiv für Reformationsgeschichte*
BM	British Museum
Cant.	Song of Solomon
CS	*Corpus Schwenckfeldianorum*
Covenant	*Covenant and Community, The Life . . . of Pilgram Marpeck*, by W. Klassen
CV	*Clare Verantwortung*, Marpeck booklet of 1531
KU	*Klarer vast nützlicher Unterricht*, booklet by Marpeck of 1531
Krebs-Rott	Manfred Krebs and Hans Georg Rott, ed. *Elsass I and II: Stadt Strassburg, 1522-1535* in *Quellen zur Geschichte der Täufer*, Vol. VII and VIII (Heidelberg, 1959, 1960)
ME	*Mennonite Encyclopedia*, edited by Harold S. Bender et al, 4 vols.
MQR	*Mennonite Quarterly Review*
RGG	*Die Religion in Geschichte und Gegenwart*
TB	*Taufbüchlein*, 1542, also known as *Vermanung* and here translated into English as *Admonition*
TE	*Testamentserleutterung*, concordance compiled by the Marpeck group but not translated here
QGT	*Quellen zur Geschichte der Täufer*
V	*Verantwortung*, lengthy book produced by the Marpeck group in reply to Caspar Schwenckfeld, 1544 and later; not translated here

Contents

Introduction

The Life and Thought of Pilgram Marpeck[1]

A. *Early Life in the Tirol*

Pilgram Marpeck was born in the city of Rattenberg, in the Tirol, some time during the last decade of the fifteenth century. His family was prominent in the civic affairs of the city and all evidence indicates that Marpeck received a good education. With his wife, he joined the guild of mining workers of Rattenberg on February 26, 1520. He was an active member of his community, serving first as a member of the Lower Council after February 24, 1523, and then as a member of the Upper Council after June 11, 1525.[2]

Rattenberg, along with other cities and villages in the Tirol, had been directly affected by the movements toward reform in the sixteenth century. Revolutionary figures like Michael Gaismair had been able to attract and hold the support of the peasants in their efforts to achieve some measure of economic and political justice. In this program religion and politics were closely related. Like Gaismair, Marpeck belonged to the class that had both wealth and the power that comes with wealth, but most important he, like Gaismair, had certain skills which were eagerly sought after by the ruling authorities.

Evidence of the high confidence placed in him by the rulers appears from his appointment as mining magistrate on April 20, 1525, which provided him with an annual wage of sixty-five pounds a year, effective on June 7. Thus while the Anabaptist movement was beginning in Switzerland Marpeck began a professional career which would save his life later when he had become an Anabaptist and such a status was punishable by death.

The office of mining magistrate goes back to the thirteenth century. Around the year 1477 there were only five mining directors in Europe. If there were only five in the 1520s then it is apparent that Marpeck had one of the most demanding and responsible positions in the Tirol. As mining magistrate he was commissioned to administer the laws regulating mining in a given region. Accordingly he was empowered to lease new mining strips or pits, and to settle legal controversies related to mining. In addition he was charged with the responsibility of arbitrating legal controversies concerning the personal affairs of the people working in the mining and smelting locations. The only exceptions were criminal offenses which the local regent alone could adjudicate. Not only did Marpeck supervise the adherence to the mining code; he was also charged with the responsibility of collecting the revenues pertaining to the mining royalty which went to the royal treasury and of keeping accurate records. Certain assistants were assigned to him for this latter task.[3]

Marpeck acquired his skill in the silver mines of the Inn Valley at Rattenberg and Schwaz, Tirol, some fifty miles from Innsbruck. As early as the year 1520 he appears in the records as a merchant who delivered ore from Schneeberg and Gossensass to Kitzbühel on February 20. He held the appointment as mining magistrate from April 20, 1525, until his release on January 28, 1528.[4] Most likely he sought the release because of the pressures being put on him to police the miners and their religious affiliations.

There appears to have been a substantial group of miners in the Inn Valley who were receptive to and eventually became adherents of the Anabaptist movement. Evidence indicates that a mining magistrate refused to divulge the names of these Anabaptists and it is assumed that this refers to Marpeck himself.[5]

His work as mining magistrate thus brought Marpeck into direct contact with Anabaptists. Although it is not possible to

Rattenberg on the Inn, birthplace of mining magistrate Pilgram Marpeck.

Kitzbühel, where Marpeck delivered silver ore.

pinpoint the exact date when Anabaptists first appeared in the Inn Valley or when Marpeck first heard of them, Ferdinand I called attention to their presence in the Tirol as early as April 24, 1527.[6] It is apparent from his mandate of April 1, 1528, that their presence in the valley had reached such proportions that the Archduke felt compelled to order that they be rooted out in his domains.

In spite of such measures and some undertaken earlier, men like Leonhard Schiemer and Hans Schlaffer had been active in the Inn Valley and had given forceful leadership to the groups of Anabaptists living there. Schiemer had been arrested in Rattenberg on November 25, 1527, a day after his arrival, and he was beheaded on January 14, 1528, two weeks before Marpeck resigned as mining magistrate. On December 5, 1527, Hans Schlaffer along with Leonard Schiemer had been arrested and both were beheaded on February 4, 1528, at Schwaz, about ten miles from Rattenberg. Both Schlaffer and Schiemer wrote inspiring treatises for their churches while imprisoned and some of these writings appear within the Marpeck circle in the *Kunstbuch* collected by Jörg Maler. It is inconceivable that Marpeck was unaware of these men and the developments within the Anabaptist communities in the Inn Valley. His later writings reflect the influence of their thought and his immediate circle collected some of the writings of Schlaffer and Schiemer along with those of Marpeck himself.

It has been suggested that Marpeck was baptized sometime during the year 1527 and since the Anabaptists may have been active in the Inn Valley as early as May 1526, this is possible. The Rattenberg congregation had seventy-one martyrs—more, as far as is known, than any other congregation. Neighboring Schwaz had about twenty martyrs and it is said that at one time 800 of its 1200 population were Anabaptists.[7]

The first evidence of Marpeck's reluctance to comply with the royal order of December 14, 1527, comes from a letter written by Bartlme Anngst, magistrate at Rattenberg, on January 1, 1528. That letter is not available but the government reply of January 3 says:

In the Upper Inn Valley two thirds of the population held Anabaptist beliefs during the late 1520s.

Your writing of January 1 in which you indicate that the mining magistrate of Rattenberg desires to be excused from apprehending the Anabaptists (den widerteuffern nachzustellen) because it does not fit his office or that it would not be suitable for the mining magistrate to collaborate thus with the provincial magistrate is hereby acknowledged, along with the rest of what he wrote.

His royal highness, however, advises us that those who are now in charge of the leases at Schwaz who have opened and read your writing have today written here that they wish to deal seriously with him (the mining magistrate) in these matters pertaining to the Anabaptists, together with you, in obedience to the royal mandates and orders. We are also confident that if he is negligent in these matters you know what is best and what is necessary. If he persists in not following the royal prescription you must report it to us.[8]

Seven days later a letter from the same source to the same destination deals with Marpeck's reluctance and apparently requests additional manpower to deal with it. The reply reads in part:

19

. . . we inform you that you have no need for additional protection beyond the court servant whom you have as part of your office. For when the assistants of our Royal Highness negotiated with the same mining magistrate recently in Schwaz, he promised seriously to prevent the mining workers under his jurisdiction from practicing rebaptism and to observe scrupulously the mandates of his Royal Highness.

In addition where it would come to his attention that one or more of the same miners was not living according to the mandates and adhering to the new sect of the Anabaptists he would indicate this to you, capture them, not hinder you, but upon your request to proceed with the appropriate punishment against such and to provide you with help and support. Therefore as the need requires you should feel free to ask the mining magistrate for assistance.[9]

It would appear from this that Marpeck had reconsidered and that he had decided to collaborate with the authorities in the apprehension of the Anabaptists. Eighteen days later (January 28, 1528) a letter came from Ferdinand I himself indicating that he has honored Marpeck's request to be relieved of his duties and instructing him to give the responsibility over to another. He requests that all books be handed over to his successor and that as soon as the latter has taken the oath of office Marpeck is free of all responsibility.[10] This letter is addressed to Marpeck himself.

No further word about Marpeck appears in the sources except that a request is made that some of the goods confiscated from him may be used for the care of his adopted children (July 31, 1529). Is it possible that Marpeck changed his mind about his attitudes toward the Anabaptists? If so, what happened? Possibly the execution of Leonhard Schiemer on January 15, 1528, just five days after the letter indicating a change in Marpeck's position was written caused him to change his mind and give all of his allegiance to the new cause. In any case after this there appears to be no vacillation whatever in his resolve to be an Anabaptist.

Marpeck received whatever education he had in Rattenberg. The evidence that he had a good knowledge of Latin which has often been cited (most recently by Harold Bender) is not persuasive. It is quite likely that the evidence of Latinisms in his writings comes in fact from the Bible that he used, for most of his Latinisms appear in biblical quotations.

Marpeck was a man of some wealth, for he lent Ferdinand I 1,000 guilders in 1528 at 5 percent interest[11] and his estate including two houses which he owned as early as 1524 was evaluated at 3,500 guilders when it was confiscated in 1528. He had easy access to members of the nobility including particularly Countess Helena von Freyberg whose castle was near Kitzbühel but he was himself not a member of the nobility.

It is not known how soon after January 28, 1528, Marpeck left Rattenberg but we do know that he relinquished his office as mining magistrate soon after that date. It is quite likely that he was one of a number who left Rattenberg secretly after the death of Schiemer.[12] One of the factors that may have influenced his leaving was the escalation of repressive mandates against the Anabaptists. Archduke Ferdinand's mandate of April 1, 1528, sought to root out all Anabaptism in his domains, particularly the Tirol. It called for the execution of all Anabaptists in prison if they would not recant and of all those who had been preaching and baptizing whether they recanted or not, and also the confiscation of all their property.[13] The vitality of the Anabaptist movement in the Inn Valley undoubtedly contributed to Marpeck's conversion to Anabaptism. For about a generation Anabaptism was more prominent in this area than was Lutheranism which never became strong. In some cases early Lutheranism merged almost imperceptively into Anabaptism. It is impossible to estimate how many Anabaptists were in the Tirol before 1550 but there is constant evidence that their presence threatened the authorities. Marpeck's successor, W. Schönmann, was warned on February 9, 1528, by the authorities to be vigilant, for among the miners they were gaining the upper hand.[14] Bender cites a report which claims that there were 12,000 Anabaptists in the Tirol before 1550 including over 600 martyrs. This is obviously exaggerated.[15]

Marpeck does tell us a little about his own spiritual pilgrimage in his discussion with Bucer at Strasbourg on December

The Mandate of Ferdinand I, dated April 1, 1528, called for the execution of all Anabaptists and confiscation of their property.

9, 1531. The Council Minutes report: "Since now in the whole world the fight and quarrel is only about the faith, he had been brought to this faith by his God-fearing parents in the papacy. Then he found a notable contradiction in the writings. For since at those places where one preached the gospel the Lutheran way, in which also fleshly liberty was felt, this made him hesitant, since he could not find peace in it" (the Lutheran gospel). Later he says that he had accepted baptism for a testimony of obedience of faith.[16] Possibly Marpeck was first a Lutheran but in any case he rejected Lutheranism because of the "fleshly liberty" he saw in it. Anabaptism was for him a commitment of faith and probably this is the reason why he joined himself to an Anabaptist congregation.

Whatever may be the origin of Marpeck's own Anabaptist convictions and whoever may have been the instrument responsible for bringing him to this conviction, it is apparent that from the earliest days of his public work he was committed to a separation of church and state. The state could expect him to carry out his work as a mining magistrate diligently and efficiently. The state, however, could not dictate on matters of faith and when it attempted to do so Marpeck refused to comply with the wishes of the state. After he became an Anabaptist he could no longer live in his own town and once he left, his property and all his assets were confiscated by the state.

B. The Years in Strasbourg 1528-1532

From Rattenberg Marpeck went to live in the city of Strasbourg. Strasbourg was a city of great religious tolerance and Marpeck had his most important encounters with the Reformers in that city, particularly with Bucer. There is evidence to indicate that this encounter was fruitful for the development of both Marpeck's and Bucer's theology and it can be described as "futile"[17] only if one assumes that it was the intention in these encounters to make each accept the other's position.

We know nothing about the movements of Marpeck from January 28, 1528, until his purchase of citizenship at Strasbourg on September 19 of that year although it can be assumed that he moved directly from Rattenberg to Strasbourg. The mandate of Archduke Ferdinand of April 1, 1528, led to the practice of widespread recantations but Marpeck took another alternative. If he had preached and baptized he would have lost his life and property, so he abandoned his property and his position and went to take up his life elsewhere. Some earlier historians have reported that he went first to Augsburg and others that he went to the martyr synod in Augsburg; some have claimed that he went to Moravia. No evidence has been found for any of these assertions.[18] It may well be that he stopped in Augsburg on his way to Strasbourg only to discover that the Anabaptist congregation there was being severely persecuted. As he arrived in Strasbourg in 1528 he may have encountered other Anabaptists who had moved there from Augsburg. At any rate it was reported in the spring of 1529 that some 100 Anabaptists who had been in Augsburg were now living in Strasbourg.[19]

Whatever the route may have been which Marpeck took to get there, upon his arrival at Strasbourg he took a public position as an Anabaptist. The Strasbourg archives record that he became a citizen on September 19, 1528, and slightly more than a month later, October 22, it is indicated that meetings of the Anabaptists were being held in his house.[20] He and other Anabaptist leaders were given a hearing before the City Council. At this hearing Marpeck reported among other things that the Strasbourg congregation had set up a poor fund to care for needy members, since the city poor fund was overtaxed. It was also reported to the Council that Marpeck and Fridolin Meiger, a city notary, gave refuge to Anabaptists and attended a meeting in Staden, a suburb of Strasbourg. At this meeting plans were made to "establish a constitution as to how the brethren were to manage the affairs of their sect."[21] Other records indicate that in early 1529 meetings were held in at least three other homes besides Marpeck's. In 1531 meetings were being held Sundays in Ostwald near Strasbourg where a large group had gathered, as reported to the City Council on April 17. Some years later the number of Anabaptists was reported at 300 and more. According to Claus-Peter Clasen, the number of converts in the Rhine Valley from 1525 to 1549 was 885.[22]

From September 1528 to January 1532, Marpeck's name appears frequently in the records of the city archives as the outstanding Anabaptist leader. On December 18, 1531, reference is made to Pilgram Marpeck, the Anabaptist leader. It is clear that Marpeck exercises the role of leadership both in his writings, as spokesman of the Anabaptists, and even as one who baptizes other people upon authorization of the church in Moravia.[23]

The historical situation into which Marpeck came is important. The Anabaptist movement was perhaps strongest in the city of Strasbourg. Here the authorities tolerated the Anabaptists, engaged in hours of dialogue and debate with them, and to this city came every stripe of Anabaptist. For Marpeck himself his stay in Strasbourg meant the first major arena in which he did battle with the Reform theologians. At the same time he saw the

Marpeck fled to Strasbourg where he became a citizen on September 19, 1528.

factors which threatened the healthy establishment of the Anabaptist movement and took pen in hand to begin to describe what the Anabaptists believed. During this period he published two booklets (in 1531) and followed these booklets with considerable writing in December 1531 and January 1532 as he left the city of Strasbourg. During the time that the evangelical Reformation was gradually beginning to displace Catholicism in the city, when the evangelical preachers Martin Bucer, Wolfgang Capito, Caspar Hedio, and Matthäus Zell were striving to find a way of relating church and state, and of expressing the values of the Protestant Reformation, the Anabaptist movement also moved into Strasbourg.

The City Council moved slowly and deliberately and did not abolish the mass until February 28, 1529. This policy of gradualism together with the commitment to a merging of the City Council with the ministerial alliance received the severest criticism by Marpeck. During this time also came the conflict within Protestantism between the Lutherans and the Zwinglians over the nature of the sacrament of the Lord's Supper in which Strasbourg took the Zwinglians' side. Marpeck's writings very clearly indicate that he stands between the extremes of those positions. It has been suggested that the preparation for the Augsburg Diet of 1530 was one of the occasions when little energy and time was left for Anabaptist problems on the part of the Strasbourg authorities and consequently the Anabaptists were relatively undisturbed.[24]

The few mandates which the City Council enacted against the Anabaptists were relatively lax; the one of July 27, 1527, specified no particular or severe punishment and was not rigorously enforced. Sometimes Anabaptists were imprisoned for brief periods of time but in no case did Strasbourg ever execute an Anabaptist or anyone else for his faith. Censorship did exist sometimes, but for the most part the leaders, particularly Capito, were friendly toward the Anabaptists, and Katharine Zell, the wife of one of the preachers, ultimately became an adherent of Schwenckfeld. The ministers in the city had a great deal of difficulty agreeing among themselves on their attitude toward the

Jacob Sturm, the tolerant mayor of Strasbourg and chancellor of the university.

Martin Bucer, a leader in the Strasbourg reformation, highly respected Marpeck even as he disagreed with him.

Anabaptists. It was not until 1534 when they replied to the writings of Rothmann that some of the preachers took a united stand toward Anabaptist teachings. Bucer agreed with the Anabaptists on the necessity for church discipline and in other areas shows their influence.

Even though a more severe mandate was issued on March 3, 1534, in an attempt to crush the movement, it was never successful. Harold Bender is correct when he writes "Pilgram Marpeck's four years of relatively unhindered life and ministry as an Anabaptist leader in Strasbourg can thus be explained in the light of a very complex and fluid religious situation in the city, and the tolerance of Burgomaster Sturm and the Council, as well as by the need for his engineering services."[25]

The catalogue of Anabaptists who appeared in Strasbourg includes the most illustrious leaders and reads like a *Who's Who* of the first few years of the movement. Balthasar Hubmaier, the Anabaptist theologian from Waldshut, arrived first in July 1525. In the following year a series of leaders arrived, often remaining a relatively short time and often being imprisoned.

In March of 1526, William Reublin, the real founder of Anabaptism in Strasbourg, arrived but left after a few months,

27

returning again in the spring of 1528 shortly before Marpeck arrived. He was in prison in Strasbourg from October 1528 until his release in late 1529. That a warm relationship existed between these two men would seem to be evident from the letter that Reublin wrote to Marpeck when he was in Austerlitz in Moravia on January 26, 1531. Others who visited Strasbourg were Jakob Gross, April 1526; Michael Sattler, November to December 1526; and Leupold Scharnschlager, arriving perhaps by late 1527 and remaining till 1534. This was perhaps the first occasion when Marpeck and Scharnschlager got together and they formed a strong relationship. During the 1540s both wrote letters to the Strasbourg brotherhood thus continuing to influence its development. The Anabaptist intellectual Hans Denck spent about a month in Strasbourg in 1526.

More significant for Marpeck's own intellectual development was the arrival in Strasbourg of the Spiritualist Hans Bünderlin in March 1529. During his stay in Strasbourg he published several booklets which were read in the group meetings. He called a meeting on March 16, 1529, at the home of Klaus Bruch apparently in an effort to take Anabaptism into a different type of emphasis. Bünderlin's books emphasized the characteristic points of view of the Spiritualists who rejected all external form and stressed the cultivation of the spirit. Marpeck himself saw Bünderlin's presence as threatening the integrity and stability of the group of Anabaptists with whom he was working and therefore it was against Bünderlin that he wrote his first book.[26]

During this time also, Marpeck must have met Caspar Schwenckfeld for the first time. In later correspondence the Silesian nobleman speaks of the warm relationship they had in the early years and laments the fact that it no longer exists.[27] But Marpeck was able to see the difference between his position and Schwenckfeld's and opted for a more activistic understanding of the Christian way. He knew that the quietism of Schwenckfeld would ultimately lead to a conventicle type of religion with its emphasis on the cultivation of inner piety. While Marpeck stressed the cultivation of inner devotion he also affirmed that all

28

genuine inner devotion must lead to external attestation.[28] The contexts in which Schwenckfeld and Marpeck met is not known but it is clear that Marpeck's other booklet (1531) was addressed against him even though the sharpest engagements they had in the realm of literary arguments came after 1542.[29]

The name of Sebastian Franck was known to Marpeck, for it appears several times in Marpeck's writings. He used Franck's historical chronicles in his discussions of the history of baptism, but it is apparent that Marpeck did not accept Franck's theological position since he tends to lump Franck into the same category as Schwenckfeld and Bünderlin. There is no evidence that the two ever met.

Marpeck's daily life was spent in the services of the city and the wider community. As civic engineer it was his responsibility to provide the city of Strasbourg with wood and perhaps also to engage in other types of engineering work. He also appears to have had major responsibility in the area of mining since the mining director in the Tirol as well as in Alsace had supervision over the use of the forest. He had been given more authority over the forest through the reforms of Maximilian earlier in the sixteenth century. The regulations on cutting, transporting, and selling the wood were complex and it was the mining superintendent's responsibility to see that they were observed. The fact that Alsace followed Tirol in these regulations may have made it much easier for Marpeck to find employment there. It is also possible that he was instrumental in bringing some of the tried methods from Tirol and instituting them in the Alsace. At least one historian of the mining methods of that time concludes "the mining operations in Alsace took from the slightly earlier and more highly developed mining techniques of the Tirol the basic outlines of a unified mining law and also their engineering methods."[30]

Marpeck built a water system for the city and wood-floating flumes in the surrounding valleys whereby Strasbourg which lacked wood attained access to the wealth of the forests surrounding it. The Kinzig River was used to bring the wood down into Strasbourg.

The Black Forest across the Rhine from Strasbourg.

Pilgram Marpeck built channel dams to float Black Forest lumber down the Kinzig River.

Every indication exists that Marpeck was an honored member of the Strasbourg religious community, so important in Reformation times. The leading ministers Capito and Bucer spoke highly of him and Bucer said that the Anabaptists honored him like a god. Bucer recognized his achievements and their value to the city. He admitted on August 19, 1531, in a letter to Margaret Blaurer that Marpeck and his wife were unblamable, adding,

> concerning Pilgram you should know that he is a very stiff-necked heretic. He has left much but he cannot leave himself. The more serious vices he has beautifully put aside but the spiritual vices stick to him all the more. I write this in the presence of the Lord. I am not uninclined either to him or any other man upon the earth being as I am a grave sinner myself. But the church is the bride of Christ. . . . The premature or untimely strictness and a giving up of temporal goods which God has given us is an ancient bait of Satan which profits no one. With this he has lured all heretics from the beginning of time even to the time of Paul which is seen clearly in Colossians and Corinthians. Surely Christ is a more transparent common Saviour than that these people could have his spirit. The years of his own acceptance and presumed knowledge of this Pilgram stand up quite straight. Apart from that he and his wife have a nice unblameable conduct. The fish hook must have its bait.[31]

Because Marpeck staunchly opposed infant baptism which he called a sacrifice to Moloch and continued to encourage Anabaptists not to take the oath of allegiance to the city of Strasbourg and because of his prominence in the city, Bucer charged him with misleading the citizens and he was imprisoned on October 22 along with a number of other Anabaptist leaders including Reublin.[32] At that time he appears to have come out of prison through the intercession of Capito who at least came to visit him in prison.[33]

His period of freedom was of short duration for at the beginning of December 1531 events in Marpeck's confrontation with the authorities of Strasbourg took on a faster tempo. Throughout this period Bucer's correspondence indicated that Marpeck continued to baptize and to teach against the oath, and at one time he even expressed the concern that Marpeck would soon be banished from the city.[34] During the beginning of this month Marpeck requested the Council's permission for a public debate with the clergy but this request was not granted. Instead on December 9 he and Bucer had a debate behind closed doors in which a number of points were discussed including Marpeck's own religious pilgrimage, his position on Anabaptism, his position on the Old Testament, and his position on the freedom of the pulpit in terms of its relationship to the princes and the city authorities. As long as the gospel was not freely preached, Marpeck argued, it could not bear fruit because it was really under the protection of princes and rulers.

This initial discussion took place on a Saturday, December 9, and the Council did not take a position in the matter. Rather they agreed that on Wednesday, December 13, Marpeck and the ministers would be allowed more fully to pursue these questions and the leader was instructed to tell Marpeck that he could bring along two more of his followers. First the leader was to inquire, however, if they knew something and if so to listen to them; if they did not know anything he was to tell them to keep their mouths shut.[35]

On the same day Bucer wrote a letter to Ambrosius Blaurer reporting on the conversations that he had had with Marpeck. The report from the City Council notes indicates that on December 13 Marpeck along with another Anabaptist engaged in debate with the four preachers—most likely Bucer, Capito, Hedio, and Zell.

The reports indicate that after the enumeration of the articles a request was made for clarification from the ministers on their differentiation between the Old and the New Testament. Apparently the same group continued during the afternoon since two entries are listed under that date. In this notation it is indicated that no public disputation was permitted even though the preachers had consistently been asking for such. This is the first indication that the ministers were pressing for an open discussion with the Anabaptists for the sake of the common ordinary man. They insisted that it would be easier to refute the public impressions that there was disunity in the Council and also to keep public order. On the following Monday, December 18, the Council took action and continued the debate with him which concluded in the decision to banish him from Strasbourg. To be sure this banishment was apparently given unenthusiastically. They preferred to have him stay on but he could only stay on if he gave up his views on baptism, discontinued his teaching about war and the oath to protect the city, and desisted from working for his own church or fellowship. They recognized that God had given him "many magnificent gifts and that in many ways he is a diligent man; that he possesses a diligent, good zeal but it is precisely these gifts which caused many good hearts to be led into error and kept there through his forthrightness."[36]

With the banishment of Marpeck a legal reality he requested a longer period of time in an intervention to the Council on December 19. He asked for three or four weeks in which to sell some property and to settle his accounts. This request was granted. At the same time on December 20, Marpeck made it clear that he would submit to the order of the Council, dependent, however, upon the way in which his spirit led him. This depended upon God's own command, for Marpeck did not seek any change with regard to their decision relating to his worldly life. He expressed gratitude for the fatherly way in which they related to him.[37]

The Council gave him another fourteen days but he was to abstain from all preaching and public assembly, otherwise he would not be tolerated. The Council further expressed reservations about the fact that he was making public statements that his position could not be refuted and that answers were not given to his questions. Later, on about January 2, 1532, he was given an additional fourteen days.

Some time after the middle of December 1531 Bucer wrote an apology for infant baptism which he gave to Marpeck. It may have come as a response to Marpeck's request but in any case indicates the desire of these two to continue the discussion of the issues that divided them. During the beginning of January 1532 Marpeck wrote his confession of faith which appears in translation in this volume.[38] A detailed rebuttal to that confession of faith is found in the Strasbourg archives written by Bucer himself. It appears together with the text of the confession in the collection of sources from the city of Strasbourg.

One of the striking tributes to the level of their discussion came when Marpeck sent this confession to the Strasbourg Council. He appended a letter to it in which he described his own reactions to the discussions. Although this is not dated it must have been written around January 12, 1532. It is also presented in translation in this volume.[39]

As a tribute to the caliber of this discussion the report in the Council minutes shortly after the presentation of these letters indicates that before Marpeck left Strasbourg the ministers once more appealed in a written intervention to the Council for a debate with Marpeck. It begins,

> Pilgram, fourteen days ago desired that we should briefly give him the bases from Scriptures for our practice of infant baptism in an attempt to see whether God could grant us the opportunity of agreeing in our interpretation of Scripture. We did this and when he received this from us he asked us whether we would permit him to write his interpretation over against our articles, in those instances where he was not satisfied with them. We asked him to do this. The day before yesterday he came to us and said that he had written rebuttals to our statements but desired that one or six of us would meet him and discuss these articles in an attempt more clearly to illuminate the truth. We are quite happy to let this happen. Therefore we told him that he should ask whomever he wished, then we would request that some of the church leaders discuss this matter with him in a very friendly manner to his heart's content. He responded to this that while he was quite prepared to do this he would prefer not to do it behind the backs of the lords of this council and therefore requested that we ask your graces for permission and we promised him that we would do so. Therefore we would ask our gracious lords humbly and submissively to help us to have such a discussion, for Pilgram complains that he has not much time left. We believe that it would further the common discussion with the Anabaptists. In such discussion we would eagerly desire to have Pilgram. In matters of faith above all we must act in accordance with God's Word. Please give us an answer. Written on Friday the 12th of January, 1532.[40]

The Council granted the request and Marpeck was given

another opportunity for a discussion. Additional time was given him so that he could remain for this occasion. However, the Council minutes indicate that eventually because he did preach in a conventicle he was banned by virtue of the previous decree and both the city and jurisdiction of the city were forbidden to him.[41]

From an external point of view these four years in Strasbourg were exceedingly important for Marpeck. All the major positions with which he would debate throughout his years as a leader of the Anabaptist movement were represented in Strasbourg, and Marpeck's own position was increasingly more fully developed in these years. Again from an external point of view, they marked the time when he began his publishing career. The report of the censors of the year 1532 indicate their suspicion that in the year 1531 Marpeck published two books.

Both of these books were intended to clarify the relationship between the Anabaptist movement and the Spiritualists. Spiritualism had been strongly represented in the Strasbourg area and the two people to whom Marpeck addressed his booklets were Hans Bünderlin and Caspar Schwenckfeld. Bünderlin's influence among the Anabaptists is evident from the fact that the records show that he and Reublin were at the same meeting in March 1529 in which discussions were held about how the Anabaptists were to order their common life.

However long Bünderlin may have stayed in Strasbourg his influence continued on and his position was shared to a large extent by Sebastian Franck. While in Strasbourg Bünderlin attempted to unify the movement and rally it around his position. Even in his later books Marpeck refers on occasion to Bünderlin's people[42] which may indicate that they were an independent group in Strasbourg although more likely it simply refers to a type of person who was attracted to the Anabaptists and the high place given to the spiritual dimension but who went on to deny the material aspects. Schwenckfeld tells us that about this time the Anabaptists called Bünderlin a squabbler.[43]

Marpeck's own writings indicate that he saw the Strasbourg period of his life as a watershed in the development of the movement. Writing in 1542 in the Preface of the major confessional volume—the *Admonition*—the writers refer to the manifold splits and sects which are a terrible error and which have been accomplished through the guile of the serpent "now into the twelfth year." This is doubtless a reference to the turmoil of the Strasbourg period and the context makes it clear that the sects are being caused by false apostles of Satan within the true members of the covenant, that is, among the Anabaptists themselves. The situation did not stabilize with the departure of Marpeck and it seems that Moravian authorities instituted a temporary suspension of baptisms until the matter was clarified.[44]

The most important dialogue of this period, however, was undertaken with Martin Bucer. The various elements of these discussions have not yet been isolated but it is clear that two of the best spirits of the Reformation met each other on these issues. The major issue from Marpeck's point of view was the question of the separation of church and state. This is an issue which comes from his early encounter with the Anabaptist movement; no more in Strasbourg than in Tirol would he permit the authorities to prescribe the shape of his Christian faith. The theological issue of the relation of the old and the new covenant, the central concern of Bucer's theology, also became a major point of discussion. Marpeck himself was just beginning to develop this aspect of his thought and Bucer was a major impetus to him in this matter. It is quite likely that the Sabbatarian influence found in Strasbourg also contributed to it. There is, however, no doubt that the major impetus for this element in Marpeck's thought came from Bucer whose discussion of infant baptism and its relation to circumcision made it essential for Marpeck to take a look at the whole question of the relation of the Old Testament to the New. Four years later the Münsterites would raise the same question in a different context, but Bucer was the first to put it on Marpeck's agenda.

C. Switzerland and Moravia: "The Obscure Years" 1532-1544

We have no direct knowledge of where Marpeck spent these years. No trace of his movements from Strasbourg has been left

Following his exile from Strasbourg, Marpeck worked for some time in Sankt Gallen.

although his correspondence with the Strasbourg church indicates that he maintained his connections with them as a leader and as a co-worker of Leupold Scharnschlager.[45]

Some traces of his activities during these years do appear, however, in the court records of Switzerland and in some of the later correspondence. The suggestion that he returned to his homeland, the Tirol, has to be rejected for lack of evidence. If he did return it could only have been for a very brief visit. It is possible that the Moravian church asked him to serve as an itinerant apostle for them. At the same time he did not neglect his skills as an engineer, for there is evidence that he built a fulling mill at Sankt Gallen. He was also most likely responsible for building a water conduit around the mountains for the rapidly expanding weavers' craft in that city. One of Marpeck's closest associates in Augsburg in the later years, Jörg Maler, for fourteen years a weaver in Sankt Gallen and Appenzell, became acquainted with Marpeck there through his genius at construction. He told the Augsburg Council in the forties that he had first learned to know Marpeck through his fame "as the builder of the fulling mill at St. Gall."[46] No doubt Marpeck developed a close relationship with Maler, for throughout the ensuing years there is cor-

37

respondence between these two men. On one occasion Marpeck writes in an attempt to iron out the difficulties between Maler and the Swiss; the very preservation of the Marpeck letters by Maler indicates his esteem for Marpeck.

Other letters written from Switzerland include one written on December 21, 1540, from the Grisons to Strasbourg and one to the brethren in Württemberg on August 15, 1544, from Chur. It would seem most logical, therefore, to assume that Marpeck spent most of his time from 1532 to 1544 somewhere in Switzerland where contacts with Scharnschlager made it possible for the two to undertake the revised translation of the *Bekentnisse*. According to the Hutterite Chronicle he undertook a trip to Moravia in 1541 in an attempt to unite the Anabaptists there with the South German and the Swiss groups.[47] A letter written by Schwenckfeld on May 27, 1543, complains that he does not know where to find Marpeck and this also indicates that his dwelling place in these years was not fixed.[48]

He did work for the unity of the church and continued to correspond with individuals and with the congregations. The abhorrence of church splits which had turned him away from Lutheranism because Lutheranism had its own split from Zwinglianism was carried over now into the Anabaptist movement. One of his basic concerns was to bring together the badly splintered Anabaptist movement. This concern for a united church based upon a united confession resulted in the publication of a major work in 1542. This book here translated under the title *Admonition* was a major factor in the attempt to draw the Anabaptists together around a common confession. At the same time it opened up a new era of debate and disagreement with the Schwenckfeld circle.

In many ways these twelve years are the most obscure and hidden ones of Marpeck's life. At no place does his name appear in the Council minutes of any of the towns where he had lived or where he was known. Perhaps the shock of the events at Münster in 1534 was so great that he could not involve himself directly in the Anabaptist movement again in a public way until the early forties.

Marpeck spent the final years of his life in Augsburg. The Fuggerei, the world's first socialized housing development, was only 25 years old when he arrived.

D. Marpeck's Life in Augsburg, 1544-1556

We can pick up the thread of Marpeck's life with certainty again in 1544 when he was engaged by the city of Augsburg as an engineer. City records indicate that Augsburg's chronic wood shortage led the city fathers to hire Marpeck and to ask him also to repair the water flumes of the city. Although in earlier days Augsburg had made every effort to eradicate the Anabaptists, by 1544 the religious concerns of the City Council lay elsewhere. To be sure Marpeck's efforts in the religious realm were neither curtailed nor were they unnoticed by the civic authorities. Caspar Schwenckfeld expressed surprise that the authorities did not apprehend him. He wrote in 1551:

Leonhard Hieber writes that Marpeck had to present his book to the Council. I did not think that he was there any more. Thus it sometimes happens when it is to your benefit, otherwise the Council would hardly give him shelter.[49]

Thus Marpeck spent his time working as an engineer for the city and at the same time giving considerable time to the writing of books for the Anabaptists and also writing epistles to the churches.

Robert Friedmann was the first to suggest that for Marpeck to survive in Augsburg he must have made certain compromises with the authorities and indeed become a quietist in religious matters. But there is no evidence that he changed his style in any direct way. It is quite possible that he was more circumspect in the way that he raised the issues and the years had undoubtedly left their mark. In one of his letters written during this time he indicated the importance of not necessarily irritating the state, for unnecessary provocation may lead to bad results. The most important factor, however, was undoubtedly the changed political and religious scene in Augsburg.

Neither Augsburg nor Marpeck had any desire to pursue the questions of the earlier years as long as Marpeck rendered faithful service to Augsburg and as long as the city allowed him the privilege of publishing and working within the Anabaptist movement. The uneasiness of the Augsburg authorities with this is evident from the warnings sent him on at least four occasions. The first of these warnings came on July 16, 1545. He had been doing work occasionally for the city during the year 1544 and on May 12, 1545, the city contractors were instructed to approach Marpeck in regard to a longer term appointment. According to J. C. Wenger he was paid sixty-five florins in coins on July 18, 1545, and hired for one year. Accordingly the first warning he received to desist from Anabaptist ways must have come two days before he entered into a longer term contract with the city.[50]

For the next five years, however, he was not bothered by the authorities and his salary from 1546 on was set as 150 florins annually.

The warnings from the City Council on the various dates are:

July 16, 1545: An order that the mayor was asked to relay to Marpeck that Marpeck was to desist from working among the Anabaptists.

May 6, 1550: A report had been given that Marpeck had published the concordance known as the *Testamentserleutterung* and the Council wished to have verification of this report.

September 26, 1553: An investigation was ordered on whether Marpeck was holding meetings, and if so that he be punished.

September 25, 1554: "If it is ascertained that Pilgram is spreading his error, he shall be told to go and spend his penny elsewhere."

Two years later, Marpeck died a natural death. While the exact date is not known it must have occurred some time in the last part of the year. The Augsburg records indicate that under the payment of his wages of December 16, 1556, are written the words, "Is dead."[51]

The life of Marpeck thus spans the first few years of the movement and the second generation of the Anabaptist movement. His contacts were with the Reformed parties, and with all stripes of Anabaptists. He was engaged in the major theological struggles of the Anabaptists for an identity which would be built upon the Bible and have a concrete meaning for the world in which they lived. His own life, lived intensely at the points where the secular world and the life of faith intersected, and the writings which emerged from that life, are a legacy to Anabaptism and to the whole free church movement today. Only as we study that life and the thought of this man can we assess what contribution if any he has made to man's search for truth and justice.

I

A Clear Refutation

Introduction

An anonymous tract attributed to Hans Bünderlin,[1] the *Clare Verantwortung* of 1531 was first discovered by Hans Hillerbrand,[2] who suspected it originated in Anabaptist circles.

The date 1531 is printed in the book, but the place of publication and the authorship have to be determined by internal evidence and by the report of the Strasbourg censors, who suspected Marpeck of publishing two booklets in 1531.

The book discusses three subjects. It deals first with the assertion by certain "erring spirits" that the children of God should no longer use the ceremonies of the New Testament, such as baptism and the Lord's Supper, Scriptures, etc., because of the abuse into which they have fallen. The author's reply is that such abuse is not a sufficient argument for the cessation of ceremonies, and he rejects Bünderlin's argument that, when ceremonies are used over a long period of time, they become perverted. In the tract, Marpeck argues that God, at times, reestablishes the correct order. He adduces evidence from the Old Testament to prove that renewal does take place. His use of the Old Testament is somewhat self-conscious, but he justifies it on the grounds that his opponents refer to the Old Testament. This first matter is dealt with in about 4½ pages.

The second topic receives a longer treatment, about eleven pages, and deals with the assertion by the erring spirits that, since the apostles are dead, there is no longer any mandate supported by the Scriptures to carry on the ceremonies. They are invalid unless an external command should come for their continuing practice. To this avowal, Marpeck responds that, if this were so, then the Lord's Prayer should also be discontinued. He rejects the argument that the words of the Bible are not meant for his generation, and insists that the "last days" are the days after the life of Christ and that, since the commands of Christ are still binding upon His people, no further authenticating signs are needed now. He also criticizes the excessive individualism of these "spirits," and reminds them that the gifts of the Holy Spirit are given for the common good of the church and not for individual edification.

The third argument, which extends to about seventeen pages, deals with the continuity of the apostolic authority. The erring spirits insist that the apostles were in no position to hand down their authority to their successors and that apostolic authority ended with the successors of the apostles. In reply, Marpeck deals with the subject of authority in the church. He argues that Christian ministers do not derive their authority from an external act, but rather from the authority of Christ who "thrusts His spirit into the bosom of their hearts" just as He did to the eleven apostles. He also briefly touches upon the accusation that the Anabaptists make the ceremonies into a form of idolatry. The accusations are those of Bünderlin and the answers to them are Marpeck's.

The booklet represents the earliest and clearest repudiation of Spiritualism by the Anabaptists, and refutes the assertion that the parting of the ways between Anabaptism and Spiritualism did not occur until the decade of the forties.[3]

The Text

by Pilgram Marpeck[4]

I

First, certain spirits (which, according to 1 John 2 "went out from us but are not of us")[5] are advocating that the children of God should no longer use the ceremonies of the New Testament, such as baptism, the Lord's Supper, and the Scriptures. These spirits think that such ceremonies are to be shunned because they have been abused and destroyed by the Antichrist, who imitates them without a mandate and without the witness of the heart. Therefore, the ceremonies are misunderstood, abused, and stained. This abomination will remain until the end, etc.

Answer:

The righteous have nothing to do with evil matters (Ezek. 18; Deut. 24) because they have not given their consent[6] (Lk. 23; Eph. 5; 1 Tim. 5; Rev. 18; 2 Cor. 6; Ps. 26; Ex. 23). Because the Antichrist is an unbeliever and a pervert, he uses all things, including the ceremonies, in a perverted, impure manner, for to him all things are impure (Tit. 1). This abuse cannot invalidate them for the believer who understands, uses, practices, and promotes them in a correct and pure manner. The ceremonies, duly instituted, are valid in themselves and cannot, as a result of the Antichrist's impurity and abuse, become impure for the pure (A ii).

Although the Antichrist uses them in a carnal manner, when man decides what is right and when they are inspired by Christ's mandate of faith, spirit, and truth, these ceremonies are also performed in a Christian manner and spiritual form. For they have been commended to the believers and not to those who follow the Antichrist. Consequently, neither those belonging to the Antichrist nor any others can defile the ceremonies so that they are weakened, or lose their power. Those who abuse them defile only themselves, but the commandment and the ordinance of Christ remain in themselves fresh, free, upright, powerful, and steadfast forever. They do not age, nor are they replaced, and, until His physical return, are not misplaced through length of time, for they have been instituted in the New Testament and not in the Old. Thus, with respect to time, they belong in the New Testament until Christ's physical return.

I freely admit that whoever, like the Antichrist, abuses such ceremonies does so unjustly and participates in the abomination. Where, however, the Spirit of Christ is present (which those belonging to the Antichrist lack and, I fear, these spirits also lack), there Christ's pure ordinance is joined to it. Among the holy, undefiled, and pure, Christ and His law are holy, undefiled, and pure; among the perverted, they are perverted (Ps. 18; 2 Kings 22). The perverted and the cursed have spoiled it as far as God is concerned, and they are not His children because of their spots[7] and blemishes (Deut. 32). Moreover, because these spirits appeal to the images of the Old Testament, I must reply using the same images.[8]

How often did the Israelites and Jews defect from God and their laws in the Old Testament! Godless kings arose who besmirched, changed, perverted, and distorted the ceremonies of the law (just as the Antichrist did, and now does, in the New). Read 2 Kings 21; 2 Chronicles 15, 34, 35; Ezra 5, 10. A few times it occurred, not through the prophets, but through the people and their kings themselves, men who were compelled by their consciences and the fear of God (2 Chron. 14, 23, 24, 29, 30, 31, 33, 34; 1 Macc. 4) and not by special signs or miracles as these erring spirits aver. Just as the Israelites, rescued out of Babylonian captivity (Ezra 2), restored the ancient ceremonies, so too does Christ today, through His servants rescued out of the prison of the Antichrist, restore and renew His instituted ceremonies (Acts 3) by means of His inner command and His bestowal of the certainty of His Spirit (A iii).

Similarly, because of the apostasy of the same Jerusalemites (2 Thess. 2), Christ is again restoring the spiritual Jerusalem destroyed by the antichristian Chaldeans. Earlier, because of the sins of the Israelites or Jews and their kings, the Chaldean and other kings destroyed the physical Jerusalem (2 Chron. 36; Neh. 1; 2 Chron. 24:23, 24; Jer. 25; 1 Macc. 1, 2). Yet, through the inspiration and awakening of God, and not through external miracles, Jerusalem was again rebuilt by King Cyrus (2 Chron. 36; Ezra 1) and also by Nehemiah (Neh. 2). For God calls His apostate people that they may again return to Him and keep His law and ordinance, that He may receive them and gather them together (Neh. 1; Jer. 3, 8, 31; Is. 31; Hos. 14). As then, so now, by breathing on His disciples and directing the shining brilliance of His countenance toward His spiritual Jerusalem, Christ will accomplish what He has promised, the revelation of His glory by means of His physical return (Lk. 21). To prepare for His coming, the King, Christ, has already begun to send ahead messengers who will ensure that His temple and the city of Jerusalem are purified and cleansed of all abuses of His commands, laws, and ceremonies. The spiritual idolatry, waste, and abomination raised by the Antichrist are to be purged from this spiritual Jerusalem, just as, previously, Josiah (2 Chron. 30, 34) and, figuratively, other kings under the law purged it. Thus, when this king comes, ceremonies, external instruction, Scriptures, all enigmas, and all that is partial (1 Cor. 13) will cease and will no longer be needed. Only then will the true leap be taken.[9]

II

Second, these spirits insist that, because of the death of the apostles, there is no longer any command or witness of the Scriptures concerning ceremonies such as baptism and the Lord's Supper. Accordingly, these practices fall away, and the erring spirits are unconvinced that restitution is called for at this time. Therefore, what is needed is an external command lest we practice the ceremonies in unbelief or with an unsteady, doubting heart and the like, etc.

Answer:

If such an argument were valid, we might well take heed not to say the Lord's Prayer in vain or many other matters (A iv) about which Jesus spoke to His disciples, internally and externally. Are we now to regard the Scriptures as words spoken only to the disciples present and as applying literally only to them at that time? That is impossible. It will be found in Scripture that such ceremonies must remain as long as there are Christians, that is, until the end of the world, for, in His command to baptize (Mt. 28), Jesus had in mind not only His present disciples but also all future disciples throughout time until the end of the world, a fact which is evident when He says: "I am with you always, to the close of the age." He also spoke to them in this manner on other matters, as He did, for example, in Matthew 24, when He spoke of the end: "Now when you see the abomination

47

of desolation," etc. Further, He says in Luke 21: "When you see all this, then know that the end is near," and in Matthew 10: "When, however, this begins to happen, then look up. . . . You will not get around to all the cities of Israel until the Son of Man comes." He certainly knew that His contemporary disciples would not live that long. He further says in Mark 13: "What I say to you, I say to all, Watch." Paul, too, when he spoke of the Lord's Supper (1 Cor. 11), addressed his remarks about Christ's physical return not only to his contemporaries but to all Christians, thus reiterating Christ's command to proclaim the Lord's death until He comes. This injunction does not refer to Christ's spiritual coming, as some have understood it to mean, for those who proclaim Christ's death must first have Him spiritually in them (2 Cor. 13), or eat the bread in an unworthy manner and thus, since they are unable to discern the body of the Lord, eat judgment unto themselves and the world.

How then can these spirits say that there is no longer any scriptural testimony or external authorization for such ceremonies? Similarly, when they affirm that at the time of the apostles the proclamation already went forth adequately as a witness to the world,[10] they refute the proclamation of the gospel. Especially in these last days, proclamation of a witness is required from all nations in the whole world (Mt. 24; Mk. 13; Acts 3; Rev. 14). But the proclamation must be the same as the one Christ and the apostles have preached (Gal. 1; John 15; 2 John 1, 2; 2 Cor. 11; 1 Tim. 6), for Christ's Word will not pass away until heaven and earth pass away (Mt. 24; Mk. 13; Lk. 21). Since such a gospel is proclaimed openly through word and blood,[11] neither is it His will that His words be changed, added to, or subtracted from (2 Cor. 2, 4; Rev. 22; Mt. 5; Deut. 4; Prov. 30; Gal. 3). Who, however, sent these preachers, witnesses, or messengers? Or do they testify to lies and not to truth? (A v).

If, then, such proclamation of, and testimony to, the gospel must take place in these last days, why then would they discontinue baptism, the Lord's Supper, etc., which are also external witnesses? Why differentiate between one external witness and another?

That Christ does not at this time once more in the flesh give a personal command as He did to the eleven disciples or, as in the case of Paul (Acts 9), perform a miracle, should not deter us. As noted, subsequent to the apostasy of Israel and the destruction of their kings, the ceremonies of the old covenant were reinstituted without miracles. If the people whom the Assyrian king (2 Kings 17) settled in the cities of Samaria had followed the Israelite priest, who came not with signs but rather with teaching or preaching, and if they had dealt with him according to the law of Moses, they would not have acted incorrectly, even though they were Gentiles. Thus, we should not yearn to have Christ, the Head, physically with us until He comes at the end of the world. Through the Spirit of Christ, there is sufficient inner command. Whoever desires more, such as miraculous signs or the like, as unbelievers always do, and does not, like the Ninevites, allow the proclamation of Jonah (who preached without miraculous signs) to suffice, is not hungry for the truth. Signs and wonders have already testified to this truth and the Scriptures have been made abundantly certain for us (Heb. 2; Mk. 16; Jn. 20; Acts 2, 7). For, although its actions deny this claim, the whole world verbally confesses Christ to be the Son of God and considers the Scripture its certification. Consequently, a destruction worse than that of Sodom and Gomorrah, who did not have such a clear revelation, could result.

Therefore, he who in these last days[12] desires miracles, and will not believe the truth without them, let him beware lest he be deceived and punished by those wonders and signs of deception referred to in the Scriptures (Mt. 24; Mk. 13; 2 Thess. 2; Rev. 13; Rom. 16; 1 Tim. 4).

I speak thus as a warning and not, as certain individuals assume, as an argument to exclude divine miracles and signs. Nor does Scripture assert this exclusion. God has a free hand even in these last days. He has performed miracles and signs before, and even does so today for him who has eyes to see. These spirits who also assert that, together with ceremonies, all miraculous signs (A vi) ended at the time of the apostles well recognize this fact and should take note how Christian baptism and the Lord's Supper are today repeated according to their original intention and institution. Not only through external ceremonies but also through the power of Christ and His authoritative teachings and of the apostles, these people bear witness both in death and blood. And they do so uncoerced—freely, deliberately, and joyfully through the abundant comfort and power of the Holy Spirit of Christ in this world. Thus, they seal and confirm the power of Christ. Many of them have remained constant, enduring tortures inflicted by sword, rope, fire, and water, and suffering terrible, tyrannical, unheard-of deaths and martyrdoms, all of which they could easily have avoided by recantation.[13] Moreover, one also marvels when one sees how the faithful God (who, after all, overflows with goodness) raises from the dead several such brothers and sisters of Christ after they were hanged, drowned, or killed in other ways. Even today, they are found alive and we can hear their own testimony.

Here and there one can find the same thing happening, even today, it takes place among those who are powerfully moved and driven by the living Word of God and the Spirit of Christ. They will continue on (as we see before us now), and no one will be able to wipe them out until the whole world, inebriated and insane with innocent blood, will bear abundant testimony to them.

Cannot everyone who sees, even the blind, say with a good conscience that such things are a powerful, unusual, and miraculous act of God? Those who would deny it must be hardened men. Yes, and even more murders now occur, executed by the devil, that is, by his children, the Antichrists and their breed, his citizens and agents with whom these erring spirits accuse us of committing adultery. These spirits further accuse us of imitating him, of paying homage to his image. How, indeed, can anyone say that such a thing is not of God? For, if it were of the devil or Antichrist, as the Jews also committed blasphemy against Christ in the Holy Spirit, it would follow that the devil is himself divided and is fighting against himself. Then, he and his kingdom could never endure, but would come to an end (Mt. 12; Mk. 3; Lk. 11). But one devil cannot be against another.

Christ bids us to recognize prophets not by miraculous signs, but by their fruits (Mt. 7). Likewise, we also know the fruits of the Spirit (Gal. 5). 1 John 4 tells us to test the spirits in order to determine whether or not they acknowledge Christ's having come in the flesh (A vii).

Nowhere do I find Christ's physical command to Philip, the deacon, who was not elected by the church to teach or baptize, and yet he preached and baptized in the surrounding lands. The same is true of Apollos and other renowned apostles who moved about, preaching and baptizing, without external command or commission, but who were sent inwardly by Christ's Spirit. Similarly, the revival and restoration of the pure order of Christ has occurred, and continues to occur, by virtue of His voluntary Spirit, not by carnal compulsion or pressure, but freely and voluntarily. Those who act differently, as lords or masters, should take heed lest they miss the goal. I fear that these spirits lack the true knowledge of Christ; otherwise, they would speak differently. They preach a different gospel than Paul, who prescribed that in the Lord's Supper believers should proclaim the Lord's death until He comes.

Thus, these spirits, through their alien preaching, call down Paul's curse upon themselves (Gal. 1). Christ also commands and directs us (Mt. 28; Mk. 16; Lk. 24) to preach, teach, and baptize not only the world of His time, but also the world which will remain and the nations which will exist until the end or the last day (Mt. 24; Mk. 13; Acts 2; Rom. 15; Deut. 31; Ps. 78). He commands us also in Luke 22 to break bread in remembrance of Him; in John 5, "Search the Scriptures," and in John 7, according to the word and content of the same, to believe in Him; in John 13, to wash one another's feet, etc. So also John, in the Book of Revelation, refers to these last days when we read in chapter 1: "Blessed is he who reads and those who hear the words of the prophecy and keep what is written in it." But these spirits shy away from such external matters, and so the judgment falls upon them, as it is described in 2 John 1: "Whoever goes ahead and does not remain in the instruction of Christ has no God." The same John 8: "Whoever does not believe in Him, as the Scrip-

tures say, from his body will not flow rivers of living water."[14]
Also Revelation 22: "If anyone removes anything from the words
of this prophecy, God will remove his portion from the book of
life." These spirits speak with neither discernment nor the support of the Scriptures, and think that, because the ceremonies of
the Old Testament have been abrogated (as for example, in Heb.
7, 8, 9, 10; Gal. 5), the ceremonies of the New Testament have
also been abrogated. They are mistaken. Note, however, that if
they do regard as abrogated (which they cannot) the ceremonies
of the New Testament, ceremonies like baptism and the Lord's
Supper, it should follow that all Scriptures, external teaching,
separation from the world, ban, rebuke, exhortation, prayer,
kneeling, the example of the believers (A viii), and all ceremonies for improvement and corporate benefit are no longer
valid. If one is invalid, all are invalid; if one remains valid, all
remain valid.

Who has commissioned only them, or ordered them to
teach, write, and travel here and there with allegations and in-
ferences drawn from the Scriptures and other creatures and
examples? Here in the kingdom of Christ, they must, after all,
renew the tangible, visible, physical body of man through the
Spirit of Christ (2 Cor. 5) and, at the same time, retain the
external visible ceremonies which have been instituted and commanded by Christ. Where Christ has come in the flesh by faith
(Eph. 3; Gal. 2), that same man, with his flesh and all external
members, indeed, the whole man obedient in external ceremonies, will confess the instruction and the life of Christ. But today these spirits desire to make the kingdom of Christ far too
spiritual, and make too great a leap, just as, on the other hand,
the Antichrist has made it too physical.

I willingly believe that they cannot in their hearts feel such
ceremonies and matters, which seem foreign to them; they are
wary and suspicious of these ceremonies. So, too, in the whole
world the pure usage of the ceremonies is suspect. They are an
abomination because of their lack of knowledge and their shying
away from the discipline of God. But it is, therefore, not so with
others as it is with them. I sense that they lack the Holy Spirit

dedicated to the common good (1 Cor. 12), who uses the gifts of the Holy Spirit for the edification of others (1 Cor. 14; Eph. 4), and thus serves them (1 Peter 4). Therefore, they do not believe in Jesus Christ, by which faith one receives the Spirit of promise (Gal. 3; 2 Cor. 4; Jn. 7; Acts 11; Rom. 12). Without this spirit, they are unable to address Jesus as Lord (1 Cor. 12), to cry "Abba Father," to belong to Christ, to pray (Rom. 8), to have love (Rom. 5), to be baptized inwardly, washed, sanctified, or made righteous (Jn. 1; 1 Cor. 6), to know the truth (Jn. 16), or to be instructed in it (1 Jn. 2; Jn. 14). Thus, they themselves have not yet been taught (Rom. 2). Nothing but error and confusion arises from such unbelieving, vain, carnally wise, fable-producing spirits and blind leaders.

If they say, however, that they have as much spirit and faith as they need, but have no command to use spiritual gifts for others, I answer: Their boast is nothing but a deceitful adornment of Satan. If they are members of the body of Christ, they will speak differently. For one member to forsake another (1 Cor. 12) in spiritual matters (to say nothing of the temporal, which is of less importance) would be contrary to the faith of the Spirit, and the nature and attributes of love. The fruit of the Spirit is love and faithfulness (Gal. 5). Faith must manifest itself in witness, fruit, and work (2 Pet. 1; Jn. 7, 15; Heb. 6; Jas. 2; 1 Thess. 1). So love is faith in action (Gal. 5); it edifies and improves (1 Cor. 8). If they do not love their neighbor, how can they fulfill the law, for such love is the fulfillment of the law (Rom. 13). Paul says: Let no one seek his own profit, but rather the profit of another. I do not seek what is beneficial to me, but rather what is beneficial and advantageous for many in order that they may be saved. Follow me as I follow Christ (1 Cor. 10; Phil. 2). Thus, the gifts of the Spirit manifest themselves not only for private but also for common benefit, service, and improvement.

Now, since they do not admit that they are commanded to use the gifts of the Spirit according to the distribution of faith (Rom. 12) in relation to others, I would very much like to see how they stand the test of stewardship over their professed gifts of spirit, faith, and love—a spiritual gift given them by the Lord as a committed trust, talent, or pound until the return of the Lord. What will be their increase (Mt. 25; Lk. 19), and how have they watched (Mk. 13)?

When Christ in Mark 13 says: "What I say to you, I say to all, Watch," these spirits say that such watching does not refer here to preaching, teaching, or action toward others, but only to oneself, and that one should be awake to oneself.

Answer: Christ says this to all stewards and guardians of His house and to the people over whom they are to watch and guard (Mk. 13; Lk. 12; Mt. 24; Heb. 13) by means of teaching and exhortation and other external service (Col. 1, 4; 2 Cor. 12; 1 Thess. 2, 3; Rom. 15).

Thus, these drunken prophets want to watch for their own benefit, like dumb dogs which cannot bark (Is. 56). They bruise the conscience of the group by means of false (b ii) teaching and retard them in their search for the truth; they teach them to watch without love when, after all, watching, not only by the masters but also by the servants, must take place if one is to love one's neighbor, as evidenced in Ephesians 6: "They are to watch, for all the saints."

The salvation of the soul depends upon love for the neighbor. Whoever does not love his neighbor does not love his own soul, and foolishly seeks his own profit to his highest damage. Therefore, no wakefulness or sobriety are manifested over either his own or over others' souls, but only slumber and drunkenness. Since one can find Scriptures about the suspension of the Old Testament ceremonies, I would greatly desire that these spirits show me clear Scriptures indicating that such ordained proclamation, teaching, baptism, and the Lord's Supper (Mt. 28; 1 Cor. 11) had been suspended, or again forbidden and discontinued. Then, without wavering and doubt in my heart, I might be able to believe their teaching. They are, however, unable to accomplish this without resorting to questionable, untenable, sophistic[15] presentations, examples, and illustrations, all of which the Antichrist does for the preservation of his abomination.

54

III

Third, these spirits say that no apostle has Christ's authority or mandate to hand over the apostolic offices to others, nor did these spirits do so. Rather, they appointed bishops to tend the flock of God. Since then, however, no one has been instructed to appoint the ruler of God's flock.

Answer:

External transmission of authority or mandate does not make an apostle, even if the apostles themselves had made the appointment. If the inner mandate of Christ is not present, all is in vain. Even the external mandate of Christ to the eleven would not have been effective if He had not afterward spiritually thrust the mandate into the heart of their bosom. Therefore, the apostles saw what was committed to them; they themselves carried out their mission and office until they died, when they were then followed by others whom the Lord (who has all authority) sent (Mt. 28).

Indeed, in the worldly realm, those in authority externally hand that authority on to others; but not so in the spiritual realm. Here it depends upon the inner power which Christ alone gives through His spirit. For (b iii) without the inner mandate, even if Christ, Paul, or Peter would today confer on me external authority, I would not undertake anything. Otherwise, I, together with all the other worldly and antichristian potentates, would be pursuing my own advancement.

Nor is it the case (as these spirits claim) that the apostles, who were sent by the chief Shepherd to gather the flock, did not appoint successors to watch over and to guard the property or sheep gathered together for the Lord. Nor was there provision that these successors had first been found adequate and placed into the confidence of the chief Shepherd. Christ appointed them over the flock so that the true sheep might not diminish but increase. For like Peter, whom He appoints as a shepherd (Jn. 21), Christ would have shepherds who love Him.

Our carnal flesh sharply opposes the right kind of apostolic bishopric. For this reason, many turn away from it and, by means of clever excuses and undisciplined, deceptive teachings, seek to evade it. For, truly, neither reason, wisdom, selfish ambition, honor, impatience, nor other weeds of the flesh have a place in the kingdom of Christ, especially in the office of leader (*Vorsteerampt*), if fruit is to come.

The authority of the apostle, bishop, and shepherd is not an authority of ruling or lordship; rather, it is one of humility and lowliness so that nothing is done out of a desire to dominate others or to advance only themselves. They are servants of God and of His community.

As mentioned, Christ left, until the end of the world, His external authority and command in the Scriptures (Mt. 28) to all His disciples, brothers, and members who possess His Spirit or mind. This same written authority was accepted by Paul, as a member of Christ, when he refers to the verse (interpreting it to refer to the body of members of Christ in Acts 13): "As the Lord commanded us, I have made you a light for the Gentiles that you might be salvation to the ends of the earth," etc. Let everyone beware lest he abuse such authority, lest he represent only himself rather than Christ, who sends him, and lest he be without the seal of authority in his heart. Let him honorably be Christ's representative throughout the whole world, wherever need exists; then he need not be concerned that he is abusing his authority. Yes, even if a dog or a cat were to proclaim the gospel as a testimony, throughout the unbelieving world (b iv) and deliver it into repentance and improvement, who could declare it wrong? For everything that leads to godliness is good, and not evil, for all visible creatures are placed in the world as apostles and teachers (Job 12). If such mute creatures could speak, Christ's sending the apostles to elucidate or preach the gospel would have been unnecessary.[16]

But, in their carnal wisdom, these spirits desire, on the basis of the verse "they will all be taught of God" (Jn. 6), the proclamation of the gospel to all creatures (Col. 1; Mk. 16), and they desire to abolish too much. For the latter was spoken by Christ *after* the former. They seek even to abolish all external order and means of God, through which and in which His invisible being is seen (Rom. 1; Wisdom of Sol. 13); in Christ and in God man is led from the visible into the invisible. Thus, with the ruse that it breeds idolatry, these spirits abominate that which God has created and provided for man's well-being. If in this way they thank God for that which is external, how would they thank Him for that which is internal? In any event, they adduce only part of the Scriptures and leave out the counterpart, have uncloven hoofs, not cogitating on what they take in (Deut. 14). Therefore, one should neither heed them nor accept them. They err in vision and stumble in giving judgment (Is. 28). They act like Joshua, the servant of Moses (Num. 11), who sought to prevent Eldat and Medat from prophesying. But Moses said to him: "Are you zealous for me? Would to God that all the people of God might prophesy and that God's spirit might be poured into them." These spirits also act like Jesus' disciples when they forbade someone to drive out demons because he did not follow after Christ with them. Jesus answered: "Do not forbid him or hinder him, for there is no one who does anything in my name, even if he speaks evil against me, for whoever is not against us is for us" (Mk. 9; Lk. 9).

With their sandy soil and sod taken from the ground, which is earthly wisdom,[17] they desire to stop up the well of the Spirit which pours from the believing hearts (Jn. 7; 2 Cor. 4; Acts 2; Rom. 10; Ps. 115). These spirits compound their sin in every way (1 Thess. 2), for, like the world, they would restrain us from preaching salvation to the heathen. The world resists us with physical force; these spirits with their false artistry and cunning trickery (2 Cor. 11) hinder us spiritually. Paul says: "I rejoice that Christ is proclaimed in every way, whether out of a good motive or accidentally" (Phil. 1). Who sent the woman (Jn. 4) into the town that she might proclaim Christ? Nevertheless, through her message (b v), the Samaritans were edified. Only if these spirits had good intentions, neither misleading others nor condemning themselves (Rom. 2; Mt. 7; Jas. 3; 1 Cor. 11; Ps. 50; Ecclus. 5, 7, 14, 22), only if they sought to warn emissaries or bishops, teachers and others to pay heed to the manner in which they themselves had been taught and now think (Tit. 1, 2; 1 Tim.

3, 4, 5; 2 Tim. 2; 1 Pet. 5), only if these spirits did not go so far as to discontinue or forbid completely instruction and ceremonies, only then could their cause be tolerated. Their cause, as it now stands, cannot be tolerated.

Christ did not restrict His command, Word, grace, Spirit, or ceremonies to the first apostles and churches. His Word and power, and the outpouring of His Spirit, have no end. Nor is the arm of the Lord shortened (Num. 11). Had the world died out with the first apostles and ceased with them, I would believe this. However, the fallen world continues even now to need apostles, messengers, and teachers, who testify and confess the sound of the gospel and the name of Jesus Christ (Rom. 10; Col. 1). Also, they must declare, remind, and testify to the world's sins and burdens, and to their own imagined, fabricated faith. The Israelites, too, after their apostasy everywhere (where they did not do right by themselves), had to be reminded again of their vices, sin, and destruction. The sound that went out, the law and the name of God (Ps. 18) had been witnessed to and confessed beforehand. For it is the will of God that recollection, testimony, and proclamation should always be made to the followers, apostate, erring, and ignorant (Is. 60; Rom. 15; Deut. 31; Ps. 78), and, as long as it is today (Heb. 3), even to those who know (2 Cor. 1; 2 Pet. 1; Phil. 3), in order that no one may be lost, that everyone may improve (2 Pet. 3), and that all men may become well, be saved, and come to the knowledge of the truth (1 Tim. 2). Just as Christ is not the atonement for the sins of a part or a half but of the whole world (1 Jn. 2), so, also, as the light which enlightens every man coming into the world (Jn. 1), through His justification, the justification of life came upon all of them (Rom. 5). Therefore, the Scriptures also are designed and intended for those upon whom the end of the world has come (1 Cor. 9, 10; Is. 30) (b vi).

We do not serve the Scriptures or benefit them; they serve and benefit us by their instruction, edification, exhortation, and discipline (Rom. 15; 2 Tim. 1). Similarly, all ceremonies have been instituted by Christ for our service and benefit, and we are not thereby to serve God in the manner the carnal Jews (Is. 1; Ps.

50) thought.[18]

These spirits ask us: why should God need such external things or services, and how is it that we are making an idol out of them, etc.? Rather, these services serve us, just as Christ the Man came to serve us (Mk. 10; Rom. 15) and did everything for our sake (Jn. 11). To be sure, God ordered that it should be so, when it is done in faith (Heb. 11; Rom. 13; Mt. 5; Prov. 15; Rom. 8; Col. 1; 1 Thess. 2) and in obedience to faith (Rom. 1, 6, 10, 16; 2 Cor. 2, 7, 10; Heb. 5, 13), and when one serves the members or body of Christ thereby (Col. 1; 1 Thess. 2; 1 Cor. 3; 1 Pet. 4; Eph. 4). If one does it in the Spirit of God (Phil. 3; Rom. 13) and for the praise of God (Jn. 7, 16; 1 Cor. 10; 1 Pet. 4), to do so is to serve Christ the Head and God Himself (Phil. 2; Eph. 6; Col. 3; 1 Cor. 8; Mt. 10, 18, 25). We would not use such ceremonies and Scriptures as the scribes of this world do (Mt. 15, 23; 1 Cor. 1; 2 Cor. 2, 4), that is false and for the sake of unrighteousness. We would use them as the scribes of the kingdom of God do, for the sake of righteousness, and godliness, piety, and wisdom, and with the faith of the elect in Jesus (2 Tim. 3; Mt. 13; Act. 18). With Paul, we believe all that is written in the law and the prophets (Acts 24), and fulfill the royal law according to James 2. We recall the written words of the apostles (Jude 1). We search daily in the Scriptures to see whether it is in fact as these spirits teach (Acts 17). From what we read and know beforehand (2 Cor. 1), we find, however, that it is not as they say. Nevertheless, we say nothing except what has already been said by Moses, the prophets, Christ, and the apostles (Acts 26). Without the Scriptures, no one knows how, why, and in what form Christ died, was buried, and was raised (1 Cor. 15). Therefore, moved by the Holy Spirit (2 Pet. 1) and by the example of Christ through His Spirit, all messengers and teachers should have witness of the Scriptures, but in humility and obedience to the gospel—as it has happened until now, God be praised, on many occasions. Thus, not entering into a situation as overlords (1 Pet. 5), they are genuinely commissioned messengers eating (Jn. 6) of Christ and living for the sake of Christ, just as Christ was sent by the living Father and lives for the sake (b vii) of the Father. Into the hearts

59

of such as the apostles, the Spirit of God is poured forth, according to common salvation, for it is one unified Spirit.

The pouring out of the Spirit is not as those spirits say: At the time of the apostles, the Spirit of God was poured forth over all the present and future world, until the last judgment, as if such a pouring out had then ceased. The Spirit of God at that time (Acts 2) was not poured out over all, but only on the apostles and Christians. The others were unbelievers. And without such a Spirit, like all men from the beginning of the world and so too, now, the unbelievers are not any better by virtue of such an outpouring than the people at the time of Noah, Lot, or Moses who had the same light of conscience as these have now. For if today a man is born and grows up without hearing external proclamation about Christ, how can he be better than the people at the time of Moses? Without external hearing or proclamation (Rom. 10), neither can he name Jesus Christ nor the Holy Spirit except through special or miraculous proclamation of God; as in former times, they could know little about sin without the written law (Rom. 5, 7).

If, however, man hears about the life of Christ, a higher light and witness comes to his conscience than the one that came under the law, just as today the believers receive a mightier spirit than before.

The outpouring of the Spirit of God on the apostles or on another man next to me does not profit me, a coarse, crude man, except it also be poured into my heart for common good unto salvation. All men from the beginning of the world, from their mother's womb, have the image and likeness of God (Ezek. 28; Ecclus. 17). However, they have all been misled, along with Adam, by the advice of the serpent (Gen. 3; 2 Cor. 2, 4, 11).

God says in Joel 2 and Acts 2 that in the last days He will pour His Spirit upon all flesh. That is the New Testament of which Hebrew 8 and Jeremiah 31 speak. The last days begin with the birth of Christ. Since then, a richer outpouring of His Spirit has taken place than ever before. Not, however, upon all men, 1 John 2 explains: Christ is the expiation for the whole world and for the sins of all men. The counterpart (b viii) says:

whoever does not suffer (meaning through a genuine act of repentance) will not rule with Him (Rom. 8). Since not all men repent, not all will share in the sufferings of Christ. Neither can God be gracious to such unrepentant, unrighteous men nor (as He promises in Hebrews 8) will He forget their sins (Ezek. 33). Thus, God would pour His Spirit over all men unto the end of the world. God desires that they would all know Him (Heb. 8; Joel 2) and desires that all be healed (1 Tim. 2). His will and desire are clear. But, where man is not willing, God cannot and will not. He does not pour His new wine into old skins (Mt. 9). He opposes the proud (1 Pet. 5). The hungry He fills with good things, the rich He sends away empty (Lk. 1; Mt. 5). Wisdom does not enter an evil spirit, nor does it dwell in those who are subservient to sin (Wisd. of Sol. 1). Therefore, the unwilling, disobedient man will no more receive the Spirit of God than he will participate in the expiation of Christ. The man who, through genuine works of repentance (that is, through faith in Jesus Christ), submits to the fellowship of suffering under God's hand and discipline will also participate in the suffering and expiation of Christ, and upon him God's Spirit will be poured (Prov. 1) by faith (Gal. 3; Jn. 7); he will receive the rich spirit of transformation, the knowledge of Christ in his heart, indeed, the Spirit of the New Testament, which He promised in these days to pour over all flesh. Wherever He has promised the Spirit and grace of the new covenant, we are to understand that it is this Spirit, even as He promised to Abraham: In his seed, that is, the seed of this Spirit, all the nations will be blessed. This Spirit was promised as soon as Adam transgressed the commandment (Gen. 3). To whomever this seed or Spirit is given, in him the Spirit crushes the head of the serpent (Rom. 16), that is, he resists his advice, deception, and lust (Rom. 8; Jas. 4; Gal. 5). For the fastest way to kill a serpent is to step on its head. Therefore, it refers to the head. While the head is being stepped on, it bites Christ in the heel; without suffering and the cross, it cannot be crushed or killed. It lies under Christ's feet and bites, not His toes, but His heel. Why? Because Christ's countenance is too sharp, and therefore, the serpent attacks from behind, for he is a murderer

61

(Jn. 8). Murderers do not attack honorably. So, too, the serpent does everything in a crafty way, seeking to deceive (c) and to kill and lead men spiritually and physically astray.

Furthermore, before the birth of Christ, the elect already possessed (Heb. 11) this promised Spirit, the Spirit of faith, (Gal. 3), but not as generously as they do now. God would willingly have given it to all the nations, since He promised it to them, but they did not want it. Just so today, the world does not want it, choosing to follow instead the wisdom of the serpent. Neither God nor Christ can be blamed for this action, only men themselves are to blame. Pharaoh himself hardened his heart, first through his disobedient, unwilling heart, as the knower of hearts testified and said in Exodus 3: I know that the king of Egypt will not let you move, etc., otherwise God would not have hardened his heart (Exod. 4). From the beginning, God's offer is upright (1 Cor. 1), and His faithfulness will not falter (Rom. 3). But, even as it is now (Jn. 1), the nations did not wish it nor believe it (Jer. 5, 6, 7, 8, 25; Heb. 3, 4).

God's order is a purposeful one. Whoever seeks Him will find Him. Whoever leaves Him will also be deserted. Whoever does not hold Him will not be held by Him (1 Chron. 29; 2 Chron. 15, 24). Before the birth of Christ, the elect looked forward to the promise of Christ's coming (Acts 2, 7; Deut. 18; Jn. 4; Is. 11). The promise has been realized; He has come for men's salvation, but, until now, they have looked only upon the Christ of the past. So take a lesson from the clarity of vision present before His coming; how much more clearly is He known since His coming. Scriptures speak more clearly of Him after His coming than they had done before. After He came, He is clearer and more powerful than He was before, as He said Himself (Mt. 13): Many prophets and righteous men longed to see what you see, but did not see it; they longed to hear what you hear, but did not hear it. Therefore, the present world, since His coming, will experience sharper condemnation than did the one before He came (Mt. 10, 11, 12; Lk. 10). For, since we are now more able to know Him and can say more about Him, we can pattern ourselves after Him, and more fully partake of the divine nature and spiritual good. Thus, revenge is no longer permitted in the New Testament for, through patience, the Spirit can now more powerfully overcome enemies than it could in the Old Testament. Therefore, Christ forbade such vengeance and resistance (Lk. 9, 21; Mt. 5), and commanded the children who possessed the Spirit of the New Testament to love, to bless (c ii) their enemies, persecutors, and opponents, and to overcome them with patience (Mt. 5; Lk. 6).[19]

Such a powerful Spirit, a Spirit promised for the last days, could not come as long as Christ was personally upon the earth with His disciples (Jn. 12, 16). Now we are to reflect upon Him spiritually, upon what kind of a mind, spirit, and disposition He had, and how He lived; the more we reflect upon His physical words, works, deeds, and life, the better God allows us to know His mind, and the better He teaches and instructs us (Jn. 6). Whoever does not think of Him, reflect upon Him, pray, or seek Him will not receive from Him (Mt. 7; Luke 11, 13; 1 Chron. 29). The more one now learns to know Him and see Him spiritually (Jn. 6, 17; Heb. 12), the more one learns to love Him, to become friendly and pleasant toward Him and, through such knowledge, receives Him into the heart and grows therein (2 Pet. 1, 2). Finally, one jumps with Peter himself, freely and voluntarily (Jn. 21), into the sea of tribulations and, concentrating on Christ, casts aside the mantle or the old garment. Through such a knowledge of Christ, man also comes to the knowledge of God (Jn. 8, 14; 2 Cor. 4) and partakes of divine nature, but only if he is willing to flee from the lusts of this world, under God's rule. In this manner, through instruction and knowledge of Christ's mind, God places His law into our mind and writes it into our hearts (Heb. 8).

All of the apostles had this Spirit, receiving it only after the ascension of Christ. The Twelve received the foretaste of the Spirit from Christ (Jn. 6) when they said: "He has words of eternal life." This foretaste of the Spirit first enlightened Peter, and impelled him to stand up and speak at Pentecost. Also through the foretaste of this Spirit, they elected Matthias before Pentecost and prayer (Acts 1). Such a Spirit already moved in the disciples before the ascension of Christ, especially in Peter when he acknowledged Christ as the Son of God (Mt. 16; Jn. 6). Flesh and blood did not reveal that knowledge to him; rather, God confers this Spirit of knowledge. Through this Spirit, they were all together in one accord at Pentecost (Acts 2). The Lord then marvelously filled them with this Spirit, not in the way that He usually gives it to men, for the common good; rather, He gave a strong witness to it at the beginning, according to His will and good pleasure. We must speak of this beginning until He returns. In the meantime, we do not need to long for that beginning; at Pentecost, in the presence of many people, external noise, wind, and strange tongues were His witness (c iii) to His promise. This testimony is contained in the writings of the New Testament. He who has this Scripture sealed in his heart, this common Spirit of salvation, he alone, and no one else, can bear testimony to it. This Spirit of promise and clarity from God is here and now in the elect an open indicator, foretaste, seal, and down payment of future glory (1 Cor. 2; Eph. 1, 4; Rom. 8).

Conclusion

Whoever retains, practices, or accepts baptism, the Lord's Supper, or anything else, even Scriptures, word or deed, according to the command, attitude, form, essence, or example of the Antichrist is a child, member, and brother of the Antichrist, worships the image of his being, and with him will inherit destruction.

But whoever retains, practices, and accepts such ceremonies according to the command, attitude, form, essence, and example of Christ and the apostles, indeed according to the instruction and urging of the free Spirit, participates without blemish, misunderstanding, or abomination in the truly reenacted, spiritual apostolic order.

Whoever practices or receives such ceremonies and matters without[20] true faith, because of an external urge or other reasons, errs even though there is, externally, correctness of words and procedures. Such mistakes some have confessed to have made, but they confess it only out of anger and not for the good, which makes them unbelieving and unloving; these I admonish to believe and to genuine confession.

Whoever has been inwardly baptized, with belief and the Spirit of Christ in his heart, will not despise the external baptism and the Lord's Supper which are performed according to Christian, apostolic order; nor will he dissuade anyone from participating in them. Rather, he should willingly accept them and practice them, not merely imitating them externally in an apish manner, but in truth and in the spirit with which the true worshipers use external means, such as the mouth, hands, and knees. For, as one can see, the heart moves our external members. Whenever the heart laughs, is compassionate, rejoices, or gets angry, then the mouth, eyes, head, hands, and feet laugh, are compassionate, rejoice, get angry, move, and grasp (c iiii) without delay the external things which correspond to anger, joy, mercy, or laughter. The opposite is also true. So it is with baptism and the Lord's Supper.

Where they are present in the heart, there they are also practiced externally and practiced according to love. Thus, the heart of the eunuch also moved (Acts 8) all his physical members and his whole body, freely and without any external compulsion, to undergo external baptism. The inner covenant compelled Abraham to accept the external sign of the covenant of the Old Testament. For out of the abundance of the heart, the mouth speaks (Mt. 12).

In summary: The believer will retain, undissolved or unchanged, the commandment of his Master and will be a faithful disciple, who does not long to be master or to run ahead of Christ; he will diligently seek to be faithful in all things (2 Cor. 2), to fulfill all righteousness (Mt. 3), not only inwardly before God, but also externally before man (2 Cor. 8; Tit. 2). If anyone acts differently, he is not to be believed, whatever boastful claims he may make. Yes, even if an angel were to come from heaven and teach differently than Christ and His apostles once taught and commanded, he should not be believed.

Whoever teaches that believers do not need external baptism and the Lord's Supper, or teaches that these ceremonies are not expected of believers or given to them, errs, for Philip demands that faith go before (Acts 8). Christ also places faith first (Mk. 16) and, according to the Acts of the Apostles, faith always precedes baptism. Also, the command to break bread is given only to the disciples and the believers, and not the unbelievers (Lk. 22; 1 Cor. 11). The believers have always practiced it (Acts 2, 20), and only they can practice it in spirit and in truth. Others practice only lies and misunderstanding.

Love has driven me to write because I discern the secrets of these spirits. The adversary would destroy the internal by discontinuing the external. To be sure, these spirits, implying that, if only the external things dropped away, love, the internal, would rapidly increase, gloss over their intentions with a great deal of pious show and denial. Yes, behind them into the land of Sodom! May the Lord keep His own, whom He knows to be on the right track to His own glory.

I desire that these spirits would become confident of their position and, if not, that they might build on the rock, securing themselves against cloudburst and tempests. I would admonish (c v) all God's children and good-hearted people to guard themselves from such errors. May God grant it to all who desire it from their hearts. May He strengthen us, build us, lead us, and keep us in His knowledge, love, long-suffering, friendliness, meekness, patience, and other fruits and powers of the Spirit. Through these powers, and through true faith in Christ by whom, and none other, we accomplish to His praise our acting and willing, life, cross, and death, we may grow and increase in divine, quiet nature without causing others to be offended by the only name that saves, the name which cannot be deceived and does not deceive, Jesus; that name will not be put to shame (1 Pet. 2). We will be without envy, strife, hatred, feuding, bad temper, ill-will, anger, insult, hypocrisy, gossip, bitter striving, evil manners, scandal-mongering, slander, and other vain fruit or work of the flesh, through the same Jesus, His only-begotten Son, who is our Savior (Heb. 7), and only mediator (1 Tim. 2), to whom is given all power and authority (Mt. 11, 28; Lk. 10; Jn. 13; 1 Pet. 3; Heb. 2), to whom the angels are subject (1 Pet. 3).

This Lamb is Lord of lords and King of kings (Rev. 17). This man and Lord is Jesus of Nazareth, a future Judge and avenger (Jn. 5; Acts 10; 2 Thess. 1) who is Christ (Jn. 20; Acts 19), who was before Abraham (Jn. 8). Whoever denies this is a liar (1 Jn. 2). Whoever does not believe that this is so will die in his sins (Jn. 7), for such an unbeliever is not born of God (1 Jn. 5). Indeed, this Jesus Christ is also true God (Rom. 9; 1 Jn. 5) and eternal life. To Him be praise unto eternity. Amen.

1531

II

A Clear and
Useful Instruction

Introduction

Although this book was known by title to be in the
Strasbourg archives, modern scholars did not discover that a copy
was in the British Museum until the spring of 1958. By bringing
together both internal and external evidence, William Klassen
argued that it was written by Marpeck and that it was one of the
two booklets attributed to him by the censors in 1531.[1] That
opinion has not been refuted. According to Klassen, the occur-
rence of the word *Stillstand* or its cognate in the text indicates
that Marpeck is directing this booklet against the position of
Caspar Schwenckfeld, whose presence in Strasbourg was felt
keenly by the total community. In a letter to Johannes Bader on
September 24, 1531, Schwenckfeld remarks that the Anabaptists
had written a booklet against him.[2] The case for Marpeck's
authorship is further adduced from the external evidence of the
censor's report, who stated that in one of the booklets Marpeck
stated that he himself had been baptized. In the *Clear and Useful Instruction*, Marpeck states: "In fact, just because it is written (that one should be), I was baptized" (KU C v recto). This
statement is one of three references in Marpeck's writings to his
own baptism.

The table of contents details the topics dealt with in the
book. Like the rest of Marpeck's books, there is an abundance of
scriptural citations and references. Thus, the book gives an important insight into the way in which the Strasbourg Anabaptists

saw, as early as 1530, the differences between their approach and that of Schwenckfeld. Although the booklet may have Schwenckfeld directly in view, its burden is to deal with all the approaches which minimize the certainty with which Christians are to conduct their mission.

There is no need to isolate Marpeck as the sole author. It may well be that Lepold Scharnschlager helped to write it, for he was in Strasbourg as early as January 1531. Moreover, Wilhelm Reublin, in a letter to Marpeck, sent greetings to Scharnschlager.[3] Thus, the contents of the book clearly indicate that it originated in the Marpeck group.

The Text[4]

A clear and very useful instruction directed toward fraudulent and sly spirits, who now go about in a concealed manner in order to lead into error and deceive many pious hearts. A faithful warning briefly presented.

- I   Concerning the office of the apostle
- II   The office of bishop
- III The ceremonies of Christ
- IV   The differences between the deity and the humanity of Christ
- V   The commission and expectation of a new prophet
- VI   The prayers and good works of Cornelius

Proverbs 21:15

It is a joy for the righteous to do justice, but dismay for the evildoer.

Not what   but that[5]
                                 1531

The pure fear of God through the Lord Jesus Christ, His desired peace attained for us from the Father, protect and rescue us from all temptation. Amen.

Dearly beloved: I am prompted to write this epistle to you because of the strange teaching of many false prophets who, in a deceptive fashion, employ the witness of the Scriptures against devoted and submissive hearts, and who (Jude 13) spew out their own shame. Some of these false prophets have gone out from us, but they were not of us, for, if they had been of us, they would indeed have remained with us (1 Jn. 2:19). They are altogether slippery, sneaking, gentle snakes, completely concealed in outward appearance; they have placed themselves under the repentance of John, and wait upon a special commission, when Christ will be newly announced with power and signs just as in the times of the apostles. God will then pour out a visible spirit upon His own.

Moreover, they say that, at present, no longer does anyone have the power to employ the ceremonies of Christ, such as baptism, the Lord's Supper, teaching, the ban, and the laying on of hands, and that those who do employ these ceremonies do so apart from God's command (A ii). They say, if those who employ the ceremonies suffer because of it, this cross is not the cross of Christ, but rather a punishment from God. The false prophets burden the devoted, submissive, simple hearts with lofty questions, none of which these false prophets themselves can answer. By such confusion, they cause those of tender conscience to be confused and concerned; they urge them to stand completely still[6] with respect to the command of Christ, and hypocritically admonish them only to prayer. Thus, many devout hearts have been made apostate by these sneaking serpents and, like the Galatians (5:4-9), have been moved to a complete standstill.

Their teaching causes me not a little reflection, and moves me to describe their error as a warning to the devout and steadfast hearts. According to human standards, it is difficult for me to take up the challenge against such scholars and scribes. Nevertheless, I comfort myself, in the simplicity of faith, with the promised consolation of Christ. This faith ranks above all

71

artistry,[7] reason, wisdom, and teaching, regardless of the degree to which their reason and thought master the Scriptures, and by virtue of which they are considered masters of the Scriptures. But the believers will remain pupils and disciples of Christ, in which state may the Lord sustain us by His grace. Amen.

First, such high-minded, rational men are to know that, had they first surrendered their reason and skill of which they boast to the true faith in Christ, had they cast them at the feet of Christ and, with Magdalene, selected the better part (Lk. 10:42) and listened attentively to Christ, they would soon have recognized in themselves such high-minded reason, cunning, and arbitrary fabrications. Such a recognition of the manner and character of faith, and of the might and power of the same, is hardly detected in their teaching; they have not recognized or felt this power. For, if they had faith and if they were not, by the decree of God (Eph. 4:18, 19), so completely darkened in their reason and thought, they would better recognize the words of our Lord Christ, of Paul, and of other apostles. They would not shorten or impair God's gracious arm (which is Christ) nor present, as the true belief in Christ, their own confused thought. Nor would they venture to receive grace and power of faith only through prayer, while, in reality, it has already been obtained through Christ for all the believers. For Christ is today, and yesterday, and forever, always in possession of the same power and glory. What has Christ not given to the true believers along with Himself (Rom. 8:32)? Who will accuse God's elect? Let the false prophets step forward and point out what the believers (A iii) still need that Christ left out. Let them point out whether the believers do wrong if, according to the command of their Christ, they perform and practice the work of faith, such as instruction, baptism, the Lord's Supper, laying on of hands, discipline, punishment, and in obedience to faith and true fear of God, the admonition and separation from the unbelievers and evil persons. Thus, given to all true believers are justice instead of injustice, truth instead of lies, certainty instead of deception, constancy instead of inconstancy—all gifts and graces granted through God's generosity, and not through their own thoughts and presumptions. These gifts must be found among true believers until the end.

Why do the false prophets accuse simple, weak hearts by attacking their conscience, saying, "Don't touch this. Don't touch that" (Col. 2:12), as though one did wrong if he employed or submitted himself to the gifts of faith? God grant that these false prophets may recognize their folly and conceit. However, if the false prophets would deal in this manner with the unbelievers, whose works are hypocritical, I would allow them to speak thus. But whoever boasts, or is able to boast, of faith, he can also with a good conscience boast of, and employ, the presents and gifts of faith through Christ. For Paul says, indeed, that everything has been given to us by Christ through faith in Him, according to the gift and measure of the members of Christ's body, in order that the foot does not present itself as an eye or the hand as a foot. This diversity of the gifts of grace each one must, in the fear of God, intensively and zealously discover and heed for himself so that the eye may not do its work apart from the foot or hand, or the foot or hands act as if they do not have the eye, lest they omit their function (as such spirits think). If the spirits were right, what could we make of Christ's words when He says in Matthew 18:8, 9: "If your eye offends you, pull it out, do likewise to the hand and the foot if they offend." If the false prophets were correct, members who did possess gifts and graces could never come into the heavenly kingdom if only one member of the body should be deficient in regard to these gifts and graces. This view contradicts the Word of Christ, given above.

Let the false teachers show me one who has not had a weakness of the flesh or who has not lacked any of the gifts of the spirit since the times of Christ—Christ who is the Head, and has rightly had to have, and still has, preeminence among all flesh since He is Christ Himself and possesses all gifts and perfect power. Paul decried his own weakness (Rom. 7:14-25), even though he was in the office of preacher, an elected vessel and light to the heathen (Acts 9:15). Therefore, Christ requires the unity of (A iiii) faith and the joining together of the members through the bond of love (Eph. 4:15, 16; Col. 2:2; 3:14). He, therefore, petitions the Father (Jn. 17:21) on behalf of His own so that they might remain one in Him, just as He (Jn. 1:1) Himself was one with the Father. In these united members, God is all in all (1 Cor. 15:28). For God the Father is not completely in any one member of Christ's body (which body endures until the end of the world) or in the single member alone; rather, He is all in all when the members are knit together under the Head and united through His Spirit, which compensates for all failure and deficiency in them. If the foot does not have an eye, in this union it receives an eye, just as the eye receives a foot, hand, ears, and all corporal members. Although members of the body of Christ are present in these last dangerous times, nevertheless, they are weak and deficient. The closer the final day, the weaker they become. Because man becomes weaker the nearer that day approaches, so Paul commanded (Heb. 10:25) that they should not, as some do, leave the congregation. Christ also said (Lk. 18:8): "Do you think that when the Son of Man comes that He will find faith on the earth?"

I fear that those false prophets who wait for a second commission will experience what the Jews experienced because they did not want, in their view, to have the son of a carpenter for a Messiah (Mt. 13:55; Jn. 7:40-44). They completely overlooked the time, for they saw and desired in Christ only the scandalous and not the true, and thus they must perish even to this day. May God grant them the recognition of their error. Although, according to these prophets, an Elijah will come who will reveal and punish all hypocrites and liars, yet he will certainly not work against the command and Word of Christ (which has its effect in faith); rather, he will bring them to justice and reveal them, just as, to their own shame, the hypocrites and liars must be exposed. Christ Himself announces that Elijah must indeed come, and He (Christ) presents Himself as Elijah when He says: "Elijah has already come" (Mt. 17:12; Mk. 9:12). Although the text seems to refer to John the Baptist alone, it cannot really be understood to refer only to him, but also to Christ. It is not John but Christ alone to whom power and glory belong, who has set all things right (Rom. 5:18, 19). John was only the evangel, and he himself said (Jn. 1:21): "I am not Elijah."[8] But whoever wishes to understand John as being Elijah, who had corrected all things, which is impossible, has Matthew 11:9-11 against him: "If you want to suppose that he is Elijah," etc. Thus, it is proved and demonstrated that our acceptance of the Word of Christ and our faith (A v) in Him is more authoritative than God's commission and requirement of John. For Christ is not sent to the unbelieving (Mt. 9:2, 22, 28; 15:28; Luke 5:33 f.), not because Christ lacks anything, but because He who rejects Him is found to be lacking. This Elijah-Christ who has been sent to us from the Father has, during the time of His humanity, drawn to Himself and saved the obedient ones who gave heed to and reverenced the commands of the Father. He has restored them, but not those who have, in lies and hypocrisy, employed the law or abandoned the law altogether. But Christ blew on the spark and the glowing wick, and brought them into a lively flame (Mt. 12:20). Those who sincerely seek Christ may hope for this divine assistance, although the fall of which Paul speaks (2 Thess. 2:3), which had to take place before the Son of Man could be revealed in His glory, is more serious than any other fall (Heb. 2:2, 3, 6:4-6, 10:26, 27; 2 Pet. 2:21; Mt. 10:33, 11:21-24, 12:38-42). Those will endure who seek Christ in true faith and from the heart according to His command and Word, of which not a tittle will pass away (Mt. 5:18; 24:35). As the Lord declared to Nicodemus (Jn. 3:10) who was, as we know, a master in Israel, a deficiency like that found in both the God-fearing Jews and in Nicodemus himself will appear. But those who now seek Christ as described above, and continue to do so, will be saved, renewed, and strengthened through Elijah, whom Christ, according to the opinion of those false prophets, will send to us. The glowing wick will not be extinguished.

I am surprised that such false teachers do not recognize their hypocrisy, which is so great that, through them, the devil needs no cunning to lead others astray; nor do they give regard to the word of Jude (13), who spoke of the spewing out of their shame. They blame the use of Christ's ceremonies. Let them blame their own hypocritical hearts and their own unbelief, which prompted them, because of the ceremonies, to join with the believers. Since they cannot look into another man's heart to test his faith, and since they cannot find true repentance or fear concerning their own unbelief in the ceremonies, it would be better not to pour out scandal designed to make the believers fall. Why do they not wait for the fruit, and punish that which is bad in themselves and others, instead of blaming, to their own condemnation, the ceremonies and the elect of God? As the Lord says, "Woe to him who offends the least of mine. It were better for him that a millstone were tied about his neck and he were sunk in the deepest part of the sea" (Mt. 18:6). Why don't they concern themselves more with the Word of Christ and such judgments which fall upon them when they attack, mislead, and confuse the weak and small with their swift, satanic cunning? (A vi) One does no wrong if, out of the deepest conviction of the heart, out of belief, and out of the inward living Word, one submits oneself to the work, teaching, and deeds of Christ, and appropriates them, not according to the letter, but according to His Word and command. The Scriptures are also a witness to the true teaching of the humanity of Christ and the teaching of the apostles; through Christ's humanity, the inward must be revealed and recognized. Since the Adamic nature and fall has imprisoned the spirit and inward life under the darkness and obscurity of the flesh (Rom. 7:17-20), the flesh cannot with assurance be set free and redeemed in anyone without the external key (which is the humanity of Christ).

Down with those prophets who say that the drawing of the Father and the unknown hidden Spirit of God have been manifested and recognized without the revelation and knowledge of Christ (Mt. 11:25; Lk. 10:21; Jn. 14:17). Down with the spirits who say that one is able to believe in the Son of God, His human voice and speech, teaching and works without being drawn by the Father (Jn. 6:44). This breath or Spirit of God would have remained an eternal secret without the humanity and the physical voice of Christ. Where this physical voice of Christ—which Christ even today channels through men and the Scriptures, which are preserved for us and are still a witness to Him—is believed sincerely our spirit is free and the drawing of the Father revealed. The Spirit of Christ, our assurance (Rom. 8:31-39) in all works, deeds, and gifts, possesses all power and authority, even until the end of the world. I defy those false teachers who teach that a really good work of faith can occur apart from the working of the Holy Spirit. Whoever believes that Jesus is the Christ of God (1 Jn. 4:2, 5:1; Jn. 20:28, 29) has the Spirit of God. "This flesh and blood cannot reveal," as Christ says to Peter: "Upon this rock I will build my church" (Mt. 16:18). Therefore, every command is made in faith, and all authority comes forth from faith. Concerning this faith, Christ says to His disciples: "What I say to you, I say to all" (Mk. 13:37); "Who because of your word believe in me" (Jn. 17:20). With such a promise and the consolation of Christ, I comfort myself, as do all believers, who are unprofitable servants that do not work, but simply receive the physical words and voice of Christ in order that we may confess them and thereby testify to His physical works, leaving the effect to God the Father, Son, and Holy Spirit (A vii), who have worked until now and have reigned from eternity and will reign in eternity.

Such authority is committed to all true believers by Christ, their Master. Christ also comforts them to act in all external commands in accordance with the gift and the measure of faith which is given to each. Not all are apostles, not all are prophets, not all perform miracles, not all are teachers (1 Cor. 12:29). But none of these gifts of faith will be lacking to the believers in their need. For whoever believes that all authority has been given to Christ, attested to by His words (Mt. 28:18), moves, speaks, and acts not out of his own authority but by the authorization of Christ (1 Pet. 4:10; Acts 3:6; Rom. 15:18, 19; 2 Cor. 3:5; 4:10; 5:20). For Christ never says to the apostles: "Go forth, all power be committed to you"; rather, He says: "To me all power is given—therefore go forth." And again Christ says that it is not you who speak, but the Spirit of your Father (Mt. 10:32) who is in heaven. This authority is not committed to any creature in heaven or on earth, nor will it ever be. The Lord alone remains in power and glory forever. Therefore, Paul says (1 Cor. 1:31):

"Whoever glories let him glory in the Lord," and it is not he who lives, but Christ who lives in him (Gal. 2:20).

Therefore, surely, no apostle or true teacher has assumed this power but, through teaching and deeds, and commanded by Christ, preach and confess Christ to be the possessor of this power (Gal. 1:12). Regardless of how much the false prophets may exalt the preaching office, this testimony is evidently, even today, not forbidden to any of the true believers. Indeed, the preaching office seems highly esteemed by them, for it is difficult for the flesh to become like the filth and offscouring of the world (1 Cor. 4:9-13), and it is because of such filth that, even today, all fleshly hearts have not perceived the foundation of faith, which is despair. Likewise, these false prophets do not feel in themselves the foundation of faith but, nevertheless, dare to pretend to be emissaries of Christ in order to make others fall (2 Cor. 11:13). I should like to know where they receive the power to preach their gospel and to proselytize. I am surprised that such high-minded people do not deliberate more, but their conceited thought is the foundation of their faith. Thus, their reason drives and sends them forth for, if the faith and teaching of Christ impelled them, they would testify to the same and would never persuade anyone to stand still[9] or to discontinue in the faith and teaching of Christ. Rather, they would warn that the inward condition of the heart must correspond to the outward confession. If the teaching of Christ impelled them, they would admonish us to ask God for that inward estate which no man can give, only God through the Spirit of Christ. For even Christ's humanity itself has left this function of establishing the inward estate to the Spirit; His humanity has only spoken, worked, and testified concerning the outward (A viii) and, without the outward testimony, no concealed or inward testimony can be made known or revealed to us as men. Nor can an inward testimony be recognized, except when it is preceded by such outward teaching, deeds, commands, and ceremonies of Christ, which belong to the revelation of the Son of God in the flesh, and which are like a new creation in Christ (2 Cor. 5:17). These things must be received and employed in a physical manner before the inner testimony can be felt and recognized. Although reason and thought and almost all conceited spirits strongly resist this act, nevertheless, they must all come under the physical feet of Christ. Such prophets do as Peter did when he saw the other disciples having their feet washed (Jn. 13:5-10). Peter wished to be wiser than the other disciples; thus, he would not permit the Lord Christ to wash his feet. Peter's assumed humility, which he possessed according to human reason, became sheer pride. Christ wished to break that pride, so He harnessed Peter's salvation to this act of washing his feet, and said to Peter's fleshly wisdom: "You do not know what I do now, but hereafter you will understand." Why did Christ not permit the inward and the knowledge of a greater secret, of which the high-minded spirits speak, to come first, to be followed afterward by the outward?

According to this captious wisdom, it is indeed a foolish thing to begin the wisdom and knowledge of God with such mundane things as outward teaching received by faith, and to testify to this teaching by simple water (Acts 8:36-38; 18:8). Immediately, they say: "What good is water, bread, or wine to me? It is sufficient if I recognize and inwardly believe." Such reason despises the humanity of Christ to which that reason should be captive. For, just as the spirit once mingled with the flesh and fell into disobedience toward God, so here, too, such a spirit, which is ruined and destroyed by fleshly reason, must come under the obedience of the unspotted, pure, mortal flesh and blood of Christ if it is to become clean and redeemed to the knowledge of its first glory. As Paul testified (Acts 17:28, 29) against the heathen, whose poets also had said that men were godlike, this spirit is a sensitive, sublime creature, and possesses its sensitivity according to the manner of God. Some, however, have attributed too much to this image of man's godlikeness, as they do, for instance, when, before the redemption by Christ, they attribute all power and ability to man's free will. But such a tribute to man's ability blasphemes the glory of God just as much as those do who do not wish to see man changed through the incarnation of Christ (B). The spirit must be brought under obedience to the flesh and blood of Christ, as already described, and His teaching and manner of life must be accepted. It is difficult for the glorious, immortal creature to submit first to a mortal form, and to be freed from sin and fleshly reason by means of physical ceremonies. It is difficult to cast all this at the feet of Christ in faith, and testify to the conviction that everything has been committed and submitted to Christ through the prescribed ceremony of water baptism. It is difficult not to confer with one's own flesh and blood (Gal. 1:16, 17) rather than to submit oneself, as prisoner, to the flesh and blood of Christ which is purity without spot or wrinkle. For, as our spirit was ruined and died in the first man (1 Cor. 15:22), it must be made alive and set right in the second Man, that is, in Christ. But first we must submit ourselves to all the physical works of Christ, and make ourselves captive to them.

Thus, Christ addresses Himself to our reason in the same manner as He addressed Himself to Peter: "We do not know what He wills," etc.[10] It is not necessary that we first experience the great secret of sublime things which the false prophets boast they have experienced. They have never sincerely made themselves captive to the humanity of Christ, under whose humanity one will hereafter learn the sublime things which the false prophets have not recognized.

One reads in many pagan histories that many, through their reason, have spoken and experienced such lofty things concerning God that even the true believers marvel. But all this occurred apart from the humanity of Christ and the coming Messiah (Jn. 4:25). This Messiah was promised, by the law, only to the Jews, and the Jews then stood and hoped for the promised Messiah. But, because the Messiah appeared in such a human and weak form, the fleshly reason would not accept such a Messiah or recognize Him. To man, He was a scandal and a folly (1 Cor. 1:22, 23). Through this denial of the humanity and deity of Christ, the Jews were like the heathen. Some desired a glorious Messiah (Jn. 7:40-44), who came only from heaven, and they would not have a carpenter's son whose person and origin they well knew (Jn. 6:42; Mt. 13:55). Some wanted only a man from the seed of David (Mt. 24:41-45), and not a Lord such as the Son of God (Mt. 26:63-67; Jn. 8:53-59; 10:31-39), who was Lord over Moses, David, the prophets, and the Law, and who could forgive sins upon earth (Mt. 9:2; Lk. 5:20-24). (B ii)

The reason of man, and of those who presume to be Christians, works even today in dividing the Messiah. Today, I find mainly three types of spirits or prophets. The first type begins to speak sublime things concerning the deity of Christ and His glorious majesty. When he expounds on the lowliness of Christ and speaks of it as the beginning of His teaching, baptism (on the basis of, and originating from, faith), the Lord's Supper, the laying on of hands, the ban, reproof, and similar gifts of Christ (which are gifts only as these things serve us and not we them), then this first type of prophet hinders others because he stirs in them pangs of conscience. It follows that the humanity of Christ is exalted more than His Deity. Thus, the highest becomes the lowest, and the lowest the highest.[11]

The second group of spirits completely rejects the incarnation of Christ, and preaches a salvation exclusive of His humanity. The third group takes only the outward ceremonies of Christ, but without the spirit, as the papists and others do, thereby directing their efforts merely to external appearance and superficiality. Oh, it annoys the fleshly to the highest degree that the Son of Man, in a physical way, should act and walk upon earth by means of His members (1 Cor. 6:9-20; Acts 13:2-47; 1 Cor. 12:4-31; Eph. 4:3-16), His body (Eph. 5:30), His flesh and bone. It annoys them that those who are regarded by the world as humble, insignificant, simple, and foolish (1 Cor. 1:18-25), who preach the crucified Christ and follow Him in the cross should have the keys to the kingdom of heaven, to bind and to loose, to forgive and to retain sin upon earth (Mt. 16:19; 18:18; Jn. 20:23; 1 Cor. 5:5; 1 Tim. 1:20), and even to capture and to destroy the high reason (2 Cor. 5:5) of these prophets and fleshly ones. They are irritated, as they were before with the Head (Lk. 5:21), that the members of Christ's body should permit themselves to be released from sin by such despised people, who embody the physical Christ or the humanity of Christ.

The secrets of God lie hidden under the outward speech,

words, deeds, and ceremonies of the humanity of Christ; as Christ Himself says in Matthew 13:35: "I will open my mouth in parables and utter what has been hidden from the beginning of the world." He has physically fulfilled this prophecy, and commanded His apostles and all His disciples who possess His Spirit to "preach the gospel to every creature" (16:15). For the secrets of the kingdom of Christ can be neither expressed nor understood without parables, as it plainly became evident when Christ spoke to His disciples (Jn. 16:25) and to Nicodemus (Jn. 3:12); without parables, they still could not understand Him (B iii).

Therefore, whoever presumes to discover the secrets of God, or presumes to be taught by God, without the outward, that is, the exterior or visible, casts away, as did the Jews, the very means by which he could be taught, could learn, or discover the divine secrets, for it is precisely the humanity of Christ which is our mediator before the Godhead (1 Tim. 2:5), and not the Godhead before the humanity. Such a person should beware that it may not be said to him, as it is to one who assumes the best position, "Yield to the more honorable one" (Lk. 14:9). For they do not wear the wedding garments and, thus, are cast into darkness (Mt. 22:12). They cannot admit any gift of faith in themselves because they have none. As lazy servants, they possess nothing and, therefore, even that which they have is taken from them (Mt. 25:29; Lk. 19:26). If they do not have any gift of faith for common use, they are neither believers nor Christian, for Paul says (1 Cor. 12:7) that, in each believer, the gifts of the Spirit reveal themselves for the common good. Therefore, because the false teachers neither have nor confess such gifts for the common good or the improvement of one's neighbor, they have a dead faith. They acknowledge God with their mouths, but they deny His gifts and powers.

To surrender both ourselves as prisoners and all we possess to the true Master in true faith, we must also surrender all our reason, powers, deeds, ability, and wisdom derived from all waters. Like thieves and murderers who (Jn. 10:1, 2) are come before and after Christ, we drank this water from putrid cisterns, the wisdom we stole from writings and from men and, as if we were our own masters, we employed them against each other without faith in Christ. If we throw ourselves at His feet (Lk. 14:10) and also testify through the prescribed witness of baptism that, as Christ died, we also die in Him and are buried by baptism into His death, only then will we be made alive in such a faith and trust in Christ (Rom. 6:3-5). Only then does the school of Christ really begin for the first time. Only then can one grasp the sublime, divine secrets which otherwise must in all eternity remain beyond all reason, regardless of how high that reason may appear. To eat and drink the flesh and blood of Christ (Jn. 6:53) means that my spirit is first freed in the pure flesh and blood of Christ. If such a transfer occurs through faith, then the Spirit of Christ, which is clothed in pure flesh, may first reach my spirit through faith and seal it. (B iiii) Only then does Christ live and not I (Gal. 2:20). Only then does the chastisement of the Father begin in earnest (Heb. 12:5, 6). Only then is every deficiency and failure revealed and recognized. Only then can one worship in spirit and in truth (Jn. 4:24). Only then does Christ become my servant according to the flesh (Mk. 10:45) and my Lord according to the Spirit (2 Cor. 4:5). For the entire physical life of Christ is a servant to the true believers, and His Spirit is their Lord. Thus, the life and deeds of all true believers serve all creatures (1 Cor. 9:19-23; 10:33; 1 Pet. 2:13). Their spirit is lord of all things through Christ (1 Cor. 10:23; Eph. 1:7-9, 19), and they are again restored to the first glory of Adam (Gen. 1:27, 28) so that nothing may rule over them, neither sin, death, nor hell (Mt. 16:25; Jn. 8:51; Rom. 6:23; 7:24-25; 1 Cor. 15:22; Gal. 5:22, 23; Eph. 2:19; Col. 2:12-14; 1 Tim. 1:15, 16; 2 Tim. 1:10; Heb. 2:14; Apoc. 20:6). All must serve the believer (Rom. 8:28), and he is lord over all (1 Cor. 3:21, 22; Apoc. 17:14). By virtue of Christ, all things are pure to the pure (Titus 1:15; Rom. 14:14, 20) in faith. Therefore, Christ said: "You are pure because of the words which I have spoken to you" (Jn. 15:3) words which were believed by the apostles (Jn. 17:6). For this reason, the true believers are lords over all outward ceremonies of Christ, and employ them for their service (Col. 2:16-23); the ceremonies are to serve them and not they the ceremonies. Thus, through

Christ, their Master, they may by His Spirit the more energetically serve the one eternal God, and live according to His will and pleasure. In doing so, they do not deify the ceremonies, as they did in the past, and they avoid esteeming the ceremonies so highly that believers do not employ them. They also avoid the opposite extreme of those who completely cast the ceremonies aside and regard them as unnecessary. For Satan cannot tolerate Christ's maintaining the correct and true means. And, therefore, even today the physical Christ serves us in His members, and He will serve us until the end of the world so that we may be able, by His Spirit, to pray, "Abba—father" (Rom. 8:15), and worship and serve God alone in a pure heart through Christ. That is the correct knowledge of God and Christ which belongs to the beginning of a Christian life.[12] If anything else is necessary for us in the future, the Lord will certainly reveal it to us (Phil. 3:15). He has indeed said that He will not leave His own to become orphans (Jn. 14:18), even until the end of the world (Mt. 28:19, 20), to which end we are closer than were the apostles. Therefore, we, like the apostles, have this comfort no matter how strongly Satan fights against this consolation through his prophets when they ask: "Where is the authority? Where the command? Where the power? Where the deeds? Where is the appearance of the Spirit, through signs, and the like?" etc.

I set over against these prophets the powerful signs and deeds (B v) of Christ. But, even if the whole world should be filled with the wonderful deeds of Christ, they will not see or notice these signs. The false prophets will take as little notice of the deeds of Christ as did the Jews, to whom only the sign of Jonah was given. They, along with the Jews, will exhaust themselves, for they do not know the physical Christ. How can they then recognize the spiritual, miraculous signs (Jn. 3:12)? How will they recognize or understand the supernatural when they have not yet recognized the natural? Who will believe them concerning their inward faith when they still despise the outward word? Whoever is unfaithful in little is unfaithful in much (Lk. 16:10). They are captives in their conscience because of an inconsistent and serious superstition, and they even dare to make others captive with themselves. They cannot comprehend the Words of Christ (Jn. 8:36)—whom the Son makes free is free indeed.

You who are free, do not permit yourselves to become their servants. Do not permit your heart to be terrified or ensnared by any such thoughts of theirs, nor by their brilliant empty words (2 Pet. 2:18). No one will tear from His hands those who are given to Christ by the Father (Jn. 10:20), and nothing can be lost except the children of perdition (Jn. 17:12). The others will be maintained by the (prescribed) means and not by the deceptive tempters who act against Christ and His own (Mt. 4:5) to try to persuade us, by the use of Scriptures, to jump from the temple when one knows well that one should descend by the steps— which is the proper way. Some tempters say, if one cannot tear them from Christ's hands neither could false teaching injure them. But Deuteronomy 6:16 speaks against this notion: "You should not tempt the Lord your God." We must employ the designated means of Christ; for instance: Ask and ye shall receive, seek and ye shall find, knock and it shall be opened to you, guard yourself against the false prophets (Mt. 7:7, 15); whoever does not work, he shall not eat (2 Thess. 3:10); whoever does not accept the teaching of Christ and follow Him is not worthy of Him (Mt. 10:37). For the Son of God is the true door through which the sheep (Jn. 10:7) go in and out and find pasture, in fullness and satisfaction. He does not contradict the created nature which is created by the Father through Him as a lord of nature; rather, He permits created nature to remain unbroken in its working power until the last time when all natural workings cease. The evil ones work evil, and the good ones work good. (B vi)

The Lord Christ thus became a natural man for natural man in order that, by the natural, the destruction of his nature might be translated again into the supernatural and heavenly nature. Therefore, the Lord Christ in all His supernatural miracles, permitted the natural and outward things to precede. After all, He was not here for the benefit of spirits and angels, but for man's sake—who has flesh and blood and natural sensitivity

(Heb. 2:14-18).

Thus, even to this day, the natural realities must precede in order to win and hold the natural man, who will then, by virtue of his natural obedience, undergo his transference (which begins in the restoration of perverted nature) into the supernatural and into Christ's prescribed order where he will eternally be held. The natural realities must precede in order that the supernatural and natural may exist together, for man is here in physical life until the translation out of the natural life into the supernatural is consummated. This physical life, however, appears in, and is opened to, its eternal unchangeable essence only after this fleeting, perishable time comes to an end. Only then will all natural and supernatural means cease to serve us (1 Cor. 13:10, 12); but we shall serve God without deficiency, without confusion, without temptation, without spot or wrinkle. And we shall serve as the elect of God—for we are bought by much deprivation, distress, affliction, fear, need, suffering, temptation, struggle, persecution—until the victory and conquest of the lamb[13] of God through our suffering, which victory will not come before the end of time. But, before the time of the ultimate victory, Christ must and will still serve us with all His powers, teaching, deeds, and works which we, as miserable, broken, destroyed, incapable, unprofitable servants, must continually recognize, every hour and minute without interruption. Such recognition is necessary for our victory, especially in this last dangerous time when our enemy, through his emissaries, sets himself with such determination against us in order to wrest from us the servitude of Christ's humanity and completely abolish it.

Either they argue that to esteem the humanity of Christ is unnecessary, an argument which leads us into the spiritual pride of the devil, for we then assume to be already what we shall only become in the future; or, conversely, in order to overawe us, they elevate too highly the servitude and gifts of Christ which He, as a Lord and Master, gives to us in our necessity, for He takes upon Himself our sufferings and sickness, and yet concerns Himself with all our illnesses and defects. Such an argument runs counter to justification by faith, which does not wish to speak nor will speak, in the hearts of true believers (B vii) (Rom. 10:6-8). Who will ascend to heaven and bring Christ down, or descend into the depths to raise Christ from the dead? The word is near them, namely, in their mouth and heart. It is the word of faith which they preach and to which they give witness. Since they confess Jesus to be the Christ and Lord with the mouth and believe in their hearts that God has raised Him from the dead, they find comfort and salvation. As the children of David's seed, by faith in Christ, they know with David that they believe. Therefore, they speak (Ps. 116), and let springs of water flow from their inmost being, into eternal life. For they have drunk from the fountain of life by faith in Christ (Jn. 4:10-15, 7:38).

It is not true, as such false spirits say, that it is impossible to possess such living water and that the members of Christ's body do wrong when they give teaching, wisdom, and information, the prescribed medicine and remedy of the true Master, to their fellow members and, in its infirmity and deficiency, to the world. We do not, as the false prophets hold, do wrong if we, who are weak and ill, employ the Great Physician's medicine, and if we extend it to one another, to those who are hungry and not to those who are gorged.

Oh, you deceptive serpent, how dare you so forcefully employ your old craft in order to throw us from the word of medicine by which we may have life and become healthy; from the beginning, through your deceptive speech (Gen. 3:1-7), you have thrown us from the word of life into death! The Lord must speak to you the word which says "I am," and so expose you and cast you down with all your cunning; you do not seek to learn of Christ; you seek only to capture the consciences. If you do not give yourself as a captive to Christ, He will nevertheless give Himself captive to your thought and reason (2 Thess. 2:11, 12) in order that you will also partake of innocent blood, for all those who struggle against innocent blood are guilty of innocent blood (Mt. 23:34-36).

Such prophets say that one should purify first the inward and then the outward. Christ addressed this remark (Mt. 23:25, 26) not to the true believers, but to the hypocrites who had no faith in their hearts (wherein, Acts 15:9 declares, lies the correct purity), who employed the ceremonial statutes and commands of God as a cloak for their guile. Nor did Christ speak this in order to take away, from the believers (B viii), the pure in faith, His outward teaching and gospel by which they were to win the unbelieving and others (2 Cor. 5:20). For all ignorant, unbelieving men have to be addressed, taught, and directed through the outward witness of others before they will be brought to knowledge and understanding (Lk. 8:4-18; 11:33; Acts 2:42; 4:2-4, 23-37; 8:4, 5, 26-40; 9:15-20, 27; 10:36, 37, 42; 11:24-26; 13; 18; Rom. 10:18; 1 Cor. 14; Col. 1:5, 6, 25-28; 1 Thess. 2:9, 13, 16; 2 Thess. 2:13-15). Only when there is belief in this outward teaching and instruction does such outward teaching become spirit and life in the inward man (Lk. 8:15; Jn. 5:37-40; 6:45-47; 7:38; 20:37; Acts. 8:37; 15:9; 1 Cor. 1:18; 2 Cor. 3:6; Gal. 3:2; 1 Thess. 2:13), as it is already to be found in the man who believes (Rom. 7:22; Eph. 3:16; 4:22-24; 2 Cor. 4:16; 1 Pet. 3:4). Only then, among those who truly believe, can the outward witnesses be added to the confession of the inward spirit and faith. If one is previously baptized by Christ, by the kindled fire of the Holy Spirit in fire and spirit, then one may also make a testimony concerning the forgiveness of sins by the sprinkling of the baptismal water, which follows the belief in the outward preached Word. For faith is the forgiveness and water baptism the witness that the comfort which is preached to the believer is truly in his heart. Therefore, Philip asked the eunuch (Acts 8:37) if he believed with his whole heart. For so it must be in order that no lies be in the heart and also that he might witness to the truth by the outward testimony.

Furthermore, the baptism of John has no comparison with the baptism of Christ because the baptism of John is a precursor, preparation and call to repentance, and not a baptism for the remittance and forgiveness of sin, which no creature could have before Christ, and also never will be able to have, apart from faith in Christ. Therefore, John the Baptist pointed to Christ (Mt. 3;11; Mk. 1:7; Lk. 3:16; Jn. 1:15), as did Paul (Acts 19:1-7), and announced Him to the twelve men who had been baptized by John; these twelve had not been baptized into the promised comfort of Christ, that is to say, they had not received the remittance and forgiveness of sin through the Holy Spirit. For this reason, they justifiably permitted themselves to be baptized in another manner. For only by the Holy Spirit, as the true comfort, are sins forgiven, and not through any passivity [14] or penitential work, which these prophets contrive and proclaim contrary to the apostolic teaching; thus, they suspend the consolation through faith in Christ. Without this faith (Acts 11:18), no one can repent or resist sin (Rom. 8:13, 14); through this faith, repentance (Acts 10:43; 11:18; 15:7-9) occurs immediately. This faith in Jesus Christ itself effects repentance (C), salvation (Eph. 2:8; Mk. 16:16; Acts 16:31), justification and purification (Gal. 3:24; 5:22; Rom. 3:28; 5:1; 10:4; Acts 13:39; Heb. 11:7), sanctification (Acts 26:18), the forgiveness of sins (Acts 10:43), and eternal life (Jn. 3:16; 6:48). In the second chapter (vv. 14-26), James speaks of this faith, which everyone does not possess (2 Thess. 3:2); this faith is the means whereby we (Gal. 3:25-29; Jn. 7:9) receive the promised Spirit, whereby we are God's children, and whereby Christ lives in our hearts (Eph. 3:17).

Therefore, the apostles have proclaimed faith, comfort, and forgiveness of sin to the God-fearing immediately after the evidence of repentance (Acts 2:38; 17:31; 20:31, 32). Sometimes, they have not even preached repentance, but only faith in Jesus Christ (Acts 10:43; 16:31; 17:3; Rom. 3:28; 4:16) and they have not, as these disciples of Moses and John do, retarded man's spiritual development by commanding him to stand still in repentance, which is opposed to Christ. For Christ Himself (Lk. 5:32) calls, knocks (Apoc. 3:20), and purifies (1 Jn. 1:9). These practice zeal apart from faith and knowledge (Rom. 10:2). For John decreased (Jn 3:30) and passed away. Christ increased, and is present in each one who believes in Him from now until eternity. Nor, as some in deceptive, sneaking talk give forth, will a new prophet come. To prove that the prophet will come, they turn to the Jewish commentaries and figurative meanings, which are not necessary to mention. They say that, as often as the Jews fell from God, they were restored and corrected through a new prophet. These fake teachers adduce many histories and accounts against the truth in order to prove that the fallen Christians of the kingdom of Antichrist also shall be brought back, in the same way, through prophets. Otherwise, as they say, one employs unwashed hands to carry out the work, teaching, and ceremonies of Christ. They introduce the fact that the apostles waited, as the Lord commanded (Acts 1:4), for the Holy Spirit (Lk. 24:49).

Against this lie and conceited thought, I set the Word, truth, life, and deeds of Christ, and also the histories and accounts of the apostles; thus, I set a light against the shadow, the Old Testament, which has passed away. I will not, because of their lies, quarrel with such prophets; the whole world argues one against the other with writings. Rather, I will strengthen the good and faithful hearts, and bring the smitten conscience to an establishment and to a planting of God through Christ.

I will first set against them the Apostle Peter and his historical deeds which occurred for and against Christ—for example, his fighting, his fleshly pride, unbelief, presumptuousness, denial, and so on—all of which occurred before the death and resurrection of Christ. These faults occur even today in all men for whom Christ has not been resurrected from the dead through faith, as well as in them for whom He has neither ascended nor sits at the right hand of God the Father, nor rules in them as He does in the faithful through His Spirit. But He will come from the right hand of God to judge (C ii) the living and the dead—that is, the believer and unbeliever. So, now the whole world is filled with Petrine and Iscariotic Christians who, in the presence of the unrighteous, wish to judge, defend, preserve, and intercede with the sword on behalf of the physical Christ. If they cut off Malchus' ear (Jn. 18:10), Christ will restore it to him (Lk. 22:5), and their faith, fleshly confidence, pride, and opinion will either result in a denial of Christ, or they will become betrayers like Judas. Such Petrine and Iscariotic Christians confess only the mortal and physical Christ, but only very few, by the testimony of their life, believe in and confess the resurrected Christ. Woe to such prophets who have allowed themselves to be persuaded by such an opinion, and I detect in some of their writings and in their own confessions that they have indeed been persuaded. I fear that such a testimony, warning, and writing may be a snare for a more serious fall, because they, uncertain in their conscience because of such false testimonies, even wish and attempt to make others uncertain. Just as, previously, the unbelieved truth has become a snare and a cause for stumbling to them, so now they make it a snare and a stumbling block to others. May the Lord redeem us all from such temptations, for these temptations are the most serious ones presented by Satan. It is only right that all true believers, in whom the spiritual Christ lives and rules through faith and the testimony of His resurrection, should fear and tremble at these temptations.

Christ, however, says that He will be with them until the end of the world (Mt. 28:20); that is their comfort. Nevertheless, it is an unpleasant message to such high prophets and spirits that the women and weak members commit their lives to the trust and faith in the resurrection of Christ as a witness to the truth. To such prophets, the cross and death of Christ must be an arbitrary act and a punishment of God. Look, they say, Jews and the heathen also die for their faith. I wish they would add: but not for the name and teaching of Christ, etc. They counsel as Peter did when he advised the Lord not to go to Jerusalem (Mt. 16:22) because He would be persecuted. May God grant that they (as blasphemers and enemies of the cross of Christ who do not grant honor to Christ and His own) may not be even more deceptive satans than Peter was, who advised the Lord out of fleshly love. The flesh seeks a quick release. Therefore, the flesh eagerly accepts such prophets. It is to be expected that the world may tolerate, according to the advice of Satan, such quietistic and retreating teachers.

Take, for example, the Lord's command which He gave to the women (Jn. 20:17; Mt. 28:10; Mk. 16:7; Lk. 24:9, 10). They were the weak and poor members (C iii) of the body of Christ who were asked to announce the resurrection of Christ to the apostles. According to the point of view of these prophets, such high apostles should not have permitted themselves to be moved by the women; merely on the word of these women, they should not have run to the tomb of Christ. In the opinion of these prophets, the apostles should simply have waited for higher and greater prophets not only to testify to them concerning the resurrection of Christ but also to dispel their unbelief with signs and miracles. After all, they had all fallen into unbelief, because the resurrection of Christ is the highest article of our faith. According to the opinion of these false prophets, the apostles, after their fall, like the unbelievers with unwashed hands, should not have believed the women to such a degree before a special testimony was given to them which would have appeared a little more glorious than that which came hurriedly as the women did. But, because of their unbelief, they should have waited for a preacher of repentance who would have called them to repentance; and they should have stood still[15] in repentance for a certain time before they would finally have believed and accepted the message.

I marvel that Thomas, who was permitted to be so bold and insolent in his unbelief, was allowed to touch the resurrected body of Christ. And I wonder that the Lord Christ did not allow the believing Mary Magdalene to touch Him, since He commanded and permitted the unbelieving Thomas to touch Him (Jn. 20:27). He was not, according to the opinion of these prophets, a true Messiah because He did not first send a glorious messenger to the unbelieving Thomas as a precursor who would, for a time, call him to repentance and command him to pray because of his unbelief. But Christ says to him from that very hour: "You indeed have faith and are not unbelieving. You have seen and have believed, but blessed are those who don't see and yet believe." I marvel that Christ, according to the opinion of these false prophets, did not say and command: "If in time you grow in unbelief and fall, you will see miracles and great powerful deeds through prophets; then believe in them. But before such prophets are sent to you, you must give yourself unto repentance and heartfelt prayer, and thereafter I will send you prophets or apostles who will restore your fall. I will then send you prophets, as in former times I always sent them to the Jews after their judging, punishment, and repentance; they have thus been lifted up and corrected." These prophets were the first to invent this approach. Christ was silent about it; indeed, He announced something different, and merely said: "Blessed are they that have not seen and yet believe" (Jn. 20:29). These prophets should certainly justify their teaching and mission with more powerful deeds than they demand from (C iiii) the blind believers. Indeed, this teaching is a new invention against the manner and way of Christ which is not commanded to any apostle or his emissaries. Therefore, they should properly justify their teaching and message with more powerful deeds in accordance with what they demand of others. Beyond this, as they always demand of others, they should reveal the authority which commanded them to proselytize men. The true believers testify according to the manner and characteristics of Christ. Forthwith, without repentance and prayer, and before belief is established, the remittance of sin is already effected (Mk. 16:17; Acts 16:31; 17:30, 31, 34) as soon as one believes, and the gifts of God's Spirit are given according to the manner and measure of faith in Christ (Rom. 12:6; 1 Cor. 12:4-11). This manner and character of faith is testified to by Christ and the apostles through powerful miracles (Heb. 2:3, 4; Mk. 16:17, 18; Jn. 20:30; Acts 2:22; 7:56). We as believers are content with these past miracles and, according to the Word of the Lord, we don't desire to see further evidence, for these words are the words of the Lord, who also says: "Whosoever will, may come and drink freely. Whoever drinks, from his being will flow streams of living water" (Apoc. 22:17; Jn. 7:37).

Christ does not say: "I will send another prophet and emissary to present miracles and signs to him who first repents and prays." Christ does not say that, after the arrival of the special emissary, they shall allow themselves "to be baptized and baptize others, celebrate my communion and separate themselves from evil." But He does say: "From this very moment, whoever believes and is baptized, he is blessed and whoever does not believe is condemned" (Mk. 16:16). Consequently, the true believers have their power from faith. From whence the false prophets have their authority, I shall let God judge. May He make it known to them. I sincerely fear that God has rewarded their waiting and desiring a special mission by sending them powerful errors (2 Thess. 2:11), and I fear that what they continue to wait for will prove to be a waiting for the terrible judgment and consuming fire which will destroy the adversaries (Heb. 10:27).

Furthermore, they accuse the simple in faith, saying that their faith is only according to the letter, and these prophets further accuse them of permitting themselves to be baptized only because it is written in the Scriptures and thus, as these prophets say, unnecessarily place themselves in danger. My answer: I have been baptized precisely because it is written that one should do so, and I have been baptized because, according to the testimony of the Scriptures (1 Cor. 15:3, 4), it is written that our Lord Christ died for our sakes, for He says: "Whoever believes in me as the Scriptures say . . ." (Jn. 7:38), which, according to the words of Christ, cannot be broken (Jn. 10:35). Therefore, upon the foundation of the strong belief and trust in the resurrection, I allowed myself to be buried, by baptism (C v), into the death of Christ.[16] This faith is a living letter in my heart. For the same reason, we are all baptized according to the testimony of the Scriptures and, also for the same reason, we employ all the other ceremonies by the authority of faith according to the Scriptures. I wish that such prophets might ask themselves, in truth, whether they themselves do not take their teaching out of the dead letter and out of Jewish commentaries and whether they have figurative meanings, of which they are full, and with which they have indeed become drunk. If they did so, they would discover their error by themselves. It is always the habit of Satan to accuse Christ and His own of just those things of which Satan himself is guilty.

They say that all this is true, but that the time is different— as Paul announces, redeem the time, etc. (Eph. 5:16; Col. 4:5)— and that today all is different from the apostolic times. Concerning this avowal, I say to them, if they seek to convert man to a better life with the shadow and night of the Old Testament (Heb. 7:18; 8:13; 9:11, 23; 10:1, 16) which has passed away, why

94

don't they seek to do so with the light which has appeared, and still appears, in order to remove the night? How can shadow and night illuminate the darkness? How can a restoration of the Jewish institutions, which were instituted because the physical Christ had to be born of the flesh, of the seed of Abraham, illuminate the darkness? But now Christ gives life, and the Spirit blows where He desires (Jn. 3:8) and awakens the spiritual children of Abraham out of stones (Mt. 3:9) to spiritual birth. This spiritual birth is now prepared for and preceded by the physical teaching, life, words, and deeds of Christ, which occurred through Him and His apostles. John has already, along with all Jewish figurative meanings, decreased (Acts 13:48-52). Just as John (Mt. 11:10; Lk. 1:76; 7:27; Jn. 1:23) was the forerunner for the physical Christ, that is to say, of Christ's humanity, so too the physical Christ, or the humanity of Christ, is a forerunner in a physical way for His own followers because of His physical teaching, life, words, ceremonies, and deeds, as described above. He himself was the way to the inward spiritual Christ (Mt. 22:42-46; Lk. 1:76; Jn. 10:41; 13:15; 14:6; Acts 26:23; Col. 1:15-20; 2 Tim. 1:10; Heb. 5:9; 6:20; 9:15; 10:20; Apoc. 14:3). And He is still a forerunner through His members (Is. 53:1-12; Mt. 5:11-16; 24:14; Jn. 10:41, 42; Acts 13:46-49; 16; 18; 24:14; 1 Cor. 4:1, 10, 17; 2 Cor. 3:6, 18; 5:17-21; Eph. 4:1; Phil. 2:5; 3:17; 1 Thess. 5:11; 1 Tim. 4:6-16). All prophets up to John (Mt. 11:13), who with his finger pointed to Christ as the Lamb that takes away the sin of the world (Jn. 1:29), have prophesied that all who believe in Him might not be lost, but have eternal life (Jn. 3:16) (C vi).

This Christ and Son of God demands neither time, place, nor person, but whosoever will, may come and drink (Jn. 7:37). As the Holy Spirit speaks through the psalmist: "Today, if you will hear his voice . . ." (Ps. 95:8). And again: "So long as it is today, do not harden your hearts" (Heb. 3:7). The place of worship is no longer in Jerusalem. The true worshipers will worship in spirit and in truth, that is, in faith (Jn. 4:23, 24). Here no individual is recognized, for Christ alone matters. Whoever believes and is baptized will be saved. Whoever does not believe will be condemned (Mk. 16:16).

No prophet is of any avail if he is sent to institute something different from that which Christ has instituted. Those who fall or have fallen away from Christ (as evidenced, for example, in the denial of Peter, the unbelief of Thomas, and the ignorant zeal of Paul) or, on the other hand, the constancy of John have all been sustained and restored by Christ. These are not figurative testimonies; rather, they occurred for our instruction and warning. All figurative Jewish testimonies and meanings are of no value or use to those who fall. For Christ is the same Christ today, yesterday, now, and in eternity.

Christ's name is known to the whole world, especially to the nominal Christians, and it is quite unnecessary to preach that man should accept the Lord as Savior, for the whole world confesses Him as Savior. Those who pretend to be Christians, however, deny Him with their lives, teaching, and works. Similarly, the Jews confessed God and His law, but denied Him with their lives. All the prophets did not change the law of God; they renewed it in their lives. Why should the Christians, who have again presented and given themselves to Christ their Lord by a renewal of their lives, not then be permitted to employ again His teaching and command and to have the same freedom as Paul? That is to say, to be a Jew to the Jews, a pagan to the pagans, a nominal Christian to the nominal Christians until such time as many of them are won to a renewal of their lives in Christ (1 Cor. 9). Paul was an Athenian to the Athenians (Acts 17:22, 23). He demonstrated to them their own superstition and idolatrous worship through these words: "Some of your poets have said that we are of divine offspring. . . ." Since Paul thus enjoyed his Christian freedom, why should we not be permitted to admonish those who pretend to be Christians, to turn their lives and teaching to the true Christian conduct and belief? And if they consent and believe (C vii), why should they not also be permitted to witness to the truth of their hearts by baptism, the Lord's Supper, and other ceremonies in order to establish the truth according to the testimony of their Lord and Master and in the freedom of the Spirit, and not according to the strictures of the law? For it is better to seek in the darkness with the light than with the shadow. I fear that, despite dangerous times, he who has not been found with the light won't be found with the shadow either. Paul did not speak such words so that, in their necessity, the faithful should not employ the teaching, deeds, and ceremonies of Christ. Rather, he spoke in the manner of Christ, who says that, when they deliver us to princes and lords, we should be as wise as serpents and harmless as doves, and also that we should not throw pearls before swine.

Oh, how earnestly Satan seeks to tear from those who believe in Him the freedom Christ bestows (Col. 1:13; Tit. 1:14)! Everything has been given to us by Christ (Rom. 8:32). Even if many have already lost these gifts, they will not be healed by any other prophet nor, as these false teachers pretend, will they be healed by returning to Jewish traditions, but only by Christ Himself, and the teaching He and His apostles planted.

I am surprised that Peter and the other disciples (Acts 1:24, 25) were permitted to elect, by casting lots, another apostle in Judas' place before the Holy Spirit was sent, for whom the Lord had commanded them to wait (Lk. 24:49). Furthermore, they had not received any other command by a special mission to elect another. They acted according to the manner, command, and testimony of the Scriptures, which Peter cited. Why do these spirits then accuse the true believers of wrongdoing when, in their necessity, they also elect leaders and apostles according to the manner of men and the testimony of the Scriptures? If such false spirits argue that too many false, deceptive apostles and teachers are elected from whom much dissension comes, and offer this as the reason for not proceeding, then I say that neither Peter nor the other apostles cited the case of Judas' betrayal, whom Christ had elected, as a reason to refrain from electing Matthias. If you argue that because of Judas the Scriptures had to be fulfilled, then I say to you that the Scriptures must also be fulfilled in order to call workers into the harvest. Where the harvest is great and few workers are at hand (Mt. 9:37; Lk. 10:2; Eph. 6:12; Acts 4:49), these reapers may turn out to be deceptive workers, like Judas. If it becomes necessary to elect another bishop, we are still able to refer to the Scriptures on which Peter based the election (Ps. 69:25; 109:8) (C viii). This fact is clear enough. Nevertheless, there are those who distinguish the apostolic office from the office of bishop. If this distinction were valid, Peter, according to the testimony of the psalmist, must have chosen a bishop and not an apostle; nor could he, in order to elect another, have employed with any truth the words "and let another take his bishopric."[17] And perhaps these prophets even think that they subsequently had the duty to remove Matthias, ostensibly because he had been elected improperly without authorization by the hundred and twenty. To such false teachers, everything done at that time would soon be rejected.

Oh, you leaders of the blind, before you pour out such lofty things concerning Christ and how He sits in heaven, I wish you would truly open your eyes with respect to Christ's humanity, and permit the Lord to rub the prepared clay (which means the outward work, teaching, and deeds of Christ done for the world's benefit) over your eyes (Jn. 9:6).[18] According to your own opinion, you have seen Him and possess the knowledge which He gives; I am truly concerned that the clay may appear to you as despicable, foolish, and shameful (1 Cor. 1:18; 2:14; Acts 13:41; Jude 10, 18). According to your opinion, you have experienced lofty things and assumed you have seen them. Those who, in their lofty artistry and thought, despise such a work of clay either find Christ too glorious and too exalted in His external work to serve men and therefore, like Peter, they resist the washing of their feet, although fleshly reason alone caused Peter to do so; or they are so high-minded that they don't believe themselves to be in need of such simple clay. One blind leader of the blind is like another; each thinks he can see but, in reality, all are blind to the truth. Would to God that they had been born physically blind rather than spiritually blind. The Jewish blindness could not be remedied, for no spiritual blindness can be healed. To them all, Christ has come as a point of decision so that the blind might receive sight and those who see might become blind (Jn. 9:1-34). I was born blind through my former unbelief, the reason for which blindness you may ask of my parents, but the desire has always been in me to be able to see. But the man

Jesus, whom God sent, also has prepared a work of clay in our times, stroked it on my eyes and the eyes of many others, and sent us to the Pool of Siloam to wash by pure faith in Christ. I have received my sight. May the Lord protect my vision, and the vision of all who are redeemed out of darkness, from all deceivers, conceit, and presumption.

The deceivers despise not only the first principles (Heb. 5:12) but also the milk (1 Cor. 3:2); they choke themselves (D) on the food, and will not learn to walk with the support of the humanity of Christ, as children walk with the aid of the bench (Mt. 11:16); they will not humble themselves under the bench, but rather sit upon it and elevate themselves upon it. Thus, they will again be humbled (Lk. 18:14).[19] They are not ill and therefore, they despise the physician, which is the humanity of Christ (Luke 5:31), whereby God Himself is despised (Lk. 10:16), for, without Christ's humanity, it is impossible for them to come to God (Jn. 14:6; 15:1-11) and, without Christ's humanity, they are unable to recognize the Godhead (Mt. 27:11; Jn. 14:6; 2 Cor. 4:6; 1 Jn. 5:10). Without this door, they are unable to enter the sheepfold (Jn. 10:9). They must either stand or fall through this cornerstone (Lk. 2:34; 20:17, 18). So then they say one wishes to preach Christ to them according to the flesh, even though Paul says: "We do not know Christ any longer according to the flesh, . . ." (2 Cor. 5:16). My answer is, their attitude determines their understanding of Paul. They themselves are precisely those who recognize Christ only according to the flesh, just as the unbelieving Jews recognized Him; they regarded His humanity, word, and deed as merely fleshly, and desired no improvement or spiritual understanding from Christ's humanity, but cast it away and despised it. The believers, however, recognize, respect, and employ the humanity of Christ; His words, works, deeds, and ceremonies serve no longer for our improvement according to the fleshly understanding, but serve for improvement according to the spiritual understanding. Until He will return (Acts 2:17-21), the believers no longer know Him according to the flesh which lived with them in the world, where He lived before His resurrection. Rather, they know Him according to the Spirit and according to the new creature, His spiritual body planted by faith, for the old fleshly nature has passed away in us, and we are spiritually minded according to the humanity of Christ (Rom. 8:5; 1 Pet. 4:1-6; Phil 2:5). For the unbelieving, all of Christ's external works, words, deeds, and ceremonies are ordained or directed for their salvation (Mk. 16:16, 17; Lk 10:13-15; Jn. 8:28, 29; 13:15-17; 17:3; Acts 13:34; 18:28; 1 Jn. 4:9) in order that their reason might be captured (2 Cor. 10:7, 17) and blended into the obedience of faith, and in order that they may see. But for the believer, these works, words, deeds, and ceremonies are erected for the freedom of the Spirit, which does not mean that they should not be employed; rather, they should be accepted and observed with a free spirit, driven by the acknowledged truth and will of God.

Some of these prophets boast that they also speak out of the power of God. But they do not have the Holy Spirit, for they are yet waiting for Him. One may then ask which power drives them to speak. They answer that Peter, although he too did not have the Holy Spirit, spoke out of the power of God when, for example (Mt. 16:16), he confessed Christ to be a (D ii) Son of God. But for all their rhetoric, they hide behind this article of Peter's revelation and confession, which occurred before the transfiguration of Christ. This revelation God then gave to him in his conscience through the fleshly words, works, and deeds of Christ, which always sustained him and the other disciples in Christ (Mk. 8:29; Jn. 6:67-69; 14:18; 17:12). But he did not yet know and believe in the resurrection of Christ (Lk. 24:9); he was still a servant and not yet a friend (Jn. 15:14, 15); he did not pray in the name of Christ (Jn. 16:24); and he lacked faith unto salvation by which the Holy Spirit comes (Jn. 7:38, 39; Gal. 3:14).

Therefore, oh, you ignorant ones, if you thus want to be Petrine, then you are still unbelieving; you are servants and not friends, for you pray apart from Christ's name. Why do you shy away from the true sanctifying power? Because you wait upon another spirit, you don't give entrance to this power. You testify that the Spirit who is already present is not sufficient for salvation and thus, you are in danger. Beware that the door is not shut before you (Mt. 25:10). Take notice that the time, from the resurrection of Christ until now and forever, is one and the same time (Acts 17:30; Rom. 13:11-13; 2 Cor. 6:2; Gal. 6:9, 10; Eph. 2:19-22; 1 Pet. 4:7), and submit yourselves to it in true faith (Rom. 12:11). Otherwise, you deceive yourselves, for the days are no longer the same as they were in the time of Peter before Christ's ascension. Christ is transfigured; the Spirit of promise is received through Him, and the testimonies to the resurrection, which Peter lacked, are present. Therefore, Christ now commands no one to wait as He did to the apostles (Acts. 1:4). He stands before the door and knocks and, if anyone hears His voice and opens the door, He will enter (Apoc. 3:20). And He says that whoever wishes may take freely of the water of life (Apoc. 22:17). Therefore, your waiting will finally be fruitless.

These false prophets also hide behind the account of Cornelius: they teach that one ought to pray and do good works without faith and baptism, and they justify their teaching by saying that, although he was yet without faith and the Holy Spirit, the prayer of Cornelius was heard and his alms were recognized before God. I answer that without faith and apart from Christ, no one can please God (Mt. 3:8, 9; Heb. 11:6; Titus 1:13-16). Without the Holy Spirit, no one can pray (Jn. 4:24; Rom. 8:26). Cornelius was a Gentile. He had not yet heard of the resurrection of Christ and the forgiveness of sins by faith in His name; nor had he heard the words by which one is saved (Acts 11:14). When he understood the words, he believed, he received the Holy Spirit, and he was baptized in the name of the Lord (Acts 10:47; 11:15-18; 15:8, 9). The false prophets, surrounded by many testimonies, are full of such preaching about Christ. Nevertheless, they don't believe as Cornelius did. How can they compare themselves with him? Like many had done who had not heard such preaching about Christ, he feared God (Acts 2:5). He who, like Cornelius, does not believe such preaching (D iii) does not fear God, for those who fear the Lord will be neither unbelieving nor obstinate toward His Word (Eccles. 2:24-26), but will be sincerely converted (Ecclus. 21). God knew that Cornelius would be converted; therefore, His eyes looked upon him as upon a God-fearing man (Ps. 33:18; Ecclus. 15). God accepted him and spoke to him through the angel; his prayer and alms were heard and recognized before Him. But God commanded him to change his life. Furthermore, God showed him another way and Word, and thereby God demonstrated the first way to be blameworthy, not pleasing to Him and insufficient for salvation; otherwise, He would not have needed to point out a new way to Cornelius.

As there is in all men, there was a struggle in Cornelius between the light, the Word, and the natural law (Deut. 30:19; Mt. 6:24; Rom. 2:14). God permitted this struggle to burn freely in him, without resistance, and perform its preaching office. This conflict revealed to him a God to whom he owed praise and thanks, and it placed him in the fear of God that he might begin to pray and to do good. But, without the Holy Spirit, he did not know what he was praying. Likewise the eunuch (Acts 8:26, 27), along with other pagans who unknowingly served God, was driven by something within him to Jerusalem, but he did not exactly know what he was doing (Acts 17:23). Such persons are still found today. Cornelius could not receive the Holy Spirit without outward preaching and faith in Christ (Rom. 10:7; Gal. 3:2). When Cornelius had received the Holy Spirit, he, from that moment on, had a clear knowledge of what he had to do. He was no longer permitted to pray in ignorance and to remain passive, as he had been before. His former prayer had occurred apart from the Spirit and truth and therefore it had not been pleasing to God. For he was not yet a Christian nor a child of God; he had not the spirit of sonship, but only the spirit of servitude. He could not pray the Lord's Prayer (Rom. 8:26); he was not freed from the fear of death (Heb. 2:15) nor was he freed from the curse of the natural law which, although he was a pagan, was written in his heart (Rom. 2:15).

If these false prophets now want to hide behind Cornelius, they must also pray with him apart from the Spirit, truth, and life which is Christ Himself, of whom they boast. Then they cannot be Christians and children of God, nor can they be freed from the fear of death and from the curse of the law. But, if they belong to Christ (as they boast), they can no longer pray as Cornelius did before he believed. They must pray in Spirit and in truth according to the manner, impulse, struggle, test, teaching, and command of faith and spirit. No true believer will remain aloof from all this. While the unbeliever is nothing more than flesh and death (Rom. 8:6; Jn. 3), the true believer will not be able to slacken the struggle between Spirit and flesh. His flesh cannot bear the rule of the Spirit until it submits itself to the discipline of the Spirit. Then the struggle between flesh and Spirit begins (Gal. 5:17) (D iiii).

Only then are all defects and infirmities revealed and recognized. Only then does one learn to pray correctly in Spirit and truth. It is evident that this prayer is quite different from that which these prophets teach. They say that Christ also taught His disciples to pray without the Spirit, an avowal which I deny. Christ did not teach His disciples to pray in this manner in order that they should immediately do so, for He was physically with them as a bridegroom, they did not yet bear any suffering (Mt. 9:15; Lk. 5:34) and He did not permit them to lack anything (Lk. 22:35). He taught them by reminding them of the Spirit who would come after His transfiguration and who would teach them inwardly (Jn. 14:26; 15:26; 16:7). Before this time, they had never prayed in His name (Jn. 16:24). But since then and forever, we are no longer taught and sustained as the disciples were before the transfiguration, that is, by Christ the Head who is present. We are taught through His Spirit, but only with respect to His physical words and works.

It is no longer as it was in the time of Cornelius. No one can excuse himself by pleading the case of Cornelius (Jn. 15:22). Since then, the preaching of Christ has widely resounded, and Christ is testified to by every man, confessed with the mouth, but denied with the life. I do not hold the argument that God, by this example of Cornelius, especially wished to demonstrate and testify to His grace, as promised to the Gentiles (Gal. 3:8).

The false prophets also base their argument upon various divisions, and contrast these dissensions to the glorious congregation at Jerusalem, where they were of one faith, heart, and soul, and where they lived in the unity of the Spirit. These false prophets say that if the recently established church were the church of Christ, it would remain constant in prayer and in the unity of the Spirit. I answer, did there not arise dissension in the Jerusalem church because of the distribution of food and temporal goods (Acts 6:1-7)? I won't pursue this argument here. Christ sought to provide the first congregation with especially great gifts and graces in order that the sound of His name, which at that time had not yet been preached nor was known in the world, might be made known. Christ abundantly bestowed upon the first congregation these gifts and graces in order that the world, through the preaching of His name, might be brought to an unusual curiosity and thereby more actively inquire after His name. Now, however, almost the whole world boasts of the name of Christ but employs Him only as a cloak for its guile. In this last dangerous time (for which the greatest deceptions have been prophesied), many, under a false appearance and through whom Satan attempts to raise up dissensions, mingle among the true believers. These dissensions, according to the words of Paul, must come in order that the righteous may be revealed (1 Cor. 11:19); so, too, Christ, also says that it was impossible to avoid offenses, but woe to him through whom (D v) they come (Lk. 17:1, 2). Neither Paul nor Christ say, however, that those made righteous by faith in Christ should suspend the ceremonies; they do no wrong if they retain and confess them, according to the demand of Christ, and out of true faith. Otherwise, Paul would have taken the Lord's Supper away from the Corinthians because of their dissension; he would not have commanded them as he does in the same chapter, to take communion in the future: "Let every man judge himself and then eat of the Lord's bread— or one otherwise eats and drinks judgment to himself." But Paul's teaching does not accommodate the thought of these prophets, for he did not take the remembrance of Christ from the Corinthians because of their abuse and their dissension, but reminded them again how they should properly partake of the communion. The false prophets say that Paul should have commanded the Corinthians to pray for a new prophet who would again establish them. I wish that such prophets blamed Christ, His teaching, baptism, and the Lord's Supper, which Christ has ordered for our use, and affirmed that, if He Himself had not established order, no one could become guilty of misusing them or damning himself. They recrucify Christ in themselves (Heb. 6:6), and make Him a mockery. In this sense, Paul would have had to make Christ a Moses figure who would have introduced the ceremonies, not to serve our faith, but to act as a judgment in addition to salvation. Likewise, the law became a part of our condemnation and not a part of our salvation, which only comes from faith. If these false teachers were correct, the ceremonies of Christ would become responsible for our condemnation, but they have been presented by Christ as a medicine and as a means to our salvation in order that we strengthen our human weakness. Yes, had the ceremonies of Christ been introduced in the same way as the law (Rom. 5:15-17; Gal. 3;11-29), sin would increase when we violated them and God would be angry with us, as He was before. But this argument contradicts the words of John (1 Jn. 2:1, 2), who says: "If anyone sins, he has an advocate with God—Jesus Christ," who stands before God and intercedes on behalf of our weakness and defects (Heb. 2:17, 18; 5:9; 7:25). I acknowledge that we would completely do wrong if we undertook such actions apart from a special call and command of God. But thanks to the Lord Christ who consoles us by His Word when He says: "Whosoever will, let him drink freely and without cost."

I would very much like to know where such prophets place Christ's words, "Whoso wills"; He does not say, "Whoever waits until I will," but says, rather "whoever wills." I would like to know whether they have the power to confine this revealed will of Christ, and whether this Word of Christ has ever been revoked, or is it still valid (D vi) as long as "today" has the significance of "in eternity." Concerning these arguments, I would like to have from these leaders their reason and powerful testimonies. Otherwise, if God wills, they, with all the objections I still may hear from them, will not tear me from the proffered consolation of Christ; Christ's will is the same will of Christ today, open and unrestricted, from His day until ours and as long as it is called today. And even if all mankind had been apostate for one hundred thousand years, if anyone today wills to come, Christ also wills it, and there will be no deficiency in Christ. Those who accuse the gracious Christ (as if He were an angry Christ, and as if one had to hope and wait until He again conciliated the Father) accuse Him of not having done enough for the sins of the whole world (1 John 2:2).

The fault is not in the employment of the ceremonies as such, but rather in the false hearts which abuse them. I leave the judgment to God as to whether the eleven disciples also should have separated themselves from Christ because of the traitor Judas. The true believers will not leave Christ and all His teachings, for Christ does not lose anyone except the children of perdition, and that is only one out of twelve (Jn. 17:12). The believers will not again accept Moses, who brought only two men out of six hundred thousand into the promised land (Num. 14:30-32; 32:11, 12; Deut. 1:35-36), and who himself, like Aaron, was to blame for not himself coming into the land (Num. 20:24; 27:13, 14; Deut. 1:37; 3:27; 4:21, 22; 32:50, 51; 34:4). May the Lord give grace that we may remain with our Christ until the end.

Amen.

Pilgram Marpeck's
Confession of 1532

Introduction

When Pilgram Marpeck was forced to leave Strassburg in December of 1531, he prepared a "defense of his faith" *(Rechenschaft seines Glaubens)*. This statement of his faith engaged him in a major parting of the ways with Bucer's reform movement in Strasbourg. The bulk of the *Confession* was written during the last weeks of 1531, and was presented to the City Council in January of 1532. The appendix which deals with Bucer's views on infant baptism can not be dated earlier than December 31, 1531. It was presented to the Council on January 18, 1532.

The *Confession* was taken seriously by Bucer and his colleagues as is seen from the fact that Bucer answered Marpeck's *Confession* phrase by phrase. Two themes recur in the statement: the radical separation of the old and new covenants, a position to which Marpeck came when he observed the status given to the Old Testament by Bucer, and the nature of baptism, where Marpeck reiterates that baptism is not to be seen as a symbol *(Zeichen)*, but as a witness *(Zeugnis)*.

The literary structure of the *Confession* is simple. A series of propositions is given at the outset of the document, and in the body of the document these propositions are defended. Although the literary style is rambling, Marpeck's position is clearly stated here. The *Confession* is an anchor point for the study of Marpeck, for we are here dealing with a document that we know to be written by Marpeck, and one which was most likely written only by him.

In 1938, J. C. Wenger prepared the first published text of the *Confession* in the *Mennonite Quarterly Review,* July and October issues. Our present text is based on the Krebs-Rott *Täuferakten.* The numbers found in the body of the text refer to the replies which Bucer made to the section so numbered.

The *Confession of 1532* appears here for the first time in English. It had been translated by Norman Baxter, president of Fresno State University, but his text was not accessible to us. This translation was done by Walter Klaassen.

The Text

1531/32

The following are several articles, in summary form, concerning the confession of my faith, and they are given for greater clarification of what the longer confession contains. I have abstracted it as follows:

1. First, that all sin, including the fall of Adam (Gen. 3:[7]), consists in the recognition of the knowledge of good and evil; where there is no knowledge, there is no sin (Jn. 15: [22]).

2. That Adam's fall is first restored through the promise of God given to Eve as inherited sin; until the knowledge and cunning of the serpent (Gen. 3: [7]) comes after the manner of the flesh, since flesh itself is not sin.

3. That the promise of God was the basis of the ancients' faith; that such faith is completed in the future through Christ and, thus, men had to wait for the Son of God.

417

4. That the faith of Adam, Eve, Noah, Abraham, Isaac, Jacob, Moses, David, and all others did not receive nor experience the power of free godliness and remission of sin prior to the death and suf-

fering of Christ, but that they lived alone by faith in the hope of it.

5. That they were all prisoners of sin, death, and hell until [the coming of] Christ. And no one has gone to heaven before Christ, who has redeemed them through His blood.

6. God promises Himself to all men, young and old. This was called a covenant of promise. For this reason, both young and old were circumcised, and the good and the evil were all included, since God was the God of them all.

7. That to the children of Abraham alone, who were born of Abraham after the flesh, was circumcision of the flesh given as a seal of the covenant, which God Himself had promised to [Abraham's] seed. Strangers who lived with the Jews as their servants were also circumcised, so that the covenant should not be regarded as ineffective.

418

8. That only those who are children of Abraham's faith are called children of the Spirit. Those who believed God's promise of future redemption to Abraham have kept the commandments of God only from fear and not from love. Why? Because the law was not yet written in the heart; consequently, it was only against them and not with them.

9. That the circumcision of the spirit took place through the revelation of Christ, the Son of God, who first gave this power to all. The [p. 2] ancients had only the desire of this circumcision, and a deep longing for the power of completion.

10. The power has been brought first by the Son of God. [This power] He gives to His own, the faithful referred to above, who desired and hoped for it, and still desire and hope, to become children of God. This hope is the free and willing spirit, and the power received through Christ. The will and the

power are now, and will be, united in all true believers of Christ.

419 11. That, for reasons given above, outer and inner circumcision are not parallel to outer and inner baptism.

12. That circumcision and the law only lay demands on men without the possibility of fulfilling them. They create only the desire to do, but not the performance.

13. The baptism of water and the Spirit of Christ, which springs from faith in Christ, demands nothing but love, and adds power and action to the desire. Whoever does the will of the Father is a child of God.

14. To him who believes that it is God's law and regulation, the circumcision of the law conveys the recognition of sin, death, and hell, together with a hope and comfort to be saved from them, which God has also committed Himself to do for them. This servile spirit the ancients have received from God.

15. To him who believes and is baptized, the gospel of Christ, of Christ Himself as the Savior for whom the ancients hoped and waited with great 420 patience, conveys salvation, and the remission and forgiveness of sin. It utterly takes away all fear and bondage, sin, death, and hell, comforts and strengthens bruised hearts and gives them strength and power to do the will of God.

16. Those who thus believe in Christ Jesus are made alive from all dead works of the law and circumcision, for Christ has made the consummation on the cross and finished what was promised to Abraham [Jn. 19:30].

17. From now on, therefore, faith in Christ can do and produce what pleases God; disease and death are undone; life and health are at hand. The

salvation of all men is accomplished, ignorance is excused, and, to children and all who have true simplicity [of spirit], the kingdom of God is given.

18. The knowledge of good and evil, preached by the natural or divine law, is a matter of the heart, provided that [the heart] is taken captive by the simplicity of faith in Christ, that the heart itself gives testimony to the truth, and that it is baptized. [Such a person] again becomes like a child, after the order of Christ [p. 3].

19. Thus, one cannot baptize young children on the basis of the figure or analogy of circumcision for this reason: circumcision is given under the promise of God, in which were included young and old. Faith in Christ only takes reason, an enemy of God, captive, and casts it into the simplicity of faith. Where the Spirit thus testifies, there baptism too is a witness and a revelation in Christ.

20. If one is baptized in infancy before pride, cunning, and self-will (which are surrendered in baptism through faith), are present, the cunning serpent has a free hand. He achieves his effect in the understanding of the unregenerate, and implies with false treachery that [the baptized one] is already a Christian. This, may God have mercy, is what one sees in all people who have been baptized in infancy.

21. Whoever believes and is baptized shall be saved; whoever does not believe is condemned [Mk. 16:16]; where there is no faith all teaching is of no avail and baptism is no baptism.

22. Where children are baptized contrary to Christ's intention, insufficient attention is given to His Word, and they are baptized only with water without the Spirit, as shall be revealed, for water and blood are given to the Spirit as witnesses [1 Jn. 5:6-8]. The creature is preferred to the Creator, who

421

422

111

Himself is the one who first gives birth.

23. The covenant from God included all [members of Israel], and the circumcision was the sign of the covenant, not a witness. God Himself was the witness; therefore, young and old were circumcised.

423

24. But not all men make the covenant of a good conscience with God [1 Pet. 3:21]. To those who make it, however, water is a creaturely witness, as also man is merely a creature. Therefore, only those who believe and who again conclude the covenant with God are commanded to be baptized for a witness to a good conscience with God.

25. Those who are thus baptized for the forgiveness and remission of sins are, together with the children—they through faith, the children through promise—in the kingdom of Christ.

26. Such true believers are kept, ruled, and led by the Spirit of God without any human aid or assistance. Those who are driven by the Spirit of God are the children of God [Rom. 8:14]. Whoever is a partner in the tribulation of Christ is also a co-inheritor in the kingdom of Christ.

424

27. Such children of God in the kingdom of Christ have authority, so that whatever they loose on earth is loosed and free in heaven, and what they have bound on earth is bound in heaven [Mt. 18:18]. This ban is externally administered by the Holy Spirit in the manner of God's love exclusively at the Supper of Christ, where love is commemorated.

Whoever is not ruled by love, and acts contrary to it, belongs outside. Whoever repents and is obedient to love in the Holy Spirit, eats and drinks worthily at the table of the Lord, which is the benediction and thanksgiving of God.

28. Here there is no coercion, but rather a

voluntary spirit in Christ Jesus our Lord. Whoever does not desire [this spirit] let him remain outside; whoever desires it let him come and drink freely, without price.

425   29. No external power has the right to rule, benefit, nor govern in Christ's kingdom.

426   That is a summary of the following confession of faith. [p. 5]

(1) God, strengthen and comfort the weak, through Your Christ Jesus. Amen.

Alpha, Omega, God, who locks and no one (Rev. 3: [7]) opens, who opens, and no one locks; I commit myself to His will.

I have not come to pretend that I am the light, but to witness to the light which lightens all men by its advent in this world.

(2) To begin with, I do not argue against [your claim] about how God deals with His people and what He does with them, nor do I argue against your claim that He is, and desires to be, their God through Jesus Christ our Lord. He is also the God of all creatures, good and bad. For through Jesus Christ everything has been made and without Him, nothing is made that was made, etc. Through the same Word, man was made lord of all creaturely things beneath the heavens and on earth, and nothing may rule over him except God alone. At that point, God first became the God of man and revealed Himself as God in the Word.

427   When, however, the creatures through man and man himself were corrupted through disobedience to God and the Word, sin, death, and hell became lord over him, took him captive, and man was sold to sin to be a slave of sin. Because he wanted to be his own lord and god, and because of the cunning deceit of the serpent, he became ashamed and fearful, and, together with all the

113

creatures, fled before God in the knowledge of good and evil. As God said: "Who told you that you were naked?" [Gen. 3:11]. Thus, man fell out of the intention and will of God into ignorance and into the intention, cunning, deceit, and will of the serpent, and became its head. Even today that serpent reigns according to his own will; he is a prince of this world, but has been overcome by Jesus Christ. The deceit in man, acquired from the serpent and which God calls the serpent's head, will be crushed by the seed of the woman, etc. The

428   knowledge of good and evil, which was hidden and secluded in the forbidden fruit, is the source of all malice. That is the old dragon, the old serpent.

(3) Since it is now obvious that the rule and power of sin, death, and hell exists in each person's own knowledge of good and evil and not in ignorance, God has set Himself against such knowledge and personal malice with a severe judgment and curse. Although man had already received knowledge and malice in his heart—"for the hour you eat of it you shall die"—it was not yet consummated. Now, through the Word of God, he received the curse, without comfort against sin, and its heritage, which was death and hell. Through this Word, man first received all remorse and dissatisfaction with himself and his sin, before God gave him any comfort. (4) (If one is truly to receive grace upon grace, recognition of sin is even today the first goodness and grace of God through Christ. Recognition of sin is of course only death and not life; Paul calls it an odor unto death).[2] As soon as man knew himself to be corrupted, God promised

429   him comfort and hope, which was also to be the heritage of all his descendants and which was given before anyone else was conceived and born of Adam and Eve. Man was an enemy of his own life for, as

God said: "I will put enmity between you and the woman, between your seed and her seed; he himself will crush your head and you will bite his heel," etc. The seed of the woman was Christ, who was to be born of a woman and who was to destroy the deceit of the serpent in man's seed through faith. This promise and assurance became for man a source of comfort and faith, to which Eve testified and said: "I have received a man from the Lord." (5) But this comfort and promise did not make him godly, nor did it release him from his sin; he had only received hope that he would be released. This same faith and hope brought the promise and assurance of God to Abraham. Thus God again became the God of all 430 men. (6) However, it cannot be said that man, therefore, became godly; he had to remain under the curse until the corruption of the world. He had to wait patiently for Christ, who is from everlasting to everlasting. (7) He remained in bondage and sold under sin, death, and hell until the work of restoration through his humanity, in which the Son of God had to be revealed for the redemption through His blood. In the hour of Christ's death on the cross, Christ made atonement for sin by Himself and to Himself through His blood.

(8) Similarly, there is no godliness nor redemption from sins in the promise to Abraham; bondage, sin, death, hell, and fear remain (9), even though He is the God of Abraham, Isaac, and Jacob, and Christ, the resurrection, issues from it. However, He shows Himself to be the resurrection and the life, the firstborn of the dead. And in the revelation 431 of Christ, God has first given Himself to be known so that they may all believe in Him and have eternal life. This is eternal life, that they know Thee, Father, the true God, and Jesus Christ whom Thou has sent. (10) Thus, eternal life exists in knowledge

115

and understanding. (11) Innocent children are not included in this knowledge and understanding because (12) they have another assurance from Christ. (13) For Christ came, as the covenant itself, only after the promise to Abraham (14). This was not the covenant which Abraham kept (15), since the prophet Jeremiah [31 ff.] would not then have spoken of another one: "I will establish a covenant, not like the one established with your fathers, but I will write my law into their hearts." (16) That is why Paul (Col. 2:11 f.) says that circumcision can be compared to baptism. When man believes in and confesses the revealed Christ, the heart is circumcised and made just (17), which infant baptism cannot accomplish. That is why Paul speaks of the circumcision without hands [p. 7] and of the circumcised heart which proceeds from faith in Christ. To this, he compares baptism; (18) it has nothing to do with children. (19) It is that circumcision to which Philip referred when he dealt with the eunuch, namely, that, if he believed with his whole heart it could be done, only then was he baptized. Even as faith consists of personal acknowledgment and confession (20), the baptism of the tribulation in Christ consists of personal acceptance of the forgiveness of sins (21), just as the promise to Abraham also states: "And I will be their God," etc.

And God spoke again to Abraham: "Keep my covenant, you and your seed after you. Now this is my covenant (22), which you shall keep between me and you and your descendants after you: every male among you shall be circumcised." Understand that this covenant is God's assurance and covenant and not man's covenant. It does not say "you shall circumcise" but rather, "it shall be circumcised." God speaks here about the circumcision without hands, which was to be accomplished in Christ through the preaching of the gospel. Here there is no woman, but only the image of God. According to the words of Paul, only through the image of God could Christ circumcise the hearts when He led captivity captive and offered, through His humanity, the righteousness which God required. Only from Christ's humanity could the covenant of a good conscience with God come, since men were sold under sin, bound and unredeemed, and had to remain so until the humanity of Christ released them. The faith of Abraham was reckoned in hope of Christ's righteousness, which only came later: Abraham believed God, and this was reckoned to him as righteousness [Gen. 15:6], for human circumcision cannot make the heart good. (23) Moreover, although his heart was circumcised, through hope of what was to come, the faith and hope of Abraham at that time were not the goodness which God required and which is now possible. As is indicated above, true godliness came only afterward, through Christ. As the Lord Himself said to Abraham: (24) "You shall circumcise the foreskin on your flesh [Gen. 17:11]. The same is to be a sign of the covenant between me and you." (25) He does not say that this is the covenant itself, for that is to come. (26) Were we to understand the covenant and faith of Abraham some other way, it could all have been accomplished in a spiritual manner without the bridegroom, Christ, who became the bridegroom of the Spirit (27) after the flesh. (28) Only then the godliness of the heart began, etc. (29) For He says: "In or through your seed all people shall be blessed"; He does not say: "In your seed are all people blessed," but rather, "they shall all be blessed," not as something already done, but as something that will be done [Gen. 12:3]. (30) Thus, Abraham could not have received the blessing of

434

435

Christ as grace upon grace (31), but he did receive the first grace of faith, as promised to him, in the hope that he would receive such future grace that produces godliness and forgives sin. (32) Circumcision was merely a word-sign of the future grace, and not a present covenant already received, experienced, and possessed in the heart. (33) Otherwise, the text would have to say: "Abraham, you are blessed, you and your seed after you, and you are justified by virtue of your faith." If such were the words of the text, then I would allow the opinion that a comparison of the old with the new is legitimate [p. 8], namely, (34) that one could baptize children in the new because of what happened in the past. But, since something greater has come, and (35) since the old was only an assurance and a promise of what was to happen, and what was to be consummated, not really even then could the baptism occur. Now a finished and complete reality in Christ is present. There can be absolutely no comparison between what is to be done and what has been done. It is a great difference (36), for now we can enjoy the completed work; before, it could not be enjoyed, since men (37) waited, believed, and hoped to enjoy it. The reason follows.

(38) To begin with, since young and old received the promise, both young and old had to be circumcised. (39) Second, since at that time there was no difference between the Gentiles and those to whom the covenant had been promised, the sign was given so that the covenant would not be regarded as invalid. (40) Third, Christ Himself is the covenant who, after the flesh, is of the seed of Abraham and is to be born under circumcision. (41) Fourth, whoever was not circumcised was turned away from the citizenship of the testament and considered a Gentile. (42) Fifth, whoever acted

contrary to the covenant was exterminated from the people [Gen. 17:14]. (43) The old covenant brought forth [men] into slavery through the fear of God, but without the future love of Christ. (44) Their understanding of the testament of promise was quite childish, and, thus, as young children, they had to wait under the tutelage of the external ordinances. (45) Good and bad together (46), they needed compulsion (47), for the freedom in Christ had not yet been achieved. (48) There was still no difference between a servant and a child; (49) in the household, as much is accomplished with one as with the other. (50) Therefore, the children and the servants together were commanded to be circumcised (51), since, as the Scripture says, there is no distinction. (52) However, in the New Testament, by virtue of the Holy Spirit received through Christ, there is a different reality. No one is born to servanthood; all are born as free adult children without fear, coercion, or tutelage as lords over all things. This will be shown later.

(53) Although the godly Jews faithfully lived in the external godliness and righteousness of the law because of the fear of God, it does not follow that the future righteousness, justification, or sanctification was promised to Abraham, nor that he or others received it. (54) That would be an insult which discounts the incarnation of Christ, His suffering, and His death. The Spirit of Christ, which is the true sanctification, was given to no one before the suffering and death of Christ, who Himself bought, acquired, and won that Spirit and comfort. As Christ Himself says: "If I do not go, you will not receive the Comforter who will now lead you in all godliness [p. 9] and truth, and will remind you of what I said to you." The way and the cause is the suffering of Christ and His blood which has been shed for the

remission and forgiveness of sin. This way of Christ (55) the apostles were not prepared to go until they had received the Spirit of power and strength, for, as Christ said to Peter: "You are not able to follow me now, but afterwards you will follow. . . ." For this reason, He (56) descended into hell, and first preached the gospel, the comfort, and the remission and forgiveness of sins to the patriarchs (57), and led captivity captive as indicated above. Thus, the law of Moses (58) is for us an odor of death [2 Cor. 2:16], that sin might be shown to be exceedingly sinful, that repentance and remorse may take place, and that man may experience a heartfelt sorrow and mourning over his sin. Not that the law made sin greater before God than it had been before, for sin is always sin. There is eternal death when sin never becomes sin, when the heart is never broken, and when acknowledgment of personal corruption and death is not present; thus, man does not sorrow and mourn and show his grief from the heart. If God does not give this grace, or if, God's having given it, in order to urge man to self-knowledge, (59) this first grace is trodden under foot, that person has called judgment on himself, and sin never becomes sin to him. And where sin is not sin, there is eternal death, and all is unbelief, as one already sees in the whole world. They are already judged. It cannot be said that a man who has truly mourned and sighed over his sin (60) has been consigned by God to damnation; rather, he has received God's grace to be redeemed through Christ, who says: "Come to me all who are heavy laden; I will give you (61) rest for your souls, for my yoke is sweet, and my burden is light," etc. Cain, Judas, and their like had no remorse for their sin but only remorse for themselves, because of their despair of God; as Cain said: "My sin is greater than your mercy; whoever passes by

441

442

will kill Cain." He was concerned only for his physical life, and not for his eternal life, of which God also assured him. For he sowed in the flesh and, from the flesh, he reaped corruption. Then a man no longer has God, and God can never be the God of such a person, nor are such persons preserved under the law. Where, however, sorrow and lamentation for sin remains, there God remains (62), a God of men. That is the difference among the ancients between good and evil men. However, the new men, who are born in Christ, have another difference. (63) They are taken from remorse, lamentation, and wailing about their sin, and removed to comfort, peace, and joy in the Holy Spirit, to remission and forgiveness of sin, and redeemed from death to life. Thus, death, hell, and sin have ruled because of Moses' sorrow and dissatisfaction over sin. And Moses even increased such sorrow and dissatisfaction. Why? Sin was even more clearly recognized in order that man would be overcome by sorrow, lamentation, and weeping; then, man would be driven to prayer, which is the prime reason for God's grace and mercy. Therefore, the right order of teaching is that God has allowed the law to precede Christ in order to show clearly the nature of sin and its fruits. Sin then becomes (64) the reason for a sincere [p. 10] prayer to God for help. For this reason, the ancients gladly accepted the law (65), and believed it would lead them to godliness. It was impossible, however, for either believers or unbelievers to keep the law before Christ (66). Although they willingly agreed to keep it, they were always found to be wanting. Why? (67) They had the notion that they had the power within themselves to keep it. Through this same inability to keep the law, God has taken from man his self-confidence and the comfort of his self-

443

121

made godliness in order that he should clearly recognize his poverty and sickness and that Christ, God's healer, might have more fully His place in man. Those who are well need no physician. Then the Scriptures must be searched, and one finds in it death and an inability to do God's will. By means of the Scripture, Christ is shown to be one who truly raises to life, and who enables us to do God's will; without Him, nothing can be done (68), for it was shown to be impossible before His coming. (69) For all their good deeds and godliness, the ancients are figurative witnesses who point to Christ as the shadow points to the light (70) which, by its advent into this world, is to enlighten all men, old and new.

444

Then only was it discovered that they had all gone astray, and that there was no one, not one, who did good. There was only this difference: some believed in the law and God and, through the law, recognized their sin. Even where sin did not occur externally, because of the fear of the law, nevertheless, the heart transgressed and remained unredeemed from sin. (71) In all Scripture, no other power to do God's will was present before Christ, only the hope of Christ's redemption which was eagerly awaited. For this reason, Christ says to His disciples [Mt. 13:17]: (71a) "Many have desired to see what you see, and to hear what you hear," etc. Moses also says: "God will raise up one from among their brethren; him they shall heed even as Moses." (71b) Christ was to become an inner teacher and ruler of the heart, to forgive sin and to make the heart alive, even as He punishes sin and kills the old man, etc. For to whom the law is unable to reveal sin, that man has no God. And whoever does not remain in the teaching of Christ, he also has no God.

John preached and taught for no other reason

than to reveal sin to men, call them to repentance, and point to Christ, who was to sanctify the heart and baptize with fire and the Holy Spirit. For Christ does not come for those who are well; they need no physician. Rather, He comes . . . [for the sake of those in whom] sin is taking over. Here, Paul does not refer to the effect the domination of sin has upon the world, in which case God's wrath rightly takes over, as it did when He flooded the whole world or when, because of their evil deeds, He razed Sodom and Gomorrah. Rather, Paul here refers to the domination of sin with respect to mourning, lamenting, weeping, and dissatisfaction over sin. And where sin thus dominates the heart, there grace also dominates, and that was the inner circumcision of the heart of the ancients. The first grace, which is the Old Testament, has brought knowledge of sin; that is, the law was given through Moses, grace and truth through Christ. The first grace of the Old Testament, through which man received only knowledge of sin, also comes through Christ. And this first grace, as has been shown [p. 11], was promised to Adam and Eve. Thus, from His fullness, we have all received grace and more grace [Jn. 1:16], which is also a complete comfort to the godliness of faith, namely, the remission and forgiveness of sin. For this was the Lamb of God who takes away the sin of the world through His blood. Before Him, there was no redemption from sin. Neither the faith of Abraham, Isaac, Jacob, or Moses nor their godliness, neither circumcision, law, sacrifices, or ceremonies [Rom. 8:38] nor angels or principalities, neither height nor depth, in short, no creature, whether in heaven or on earth, proved effectual or sufficient to redeem us out of this prison. (It cost too much for one brother to redeem another; he would eternally not be able to

445

accomplish it.) Everything remained under the curse and, whether good or bad, believing or unbelieving, all had to wait for the Son of God, for the coming of Christ (72) Himself in His humanity. John [Jn. 1:29] points to Him as the Lamb of God who takes away the sins of the world. For sin, death, and hell have all been made subject. So, also, the Son of God Himself had to be made subject, for He appeared in the form of a mortal and sinful body. Without sin, He bore our sin and our weakness, and fastened it to the cross. Since He has made everything subject to death, even to the death which never ends, He Himself has been made subject to the redemption through death. And because the Son Himself had to become subject and innocently bear our guilt, all the others have had to wait in their guilt for the redemption. Then God loved the world so much that He did not spare His own Son, but gave Him up so that all who believe in Him may not be lost but have eternal life [Jn. 3:16]. In this hope, all the ancients who have been redeemed by Christ stood, believing that God's promise of redemption and sanctification would finally come. Such faith is reckoned as righteousness to Abraham and all the rest, but they, along with us, have been redeemed into a new people only through Christ. (73) God has not established with us the kind of reality and covenant which He established with the ancients; Jeremiah says [31:18]: (74) "Convert me and I shall be converted, for thou art my Lord and God." Here Jeremiah was thinking about himself and his people, for he said: "As soon as you convert me, I will improve myself," etc.

Further: "for the Lord will do a new thing upon earth," etc. Again, the Lord says [Jer. 31:31]: "I will make a new covenant, not like the covenant made with their fathers," etc. Now everything has

446

become new in Christ Jesus our Lord, who finally made the consummation or fulfillment on the cross. Then the light of victory or conquest appeared in the darkness of death, sin, and hell. But the darkness has not put out the light [p. 12]; it shines in the darkness. There, the face of Moses, which had received its radiance from the law, was uncovered. There, the light and the radiance itself appeared; the people may look in his face and he in the face of the people. There, life breaks forth out of death, and the ability to do the law is granted to all people. Christ has become the fulfillment of the law, and has gone into the holy place for us. There, the curtain of the temple's sanctuary was torn [Mt. 27:51] in order that the Priest Christ may see us and we may look to our King and Priest. There, nothing remains hidden or segregated, but the Priest is like we are and we are like the Priest. We are a royal nation and priesthood in Christ Jesus our Lord, who became a sacrifice to the Father for us. This day Abraham saw, and was glad for his and his people's redemption. Before Christ, no one ascended into heaven; only He who descended has ascended. Prior to the humanity of Christ, no one had any freedom, neither believers nor unbelievers, neither good nor bad (75); all were detained and imprisoned, both, internally and externally, by law and prohibition. Because of fear of sin, death, and hell, everything had to serve the slavery and coercion of consciences. All went down into the pit; the faithful were comforted in the hope of the promised covenant and Abraham's seed (which Christ calls Abraham's bosom), but all were shackled, bound, and imprisoned until the time of the Son of God, who Himself (76) preached the gospel to them in the lowest places of the earth. He has led captivity captive in the heights, and He has seated Himself at

447

the right hand of God, His heavenly Father. He has the radiance of His Father, in a transfigured immortal body; He is a Monarch and Ruler in eternity because He is the Son of Man. He will judge the living and the dead until all His enemies become His footstool.

From now on, all those who believe in Him will have eternal life [Jn. 3:15]. (77) Such assurance was never given the ancients. For this is eternal life: that they confess You Father, the true God, and Jesus Christ whom You have sent. (78) This acknowledgment has been hidden from the foundation of the world, and revealed only to us. This faith and confession gives birth to godliness, freedom, and truth, for he whom the Son sets free is free indeed. For whoever believes that Jesus is the Son of God, his heart is sanctified, and whoever openly confesses and testifies with the testimony of Christ as here explained (and not from human fabrication or testimony) will be saved. For the testimony of God is greater than man's testimony. (79) Therefore, one can no longer say in his heart: "Who brings [p. 13] Christ from heaven or the dead?" [Rom. 10:6 f.]. No longer are we like the ancients, who longed [for Him] (80) and cried: "Rend the heavens and come down," etc. As Paul says [Rom. 10:8]: "The word is in the hearts of the faithful." Whoever wants to remain under the literal law, to him Christ is of no benefit. (81) Both John and the law, by God's bidding and command, are gone, for they could only produce sorrow and tribulation. However, He who came after John, the laces of whose shoes John was not worthy to untie (although, according to the witness of Christ, John nonetheless was the holiest man born of woman), (82) was Jesus Christ—Jesus Christ, the living power of God Himself who baptizes with fire and

448

449   the Holy Spirit [Mt. 3:11]. (83) I fear that he whom Christ has not baptized into godliness with fire and the Holy Spirit can say little about the might and power of Christ. For him, Christ is known only in the letter, like Moses, and Moses like Christ, and he finds himself still under the curse of the law. For those who have been baptized by Christ with fire and Spirit know Christ and His people differently from the others. They know, to begin with, that Christ is the living power of God, and the end of the law, for the sanctification of everyone that believes. They have the forgiveness of past sins, a certain comfort, (84) security and rest through faith in Christ. (85) Those who are thus baptized must be persons who have recognized their sin and inability in the law, just as the ancients and those who knew the law, as I have explained earlier, knew that the law is given for those who can know and not for those who cannot (such as children or idiots, for whom there is no law either with man or God). For people who have thus been shattered, beaten, and broken by the law, Christ is the Physician and

450   Savior. All who know and recognize their sin can only then receive comfort and security. To this part of man's recognition and faith belongs the (86) baptism of the apostolic church (87), and not to young children or the ignorant, who have no law or knowledge of sin even though they are under law and sin. (88) That is why the young children had to be circumcised under the law (89), for whoever received circumcision is responsible for the whole law, but only after he knows it. Where in the old law was any (90) child punished for his own transgression? Much less so in the new (91), where the children never bear the penalty of the parents

451   nor the parents of the children. (92) However, that God's grace and mercy, because of the godly, lasts

127

into the thousandth generation is illustrated by the story of Sodom and Gomorrah. Abraham's prayer was granted that, if ten godly persons could be found, the others would all be spared. I admit that, because of one good Christian, not only a thousand generations but a whole land may be spared, as it was granted to Abraham. (93) That one person, by physical birth, will be godlier because of another's godliness is, however, not witnessed to anywhere in Scripture. (94) Otherwise, it would follow that [p. 14] godliness could be acquired by the inheritance of physical birth and not by faith in Christ, who is Himself the sanctification. (95) In matters of faith, there is with God no respect of persons. (96) All men have been included in sin in order that He could have mercy on all.

(97) In this matter, he sets father against son, the children against the parents, the son's wife against her mother-in-law, and the enemies of a man who is born in Christ will be the members of his own house. This enmity is found only in the children of malice and unbelief who, as children of the flesh, persecute the children of the Spirit, the believers, and the godly. (98) They are of the fellowship of Satan. The children of the Spirit are faithful, loving, and patient people, walking under the cross of Christ; they are the sanctified and the church of God. (99) No other difference is to be seen than in the fruit. In this respect, one cannot mark any difference in children; they are without justification pronounced blessed by Christ, and regarded as belonging to (100) the sanctified of the kingdom of God: "For to such belongs the kingdom of God." (101) Christ gives no reason from either the Old or New Testament; He simply says, to such belongs the kingdom of God. (102) Furthermore, there is no Scripture to prove whether these were

452
453
454
455

Jewish or Gentile children. It is a matter of conjecture. Nothing can be proved by it. (103) Thus, in all eternity, you will not find in any Scripture that circumcision or baptism is called a sacrifice; nor was anyone, either in the Old or New Testament, commanded to sacrifice under these signs and testimonies. (104) Circumcision is the true sign of the assured seed of the woman and the covenant of the future reality of Christ, under which young and old are made blessed, the young and the ignorant who are without law and all external witness and ceremonies, but who are put under the law (105) because, at that time, young and old were regarded in the same way. Now, however, those who know good and evil are distinguished through faith in Christ, in whom they learn, etc. that whoever believes and is baptized shall be saved; whoever does not believe will be condemned. It does not say "he who desires to be"; rather, it says that he will be condemned or judged. See John chapter three [18]. (106) Here, election comes from the knowledge of faith and the distinction between good and evil. In the New, the children are pronounced holy without baptism, without sacrifice (107), without faith or unfaith; they are simply received by Christ, although Paul says: "Without faith no man can please God." Children and the ignorant are not required to believe or disbelieve these words, but those who are born from the knowledge of good and evil into the innocence and simplicity of faith are required to believe. The witness of God and Christ belongs to the process of becoming like children; but human understanding, all fleshly pretention, deceit, and desires are to be crucified with Christ [Gal. 5:25] and, through baptism and confidence in the future life, they are buried into the death of Christ. Here, reason is again included in faith in the true sonship

456

of Christ. Christ has accepted the children without sacrifice, without circumcision [p. 15] (108), without faith, without knowledge (109), without baptism; He has accepted them solely by virtue of the word: (110) "To such belongs the kingdom of heaven." That is the difference between the children and understanding. (111) And, even if the children were referred to here, it would not follow that they should be baptized, or that they should be sacrificed in baptism; rather, they should be left in the order into which Christ puts them. (112) No one can teach anything which is wiser or better with respect to what is needful for adults and children than Christ Himself. For He came for our sakes, and He knew best what was useful to us and what we needed. (113) Paul curses those who teach differently to that which Christ taught. (114) Thus, one may never confuse the reasons for ancient usages with the Word and kingdom of Christ, nor accept them (115), especially those that have been the source of that idolatry which is firmly fixed in the hearts of most men: "If children are not baptized they are condemned," which is not the least apostasy in (116) so-called Christendom; (117) in fact, it is very nearly the mother and root of all the others. (118) Since the mass and the images have been removed from the heart and the sight of man because of offense (119), and since the water itself is of no significance, why is not the root of all offense also torn out of the heart?

(120) For it was traditional, and it is still the case, that all those baptized in infancy had to be Christians. (121) If we baptize the children, we throw them, together with sinners and unbelieving deceit, into damnation and death; such an act is contrary to Christ's grace, for the children cannot know and confess any sin, faith, or unbelief. (122)

457

458

459

For baptism is a witness of the death of sin and unbelief into which we have come and in which we have lain. [Sin and unbelief] are to be crucified with Christ and buried in His death. For in dying, we have died to sin only to live in Christ, in whom is forgiveness of sin and the assurance of eternal life. (123) This assurance Christ has promised to the children, and it is demanded of those who know how, through the simplicity of faith, as stated above, to become as children [Mt. 18:3].

When the children attain the knowledge of good and evil, the pretentious knowledge of the
460 flesh and the deceit of the serpent which is enmity against God (124), only then do sin, death, and damnation begin. (125) When one again becomes a child, through faith in Christ, and is baptized, one is again of the seed of Abraham, and a child in and with Christ through faith. From now on, therefore, since the man Christ Jesus, the Son of God, has appeared and (126) has restored the fall of Adam and Eve (127), every man himself takes and eats of the forbidden fruit, the knowledge of good and evil (128), and does not eat through the fault of Adam
461 and Eve. Otherwise, it would have to follow that the fall of Adam could not be restored in us, as in the innocent children, through Christ. (129) Since, however, the guilt of sin consists of knowledge, Christ has taken away the sin of the whole world through His blood, the sins of the innocent through the word of promise, and the sins of those who have knowledge through faith in Him. Although, after the manner of the flesh a root of sin is to be found in ignorance (130), ignorance is in itself not sin; it is washed by the blood of Christ, by the promise and assurance. (131) Such promise is [p. 16] not faith it-
462 self either, but faith is caused by the promise and assurance. When the flesh bears its fruit as sin, the

promise and restoration of Christ begin to preach the law and the gospel. If they are accepted, the promise bears its fruits (132), that is, faith which gives birth to sonship. Although Christ came to His own, but His own did not receive Him, He gave, to as many as received Him, the power to become children of God, who were born not of blood, nor of the will of the flesh, nor of the will of a man, but were born of God. (133) Thus, the innocent children cannot accept Christ; rather, Christ has accepted them as children in His kingdom (134). The law was given to those who had knowledge as sinners and, as shown above, they waited for the future promised Messiah who was to redeem them, who was to be born of the seed of Abraham after the flesh, and who would make a heritage of the Gentiles and all peoples. For the Lord first (135) accepted the Jews as a bodily, fleshly heritage, and He also assured them of a fleshly heritage and land (136), as well as physical rules, laws, and prohibitions which concerned the flesh only, in order that they might be held together in unity until the coming of Christ. To the ancients, He also promised the Spirit that gives life, in order that, through such spiritual life (137), He might also become the God of the Gentiles. For the first man was made for the earthly, the second for the heavenly; as Paul says in Romans [1:3 f.], at the beginning of the epistle: "Who was born of the seed of David according to the flesh, and (138) revealed a Son of God through the power of the Spirit who sanctifies, since . . . [Christ] was raised up," etc. Again, in Romans 9 [5]: "From whom Christ came after the flesh, who is God forever blessed above all." Amen. (139) Paul does not say that He came after the Spirit, etc. Because of the promised bodily Messiah, who was believed to be coming in the future and who was to

463

464 redeem the people (140), John calls it the property of the Lord. (141) Although He was their God and the people were called His own, it did not follow that they accepted Him (142), and those who did

465 accept Him did not yet have the power to become children of God. He first gave them power to become the children of God. (143) Here, it is clearly shown that the faith of the ancients was not sufficient for the sonship of the Spirit. Such power first came through Christ.

466 And there are those who become children, not of the blood, flesh, nor will of man, but are born of God. (144) The Old Testament says not one letter about this birth; not one single person was born

467 thus before Christ, for He was the first to make it possible. (145) They are children of the testament, of the promise and the assurance which they have believed. (146) In this old covenant, God commit-

468 ted Himself to them (147), for He promised that in the seed of Abraham He would bless all peoples. In Ephesians 2:12, Paul calls it (148) the covenant of promise, but this covenant (149) never had the power to make children of God [Jn. 1:12], for [p. 17] the Holy Spirit (150) was not yet present and Christ had not yet been glorified. This verse deals not only with the gifts of the Spirit (151), but also with becoming children of the Spirit. Christ preserved His own in the body; (152) while He was with them as the Word itself (153), He prayed to the Father to

469 keep them spiritually. He also says: "If I did not go away, the Comforter (154), who will lead you in all truth and call to your remembrance everything I said to you, would not come" [Jn. 16:13]. Only then was the Word (155) made alive according to the understanding and recognition of the truth, and only then was the Spirit given to forgive sin in Christ Jesus. John gives evidence (156) that, before

133

this Word was given, they did not understand nor recognize the truth. (157) Therefore, they were not yet children of the Spirit, but were only children of the bodily word of Christ (158), which gave them the power to become children of the Spirit, of the resurrection. And because of the bodily word of Christ, Paul (159) also calls this resurrection the birth through which, by virtue of the washing of the Word, faith first begins. Paul (160) calls this power to become children the first fruits of the Spirit Christ also told the Jews, who believed in Him through the Word that He had spoken to them: "If you remain in my teaching, you will be my true disciples, and you will know the truth and the truth will make you free." (161) Here, Christ also speaks of the distinction between the birth of the washing of the Word and the birth of the true liberation of the Spirit, who gives life and power and who, as Paul says [1 Cor. 6:12], has the power to do all things. However, love and the improvement [of life] is bound up with power. For he whom the Son who is love itself, sets free, is free indeed [Jn. 8:36] (162) Consequently, we find mainly three births in the Old and New Testaments, as God even today uses three births with mankind. Only the first birth of the Jews or the ancients, which even today occurs through the law, rejects the Jews' external ceremonies.

471 The first birth is accompanied by the dead letter (163) in two tablets of stone (164), which is the severe demand of God and which He requires of man on pain of eternal death and damnation. (165) And, if a man carefully searches himself, he immediately finds contrariness in him, namely, that he does not accomplish either the least or the most; he acts contrarily and, instead of the good, he accomplishes only evil. He is too corrupt to do the good

he sees and knows that he has deserved and incurred eternal death and damnation, for the good is not in him, neither is comfort nor life. Nor is any help available for him. Thus, he looks around and falls into lamentation, grief, and brokenness of heart, and seeks to flee and look for help everywhere. Why? He is condemned to death, a fact which drives a man either to God, that He may have mercy on him, or to his own resources, comfort, and apostasy according to the fabrications of his own heart and mind, the source of all apostasy even today. The ancients' lamenting hearts seek God. To them, God gives Himself, for He has become their God; to them, God has promised redemption through Christ, but this redemption was to happen in the future, when mankind, through repentance, was fulfilled. In the meantime, the figurative [p. 18] ceremonies were commanded (166) as a strength and a comfort, and they were to be confident in the divine assurance that they would in the end be redeemed, and that He would be their God through Christ, in order that they might not fall into the apostasy of depending on their own resources, from which destruction always follows.

472

Therefore (167), since Christ, the Son of God, the true comfort and Redeemer, has Himself come, all ceremonies have utterly fallen and passed away. The birth and circumcision of the ancients occurred in order to serve the laws and the ceremonies as a sign of assurance; this Paul [Gal. 4:25] (168) calls a slavish birth.

Now, however, the righteousness which is acceptable to God has (169) appeared without any help from the law, which is witnessed to by the law and the prophets. Paul speaks of righteousness before God, given to all and upon all who believe,

473

135

which comes from faith in Jesus Christ. For here there is no difference; they are all sinners and lack the praise which God desires from them. They are made righteous without any contribution on their part [Rom. 3:23 f.]; understand clearly that they were made righteous through the (170) redemption which took place through Christ whom God has set as a mercy seat through faith in His blood; Christ demonstrates the righteousness which God demands in that He forgives sin. (171) Before Christ, no sin was forgiven; He Himself, Christ, forgives sins which (172) occurred before, under the patience of God [1 Pet. 3:20]. This sin He carried in order that the righteousness which God requires be demonstrated only in these times and in order that He alone might be just and justify him who has faith in Jesus.

Here, the extent of the ancients' ability under circumcision [to do God's will] is seen clearly (173), for God has been patient with their sin until the righteousness of Christ. As the psalmist says: "Blessed is the man (174) to whom God does not impute sin, whose sin is covered (175), and in whose spirit is no falseness." The ancients have stood in the time of repentance and remorse (176) until given the righteousness which alone, as Paul says, counts before God [Rom. 3:21].

To us, however, the law has been announced through the gospel in Christ. When, through the brokenness of the heart, we recognize and confess sin, we may not ask, as the Jews asked Peter, what shall we do? The Jews, who were responsible for the whole law, could no longer find in the laws, nor could they obtain, any comfort from them. Then Peter told them about the other birth; he testified that Christ alone did not see corruption and was not like David and the others left in hell, but had

474

arisen from the dead. He says: "Now that He is exalted through the justice of God and, having received the promise of the Holy Spirit from the Father, He has poured out that which you see and hear. The Lord said to my Lord: Be seated [p. 19] at my right hand until I make all your enemies your footstool. Therefore, let all the house of Israel know assuredly that God has made this Jesus, whom you have crucified, both Lord and Christ. When they heard these words, they were cut to the heart, and they said to Peter and the other apostles: Men and brothers, what shall we do? Peter said to them: Repent, and let every one of you be baptized in the name of Jesus Christ for the forgiveness of sins, and you will receive the gift of the Holy Spirit" [Acts 2:33-38]. The birth of the washing with water began when they believed in the words of Peter, for those who gladly accepted his word were baptized [Acts 2:41]. (177) Now, this birth of the washing in the Word, because of the physical word and water, gives one power to become a child of God. (178) For, when one surrenders to it and believes in it, first one has to be born through the Word. (179) After the Word, one is born through the water. Then the power to become a child of God here in the present life and then in the future life is present. If one perseveres until the end, one is saved, as those who now accept Christ, through faith, may become children of God and do His will. For he is Christ's brother and sister who does the will of my heavenly Father. This, however, is the will of his heavenly Father, that He has given all judgment to the Son so that they may all honor the Son as they honor the father. Whoever does not honor the Son does not honor the father who sent Him, the true one. And, whatever Christ heard from the Father He testifies to the same and speaks before the

475

137

world. As His Father taught Him, He has spoken and testified.

What Christ says in John 3 [3] follows from this fact; no one can enter the kingdom of God (180) unless he is born again of water and spirit (181), that is, of comfort and tribulation after the manner of water and spirit. (182) There are now many teachers in Israel who do not know, nor do they desire to know, [Jn. 3:10] this truth. May God have mercy on us all, and grant us knowledge of His will. (183) Here, it appears, men cannot understand that they accept the birth of the flesh because of the faith of father and mother, or the faith of others. (184) However, Christ says; "Whoever is not born a second time (185)"—a witness that concerns believers and unbelievers— "cannot enter the kingdom of God" [Jn. 3:3].

(186) Thus, he has not distinguished the two substances, God's Spirit and earthly water; otherwise, he would have said the children have to be born of water. Rather, he clearly mentions Spirit and water. Since the Spirit of God, to whom the elements and all creatures are witnesses, and since the greater rightfully takes precedence, it follows that the Spirit is the first witness (187), as recognized received, and believed in Christ. (188) To suggest that the Spirit should witness only after the pouring of water is a blasphemy against God, for it likens the Spirit to a dead element or ignorant object. Is not that substituting death for life? For the second birth means that one is born out of flesh and death into spirit and life. It is the faith, knowledge, witness and revelation that the flesh, with all its desires and lusts, is killed [p. 20]; it has died, been crucified fastened with Christ to the cross, and buried in His death. The birth of the Spirit is the comfort of future life, and itself brings to life. (189) This birth

476

477

478

479

cannot be detected in any child, for it is a concealed, unrevealed creature, knowing neither good nor evil; it is looked after and cared for by the Word through Christ in God. (190) External ceremonies belong to the external revelation of faith. How can one give witness to the Spirit if one does not know Him and is not included by Christ?

Further, this birth is described in two parts, namely, water and spirit, both of which contribute their own characteristics as surely as the Lord lives and his Word is true. The first, water, conveys the secret of the cross. (191) Wherever water is mentioned in the Scriptures, it refers to tribulation, anxiety, distress, and suffering, and the depth of water is spoken of as physical death. That is the sign of Jonah [Mt. 12:39], in which the whole world is corrupted and condemned to death. Through these portals of hell, we all have to go with our flesh and bodily life. However, she cannot be victorious over us, for whoever is born of God overcomes the world. In this connection Christ says: "Rejoice, for I have overcome the world," and these words are the source of all Christ's words about the cross: "Enter into the narrow gate, for the way is narrow that leads to life, but the other that leads to damnation is wide. Whoever, for my sake and the sake of the gospel, (192) does not leave father and mother, wife and child, house and plot, meadows and fields, and finally life itself, he is not worthy of me." Thus, in order to believe, I am forbidden these things, and commanded to leave them, and life itself, all behind me and depart in patience. In summary, whoever would save his life will lose it, and whoever loses it will find it. The disciple will not be (193) above his master, nor the servant above the lord [Mt. 10:24].

The tribulation of Christ began in the hour of His baptism and lasted until the end according to

480

the witness of the Father. This tribulation is conveyed by the birth and by character of water. Paul also says: "I preach Christ crucified, a scandal to the Jews and folly to the Gentiles."

This is the one that comes (194) with water and blood, not with water alone, but with water and blood. And the Spirit (understand that this means the Spirit who offers the blood together with the water) witnesses that the Spirit is truth (195), as one can see today with one's own eyes.

481

All of what I have said is applicable to the baptism of infants. It is too grave a matter for children, they cannot consent to it (196). Thus, no one should be born of this water birth unless he has himself consented to it. Flesh and blood cannot give this consent, only the birth (197) of the Spirit, who is the power and who rightfully has precedence. (198) Nor may any one promise such matters on behalf of someone else. Through the fellowship of the tribulation of Christ (199), to which in their innocence they already belong, are the children, without consent and without water, taken into the covenant, for to such as they belongs the kingdom of God. Therefore, contrary to what has already been said, it is not through water [p. 21] (200) that they, without their consent, are received into the covenant. (201) No other innocent creature, animate or inanimate, only the child, was blessed by Christ and pronounced clean. When those whom Christ has praised and blessed as clean and precious creatures of God, and when, in spite of Christ's assurance, they are offered to God in the hope that God will accept them, they are made unclean (202) for God has already accepted them, and Christ has, for them and for us all, become a sacrifice in order that we ourselves would all become a sacrifice. (203) According to the word of Paul, we can sacrifice only

482

ourselves and not someone else: "Give your own bodies. . . ." (204) He does not add: "and your children, as a sacrifice," etc. (205) Whenever we sacrifice our children or anything else, we consign them to death without their consent (206), for all sacrifices have to be killed. (207) Here, without a command of God, there is nothing but a sacrifice to Moloch, an apish copying, a serpent sign [Num. 21:8; Jn. 3:14] (208) when no one has been bitten (209),—a killing of reason and sin when as yet neither are present. (210) To do so is nothing less than to sacrifice the Son of God as the papists did, and to pray to the Father that the Son may be acceptable to him. This act you have decried as the greatest apostasy—and it is. (211) Similarly, you have decried the baptism of water, salt, oil, fire, food and drink, and other matters, etc. The Word says: "All things are clean and blessed to the clean, for God has created all things good"—which is true. How much more so is that which has a special word and blessing from Christ.

You have regarded the blessing of the above-mentioned things as apostasy and great folly in the papists. (212) When you dishonor that with which God was already pleased, namely, His Son, how is your action different? For, as witnessed to by the mouth of Christ and the mouth of the Father: "Whoever dishonors the Son dishonors the Father." The papists have always prayed in the canon of their low mass that God would be pleased with His Son, in whom He was already pleased. (213) How is your action different when you are not satisfied with what has pleased God through Christ, and you pray God that, through Christ, He might be pleased with it? (214) Paul's admonition [1 Tim. 2:1] to pray for everyone has nothing to do with this matter, otherwise one would also have to pray for the dead.

You say that you receive them into the divine covenant through baptism. (215) Where is water baptism called a divine covenant? Show us even one word which supports this assumption! Even circumcision done with hands was only a sign of the covenant. That can be called a covenant when God assures man of Himself, and assurance is given to young and old, yes, to the whole world. Both young and old, among those to whom the covenant had been promised, received the sign. However, now that Christ has come, who has given man the ability . . . [to do God's will] without man's merit, Peter mentions a covenant on man's side: the covenant of a good conscience with God, to which the Spirit Himself testifies, and of which [p. 22] water and blood also are signs. In the first place, God's covenant depends on God's assurance and not on man, for man has not been able to help himself. (216) However, our covenant which we make with God is real only for him who is united with God and who has consented to it in the power of the Holy Spirit in faith (217), of which the water is a witness and not a sign. For Paul says that not everyone has faith; he who has no faith has nothing to do with the witness. Along with him who has no faith, whoever gives it to the innocent is a liar although only he remains a liar who is baptized on confession of faith and then apostasizes. Herewith, a man departs and separates himself from evil through faith. (218) Baptism of children on the basis of opinion, custom, friendship, piety, and faith of the parents may not be (219); the Spirit is not bound by natural desires, although God does not root such desires out of man's nature but allows them to stand. (220) Such desires are not contrary to God, but neither do they accomplish anything special before God. Paul was prepared to be cut off

487

488

from Christ on behalf of his friends, but that would not have made them believe. Thus, there is from now on no respect of a single person (221), be he good or evil, believing or unbelieving; all flesh is subject to unbelief in order that the grace through Christ might prevail without any human respectability. Thus, all human flesh is one flesh before God, for He died to flesh that we might live in the Spirit. There has been no godly man except Christ Himself (222), since even His relatives and brothers in the flesh did not believe in Him, for mockingly they told Him to go to the given feast in Jerusalem [Jn. 11:56]. Christ could rightfully have given privileges to the sons of Zebedee, but He left to His Father the seating to His right and left. Certainly, Christ would have been better qualified to assure them of this seating than we, who take children into the covenant of the sanctified, on the basis of physical birth, before Christ has shown Himself to them in the baptism of the Spirit, of which water baptism is to be an earthly and elemental witness. (223) Since man's blessedness and damnation is at stake, one ought to take care in divine matters of such seriousness. (224) So that he would not be found out to be a liar, no one would allow his name to be placed as witness on a deed for a cabbage plot unless the sale was legal on the part of seller and buyer. It is written: "You shall believe in one God." He who gave that command also commanded: "You shall not bear false witness" [Ex. 20:3, 16]. (225) I would not take this whole world should God forsake me to the degree that I would in baptism, for reasons indicated above, give witness for or speak for an innocent child. (226) Should you say: "If the child believes, it is a good work; if not, it carries its own guilt. There is no respect of time, state, or person before God as there is in the Old Testa-

489

490

143

ment when they prayed in Jerusalem, and similar matters. We are now in the New Testament and, therefore, free to baptize before or after the presence of faith, since we are not bound by time or age. It is not written that it is forbidden to baptize children," and other such excuses which you offer. For God, all this is true (227), but people and crea-

491 tures [p. 23] still have beginning, middle, end, order, and time; otherwise, it would follow that the external Word was enough for children in their infancy.

Since, however, the Word does not ignite itself where God does not make it alive, everything must remain in its order and time. If this is true in one matter, why not in the other? Apart from the working of God, one is the same as the other. (228) The child knows as much about baptism as about learning. Whatever is bound to Christ's Word and order, no one will be able to sever in all eternity. Heaven and earth will pass away before one tittle or iota

492 falls or passes from His Word [Mt. 5:18]. (229) Does this not mean binding to time, place, and person, even without divine order? First: "All power is given to Me; therefore, go and teach all nations to keep everything which I have commanded you, and

493 baptize them," etc. Whoever believes and is baptized is saved; whoever does not believe, is condemned. First: The power belongs to Christ;

494 the messengers to the believing and unbelieving people, who are to be taught to keep what Christ commanded, are the disciples. Whoever believes and is baptized shall be saved, etc. (230) In this text it is clearly stated what one is to do. Thus, there is no freedom, indeed no God, where one does not abide in the teaching of Christ, etc. (231) I would

495 be delighted if someone could show me just one letter which demonstrates that, by transgressing the

assurance of Christ either because of their own free act or because of heredity, the children thereby excluded themselves from His church and must again be received into the church of Christ. (232) Oh, mystery of wickedness, how subtly you disguise yourself until the Lord reveals you! Paul is speaking here not about vices, but about teaching, etc. I believe and witness to it before my God in Christ Jesus our Lord that is is the devil, and not man, that again includes them [in the church]. (233) Christ says to the knowledgeable: "Unless you become as children (to whom the kingdom of God belongs) you will not enter the kingdom of God" [Mt. 18:3]. Here, He commands man to submit reason to the childlike simplicity of faith. (234) In contrast, today the children are subjected to the craftiness and wickedness of the world. (235) I testify before my God and Lord, I have no desire to be (236) in the community in which parents allow their children to be baptized, for I do not want to have anything in common with, or any part of, their evil works. (237) It is the root of the Roman harlot, for such is what I find the water baptism of children to be, since it is outside of the Word.

(238) In contrast, the true assurance of God and Christ which is received with certainty and which is written in the heart, believed and trusted even to death, characterizes the birth of the Spirit, to which water baptism is only a witness. As Paul says [Gal. 5:22], being made alive in the Spirit was a clear revelation, apprehended in peace, joy, comfort, confidence, and true love, with a clean heart and sincere faith, with patience, meekness and lowliness of heart, with mercy and peacemaking [p. 24], friendliness and true godliness, with the whole heart, which is kindled by the fire of the Holy Spirit, with a burning love for God and the brothers,

with faithfulness even unto death, which witnesses, reveals itself, and believes all the words of Christ to the pleasure and praise of the Father. For it is the Spirit which testifies to Christ [Rom. 8:16] and reveals the gifts of the service of the body of Christ and the whole world; He does not strive to rule, but denies Himself. He divests Himself and surrenders everything at the feet of Christ, and is given only to service. Although in Christ He is a Lord and child of all, He does not consider all things as things to be grasped; rather, He humbles himself for servanthood, for Christ the Son of God did not consider His divinity as spoil but served friend and foe, did good and loved even to death [Jn. 13:1]. In summary, the Spirit's witness, life, and birth is of Christ, and hidden with Christ in God, to the eternal praise of the Father, to do your will, O God. These and similar things are the witnesses of the Spirit, water and blood, who give witness on earth through men when they give evidence of such working, etc.

499

Those are the testimonies of the two parts of birth, and the consummation of that birth is the testimony of blood. Together, they all serve as a witness on earth to the revelation of the Lord Jesus Christ. (238-sic) Such a birth may not be accomplished in innocent creatures.

(239) *Testimony of my faith in Christ.*

(240) First, whoever confesses faith in Christ, according to the witness of Christ, shall be baptized upon his own professed faith, and whoever believes thus and is baptized shall be saved [Mk. 16:16].

(241) Second, no one can have faith for anyone else, neither wife for husband, husband for wife, children for parents, nor parents for children, but everyone will believe or disbelieve, be saved or condemned for himself. For the believer all things

146

are clean through faith. Thus, when one is a
500 believer, the man is clean for the wife and the wife
for the man [1 Cor. 7:14]. (242) So, too, are the
children in their bodily works; otherwise, the
temple of God might not have fellowship with unbelievers, and be similar to a temple of idols [2 Cor.
6:16] (243), for without faith no one can please God.
501 Whatever familiarity with the Word, eventually
believed, may accomplish, is a matter of hope, for
there are twelve hours in a day. Paul means that,
regardless of what man and wife know or do not
know about being saved, one should always [p. 25]
hope for the best from God (245). But this hope
(246) cannot be established by a witness until it is
realized and revealed. Only then should baptism
follow and, where faith is recognized, no one
prevent it (247), as Peter says.

(248) Third, the infants shall be named before
a congregation and God shall duly be praised for
them; thanks and blessing shall be given to His
502 fatherly goodness that, through Christ Jesus our
Lord and Savior, He has also had mercy on the innocent creatures and that, without discrimination,
He has taken them in His hands and assured them
of the kingdom of God. We rightfully owe him
gratitude at all times for His goodness. In the
liberty of the Spirit and Word of Christ, we should
pray for everyone, and also for the child, that God
would also in future give us knowledge of His
gracious will, etc. We admonish the parents to
cleanse their conscience, as much as lies in them,
with respect to the child, to do whatever is needed
to raise the child up to the praise and glory of God,
and to commit the child to God until it is clearly
seen that God is working in him for faith or unfaith.
(249) Any other way is to be like thieves and
murderers and to be ahead of Christ.

Fourth, in the commemoration of the body of the Lord, our testimony to His death, the believers and the baptized are to remind one another to be mindful of such love and of His new and eternal commandment. He is the first among them [1 Cor. 15:23]; He died and was given for us for the sake of love in order that we might live eternally. He commanded that we love one another as He loved us, and He goes on to point to death as the culmination of His love: no one has greater love than he who 503 stakes his soul on behalf of his friend. That is why Paul commands the proclamation of the death of the Lord until He comes. In this bond of love, the Lord keeps His own in the unity of faith, which is the fellowship of the saints. In this fellowship, forgiveness and remission of sins through the Holy Spirit are practiced. He gives the life of the resurrection from the dead, an eternal life. In this commemoration, according to the practice of Christ, bread and wine are used as a parable of the mystery of Christ's body and blood, as a spiritual food which is eaten in faith and not in bread and wine. (250) According to the opinion of Martin Luther and others, He would be of little use to us in bread and wine. Whoever thus eats of His body and drinks of His blood has eternal life through this Spirit who brings to life. And whoever walks among this people of God and true Israelites with an [p. 26] uncircumcised heart, the same shall be rooted out from among the people (251), that is to say, from the remembrance of the Supper of our Lord Jesus Christ. For none of these men shall eat His Supper eternally. Who has ears to hear, let him hear, and 504 eyes to see, let him see, etc. [Mt. 11:15]. (252) It is proper to exclude that which is evil (253), and not to urge anyone to enter according to the teaching of Christ and Paul. Whoever lightly excludes himself

148

from the remembrance of Christ is not taking Christ seriously. And whoever excludes lightly, without some deep pain, has no power to exclude.[3] (254) If at the Supper there is no distinction made between the body of the Lord as a spiritual body, comprised of children and members of Christ, and the carnal body, comprised of children and members of the world and Satan, there men eat and drink judgment to themselves because the body of Christ is not discerned. (255) Even if we judged one another, we would not be judged by the Lord. And even if we were judged, we would not be condemned along with this world [1 Cor. 11:31]. Would to God that those who have, until now, observed the Supper of the Lord would from now on do it with better discernment, and would remind and examine themselves better than formerly before they eat this bread of the Lord. If not, they should take care that judgment and condemnation does not take them along with the world, and may God have mercy on us. I hope, however, that the Lord will have mercy on us all, and convert us to the pleasure of His divine will, that we may obey His voice and Word. (256) May we also warn, admonish, teach, discipline, hear, and understand one another in integrity and truth, and live in obedience to the Word in faith. (257) For this reason, I have surrendered to God and all true believers, and try to serve all men with whatever I have and can accomplish through His Son Christ Jesus. Amen.

In this house of Christ, there is no lord after the flesh, but only vassals and servants in Christ Jesus, for He Himself served. (258) There is no Christian magistrate except Christ Himself.[4] For men, the title lord is too great; it minimizes Christ, although that is perhaps not the intention. Therefore, the title ought to be renounced for the sake of the honor

505

of our Christ. (259) It is he to whom I grant all honor.

I admit worldly, carnal, and earthly rulers as servants of God, in earthly matters (260), but not in the kingdom of Christ; according to the words of Paul, to them rightfully belongs all [p. 27] carnal honor, fear, obedience, tax, toll, and tribute. However, when such persons who hold authority become Christians (which I heartily wish and pray for), they may not use the aforementioned carnal force, sovereignty, or ruling (261) in the kingdom of Christ. It cannot be upheld by any Scripture. (262) To allow the external authority to rule in the kingdom of Christ is blasphemy against the Holy Spirit (263), who alone is Lord and Ruler without any human assistance. (264) And if false teachers desire to lead astray, the true sheep do not listen to the voice of strangers; they are soon known by them. (265) Where the governmental authority is used, as it was in the Old Testament, to root out the false prophets (266), Christ's Word and Spirit are weakened, and are turned into a servile spirit designed to uphold insufficient and weak laws. (267) For the Word of God is the sharp, two-edged sword, separating and chastising false and true, good and evil. (268) It is to be feared that the wrath of God comes chiefly (269) because man, with a semblance of faith, attempts to protect the kingdom of Christ. (270) It is further to be feared that a faith will again be adopted like that of the pope, or Turk, or others, who maintain their so-called carnal faith with only an appearance of the Spirit and with the external sword. (271) If all authorities had no other example than that which, from the beginning of the world until Christ, always persecuted and killed only the godly prophets and not one false prophet— (272) other than what God punished with miracles

506

507

508

509

510

through Elijah, etc.—and if the ancients were called (273) to exercise authority, however much they erred in righteousness, (274) then what will happen to those who have not been called (275) and who fight against it [righteousness] even though they do not kill or send into exile? For whoever speaks against or judges the innocent is guilty of his blood. May the Lord preserve us all from fellowship with the bloodguilty. (276) Take care! Take care! It will happen that God will give innocent blood enough in order that they may all be filled who desire it. He gives His people at the lowest price and takes no money for it. For they are being killed all the day long, as long as it is called day, for His name's sake. He who purifies himself let him be clean; he who defiles himself, let him further defile himself. Christ's cleansing of His bride through His cross and blood has already begun. All hypocrites, deceivers, liars, and unbelievers (277) will run against it and be cast out, and will defile themselves in the blood of the saints to their own damnation. Because they have not believed His Word, God gives them up, etc. [p. 28]

511

(278) The pope of the old church, although now for his own benefit, in a false spirit and appearance, still considers the kingdom and rule of Christ to be higher and greater than earthly rule, for he allows no worldly power to reign or rule over him, neither emperor nor king.

Because of this recognition, I conclude before my God that worldly power, for all its work (279), is not needed in the kingdom of Christ (280), whose kingdom is not of this world (281), and I further conclude that all who attempt to preserve the kingdom of Christ by stooping to the governing authority will be punished for it and come to shame. For our citizenship is in heaven. (282) The earthly belongs to those of earth, the heavenly to those of heaven. The Lord Christ was raised up from the dead through the power and glory of God, and set on His right hand in the heavens above all rule, authority, power, and dominion and everything that is named, not only in this world but also in that which is to come; God has put all things under His feet and has set Him over all things, as Head over His church, which is His fellowship and gathering, His body and fullness, who fills all in all. (283) To Him alone be the honor from now until eternity. Amen [Rom. 11:36].

512

About the ancients I give no answer, since one can only use them to prove what happened in their time. (284) The mystery of wickedness, already evident in Paul's time, cannot be interpreted to mean vices which, as far as the world is concerned, have always been rampant; rather, Paul means idolatrous teaching, etc. Therefore, I commit everything to Christ the Judge.

Finally, after the above was completed, I again received several articles which were sent to me by Martin Bucer in a letter.[5] Only briefly will I answer the main points as follows. [p. 29].

(I) Where there is no intention to believe the external teaching of Christ, it is like the external baptism; where there is no faith, all teaching is no teaching, and all baptism no baptism. (II) Where, however, there is intention of faith, the more important has precedence by virtue of its own testimony, namely, the Word which is the sanctification. The children have been assured of the kingdom precisely by the Word. According to your teaching, they are insured, (III) but not assurred, so that they may not be bitten or poisoned by the serpent (IV), which, in your view is to acquire their own understanding and unbelief before they come to the

513

promised land. (V) The function of the preaching of the gospel is to lead people to faith in Christ, to bring reason and presumption under control, and to crush the head of the serpent through the seed of the woman. Through teaching, Christ must first be raised up again as the bronze serpent [Jn. 3:14]. Whenever man's own understanding, and not someone elses's, comes forth, and the face is turned again toward the bronze serpent and believes the Word, healing comes. One cannot preach the crucified Christ to a child as a scandal and as foolishness [1 Cor. 1:23]; namely, the predestined child, according to your view, will again become healthy and whole after the bite and poison of the serpent, which is all our own reason as an enemy of God, and this wholeness is the forgiveness of sin and the receiving of comfort in Christ. (VI) Through faith in Christ, in immersion and in putting to death one's own and not someone else's presumption, and through one's own faith, and not that of another, baptism is a witness to the inner conviction that one's sins are forgiven. (VII) And for this reason, the Lord Christ gave precedence to teaching, not solely because teaching is more important than baptism (VIII); such precedence was given because of the order of God and man, which is first to learn what can be learned. Of what value is it that teaching is more than baptizing? If I taught a stick, would it not be as though I baptized it? (IX) In what manner would the teaching be more important than the deed? If the teaching is primary, it must be so in the deed; otherwise, it is dead, and the words are spoken into the wind and accomplish nothing. If teaching, therefore, has precedence to the deed, then faith also has precedence to the deed, for the spirit bears witness to the teaching, in the inner man, which is believing the teaching. If the teach-

514

ing is believed, reason and human presumption are taken captive; otherwise, faith would not be faith. Under this condition, sin is forgiven, and the advice of Peter applies: Let everyone be baptized in the name of Jesus Christ for the forgiveness of sins. Those who gladly accepted his word were baptized. There the order of God and man was observed: first teaching, then faith, and only then baptism. (X) Baptism may not be called sacrifice, for no Scripture supports such a conclusion [p. 30]. However, Scripture does speak of being crucified with Christ, of putting off, putting to death, and burying in the death of Christ the old man, that is, all desire and deception, mind and reason. (XI) For in that Christ died, He died to sin. Along with similar metaphors, baptism is spoken of as taking off the old garment and putting on the new. (XII) A fine sacrifice it would be if I gave the Lord the stinking, sinful, carnal old slag, self-will and reason, sin and unrighteousness, all of which are an abomination before the face of God. All of these are put to death in baptism; they are condemned, judged, and turned over to hell, and laid on Christ, who has condemned our sin in His death. In that we now live, we live in the righteousness of Christ (XIII), who became a sacrifice for us in His righteousness and innocence which is valid before the face of God. It is clear that baptism is no sacrifice, for this is contrary to all Scripture. It is simply a putting to death of our desires. (XIV) If baptism is a sacrifice, then the baptism of children is a sacrifice to Moloch. (XV) Each one is to sacrifice his own body, cleansed through the blood of Christ. He says: Give your bodies a living sacrifice; He does not say: Your children, too. He would not have had to use the little word "your"; He could have said: give the bodies of your children. Even that would not be sufficient grounds for offering the children in baptism.

(XVI) Paul says that God has consigned everything to unbelief in order that He might have mercy on us all. It follows, then, that unbelief must first make its appearance in all men. Even though the child were born of a Christian a thousand times over and even though it were predestined by God, the first fruit of its self-recognition and knowledge (XVII), provided the child comes to that time, is unbelief and sin. This fruit is alien, for it proceeds from flesh and blood and is the offspring of an alien birth; it does not belong in the kingdom of Christ [1 Cor. 15:20]. Unbelief will show itself in man, unless, of course, he is not accountable. We can all see that there is no better way in man than unbelief and sin. And if the parents' teaching of Christ were not absent from him for one moment, it would be to no avail; unbelief would first show itself. (XVIII) Thus, he is already outside the kingdom of Christ. Therefore, all unbelief is the same with God, whether they be the children of Christians or otherwise. (XIX) Whoever does not believe is condemned and already judged [Mk. 16:16]. If you consent to the desire to baptize adult strangers [p. 31] (XX), why not also those in your own homes (XXI), since all are consigned to unbelief [Rom. 11:32]? (XXII) Therefore, teaching is of primary importance for . . . [your children]; so, too, for the children of Jews and Gentiles. The command to teach, believe, and baptize applies to all unbelievers (XXIII), since God is no respecter of persons [Acts 10: 34]. (XXIV) Unbelief is unbelief, whether in the children of Christians or strangers. (XXV) I won't mention the wretched nurture and teaching parents provide. Well and good that they have faith and teach. Indeed, although I don't say it of all, parents do display pride and avarice, usury and gluttony;

516

155

they lie, deceive, and gossip; they blaspheme; they are drunkards, gamblers, and murderers. Yes, burdened with all vices, how can such parents teach children the teaching of faith? (XXVI) But you baptize the children of all, even children of parents (XXVII) who have no faith. (XXVIII) If they are not alien guests in the kingdom of Christ, I don't know what alien means. I commit it to God's judgment.

(XXIX) I agree when you say that individual surrender, offering, and confession accomplishes nothing before God. Indeed, personal confession and carnal reason avail nothing. However, personal confession of faith in Christ does avail. If such is not the case, Paul is a liar when he says: Faith justifies, and confession brings salvation, etc. (XXX) If you say that the confession of aliens and the faith of aliens (which you believe avails for something) is nothing, that would be well and truly confessed. But you offer your children under such alien confession and witness.

When you say that the commandment of love is the principal tenet and work of Christians which accomplishes every improvement [in man], I agree, but with this difference: In Christ we have a true God (XXXI), and we must remain in His teaching and order. Whoever does not remain in the teaching of Christ has no God. Thus, the beginning of love is to believe in and hold to God and His Word, as John 8 [21 f.] advises: If you remain in my words, you will be my true disciples and you will know the truth, and the truth will make you free. (XXXII) Here is the love of the believers rooted. Where this commandment is kept, I will never separate myself from them any more than I would separate myself from my Christ. I am prepared to show human love to everyone according to the word of Paul [Gal. 5:13], to serve everyone from the heart (XXXIII),

518 and not to hurt anyone's feelings. If I have, un- aware, not followed these strictures, I ask for for- giveness from everyone. (XXXIV) However, I will in matters of faith [p. 32], God willing, not yield to anyone for the sake of love; in the same way, you (rightly) did not yield to the papacy, in spite of nu- merous admonitions by the papacy that love might be spared, which is not rightly to be spared. (XXXV) But the fruit of love delivers the verdict. As the pa- pists have practiced love with you, so also love will judge between us. (XXXVI) If we prejudge, perse- cute, and do evil to you, love, which demands the patience and faith of the saints, will certainly not be found in us [Apoc. 13:10].

The false apostles will be judged by God.

(XXXVII) Now, then, to God be the glory.

IV

The Admonition of 1542

Introduction

The *Vermanung* of 1542 is the longest and most detailed statement of the Anabaptists on baptism and the Lord's Supper. Authorship of the book was attributed to Marpeck by Caspar Schwenckfeld, who replied to it in his *Judicium*.[1] The spirited discussion between Marpeck and Schwenckfeld, which resulted in numerous letters and books, clearly indicates that, although large sections of the book were in fact taken from a book of 1533, *Bekenntnisse van beyden Sacramenten*,[2] Marpeck and his colleagues saw it as their work and stood passionately behind it.

It was initially published by Marpeck's group, and was most likely printed on his own printing press. Only two copies are known to exist. One rests in the British Museum, a photocopy of which has been used to check our text, and the other is in the Württemberg Landesbibliothek, Stuttgart, from which a modern edition has been prepared.[3] A manuscript copy was discovered by Robert Friedmann among Hutterite codices in Austria. It is not clear how widespread its influence was in the sixteenth century, but in a letter of 1553 Marpeck mentions that he is sending twenty *"Bundszeugnisse"* to Moravia (*KB* fol. 167). Since the *Vermanung* was also called *"das Buch der Bundesbezeugung"* (the book of witness to the covenant), it is quite possible that he is here referring to the *Vermanung*.[4]

One of the most fascinating aspects of the book is the fact, first discovered by Frank Wray, that approximately two thirds of the book was taken from *Bekentnisse* of 1533, the authorship for which Rothmann receives major credit. Although the introduction indicates that other sources have been used, no one had suspected that such a large amount of material was in fact appropriated. In effect, the book must be treated as the Marpeck group's revised edition of the *Bekentnisse*. In this translation, an effort has been made to indicate each point where changes have taken place even though, on a number of occasions, it would appear that the changes are not significant and, in fact, represent merely a misreading of the text or a mistranslation. Those relatively few instances where deletions from the *Bekentnisse* text do occur are also noted. A detailed study of the relationship of the two works to each other is needed, and a collated edition of the works, in the original, would greatly assist such a study. Until such a collated edition is available, this English translation will assist the general reader's ability to recognize the individuality of the Marpeck group, exemplified by its deletions from, and additions to, the text.[5]

The outline of the *Vermanung* is simple. It deals first with the term "sacrament" and whether or not it is a term which may legitimately be used. The author concludes that, although it is not a biblical term, it can be used, provided that one brings a correct understanding of its meaning to its usage. There then follows a lengthy discussion of baptism, and a summary treatment (about twenty pages) of the Lord's Supper.

The Text

Admonition[6]

A QUITE CLEAR, THOROUGH, AND
IRREFUTABLE ACCOUNT, AIMING AT A
TRUE CHRISTIAN, ETERNAL UNION OF
THE COVENANT OF ALL TRUE
BELIEVERS, AND GIVING COMFORT AND
HELP TO ALL THE WELL-MEANING
PEOPLE ON THE BASIS OF HOLY

SCRIPTURES. FURTHER, A DEFENSE OF
TRUE BAPTISM AND THE SUPPER OF
CHRIST ALONG WITH ATTENDANT
EXPLANATIONS OF THEIR
COUNTERARGUMENTS AND REBUTTALS
AGAINST ALL PRESUMED CHRISTIAN
COVENANTS WHICH ARE CARRIED ON
UNDER THE NAME OF CHRIST.

Because the Lord lives, we will speak what the
Lord tells us against all ahabic prophets[7] (1 Kings
22:14, 15; 2 Chron. 19) who, to please Ahab (we
mean all the authorities and rulers of the world),
have united against the Lord. Nevertheless, even if
all the messengers of Ahab were to compare our
words with those of the false prophets, such an action would not happen.

Christ the Lord says: "Whoever will confess
me before men, him I will also confess before my
Father" (Mt. 10:32).

All cry, "covenant, covenant," but deny the
Lord according to the truth and become apostate
(Is. 3).[8]

TABLE OF CONTENTS

Lord's Supper.

22. That the primitive church followed apostolic usage in keeping Christ's Supper pure.

23. Concerning our understanding of the words, "This is my body; this is my blood."

24. Concerning the common usage of baptism and the Lord's Supper, and what end they serve. Also, concerning the establishment and preservation of the holy church of Christ, and who is to be admitted into it.

25. A Summary and Conclusion of the whole matter.

Admonition

Aiiii

186
1
Grace from God and the true knowledge of Christ in the Holy Spirit to all believers and *sincere* lovers of the truth from us as *members of the covenant community and brothers in the unity of faith in Christ.* Amen.

Dear, believing, and good-hearted people, we have been subjected to the terrible errors of many sects,[9] and to divisions and disunity, through the agency of the terrible enemy, Satan, and his ilk. *What hindrance, insults, and apostasy have taken place because of the poison and stealth of the serpent, now into the twelfth year![10] So it was in the beginning of the church of Christ, at the time of the apostles, when false messengers of Satan mixed with the members of the covenant of the truth in Christ in order to hinder, cover up, and despise the truth; they joined themselves with the members of the church in order to spoil, blind, and embitter. Through such methods, the insidious serpent, a true enemy of human salvation, has worn out and brutally oppressed the zealous and sincere people.*

187

Almost every sincere person is repelled by the confusion, and has come to the point of despair and doesn't know how to escape. Nevertheless, it is still our sincere and hearty prayer to God, as Christian members of the covenant and on behalf of all sincere people, that God the Father, through Jesus Christ, may rescue them from the prison of conscience and free them for genuine piety.

We also exhort all erring, weary, wounded, weak, and discouraged hearts to raise their heads together with us, for our redemption draws near. It is also our prayer to God, for them and for us, that, in these last dangerous times, He may keep us in His undiluted and unadulterated Word, in His truth and in His will, as it is in His true kingdom. May He increase and bring His Word to us more fully so through it the banner of divine righteousness, grace, and truth in Christ may be made available to all sincere people for their comfort, so that, afflicted by the devil's many attacks which have wounded, dispersed, and made them tired, all wounded and tired consciences may be restored, healed, and gathered together and united into one. We have dedicated ourselves as those committed to the covenant of the banner of divine righteousness and truth, which arises out of the grace and mercy of God through Jesus Christ our Lord and Savior. We are committed to fight in this battle with the weapons and sword of the Holy Spirit, and we are heavenly and not earthly knights, for our citizenship and loyalty is not to the earthly but to the heavenly Jerusalem from above, not to the earth as a transient kingdom but to the intransient one, not to this world, whose soldiers and weapons are of the flesh, but to the spiritual, which is mighty before God in Jesus Christ our Lord and General. We fight as in the light and not with physical power, as do

A v

the rulers and lords of the darkness of this world, but rather as those who war against the attacks and the pride of the devil, and put him to shame.

188   This we do in humility, meekness, and patience, with tribulation, distress, and anxiety, with blows, prison, work, and watching, with fasting and praying, with purity, knowledge, and nobility, with friendliness, with the Holy Spirit and the Word of truth, and with the power of God through the weapons of righteousness to the right and to the left, which take into captivity all reason under the obedience of faith in Christ (2 Cor. 10:1-6). Through praise and blame, through bad report and good report, we are like those who mislead and who yet are truthful, as the unknown and yet known; we are like the dying and yet we live, like those severely beaten but not killed, like the sorrowing and yet at all times joyful; we are like the poor and yet we are they who make many rich, like those who have nothing and yet possess everything (2 Cor. 6:3-13). Even though we walk in the flesh, yet we do not fight with physical means, for the weapons of our battle are not of the flesh, but rather are mighty in the presence of God. This we do to disrupt the fortress, and so destroy all attacks and all heights which raise themselves against the knowledge of God. Thus, we take captive all reason under obedience to Christ (2 Cor. 10:1-6). Our victory is not won with our own power and might, nor is it done with earthly or physical power and sword, but rather with the power and might of our Lord Jesus Christ. He, through patience, conquered it all, just as we also overcome, even in death, through Christ our Lord, if we are truly related to Him in the covenant by His grace, and we persevere until the end. For to this battle we have been called even from the beginning of our covenant in Christ Jesus,

and our covenant witness referred to earlier, and it exists by the grace of God, which has always been and is now evident. This continues to be our hope through the grace of God, to which we will testify without wavering unto the end.

According to our duty and covenant in Christ we have felt the need to send forth this witness along with other witnesses included herein, published by others and (according to the words of Paul) tested by us and purged of all the errors which we have in part found among them (1 Thess. 5:19-22), for these errors do not agree with our faith, love, and patience in Christ. These other witnesses we have cleansed and corrected, omitting the mistakes and errors in them, in order that we may give a free testimony only to that which is good and pure without any mixture of error. In this way, truth will not be mixed with its opposite, nor will it be despised through the blasphemers and impure judges of the truth, who habitually spoil the good by mixing it with the evil and cast it aside without distinguishing or protecting the good and the truth. Thus, we have now written, for all true believers and sincere seekers of the truth, an unmixed and purified witness and our co-testimony in order that love may be built up, [God's] praise may be extended and [His] truth furthered. We have written against the recent errors as well as against the errors of the past. Though they pretend to represent the truth, these errors only lead away from it, for they have divided people and brought into being destructive sects which, in the appearance of truth, call themselves by the name of Christ, but merely parade under this name. Nearly the whole world, to its destruction, follows these many sects so lately arisen and established in the church.

Consequently, we submit ourselves to the obe

189

dience of the saints, even to the Holy Spirit and to your judgment, as we humbly want to do at all times with this witness. We hope that each member of the covenant of the pure conscience with God will discriminate on the basis of unity of faith in Jesus Christ, and will judge us gently. If, however, God the Father through Christ gives to anyone anything clearer or better, we hope that it will not contradict our testimony, but bring it to the light more purely and more clearly. But, if our testimony is found to be true and pure, we especially admonish everyone who reads or hears our covenant, and the union of the faith in Christ, not to strive against the truth, for all who are like Saul will find it hard to kick against the pricks (Acts 26:14).

Those, however, who would like to join us in our witness, testify with us, and become fellow members of the covenant in Christ, wherever they may be in the world, whether two or three or more, may gather in the name of Jesus Christ according to His Word and enter into his binding covenant of the good conscience with God. If they do so, their General, Christ Jesus, will be in the midst of them; what they pray for in His name or ask of the heavenly Father according to His will, Christ will give them, as long as they unite together in upright heart in the covenant of a good conscience with God. For our Lord Jesus Christ has the power, which has been given to Him, over heaven and earth, as long as we walk according to the truth, to Him we are obligated to live, under the banner of divine righteousness, as true members of the covenant of the pure conscience with God in the truth.

In this covenant, every sincere (believer) can unite himself, his body and all that he has, to God in Christ. He may give it to God as a pure sacrifice. As

167

Christ says: whoever does not deny everything that he has is not worthy of Him (Lk. 14:33). And Paul admonishes us to give our bodies as a living sacrifice which, he says, is our reasonable service, acceptable and well pleasing to God (Rom. 12:1, 2). May our heavenly Father, through His Son Jesus Christ, give grace that all sincere men, through pure understanding and knowledge, may commit themselves to this sacrifice, for it is in the knowledge of Christ and the Father that eternal life consists. As Christ the Lord said: "Father, this is eternal life: that they recognize you, Father, as true God and Jesus Christ whom you have sent" (Jn. 17:3). May the heavenly Father, through and in Jesus Christ, help us to attain such an understanding and knowledge. Amen.

Since, at the present time, the whole world argues about the word "sacrament," and nearly all the breaches and greatest idolatry follow from this disagreement, it is necessary for us to indicate what the word "sacrament" really means.

190

3   In the light of not only the widespread discussion but also the widespread usage of baptism and the Lord's Supper, the word sacrament, which designates them, must be explained, especially since the common, uneducated man considers this word so highly and pays such tribute to it; he understands something special and spiritual therein and, through it, takes God's name in high respect and honor, and uses it in the form of an oath.

Therefore, since we note that this word, if it is correctly understood, makes the whole matter more easily understood, especially to simple people whom we here seek mostly to serve, we want to begin with a discussion of the word sacrament. We must look briefly at what it really is. Although the word sacrament is never expressly used in the Holy Scriptures to refer to either baptism or the Lord's

Supper, nevertheless, the ancients understood this word in its correct, natural meaning, and we shall show below that, when their understanding is taken into account, the term sacrament can be used correctly.[11]

We look first at the Latin word sacrament.

What the Word Sacrament Really Means and Is

Sacrament is a Latin word derived from *sacer, sacra, sacrum,*[12] and means holy. *This aspect of the word we must now discuss.*

Sacrament refers to anything done in connection with an oath or a similar obligation, and refers to an event that is special and holy or a work that has that kind of connotation; similarly, the knight commits himself to serve his lord by the raising of a finger in battle where, on his honor and with his oath, he commits himself not to yield in combat. *Now, the raising of his finger is not the battle, nor a fight, nor endurance, nor is it victory; the action is a covenant, made in the firm hope that, according to the command and the desire of his Lord, he will diligently attack the enemy of his Lord, even risking his life until death.*

191

In the same way, when friends shake hands and receive a guest with gifts and presents, *all that is done thereby is to indicate the friendliness, love, and faithfulness of those who give them toward*

B *those who receive them. In the same way, love and faithfulness are not the gifts themselves but are, rather, the heart which the gifts indicate. Unity and trust are indicated to the receiver of the gifts, and all goodness, love, friendliness, and faithfulness to the one who gives it. Similarly, the word sacrament has no other meaning, sense, or interpretation. He who receives the gift receives that for which it was given: sanctification. The reason for the gift is recognized when one demonstrates help, advice, faithfulness, and love. The gift must come spontaneously[13] as an act of love and an inclined will, and it must come from one who could very well neglect it without any shame or disrespect. Even if he were not to do it at all, he would not be punished for it. It is also done without hope for reward. To recognize in the gift the faithfulness of the person from whom it was given is to have all these things demonstrated. He who receives the gift reciprocates in turn with his whole heart and being, and that is called sanctification. God has also commanded that we should be holy just as He is holy, and this, in brief, is what it means to be holy.* Thus, people often act because of obligation. Such actions may be called sacraments in their natural sense.

4

Now, note this well. Sacrament really means an essential thing[14], like body, bread, wine, or water. Sacrament signifies all kinds of events which take place in the presence of an oath and are handled, or are dealt with, by an oath. Thus, sacrament is not to be understood as a single essential thing, but only as the act that is carried out. If the act is carried out with an oath or a similar commitment, then it can be called a sacrament. The ancients called an oath a sacrament because the oath is a sign of something holy, that is, it is the divine truth in the same way that God is truthful and the truth. In this way, the oath must also be true and without falsehood. When, now, the word sacrament is correctly taken in this natural meaning, it is not used incorrectly when baptism and the Lord's Supper are called sacraments, for they are, after all, instituted by Christ and, as mentioned above, are commanded with the same kind of force and binding quality as the oath. Therefore, the sacrament must be practiced with the deep earnestness which Christ has ordained; how, and in what spirit, it happens are more important than any other considerations. Both baptism and the Lord' Supper are to be carried out according to the command of Christ. The words themselves indicate this interpretation, for what is baptism other than immersion?[15] What is the Lord's Supper other than eating, an activity to which one must pay more attention, and especially to the spirit in which it is carried, for the spirit of the action is more important than the elements which are used, a fact to which Scripture also openly testifies. It not only commands us to do both of them, but it also commands us as to how we are to do them and in what kind of attitude and heart they are to be used. Christ says, with reference to baptism, that we are to baptize them in the name of God (Mt. 28:19). It is the same as if He would say, baptize them in such a way that they may call upon the name of God and remain in God. With reference to the Lord's Supper, the Lord says, "Do this in my remembrance" (1 Cor. 11:24), as if He were saying that, as often as you eat with one another, think of me and think about the way I feel about you so that you may have the same mind among yourselves.

Paul, and all the other apostles, do not place a high value upon the elements and, indeed, attribute no special holiness to them; rather, as we shall see in a later time and place, they consider the total action and usage. Thus, you can see how both baptism and the Lord's Supper are called sacraments, namely, because both of them must take place with a commitment and sanctification, which is actually what sacrament is, for merely to plunge somebody into water or to baptize them is no sacrament. You must baptize in such a manner that the one who is baptized dies to his sins in a sincere way and in the power of a living faith in Christ. From henceforth, he commits himself to a new life, and only then is baptism truly a sacrament, that is, when the *content and action* of baptism happens with the commitment to a holy covenant. It is the same way with the Lord's Supper. When this matter is thought through carefully, it becomes easier and clearer. For the present, these comments are sufficient on the word sacrament *and sanctification*. Now we must proceed to the essence of the matter, and speak first of baptism.

What the Word Baptism Means

Every German undoubtedly knows very well what baptism means and what it means to be baptized. To baptize means the same as to immerse in water or dip in water, and baptism is the same as immersion or sprinkling with water. In other words, baptism, because of its natural *understanding*, can be used to define all kinds of immersion or dunking under water. But, according to Christian understanding, there is really only one kind of immersion under water which may be called baptism, and that is when someone is baptized according to the command of Christ. If, however, this takes place in a different manner and with a different understanding than that which Christ commanded and the apostles practiced, then we can say that, in a grammatical and natural *sense*, it can still be called baptism, but not according to the catholic, that is Christian,[16] way of understanding baptism. For all immersion into water can indeed be called a baptism, but it is the true and correct Christian baptism only if it happens according to the command of Christ.

Concerning the Difference Between
the Baptism of John and Christ

Since, in Holy Scriptures especially, there is reference to two kinds of water baptism, the one kind whereby John was baptized and the one which Christ commanded to His disciples after the resurrection, the question arises what is the difference between John's baptism and Christ's? This matter has been discussed in many ways by learned people and others both in ancient days and in more recent times. We think that, if you take the simple text of the Scriptures and view it directly by faith and leave all subtle, complex speculations behind, then this question can be quite easily solved.[17] Since many people use only their reason and bid farewell to the simple, clear explanation of the text, and force the Scriptures more to their own understanding and pay less attention to the meaning of the Scripture, the matter has become so confused and disturbed that the simple people cannot easily understand it. Therefore, we want to leave alone all allegory and interpretations, and discern the difference between the baptism of John and Christ simply according to the express words in the Scriptures. In the first place, note that we are dealing here not with the baptism of Christ, that is, the baptism which He Himself gave; the Scriptures say that He baptized not with water but with the Holy Spirit. We must distinguish here between the baptism of Christ, which He commanded His disciples to do and which they practiced, and the baptism which John used. It is these two kinds of baptism which we want to look at simply on the basis of Scripture. The words concerning the baptism of John are spoken by John himself in Matthew 3, where he says: "I baptize you with the water of repentance" (Mt. 3:11).

The baptismal words of Christ, however, are to "baptize them in the name of the Father, Son, and Holy Spirit" (Mt. 28:19).

There is much difference in these words as there is between the two baptisms. The work is one, or the same, if both of these are themselves one baptismal work. John says, "I baptize." The apostles are also commanded to baptize and, al-

though John expressly says, "I baptize with water," which Jesus does not expressly say, yet, from other portions of Scripture, it is clear that the apostles also used water. Thus, the material element is the same; there is no difference, for John baptizes with water in the same way that the apostles do.

Now, although the external work in both baptisms is one, nevertheless, the meaning and the correct understanding of purpose (for in all matters, the principal thing is the purpose of the thing) in each baptism is widely different. The example of raising one's finger, which is a sign at certain times of a correct, lasting covenant and intention, and which at other times takes place for a different reason, illustrates how purposes can differ. The work itself is, however, the same, but the purposes for which it is undertaken are quite different.

So, also, in the case of the baptism of John and Christ. The work, the baptizing with water, is the same, but the purpose and reason for which it is done are widely separated from each other, both of which are exemplified very clearly in their words. John says: "I baptize unto repentance." Jesus says: "Baptize in the name of the Father, Son, and Holy Spirit." Briefly, then, as the Scripture indicates, the baptism of John means repentance. John preaches repentance, teaches the people to be converted from their sins, and warns that the kingdom of God is present and available to those who are poor in spirit, that is, only to those who are repentant; they came to John, listened to his teaching, and desired to be baptized. These he baptized unto repentance, that is, he baptized them on the basis that, from henceforth, they would turn from their sins, repent of their sins, and bring forth worthy fruits of repentance. Thus, Christ, as the one Healer or Master of the sick, might comfort both those who were poor in spirit and those who *confessed*[18] with their whole hearts. Christ had been sent, and He came with His gospel to comfort them, to make them whole, and to reunite them with God. In the same way John, in his office, prepared the way for the Lord, preparing and inaugurating a perfect people for the Lord. However, he did not go be-

B v yond baptizing unto repentance in order that they might repent of their sins; he let it be at that.

Christ, however, commanded His disciples, the apostles, to baptize in a different way than John, for He says: "Baptize them in the name of the Father, the Son, and the Holy Spirit" (Mt. 28:19). Accordingly, the apostles, who received the command and who in turn commanded others, proclaim the gospel that Christ had been sacrificed for the sins of the whole world, had assuaged the wrath of the Father, had repaid unrighteousness with His blood and saved men from eternal death. They proclaimed that, from now on, every believer could be reunited with God the Father, the Son, and the Holy Spirit; every believer could have a new and eternal life, and could lead a blameless life.

195 Whoever accepted the teaching of the apostles was baptized in the name of God. Henceforth, in view of the fact that God had atoned for sin through Christ, who had reunited them with God the Father, Son, and Holy Spirit, they no longer needed to live according to the flesh; now, they could

175

conduct themselves in a divine way of life.

Accordingly, in brief, the following difference can be made between the two. John proclaimed repentance. Whoever accepted his teaching and wanted to repent, or at least wanted to be considered for it, allowed himself to be baptized, and John baptized them unto repentance and told them to bring forth fruits worthy of repentance, for the ax was laid to the root of the tree (Mt. 3:10). The apostles, however, proclaimed the gospel. Whoever received it and believed that, through Christ, he had been reconciled with God and whoever then recognized the will of God, through Christ, was baptized in the name of God, that is, they were baptized with the intention of finishing their lives with God, through Christ,[19] to do His will until the end. Thus, the first consideration of baptism involves a commitment to follow the teaching which precedes it. Those who were baptized by John were committed to keep his teaching, and those who were baptized by the apostles submitted themselves to their teaching.

In summary, John baptized people unto repentance; they should confess their sins and improve. The apostles, however, baptized believers in the name of God or of Christ; those who were baptized turned themselves over to God and were joined to Him in Christ, whom they confessed by faith in the gospel, and according to whose standard they were to conduct themselves. And this, then, is the difference, which we can discern from the Scriptures, between these two baptisms. May those who are spiritual judge whether this distinction is true or not. As in the baptism of John people confessed their sins and allowed themselves to be baptized unto repentance, so, too, is confession made, concerning the faith, in the baptism of

Christ. To be baptized is to proclaim a good conscience and an eventual desire to do the will of God, which is the nature of rebirth and the certainty of God.

We are unable to find any other difference in Scripture, or in anything else that agrees with Scripture. We trust that those who truly believe will find this explanation acceptable. We would not wish to prejudice or reject anything better that may come out of the Scriptures which disagrees with this our statement. We are doing here simply what we are able to do, and as much as God has permitted us to do. Let each man invest his talent and wager to the Lord. We do not speak against anyone, but simply confess our own faith and, if anyone can teach us something better, we shall give diligent and sincere thanks at all times. Enough has been said about the difference between the baptism of John and Christ. Further enlightenment, by the grace of God, may come in the following.

Concerning the True Baptism Which Christ Instituted and Commanded to the Apostles

In the above, we have defined the meaning of baptism, and differentiated between the baptism of John and of Christ. Now we want to look further at the one true baptism of Christ, inaugurated by Christ and commanded to Christians.

It is generally well known that to baptize means to dunk into the water and, concerning this fact, there is no controversy, nor does it need further discussion.[20] We know also that it was inaugurated by Christ and represents His commandments, and there is no lack on this account. Christ confirmed this form of baptism with simple and brief words; but, for those who are not satisfied, the meaning and content of the words is not as openly and clearly discerned as they are for those who are upright and who truly believe. Thus, the lack of clarity consists of the reason why Christ commanded baptism, what good it does, and how it is to be used.

It is certain, after Christ had commanded it, that baptism would not be in vain, but would be useful and to some purpose. For Christ did not want to burden His own with vain or useless things. However, since those who want to press distinctions do not consider Jesus' command to be open and clear, each has his own interpretation of baptism, be it of the spirit or of the flesh, which he has either added to it or found in it. Thus, baptism is not only confused by all kinds of interpretations, but it is also terribly destroyed, as we shall discover in due time when we discuss infant baptism. As we have said before, we want to uncover this instruction for the benefit of both the learned and the common man in this time, for neither knows basically what he is to think of baptism, since these recent and diverse meanings, arising as they do from the many people philosophizing about it, hide the true intent of baptism. With each new discovery, these discussions have covered up and hidden the true and right understanding beneath it all. Even though Christ commanded baptism with simple words, the meaning was already present and, even though its meaning is neither profound nor extensively specified, the disciples could not, before the sending of the Holy Spirit, fulfill Christ's command. After the sending of the Holy Spirit, how they were to use baptism became clear in unambiguous holy Scripture. Thus, the right meaning of baptism could be easily derived if one would be satisfied only with the apostolic teaching and with the example and

11

197

witness of the Holy Scriptures. Since we have nothing more from Christ than the simple command and since we do not have the exposition of the command, each "wise-acre" or *sophist* thinks he has the authority to understand the commandment as he pleases. In interpreting and using it, little attention is paid to either what the apostles themselves wrote about it or to how they practiced it. In fact, the commandment is totally rejected.

In view of the fact, however, that the apostles proclaimed the unambiguous truth and that their writings undoubtedly contain that which Christ commanded them, we want to look first at Christ's command to baptize and, thereafter, to consider what our understanding of it may be. This understanding we want to uncover diligently, simply according to the words and apostolic usage. We need not allow ourselves to be guided or diverted elsewhere. We shall be suspicious of everything that is not in accordance with the Scriptures and apostolic usage. Indeed, to do otherwise would simply be an abomination to us in light of the apostolic curse upon teaching that which is different to their teaching (Gal. 1:8), and we must take heed that no Christian may take us from our course. We shall faithfully advise every Christian that he open his eyes, and that he thoroughly scrutinize the Scriptures himself and take heed that he does not easily allow himself, by any foreign understanding or meaning, to be taken away from the Scriptures or apostolic teaching. To do the will of God, he must work with earnest diligence through the Scriptures and apostolic teaching. The words of truth cannot fail or deceive for, if anyone seeks to do the truth with intense desire, God will see to it that he surely finds it. In order that we do not diverge too far from our intentions, let us take up the subject and look at the institution of baptism by Christ. Then, using our understanding faithfully and confessing it with God's help and grace, we can look at why He instituted it, at what is useful about it, at how one is to use it, and at anything else which contributes to the understanding of baptism according to the evidence of Scripture and apostolic usage.

Concerning the Institution of Baptism and Christ's Command to Baptize

Christ gave the commandment to baptize only in Matthew 28. Therefore, we want to talk about His command and institution of baptism only on the basis of Matthew 28. In order that we may make the matter all the more clear, we want to look at this commandment in its context and also to look at the total command which Christ gave to His disciples.

After Christ had been raised from the dead and had demonstrated Himself to His disciples with many signs and words, Jesus came to His disciples and spoke with them, saying: "All power in heaven and on earth has been given to me. Go, therefore, and teach all peoples, baptize them in the name of the Father and the Son and the Holy Spirit, and teach them to observe all things I commanded you" (Mt. 28:19, 20).

Here we have the clear command of Jesus Christ concerning baptism, and the disciples are charged, not only to perform baptism, but also to teach and preach. Therefore, the apostles are to take preaching as seriously as baptizing, as indeed their writings abundantly testify.

Now, as far as baptism is concerned, we find two things in this commandment which must be especially observed. First of all, the order: how one is to come to baptism in an orderly manner. Second,

12

198

the meaning of the word concerning baptism in its simple and actual understanding.

Two Considerations with Regard to the Commandment to Baptize

As mentioned above, baptism is actually a sacrament; it is something sacred and it entails commitment. Through baptism, *a man commits himself or obligates himself with respect to an action of God.* Baptism is an action between God and the believer which benefits no one unless he is able to understand it, and no one is able to understand it unless he is first instructed and taught about it.· Consequently, Christ gives this orderly command that one should teach all nations, preach the gospel to all creatures, and make disciples, pupils who willingly and eagerly accept His teaching. Those pupils are to be baptized, that is, they are to be instructed to observe everything (*and nothing else*) which Christ has commanded. Therefore, whoever would come to baptism in an orderly manner must first be instructed in the teaching of Christ, for instruction comes first so that the people know what has to be done. How could the apostles have moved the people to be baptized if they had not first taught the people concerning baptism, and the people had learned why they were being baptized? Indeed, it would have turned out rather badly for the apostles if they had taken the ignorant, the uninstructed, and the unwilling, and attempted to baptize them before these people had any knowledge of the gospel. First and foremost, the apostles had to teach the people with the instruction of truth so that they would be willing to come to baptism, be moved to be baptized, and then rightly allow themselves to be baptized.

Why Christ Instructed That People Should Be Taught Before and After Baptism

We must note further that instruction is mentioned both before and after baptism and, thus, baptism stands, in an orderly way, in the middle. Such an order has the following meaning. All men by nature are unacquainted with divine matters, so they must first be made aware of the teaching of the gospel, through which a man first comes to true faith, as is witnessed in Scripture. Before anything else is done with respect to divine matters, they have to be, through the word of teaching, taught and enlightened in the knowledge and the will of God. This is the first instruction, namely, that the gospel is openly proclaimed to all creatures and salvation is freely offered to everyone. This proclamation is included in the words that the Lord speaks: "Teach all nations." Wherever, then, the Holy Spirit touches the heart, so that man can truly believe the gospel, a child of God is born and his birth is witnessed in baptism, openly revealed and carried out as we shall note later.

C ii

After baptism, a different kind of teaching follows, a teaching which is directed to the regenerate and baptized children of God; they are taught to observe all that Christ has commanded, as is fitting for obedient children, and at all times to seek to do the will of their Father. These same baptized people are now given a command which Peter, in his second epistle, the second chapter, refers to as the holy commandment (2 Pet. 2:21).

14

And they are instructed to accomplish the will of God and to complete their life in the way of righteousness as exemplified by Jesus Christ. For them never to have known the way of righteousness would be preferable than for them to fall back and return to their old way of life, which, after all, they abjured and put away in their baptism. Through baptism, they fled from the sins of the world and turned away from the life of the world.

Thus, briefly concerning the order: first, to learn; we are instructed to know the will of God and to believe Christ. When we have been taught that we can know Christ and believe in Him, then it is time to be baptized, to take off our old fleshly lusts and to put on Christ, a new spiritual life. After that, just as we have agreed, in being baptized, to complete the will of God, we learn, or are instructed, to be obedient in all things, and not again return to sin, as a dog does to his vomit or as a washed sow again to its dirt (2 Pet. 2:22). Let each Christian judge what we say, and especially consider Romans 6, Galatians 3, Ephesians 5, Hebrews 6, 1 Peter 4, 2 Peter 2, John 3, 1 John 5, and other passages of Scripture; he will clearly discover this meaning.

The Commandment to Baptize Interpreted in a Number of Ways

Now let us look at the correct understanding of the words, "Baptize them in the name of the Father, the Son, and the Holy Spirit," and see what they contain. Some pay very little attention to the meaning of these words, for they divide baptism into two parts, namely, material and formal. The material they call the water. Form, however, they refer to as the above-mentioned word. These are the *sophists*, papists, [21] and others who claim that if anyone is cast into the water (that is, the material) and the following words (that is, the form) are spoken over them, "I baptize you in the name of the Father," etc., then that is a correct baptism. There are also some who understand these words about the name of God to be really an appeal to the name and confession of the Holy Trinity.

In the third place, there are some who say that "in the name of God" means on God's behalf or in the place of God, just as, when a man says, "do that in my name," he means "do it for my sake." We grant this understanding its value for, if one looks correctly at the manner of speech and at the mystery of baptism, it turns out that to say, "In the name of the Father, the Son, and the Holy Spirit," is the same as to say God Himself. It carries this meaning: we are baptized in the name of God, and then we actually confess by faith that God has been gracious to us through Christ, who has forgiven us all our sins and has reconciled us to God so that, thereafter, we may also rely upon Him and seek to fulfill His will. Consequently, we are baptized in the name of the Holy Trinity. When we are baptized, we fully commit ourselves to God and into Him and, through baptism, we make the commitment to deny ourselves and to no longer carry on by ourselves but, rather, to let the self die. Then, similar to its meaning to other places, the little word "in" refers to the covenant.

Accordingly, the Apostle Paul says: "They have all been baptized in or under Moses" (1 Cor. 10:2); they are completely drowned, and are thus comforted by Moses and united with Moses, that is, added to his word and prepared to commit themselves to his word.[22]

Moreover, in Romans 6:3 Paul says: "Do you not know that all of us, who have been baptized in Christ, are baptized in his death?" We were baptized in Christ and, therefore, we belong to Christ, have been united to Him, have been committed to Him; with Him, we are obedient unto death to the Father, and are dead to all unrighteousness. That, then, is the understanding of the words of Christ: Baptize them in the name of God that they may commit themselves to God, and unreservedly commit themselves to remain with Him. In the following, we will try to explain this concept even more *brightly and* clearly; therefore, we will talk here only of the order and the understanding of the meaning of the word "baptism," and we shall now proceed to say what baptism is.

What Baptism Is and What a Christian Baptism Demands

We have already spoken about, *and adequately indicated,* what it means to baptize; *in its natural sense, the meaning of the word "baptize" is* to dunk into water *or to thrust* into water. Now we want to look further into what a Christian baptism is, for not every action which involves dunking into water is a baptism of Christ. Although it may in a natural sense be called a baptism, merely to thrust someone into water, and thereby "baptize" him, is not to be understood as a Christian baptism. A Christian baptism is one which is carried out according to the command and order of Christ. In order to understand or discover what a Christian baptism is, we must discuss both why Christ commanded it, and with what understanding or meaning it is to be used. Not the act itself, but the understanding and meaning of it are most important. For it is a comparatively simple thing to thrust someone into water *or to pour water over him;* indeed, it does the soul no good nor is the pollution of the flesh removed. Rather, in true baptism there is a certain assurance of a good conscience with God, a removal of the old being, a shedding of sin and the lust of the flesh, and the intention henceforth to live in obedience to the will of God, all of which pertain to salvation and to what is demanded in baptism. Therefore, since we have heard enough about the command of Christ and its understanding, we want now to look more fully at the understanding of the usage and why, or to what end, baptism is to be used.

As the apostles write of it and also practiced it, baptism shall take place in this manner.

Those baptized shall thereby confess their faith and commit themselves, by the power of their faith in Christ, to lay aside their old being entirely and, henceforth, be inclined to live a new life; it is upon this basis that baptism is to be received by everyone who is baptized. He is to be renewed in the assurance of a good conscience and born again through the Holy Spirit, and he is to forsake all unrighteousness and be dead to all works of darkness. Accordingly, baptism is a burying of the old being and a resurrection of the new. *Likewise,* it is a portal of entrance into the holy communion or church of Christ. *Likewise,* in the baptism of the believers, it is all together to put on Jesus Christ. Without it, no one is able to have an assurance of a good conscience, nor is one able to forsake or to deny sincerely the old sinful life, and accept a new life and be in Christ Jesus. Baptism is similar to a betrothal or a marital union between the believer and Christ; the believer is cleansed from all sins, has given himself over to Christ, and has committed himself to live and die according to His will. This account of what baptism is should be carefully studied and understood. When this understanding takes place, you will discover that our account harmonizes with all Scripture that speaks about baptism, *agrees with it, co-witnesses to it,* and coincides with it. For further confirmation, we will cite the

202

17

C v

Scriptures and the Acts of the Apostles, insofar as it is necessary, and will scrutinize them.

We want to look first at the witness of Peter concerning baptism, and to study the manner in which he testified to it after he had confessed the cornerstone, upon which the holy church is built and by which it is baptized into one body in one spirit. In the third chapter of this first epistle, Peter speaks as follows: "And now baptism saves (as prefigured in the ark), not by the washing away of bodily pollution, but by the covenant or union of a good conscience with God" (1 Pet. 3:21).

Now listen to what Peter says. He says that baptism saves us. Why? Is it because we are dunked into water or because *it is poured over us?* Oh no, for he differentiates between true baptism and the mere shedding of the pollution of the flesh. This last act alone cannot do it; only the covenant of a good conscience with God has the power to save. Therefore, baptism saves when, through it, the believer unites himself with God and henceforth denies the desires of the flesh and the lust therof, and desires with his whole heart to carry out the will of God. Such a conscience, however, can be created and achieved only by the Spirit of God, who cleanses the heart and *unites us* through faith. Insofar as this covenant of the conscience is sincere, when they in baptism totally commit themselves to God and to the obedience of the truth, the believers thereby purify their souls and are washed from all sins. Otherwise, baptism is of no use and is only a mockery in the presence of God.

Previously, *sophists* have divided baptism into two parts: matter and form. They call water matter, and consider the form to be found in the words: "I baptize you in the name of the Father, the Son, and the Holy Spirit." They dunk persons into the water, *or pour water over them;* whoever is thus dunked into water, *or has water poured over him,* is considered a baptized Christian.

203 Unfortunately, the papists and the *sophists*[23] are not the only ones who have distorted the meaning of baptism by conceiving this *false and fabricated* interpretation. Those, *and it is almost terrible to say,* who today are considered the foremost and best Christians have also done the same. Although they are not united with papists in everything, yet they share with them almost completely this understanding of baptism. Thus, when, with these words, a child is *sprinkled with water* or dunked into it, that action is considered to be such an inexpressible grace that the child, from that hour on, is considered a true Christian, freed from original sin, and, through that action, has become a member or an organ of the body of Jesus Christ. These people insist that, when they face the temptation of sin, the devil, or confront death, persons baptized as infants 18 should remember that they have been baptized, in the name of God, with water; on this basis, they comfort the person by saying he has been baptized. The fact of baptism is used as a true sign by which we are to know that we are with God, will inherit all good things, and possess His grace. Now, Peter also divides baptism into two types, but quite differently from the *sophists.* Peter also ascribes salvation to baptism, but not in the way the *sophists* speak of it. Therefore, let us look more closely at Peter's words, and see how his understanding is to be differentiated.

Peter relates how Noah and his family were saved before the flood, because he had faith in the Word of God. He built the ark; therefore, along with his family he was also preserved in the ark, and was joyous and free in the face of the rushing floodwaters. Thus, says Peter, we too are saved by baptism, in that we believe the Word of God and obediently enter into baptism. In the act of baptism we adjure evil, we put off the old being and put on the new, yes, Christ Himself, by committing ourselves, with a good conscience and before God, henceforth to live, not according to the lusts of the flesh as we did in the old being, but according to the will of God. And this is the covenant in baptism; through the knowledge of our Lord and Savior Jesus Christ, we lay aside the filth of the world and flee from it, and, just as Christ was raised from the dead, we unite ourselves with Christ into a new life. Thus, like those who are born again from the dead and who enter into a new way of life, we too are reborn, and this is actually how the words of Peter are to be understood. Accordingly, one can see, from the words of Peter, that baptism consists of two things: 1. The pollution of the flesh is removed, namely, through water. And Peter says that salvation depends upon this removal.[24] 2. The other is the covenant of a good conscience with God, and that is what, through baptism, saves us; as Christ the Lord says: "Whoever believes and is baptized shall be saved" (Mk. 16:16).

204   There are some who interpret covenant to mean, not only that God establishes with us a covenant by grace, but also that God commits Himself to grace. Thus, when we accept God's covenant, our receiving an unambiguous word-sign, baptism, is an assurance of His grace. As indicated, then, these individuals make out of baptism a sign of grace. However, no Scripture can be used to prove or maintain that baptism should be a sure sign of the grace of God for us.

20   God sends us His Son out of tender love and, when we believe in Him, God establishes His

covenant with us, and commits Himself to us in grace. As a clear sign of grace, Christ has been nailed to the cross on our behalf. The Holy Spirit, who has been poured out in our hearts, through Christ, to all true believers, comes as a guarantee of the assurance of such grace. Such a covenant or sign of the grace of God has been given to us, and is not at all tied to baptism or any other element or work; such a sign is received only by the believers through faith or through the Holy Spirit, *who is the assurance, says Paul, and the surety of our spirit* (2 Cor. 1:22; 5:5). For God has loved us in order that we in turn may love Him; He has given us His Son in order that we may give ourselves in Jesus Christ as a holy, well-pleasing sacrifice unto all righteousness. This sacrifice is exactly what *happens* in the covenant of baptism, which we, committing ourselves, through the knowledge of Christ, and in the strength of a good and complete trust with Christ, erect with God. And thus, being washed of all sins, we bury the sinful man and continue in the way of righteousness to live in a new life. Consequently, Christ also says: "He who believes and is baptized will be saved" (Mk. 16:16). For it is not enough to be purified and united through faith. The old life must also be removed and buried. Now the burying of the flesh shall take place through baptism. If the old being is to be removed, surely, then, first another and a new birth, a spiritual birth, must take place which will displace the old one before another is laid upon it. Similarly, Jesus says in Luke 11;22: "One who is armed more mightily drives out the other." Accordingly, as Peter says, baptism saves us, not through the putting away of polluted flesh, but rather through the agreement or *covenant* of a good conscience with God, through the resurrection of the Lord Jesus Christ *who is at the right hand of*

God.

Nevertheless, whoever seeks to bind himself with God in baptism must first be a newborn spiritual man. Whoever is not, may wash his flesh, but baptism will not be truly accomplished. If baptism is to be done correctly, and accomplished fully, both parts must be there at the same time. The believer must receive the washing of the Word so that he may henceforth bury the old being and walk in newness of life. And such is our understanding of Peter's word, which has moved us to give the above account of our understanding of baptism. Now we would like to look at a few other passages to see whether or not they harmonize with our understanding.

Paul's Understanding of Baptism

Paul also writes of baptism, and his point of view harmonizes with that of Peter. The words of Paul are as follows: "Do you not know that all who are baptized into Christ Jesus were baptized into His death; through baptism, we were buried with Him in His death. Just as Christ was raised from the dead to the glory of the Father, we, too, are to walk in newness of life" (Rom. 6:3, 4).

Listen to what Paul says here. We are, he says, buried with Christ in baptism. How so? Is it because we were thrust into the water and because the words, "I baptize you in the name of the Father, the Son," etc., were spoken over us? No, my dear friend, more is involved here. When we allow ourselves to be baptized with our whole hearts, we deny the devil, lay aside our fleshly lust, and, henceforth, desire to live a new life, with good conscience toward God. But only the power of faith, and not the act of baptism, will accomplish this rebirth. When such things happen in our baptism, we bury the old being and commit ourselves to live in a new way of life. Without commitment, baptism is *useless* and incorrect. Only the flesh is washed and thus, baptism is without power and becomes vain child's play. God is mocked; God's eyes look *only* and primarily upon the heart, and not upon the external work, to see with what kind of faith His will is sought.

Paul, in Colossians 2, further testifies to baptism's being received with a good conscience and used for that kind of goal. "And you are," he says, "perfect or fulfilled in Him [that is, in Christ], who is the Head of all principalities and powers, and through Him you have been circumcised, not with the circumcision made with hands which removes the body of sin in the flesh but through the circumcision of Christ; you are buried with Him through baptism, and, through faith in the power of God, who has raised Him from the dead, you have also been raised" (2:10-12). Here, it is clearly understood how Paul interprets circumcision. He says that the Colossians have been circumcised by the circumcision of Christ; they have taken off the body of sin, which happens through faith in the knowledge of Jesus Christ. When, therefore, we confess and also believe that we have desire only toward Him, flee from all sin and totally lay aside the sinful body, which we have taken off, then we, too, are buried with Christ in baptism. If we henceforth walk in a new life, commit ourselves to do so with Christ, and seek no longer to walk in the old sins, we are raised up with Christ.

This understanding is also found in Galatians 3:27. There Paul says: "All who have been baptized into Christ have put on Christ." What else do these words mean than, as Peter already said, to put on

22

206

Christ, to walk, and be armed, with the same meaning, thoughts, mind, and spirit as the Lord Christ: to walk just as He did; we are to follow Him. In summary, insofar as we can search the Scriptures and understand them, we find that baptism takes place when believers are baptized and leave the realm of the will of flesh, give themselves over totally into the will of God, and commit themselves to it. That means to be born again in Christ and to be baptized in the name of God, to bury the flesh, to be raised with Christ, to wash off sin, to put on Christ, and similar expressions which the Scriptures use with reference to baptism.

23

We take for granted that no one is so lacking in understanding that he would insist or believe that water (which is poured over one, or into which one is thrust, with the words: "I baptize you in the name of the Father, the Son, and the Holy Spirit") would have such power, and would bring such grace, as we have described above. In the believing heart, such a thing must be achieved through the Holy Spirit and accomplished through Him, for it would take a very long time to thrust or dunk a man into water, *or pour water over him,* in the name of the Father, the Son, and the Holy Spirit until the old, fleshly, sinful man is washed away and buried, and the new man raised up. Therefore, Peter admonishes us to have "a good conscience towards God" (1 Pet. 3:21); that is the only thing that matters.

D ii

But, you answer, baptism is actually not a dying nor a burying of the flesh; rather it signifies, and is a simple sign of, this death. If that is so, then let also *the pouring* of water or thrusting into water be a sign. We also hold that, to him *who considers it as such,* water brings with it no more than any external sign, *through which one cannot be brought to faith nor can he be made good.* We ask you, however what does the sign signify when the essence[25] is not there? Whoever gives a sign of a certain thing or matter, and pays no attention to the essence, is he not a traitor? Kissing is a sign of friendship *and of love.* Judas gave the sign to Him; he did not, however, have the essence *of this sign,* and what happened to him? Similarly, if in an agreement of trust you receive the right hand of your friend as a sign of his loyalty and if in actuality he is found to be unfaithful to you and you discover that he does not have *the essence of* the sign, and the loyalty to which he gives witness does not exist in his heart, my dear fellow, what would you think of such a man? The Lord's Supper is observed, and is to be considered, as a true sign of the remembrance of Christ's death and as a sign of the true participation in the suffering and the blood of our Lord Jesus Christ. Where the mouth alone receives the outward sign and the essence is missing in the heart, which has little or no regard to the essence, then it would certainly be better for him if he had never partaken of the sign. Therefore, Paul also says: "Let each man examine himself and thus eat of the bread and drink of the wine" so that he may eat worthy of the Lord (1 Cor. 11:28).

24   Moreover, to dunk into water or to *pour water over* someone in baptism is a sign, namely, a sign of the burying of the flesh, of the laying aside and washing of sin, and of the putting on of Jesus Christ. *Whoever has the truth in the heart, the truth which is pointed to and signified by the external sign, for him it is no sign at all, but rather one essential union with the inner.* If, however, I receive the sign and do not have the essence in my heart, what would this sign benefit anyone? Would it not be a mockery of Him in whose name I receive it?

Accordingly, if one desires to receive the external sign correctly, he must certainly bring with him the inner *and the outer* essence together; *wherever and whenever that happens, then the signs are no longer signs, but are one essence in Christ, according to the inner and outer being. For that which the Father does, the Son of Man does simultaneously: the Father, as Spirit, internally; the Son, as Man, externally. Therefore, the external baptism and the Lord's Supper in Christ are not signs; rather, they are the external work and the essence of the Son. For whatever the Son sees the Father doing, the Son also does immediately.*

D iii

Thus, the children born of the Spirit and nature of Christ also do that which the Father, through the Spirit, performs in the inner man; they also perform externally as members of the body of Christ in baptism and the Lord's Supper. The Father loves the Son, and has committed all things into His hands; as the Father works as Spirit inwardly, the Son of Man works externally. Thus, in Christ, no longer does any sign exist, only essence, one baptism, one faith, one God, one Father of us all. Therefore, baptism is done in the name of the Father, the Son, and the Holy Spirit, for the Son of Man cannot be without the Father and the Spirit, nor can the Spirit and the Father be without the Son of Man. Consequently, the external essence of the Son is one in essence, and works in the Father and the Spirit. Therefore, whenever a spirit comes who does not bring with him the external things, such as teaching, baptism, and the Supper of Christ the Man, whatever he has spoken, acted, and done are denials of the Son of Man and not the Spirit of the Father. Furthermore, whoever would merely steal external teaching, speech, deeds, baptism, and the Lord's Supper out of the Scriptures acts like a

208

195

thief and, upon hearsay, would practice the external. He would promote them without true faith, which is the true and correct co-witness of the Father and the Holy Spirit, and in him the truth does not exist. It is evident now that, in Christ, no longer is a sign a sign, but only pure essence through faith.

Just as Christ Himself, according to the external man, was only a sign to unbelievers and hypocrites, now let a sign be merely a sign for those who would have it that way. As with Simon, who prophesied about the child Jesus and called Him a "sign that is spoken against," they will be contradicted (Lk. 2:34). However, nobody should give a false witness through a sign as Judas did; otherwise, the sign will be false, useless, and condemned, and will be a contradiction of Jesus Christ. Since, however, baptism is to be a sign of the burying of the flesh, the washing of sin, the putting on of Jesus Christ, and the incorporation into His holy community, not only must baptism always be received by the hearts of those who would use and appropriate the sign but it must also be true before the sign can be correctly received. Whoever receives, without love, this sign of the covenant of a good conscience with God is a liar in his heart. To him, it is a sign of contradiction. It would have been better for him had he never received it, for he will surely be cast under the judgment of God.

Observe and consider here, too, that Paul compares baptism with burial. The flesh is to be buried so that, as Origen says: "Just as no one is to be buried alive with the dead, so, too, no one who lives in his sin is to be buried with Christ in baptism, for he has not yet died to his sin."[26] Therefore, those who hurry to be baptized should first ask whether they have died to sin; then, through bap-

D iiii

tism, they are buried with Christ.

Tertullian says in his book on penance: "This bath is a sealing of faith, which has been initiated and commended by faith in repentance."[27] Not only are we to be washed in order that we may discontinue sinning, but we have already been washed beforehand. Baptism (the external immersion *or sprinkling*) is a *co-witness*[28] of the inner essence, namely of the covenant of a good conscience with God and whatever Scripture testifies to in addition to this. The essence must coincide with the witness. And, as in all other matters, the essence must be there before *the witnessing* in order that the symbol may be correctly understood or given; otherwise, the symbol would be false and would be a vain mockery. When the essence is there and is given testimony to, then the symbol is true and useful, and the symbol is what it claims to be. *It really is no symbol at all, but is true essence. Thus, the Father is in the Son and the Son in the Father for the sake of the work in which a man has come to faith.* As stated above, so, too, in the case of baptism, which may be called a cleansing from sin, a burying of the flesh, when those who receive baptism testify thereby that they have died to their flesh, abjured the devil, and totally put away the old being.

In short, we conclude our discussion of baptism as follows: Baptism is an immersion *or sprinkling with water* desired by the one who is being baptized. Baptism is received and accepted as a sign *and co-witness* that he has died to his sins and has been buried with Christ; henceforth, he may arise into a new life, to walk, not according to the lusts of the flesh, but obediently, according to the will of God. Those who are thus minded, and confess this intent, should be baptized. When that is done, they are correctly baptized. Then, in their baptism, they will certainly attain forgiveness of sins and thereby, having put on Jesus Christ, they will be accepted into the communion of Christ. The one who is thus baptized experiences this communion, not through the power of baptism, nor through the word that is spoken there, and certainly not through the faith of the godfathers, the sponsors; as his fleshly lusts depart and he puts on Christ, he experiences it through his own knowledge of Christ, through his own faith, through his voluntary choice and good intentions, through the Holy Spirit.

In brief, such is our understanding of what baptism is and to whom it can be usefully administered.

The Value of Baptism

210   If we have noted diligently and well this usage of baptism, in which those who are baptized are cleansed of sin and, by virtue of their faith, clothed with Christ, we must note some other advantages to baptism, which we shall now explore. There is

26   another special usage and value of baptism which we now want to treat in particular, one which we hope will be no less useful to our understanding of baptism, but one which we have heretofore not treated adequately. There is another understanding of the usage of baptism in the Scriptures, on which account we can refer to baptism, not unjustly, as a door or entrance into the holy church. Pauls says in 1 Corinthians 12:13: "By one spirit were we all, Jews or Greeks, slaves or free, baptized into one body." Paul says here that there is one Spirit which has led us all to be baptized into one body. Furthermore, we have been united into the unity of faith and the covenant of love, and are henceforth one body, for Paul says we have been baptized into one

body. This one body is the holy church into which we have been baptized, that is, through one Spirit and in one faith; we must be united into one confession of God. But such unity does not happen through immersion or *effusion of water;* rather, it comes into being because we are united *through the Spirit of Christ* in faith. The prayers of the ancients, called collects, also bear testimony to this. It was their practice to offer these prayers, on behalf of the baptized, on the Thursday after Easter, for the ancients practiced baptism only at Easter and Pentecost. One of these prayers goes as follows: "God, You who have united the variety of heathens in the confession of Your name, grant that those who have been thus born again and redeemed from the hand of the devil may be of one faith in heart and holiness of work."[29] The content of this prayer is as follows: The Holy Church is a gathering and a communion of believers in Christ who live by the fruits of God. Accordingly, no one is to be admitted into this assembly, *communion,* and society unless he first has been so minded as to confess such a faith, and bears testimony to this faith externally with his works. When this happens with true earnestness and total commitment, it is good for him. He becomes saved and, without doubt, cleansed of all sins; he puts on Christ, commits himself to Him, and is enrolled as an heir to the eternal kingdom. If it happens, however, in a mechanical way, or with a false heart, woe to them, for cursed are all those who try to do the work of God with contempt. Thus, baptism is a door, an entrance into the holy church, and this is certainly the narrow gate of which Christ speaks (Lk. 13:24); no one goes justified through baptism into the church or into the kingdom of God, except he who in baptism has taken off and laid aside the old life of sin,

27

211

199

and has been raised up to a new life. This portal without doubt is very narrow, for you cannot go through it with *the old sinful man*[30] of the old life; everything must be laid aside and buried before one enters through this gate. *For when the two sons of Zebedee asked to sit, the one at the right, the other at the left, Christ answered: "Are you prepared to drink the cup which I drink? Are you prepared to be baptized with the baptism with which I am baptized?"* (Mk 10:35 ff.) *Christ's is the baptism of death, to which the water baptism also bears witness. Through this narrow gate, Christ beckons His own* and, since to enter is impossible for the carnal and those who have only little seriousness, Christ says, therefore, that only a few enter it. To be sure, many are immersed in water *or have water poured over them,* and consider themselves baptized Christians. But it is to be feared that, when the king will inspect His guests, many will need to be cast out who have entered in, for they have not put on the true wedding garment with integrity (Mt. 22:2-14).

28   In the same sense, Paul also writes: "You husbands, love your wives just as Christ has loved His church and gave Himself for it so that He could sanctify it and cleanse it with the water of the word. He sought to prepare for Himself a church that is holy, with no spot or blemish or the like, but one that may be holy and blameless" (Eph. 5:25-27).

Here, note what Paul says: Christ sanctifies His church and gives Himself for it; through the water of the Word, He purifies and prepares it for Himself that it may be holy and unblemished. Now the bath is baptism, in which the believers are sanctified in Christ and, in the power of faith, they are totally cleansed.[31] Peter also bears testimony to baptism when he says: "In the ark there were eight people who were preserved through the water and, in the same way, baptism saves us" (1 Pet. 3:20 f.); we enter into the holy church by baptism, obedient to God and fulfilling His will. In the same way as it happened to those who entered into the ark, *so, too, through baptism with water, the world is condemned and the children of God preserved; through baptism, a man enters into the body of Christ, that is, the church of Christ, yes, into Christ Himself, as the true ark wherein, through the word of obedience, one can be preserved from the flood.*

212 From these words, we deduce that, clearly, holy baptism is not to be lightly considered as an entrance into the holy church, and there is no other entrance to eternal life than the one Christ Himself prescribes: "Whoever would follow me, let him deny himself, take up his cross and follow me" (Mt. 10:38; Mk. 8:34; Lk. 9:23). That is to happen in baptism. We are then correctly consecrated into the Christian church, purified of sins, incorporated into Christ, and clothed with Him; only then may we appear, without shame, at the wedding of the highest King in honorable clothing and adornment. If, at this time, the entrance to the church were to be correctly confessed and practiced, then we would surely sense a holy and unblemished church. However, when this entrance has been destroyed, and almost everybody is confused about it, the holy church has also been desecrated and disrupted. It is to be assumed that the holy church will never come to its holiness unless this entrance to the church will again be rebuilt, reinstituted, and cleansed of all in-
29 famy.

We beseech each well-meaning servant and lover of Christ that he may mark this diligently, and may very seriously reflect upon what we have said here. All of Germany boasts about the gospel, all wish to be called Christians and evangelicals, and all wish to be considered as such. But the purpose of the proclamation of the gospel, to be attained here upon earth, is that a holy community of God or church be founded in which all dealings and actions may be guided, to the praise of God, according to the proclamation of the gospel. Such is not to be found anywhere nor is it to be seen. To be sure, Christ is proclaimed everywhere, and many people take it quite for granted. In life, however, one has a feeling that everywhere the Antichrist or the opponent of Christ is present. How is that possible? The reason is that men do not hurry to come to the house of God, nor do they consider that the holy church can be correctly instituted, and, thus, they do not enter by the right gate into the kingdom of Christ. Therefore, beloved Christians, you who seek seriously the honor of your Lord Jesus Christ, awake and open your eyes. Let us diligently look at the institution of our Master and the Bishop of our souls, and let each bring his talent to invest[32] so that the correct entrance into the holy church may again be opened. Then the kingdom of God will be opened to us through the true door, that is, through Christ.

The Twofold Misuse of Baptism

Baptism is misused, especially in two ways First, when unwilling, innocent people are brough to baptism, people who do not desire, nor are in clined to be baptized, or people who know nothin about baptism. Baptism is a mockery and is powe less for such people; indeed, it is not Christian bap tism. Baptism is either right or wrong, good or bac according to its usage, according to the attitude i which it is received and used.

213

30   We read that, at the time of Paul, baptism was
also misused when the living allowed themselves to
be baptized for the dead. But, even more, it is being
misused in our day, when, out of long habit and
ancient practice, everywhere the innocent, unwilling, unknowing children, who cannot even speak,
are baptized with reference to salvation. This certainly is a terrible iniquity, as we shall discover later
E   when we talk about infant baptism.

Second, baptism is also misused when someone
with a false, impure heart desires to be baptized,
and such people will not *have a better fate than did
Ananias and Sapphira. One who is baptized after a
false confession will lie not only to men, but also to
the Holy Spirit* (Acts 5:1-12). The one who baptizes
will not be harmed, for the one who is baptized will
carry his own judgment, and the guilt remains
solely upon his head. In the same way, when the
one baptizing and the one who is baptized use baptism in a different spirit than used by the apostles,
and with a different intention than Christ commanded and the apostles used it, then they are committing a sin and abusing baptism. Those who do so
will not be able to escape the punishment of God,
especially after the truth has been confessed and the
abuse cannot be evaded.

Concerning Infant Baptism

Since we have spoken of the true baptism and
its usage, we assume that everyone has been fully
informed about a true understanding of baptism.
Now we want to share our understanding of infant

baptism so that each Christian may have an opportunity to judge it.

It is a common question, treated in many ways today, whether infant baptism is correct or not. Especially at this time, many people have raised this question and, if we wanted to allow ourselves to be swayed by *literal* cleverness and the cry of many people, then we would consider infant baptism to be right and good, for the most learned people of this time confess and consider it as right, and fight and argue for it. If, however, we thoroughly weigh the testimony of Scripture and bring the matter into the light to look at it, we can in no way consider infant baptism good nor recognize it as such. Rather, we must admit and say that innocent small children, who know neither good nor bad, can in no way be baptized as Christians. We also consider infant baptism to be a prelude (when we examine and recognize the truth) to the destruction and the total apostasy of the holy church. Unless infant baptism is discontinued and the correct baptism again reinstituted and correctly practiced, the holy church cannot again be brought into its true status and glory. We now want to look at the question of infant baptism. We will study the Scriptures, and commend our results to the judgment of every well-meaning person. According to the capacity of his faith, let each man see whether or not it is so.

First, we must take into account that, in the Scriptures, there is no command to baptize children who cannot even speak, nor is it contained in any divine Word that unknowing children are to be baptized. For the command to baptize, which was given to the apostles, applies to those who have been instructed with the Word, who believe in the teaching of the gospel, and who desire to be baptized. As stated in our previous exposition of the

31

214

E ii

32   command of Christ, the total office of the apostles is not directed to innocent children, but to those who understand, who have ears to hear; the Lord earnestly commanded them, saying: "What I command you, you are to do only for the sake of the Lord, nor are you to take anything from it nor add to it" (Deut. 12:32; cf. 4, 2). Thus, that the Lord Himself did not command the children to be baptized is reason enough to allow infant baptism to fall into neglect and be discontinued. *The removal of the practice of infant baptism does not, however, belong to an external or human power; it belongs to the obedience of the Word in faith, without any human coercion in matters relating to freedom of grace.*

     Further, as Paul teaches, and concerning which we have spoken earlier, the true baptism is a burial of the old being and a resurrection of the new to a new life. However, this resurrection does not happen because of the power of a work, be it *pouring over* with water or immersion in it but, rather, because he who is baptized correctly confesses that he has died to sin in true repentance. He is being baptized in order that he may, cleansed from sin, and in obedience to God by the power of faith, henceforth walk in a new life. To attempt to accomplish this with unknowing and unspeaking children is effort, work, and labor lost, for the children have received no law. How, then, are they to reject the

215 evil and accept the good when they know nothing
33 and, indeed, cannot distinguish between good and evil? For whoever would enter into baptism, and lay off evil and be cleansed from sin, he must assuredly first be converted, through true repentance, and he must die to sin; otherwise, baptism does not wash away sins. We read in the Acts of the Apostles that, after Peter had admonished the people, they were

pricked to the heart, and said to Peter and the other apostles: "Ye men and brethren, what are we to do?" Peter answered, and said to them: "Be converted and be sorry for your sins, let each man be baptized in the name of Jesus Christ unto the forgiveness of sins, and then you will receive the gift of the Holy Spirit" (Acts 2:37, 38). However, children who cannot speak or think cannot be converted; *they have not yet been perverted by their own fleshly mind and thus, do not know the difference between good and evil. This knowledge led to sin in Adam and Eve, and was the beginning of God's enmity toward man.* In baptism, children can receive no forgiveness for sins *because, in the presence of God, they have as yet no conscience, nor do they have guilt related to sin.* Thus, such a baptism is completely empty and perverted, and is a mockery in the presence of God.

E iii

In addition, many people, both educated and uneducated, young and old, have written and held the position that, because of penance, faith by proxy, the anointing by holy water, and baptism, children are cleansed of original sin and made Christians. If such were the case, then infant baptism is a terrible horror and mockery of the blood of Jesus Christ. After all, both original sin and *actual sin*[33] are forgiven and removed, and hearts, even of those who themselves exercise faith, are cleansed only through true repentance and faith in the blood of Christ. *Original sin is inherited only when there is knowledge of good and evil. Adam and Eve, our father and mother, inherited it when, contrary to the command of God, they ate the fruit of the knowledge of good and evil. Such is the inheritance of all men. But, prior to the knowledge of good and evil, neither inherited sin nor actual sin is reckoned before God. Only when man, in his carnal nature, leaves the good and adopts the bad is God's reckon-ing forthcoming. Man may only be born anew by faith in Christ who, according to his nature, leaves the evil and does the good. For the proclamation of faith in Christ captures the knowledge of good and evil (that is, the physical understanding) under the obedience of faith, to leave the bad and to choose*

the good (2 Cor. 10:6). First of all, this knowledge must be in the heart before anyone can be baptized for the forgiveness of sins. Listen, then, to what the true and right baptism is so that each one may come to faith himself; having died to sins, you henceforth live a new God-fearing life and, willing to walk in it and abide by it, continue therein *until the end of your life*. That signifies the correct Christian baptism, which is confirmed by scriptural authority. Whoever then baptizes differently, or is baptized differently, does wrong, and not only slanders baptism, but is not practicing it. For the Scripture gives no evidence of any other baptism before Christ or in

the same true church than what we have mentioned

before. Since infants cannot even speak, know noth-ing of all this, and are unable to do anything about it, infant baptism cannot exist. Those, however, who think that, by baptizing, they can make Chris-tians and get rid of sin in that way (as the pope with his group has maintained until now) place themselves in the position of Christ and are themselves the true Antichrists.[34]

In brief, no one can be baptized in a Christian manner unless he first shows repentance for his sin, has faith, longs for baptism and receives it, consents willingly to the covenant of a good conscience, and is inclined to walk henceforth in newness of life in obedience to God. Since, however, children are un-qualified and unequipped to do this, no child can correctly be baptized in a Christian manner. Provision must be made, first of all, for the child to be instructed so that he may believe, and may turn with his whole heart to Christ and walk worthily before Him; only then, and not before, is the time right for him to be baptized.

Finally, Scripture bears witness that there is only one baptism with which the repentant and believing (those who desire and receive it voluntarily) may be baptized. Infant baptism, however, is something quite different, and is administered in a different way. Therefore, it is wrong, *and it is a concession, not to Christ's baptism, but to the children, for it takes place childishly, ignorantly, and without all knowledge of Christ*[35]; *only in the confession of Christ does salvation by faith consist. It should be called anti-baptism,*[36] *for it is practiced against Christ's Word, against His will and work; there is only one baptism, and it is not infant baptism. Let the children remain in the promise of Christ until they can be instructed, and until they can believe, confess, and desire baptism. Prior to their belief and confession, they are like Adam and Eve before the transgression, and woe to him who attempts to improve them with baptism. The Lord Jesus freely allowed them to come to Him and to depart from Him, but without baptizing them; nor did He command them to be baptized, but said to the adults: "Except ye become as little children,"* etc. (Mt. 18:3).

That infant baptism opposes the correct and true baptism of *Christ* is reason enough for us not to conceive of it as Christian *nor to consider* it as such. Indeed, we would need to confess, on this account, that infant baptism is no Christian baptism. How should the unknowing and unspeaking children be baptized when we note that intelligent, well-educated believers, and *those who know much about*

217

35

E v

208

Christ and are experienced in living with Him, have enough to do *to oppose and to resist sin, the devil, their own flesh and blood, the world and its regents, false teaching, errors, and false prophets which are spawned out of the truth to mislead men? Although it has taken place since the apostolic time, this we have seen in our own time and experienced it. Therefore, we are sharply aware of it, especially among those who have, according to the practice and the command of Christ, allowed themselves to be baptized externally and seceded from those truly baptized. They were not, however, of the truth. Had they been of the truth, they would have remained with the truth, as John himself says (1 Jn. 2:19). Thus, when, according to the Word of Christ and His example, the gospel was first preached by many faithful men of God, who suffered in patience and against whom Satan raised his portals in the appearance of the gospel, they wanted to fight with the physical sword, as if they were fighting, like the Jews, for an earthly kingdom or land. The Peasants' War and, after that, Zwingli's and, now in the appearance of the true baptism of Christ, the Münsterites in Westphalia have done the same. All of these Satan raised up in order to confuse and disrupt the true baptism of Christ which, through patience in faith and love alone, can do good to friend and enemy alike by fighting with the sword of the Spirit in the Word of truth. There need be no external power or sword, for the kingdom of Christ is not of this world. Thus, no true Christian needs to occupy or defend either city, land, or people, as earthly lords do, nor to carry on with violence, for such belongs to the earthly and temporal rulers and not at all to the true Christians, who show forth the faith in Christ. Many false people in our time have attempted, as the papists and the so-called evangel-*

icals still try to show today, that city rulers, princes, and lords (in the appearance of defending the faith) use all earthly power. It is to be feared that they shall suffer the same fate as did those who engaged in the Peasants' War, and the fate of many who have fought against the Turks. These people do not lose their lives, nor do they suffer for the sake of Christ. Because, like revolutionaries, they impatiently oppose temporal power, they are being punished for their transgressions. Their fate is the same as Korah's and his clan (Num. 16:33). Those who are truly and correctly baptized in Christ are baptized with Christ in patience under tribulation. Committed to suffer even unto their physical death, every Christian who is baptized with Christ is a participant in His tribulation. He commits himself to hate all temptations and to resist all evil, and he opposes it, in faith and patience, with the word of truth. To this tribulation no young child, unable to speak, can commit itself. Therefore, infant baptism is nothing else than the work of hypocrisy or idolatry for, if baptism is given with the assumption that it will wash away original sin in a child, and the child thereby is christened, that is, made into a Christian as the common people think, it is slanderous idolatry and abomination before God and, as said before, a blasphemy and a mockery of the blood of Jesus Christ. Only the blood of the unblemished Lamb, Jesus Christ, confirmed by each one's own faith and heart, purifies the believers of all sin, and not baptism. *Similar to an adult who, knowing good and evil, is a sinner and yet does not recognize his sin, children are unable to see themselves as guilty, for they have no sin in their conscience. Neither the child nor the adult has need of baptism and thus, one should simply commit them to the secret judgment and verdict of God.*

Concerning the Nonsense, and All Kinds of Vices and Evil That Have Derived from Infant Baptism

The first, and perhaps the worst, abuse which has grown out of infant baptism is that, through it, the true baptism and institution of Christ is ruined and completely laid waste. Christ prescribed to the apostles, and consequently to all His true servants, one command *or order, and prescribed to His own* how they are to lead all people and bring them to the kingdom of God. In the beginning, everyone who would be saved must have his own faith, and must himself come to a true knowledge of Christ and be added to Him. Since, however, faith and knowledge of Christ come out of teaching and hearing the divine Word, Christ, for that reason, first commanded that all nations should be taught and the gospel should be proclaimed to all creatures, that is, in His name, repentance and forgiveness of sin should be proclaimed, and those who then believe the gospel would receive power to become children of God. *These people, through faith and baptism, become children of God, and are children of God as long as they continue faithfully to the end;* in no other manner, *neither here nor in the beyond, can anyone be called a child of God. For being a child of God not only includes birth, through the Word in faith and baptism, but also the agony and pain of flesh and blood, until the birth is completed and ends in physical death. Thus, the mother, that is, flesh and blood, represents that which is earthly, and in her is a child of God carried. This process includes a time burdened with much pain, and it is only after such a time that this pain is alleviated. Thus, one becomes a child of God here, and enters into the inheritance only in the beyond. For, while we walk on this earth, says Paul, we walk*

36

219

211

as those exiled from Him (2 Cor. 5:6; 1 Cor. 7:29 f.). *Although it is lived according to the Spirit derived only from God, childhood is nonetheless received in flesh and blood so that, through baptism, flesh and blood is born, under the Spirit, into obedience, never again to live according to its lust. Thus, here and there, the children of God and of men are spirit, flesh, and blood, and they are also eternal after the resurrection. Just as Christ is the Word, Spirit, and God, so, too, is He a man born from the seed of woman, but without the seed of man, born of a generation of human flesh and blood, and raised again according to the flesh of the seed of David. So, too, we are spiritual and physical children of God and of men; we are included in the Spirit and Word derived from God, but we are also flesh and blood, derived from man, and we remain such with Christ eternally.* This childhood comes, not from corruptible seed but, rather, from incorruptible seed, through the Word of the living and eternal God; that Word, however, has come to us *through the humanized word from the seed of woman*, and it is to be proclaimed through the gospel.

Accordingly, the command and the institution of Christ are to be given this meaning: if a man is to come in an orderly way to salvation and to the kingdom of God, he must first of necessity hear God's Word and be instructed in it. It is then the task of man to believe the gospel, to receive willingly the knowledge of Christ, to be obedient to the truth. *Only then does it follow* that a man is to be baptized, deny himself, and commit himself to Christ. After all, it is not possible that anyone would be correctly baptized who has not first learned of Christ, knows the will of God, and believes with his whole heart in Christ. How is anyone to abjure or *deny* unrighteousness and sin in baptism, and *sub-*

mit himself obediently to the will of God, if he has not learned first, through the knowledge of God, to be obedient to His will, and to be inclined and equipped to do it? Therefore, whoever would be truly baptized must first be instructed according to what Christ Himself also taught and commanded. This institution and order, which Christ instituted for His apostles and commanded them to follow, was indeed followed by the apostles, for their Lord and Master had commanded it; their Scriptures and history everywhere abundantly illustrate their obedience to His command. If people would have stayed with Christ's one simple order or command, it would not have been necessary to raise so many other orders of baptism; His alone would have been sufficient. It would not have been necessary for Christians, with great cost and harm to souls, to erect new orders and to promote them. But, because of infant baptism, this command and order has been totally *obscured* and darkened, yes, *even completely destroyed* and rejected. In the hope that they will put on Christ and become acquainted with Christ, baptism is placed before learning; they will be "correctly" baptized before they have ever heard of Christ, understand Him, or know anything about Him. Thus, while the order of Christ is inverted and despised, this supposed baptism has become an idol; everyone intended their children to become saved, to be made into Christians. Where such a baptism was not performed, they remained Gentiles *and Jews*, or other unbelievers, like the lost and damned who could not attain salvation. As is *clearly* seen today, the teaching of, and obedience to, the gospel, by which alone the disciples of Christ and their followers were reckoned and known, and not infant baptism, has been thrown totally to the wind and despised.[37]

220

37

Therefore, infant baptism is the root of all kinds of nonsense, and is itself the origin of godless practices which have been instigated in the holy church. In order that no one thinks that we are flatulent and speak incorrectly about it, let us try to demonstrate this principle.

First, the true baptism of Christ is, and should be, a door and entrance into the holy church. For no one should be allowed to enter the holy church of Christ unless it be a fact that he who seeks to be incorporated into the body of Christ confesses the true faith by baptism, denies the devil and all his fleshly lusts, and is incorporated on the basis of this confession into the holy fellowship of Christ. But, whenever this orderly process is neglected, whenever the innocent children who are unable to speak are baptized, or another serves as sponsor for him, *or whenever faith without any prior teaching is promised for the child, a man puts himself in God's place. Acting as if it is in the sponsor's power to give the child his future faith, the sponsor promises to deliver that which God alone can give. For that reason, they become a sponsor, and act as if they knew the secrets of God. That really is the same as ridiculing the providence of the highest God; speaking for the child and acting as if they knew, they promise that the child will and should believe. In fact, the opposite takes place among most people; the highest unbelief is found among them. They even promise to resist the devil and reject evil habits. However, when the child comes to the knowledge of good and evil, it runs to the devil, and practices all kinds of vices and bad habits, such as reviling God, adultery, overeating, overindulgence in drink, idolatry, fighting, murder, pride, stinginess, envy, hate, etc. Yet, such people are considered Christians simply because they have been*

F

221

baptized in their state of ignorance. Woe, woe to the practice of sponsorship, for it represents great vilification against God the Father and the kingdom of Christ; out of this practice, it has come to pass that neither faith nor the obedience of faith remain hardly anywhere anymore.

38   If, however, baptism had remained steady, according to the command of Christ and the usage of the apostles, and if it had remained unchanged, so that no one had been baptized and accepted into the holy church unless he himself had first confessed his faith, himself denied the devil, committed himself to Christ in baptism, as is proper, and committed and pledged himself to live a new life, surely the holy church would have remained honorable and in a healthy state. But the church departed from God's order, and undertook to baptize the unknowing and innocent children, the majority of whom, when they come of age, testify by their deeds that they belong to the devil. Thus, the church, by committing the ignorant and the unwilling to Christ, mocked the secret of the covenant, which in actuality takes place between Christ and His believers, and made it into a children's game. Accordingly, God too has turned away, left them, and plagued them with worthy and well-deserved punishment. This impure adultery paid little or no attention to the faithfulness of the man he has cast aside, and thus, has fulfilled what he promised to the Prophet Isaiah (Is. 5). Isaiah spoke of the Lord's having planted a vineyard, which he assumed would bring forth grapes; rather, it brought forth wild grapes and useless fruit. Therefore, the Lord did away with the gate and the walls, and opened the vineyard to all wild animals. It has become a desolation and is trodden under foot.

F ii

      In the same way, monasticism and convents

215

have literally grown out of infant baptism. The unknowing children did not yet understand what was to be done and did not know[38] Christ. Therefore, neither did they desire to be entrusted to Christ's righteousness,[39] nor were they committed to Christ but for the promise *made by the godfathers or patrons.* Such a promise is reckoned to be a foolish sport or child's play. Nevertheless, the children were baptized. Such a baptism of children is also a vain thing, and can be seen as a useless thing, for adults know as much about it as do the children. Therefore, those who are baptized in this way departed easily from Christ and Christ from them. The profession and order of Christ have been forgotten and set aside. Consequently, all monks and nuns have turned to a different order and profession, namely, to the regard others have for them, for their opinions, discoveries, institutions, and regulations, and have with great difficulty practiced their profession. They allow themselves to be dedicated to the obedience of men rather than obedience to God. Thus, supposedly spiritual individuals, like monks and nuns, have raised, through their own profession, a different baptism and, by doing so, denied the original baptism and departed from it. Instead of water baptism, they allowed themselves to be baptized, wearing special clothing, in obedience to their patron.

It is beyond doubt that so-called Christianity would not have come to such abomination if unknowing children had not been baptized. If each one would knowingly and willingly, in a covenant of good conscience, receive the baptism of Christ and enter freely into the holy communion, he would without doubt have had so much to do in the holy commandments and obedience to God that he would not have desired to commit himself to be baptized according to any human teaching and human obedience. It is a shameful and lamentable thing[40] when a man becomes committed to serving himself and teaching the rules of men who, after all, serve the devil. In no case or in any sense will he be accepted by God until he is *rational* and comes to the age of accountability, until he has learned well the rules and the orders which God commanded so that he will know what he is to do. Even then, he will have a year of testing before he may give his confession and, when the confession is accomplished and he has been consecrated into the order, he will neither recant nor again turn back. However, in the holy church, that is, in the order and obedience to God in Christ, the unspeaking, *unknowing*, innocent children, who know neither good nor bad, are accepted in a *slovenly* fashion, without differentiation and, indeed, without any attention paid to them. Their baptism is conducted as though it were a *monkey show*, a joke or as if it were an insignificant, slovenly thing for a man to commit himself to Christ and be accepted into the holy church unto the obedience of His will. In fact, baptism *is a superbly earnest matter which pertains even to our salvation.*

What should we say about those who call themselves godfathers, who run and become sponsors for the child, as mentioned above, and, on behalf of the child, confess the faith, abjure the devil, and whatever other blasphemy they may commit? Is this not presumptuous nonsense? What do the godfathers or patrons know about the eventual intentions of a child? As soon as he grows up and thinks for himself, even though they do not now know him and indeed cannot know him, for God alone knows him, why do they run and promise good and deny the evil for the child?

Two kinds of nonsense originate from this action. First, God is mocked when, as it often happens, the godfathers themselves, as patrons, do not believe or know anything about faith. Indeed, they do not even know or consider what they are doing, nor do they understand that to which they are answering, what they are promising, contradicting, or rejecting. They reject only with the mouth, and it happens very often that these very same people are God's enemies in their hearts, that they are friends of the devil and the world. How, then, can they stand in the place of a child before God?

In the second place, even if the godfathers undertake the matter with true earnestness and with good intentions, still, as said above, it is dangerous to speak for another and, especially in matters of faith, not only to promise good things before the face of the highest and most powerful God, but also to reject evil, *when it is natural to expect only evil.*

The Lord Christ did not entrust Himself to any man, for He knew what was in man (Jn. 2:25). Neither did He make promises to His own Father on behalf of others, or in the place of any one, with respect to their future good deeds, faith, piety, or eventual rejection of evil. Certainly, He prayed for them, but He did not predict that they would become believers.

F iiii *The godfathers, however, take their place alongside those who baptize the children before Christ and God the Father, and undertake to act with a higher and greater power than the Lord Jesus Himself had. Is this not an abomination, placing oneself in God's place, and presenting oneself as Christ the Son of God?* The common proverb, *known in all circles,* says: "The pay and the punishment is before the door. The patrons shall be purged."[41] If such a saying holds true in temporal matters, then not only those who make promises in matters of faith (to the glory of God and the salvation of souls), but also those who baptize, and demand that such promises be made, invite upon themselves an inconceivably terrible punishment when they pledge for another, and especially for children. Such promises they are neither able, nor entitled, to demand. Therefore, we reckon that, if each man could look at himself clearly, and would in fact do so, he would see that it was enough to carry his own load and to deal with that; he would then find it unnecessary or unbearable to load himself with the sin of a stranger. We will not even mention here all kinds of hypocrisy and magic, such as blessing and smearing with oil, adjuring the children, exorcising the devil from them, and stroking them with spittle, ashes, and salts, and other forms of papery.[42] However, we do request all good-hearted men to reflect diligently on how the devil has spewn an abomination out of infant baptism.

We will also leave unmentioned what kind of pomposity, lofty behavior, ostentatious vanity, incontinent eating and drinking, and other practices derive from infant baptism. In summary, then, infant baptism is the true beginning, ground, and root of the total antichristian regiment and realm, and an abrogation of the true covenant of Christ, and of His cross and tribulation, under which the treasure of Christ is hidden. If, along with other children, the children of the rich and powerful were baptized only when they bore true witness, repentance, and fruit, and these children did so together with all true believers, to whom baptism belongs, and who themselves, according to the correct order of the baptism of Christ, bear witness with their own confession, then many others would be better able

41

224

*to point their children to the knowledge of Christ.
If, however, the child does not wish to allow itself to
be directed toward the teaching of Christ unto
obedience of faith, then surely each true Christian
would not, even if it would have come from his
body a thousand times, desire to have such an un-
qualified child baptized into faith. In such a way
and for such a reason, the unbelieving and the unclean would remain outside. Whoever desires to become impure, even after having been baptized
upon his own confession, would be dealt with by
the ban and the sword of the Spirit, because of love
for the betterment, and punished after the order of
the Spirit and teaching of Christ. Whoever, then,*

Fv

*would not be obedient to the Word, and would not
listen to the community of Christ, would be committed to the world and its princes, and be considered as a pagan until God again would give him a
penitent heart. And if that were to be practiced
toward everyone, without respect to his position or
power in the world of the flesh, and if we were to
leave it to God to protect them from tribulation and
persecution, then baptism would still remain. So,
too, would the fellowship of Christ and the correct
Lord's Supper remain in faith and love, through
patience in tribulation, and we would be true participants in the tribulation of Christ. Under these
conditions, baptism would remain pure, unstained,
and good; it would be in the world before the face
of God and men.*

This purity has been destroyed by infant baptism, ruined, perverted, defiled, and abrogated, and
has led into an antichristian practice. The harm to
the church that has been brought about by infant
baptism has now been adequately and briefly described. If, as the situation justifies, we were to try
to describe all of the nonsense and abomination

220

which has grown out of infant baptism, it would certainly take too long. Therefore, we shall leave it for now, and allow each one to think about the rest for himself. We hope that by now we have said enough to persuade every well-meaning Christian that our reasons for attacking and rejecting infant baptism are important and sensible. From now on, we want to deal with the foremost arguments and objections by which the intellectual and learned theologians presume to protect infant baptism and defend it. In order that we serve neither the learned nor even ourselves but, in doing so, come to the assistance of others, we want to analyze these arguments and answer them. Thus, as the case may be, when these arguments are addressed to people, at least they will know better how to answer them. The well-meaning will then know how to protect themselves against human trickery and deceit, which is based upon hair-splitting distinctions, and may more confidently adhere to the truth.

A Rebuttal to the Objection Which Seeks to Protect and Preserve Infant Baptism

42

Since infant baptism has no divine commandment and is supported by no word *at all* in the Holy Scripture, the infant baptizers seek all kinds of excuses; they devise many hair-splitting, *sophistic*[43] *and scriptural (as they claim) arguments* and proofs, heaping them up in order that they may smear the eyes of those who do not understand, and seek to defend harmful infant baptism. At first glance, these arguments appear to be valid, particularly to those who lack understanding; but, as soon as they are exposed to the light of understanding, these arguments are seen to be false. As we shall now see, when we look at each of the articles in turn, they in fact lack substance.

The first, and perhaps the foremost, argument is taken from the Old Testament, and *is introduced in order to justify the matter as follows:* Abraham and all believers are under the same promise and command of God, and were buried *through the same faith.* Now Abraham's children were circumcised, in infancy, that is, on the eighth day; on the basis of this circumcision, *it is concluded* that one should also baptize the children of believing Christians, for baptism has taken the place of circumcision. It is true that Abraham and all believers are under one *covenant* and stand under one command, *namely, in the covenant of the promise and pleasure of God.* Similarly, since the time of Adam, all believers were included in one promise. Nevertheless, insofar as the external promise is a symbol or an image, which Abraham's kinship portrays for us in a figurative way, it is not true that now this covenant is meant to include the believers and their children *and that, therefore, the baptism of children of the New Testament parallels circumcision.* After all, in the Old Testament nearly everything was done in a figurative way and experienced in that way, as Paul bears testimony. But this makes us equal *neither* to Abraham *nor* to his generation.[44] The external and figurative promise is directed only to Abraham and his generation, was fulfilled in them, and does not include the Christians.[45] *And even if it did include Christians in a figurative way, one cannot deduce therefrom that the baptism of Christ is to be compared with the ancients' physical circumcision, done by hand and confined to the flesh,* and done to the children of Abraham, born from his seed and generation according to the flesh. This seed took everything from the *external* covenant, and dealt only with *external* circumcision.

For the Christians, however, it is quite a different matter, and in the New Testament there is no such promise or covenant erected by God. For whoever would enter into a covenant with God in the New Testament and be confident of His promise, must believe for himself, each one individually. It makes no difference whether he is born of Christian parents for, in the same way as illumination is differentiated from the light, so the essence is differentiated from the picture. Similarly, a great difference exists between Christians, and Abraham's promise and his people, a difference everyone, who can understand clearly the difference between the Old and New Testaments, can easily perceive. Thus, there is a great difference between circumcision and the *true* baptism of Christ. Abraham was given a commandment by God that he should circumcise his child, *servant*, and kinsmen; henceforth, every male born to him should be circumcised on the eighth day.

Now, however, like most other things in the Old Testament, circumcision is a figure and an image[46] of the fact that God said to Abraham that He wanted to *be his God and the God of his generation.*[47] *From such a basis, the opposition argues that the Old and New Testaments are one. But one cannot extrapolate from this promise to Abraham that children are to be baptized. Later, we shall try to demonstrate this fact at greater length.*

First, on the basis of this same promise of God, they attempt to compare the Old Testament with the New, and maintain that the old people can be compared with the new, the old practices and ceremonies with the new practices and ceremonies. Indeed, what is contemplated here has already

223

taken place. Although they see the old people as somewhat more childish, possessing more understanding,[48] and gifted with less love and with more ceremonies than the new, they can see no difference between the old and the new people and, as a consequence, they maintain infant baptism because the ancients were commanded to circumcise, on the eighth day, each male child or boy born of the seed of Abraham. Since they come from the true seed of Abraham, by faith in Christ, the new people are also to baptize their children. Therefore, they feel it is incumbent upon them, even more than it was on the ancients, to include the children by baptism in the covenant of God. They do so in the confidence that God will also be the God of their children just as He was the God of the children of the patriarchs, Abraham, Isaac, and Jacob. They even base infant baptism upon the belief that, just as the fathers at that time circumcised their children upon the commandment and order of God, the very same Spirit which the ancients had, the new believers, as a new people, also have, yet in fuller measure and in a more perfect way.[49] Hence, it is even more incumbent upon the new people to baptize their children as soon as possible. Thus, they commit them to God and offer them to God in order that He may accept them into the fellowship of Christ. The Spirit of God and of Christ are one Holy Spirit.

You have seen briefly the main basis upon which infant baptism rests: "Paul sees circumcision and baptism as virtually one and the same thing."[50] We must now look at the divine and biblical writing to see whether or not there is any foundation for this position, and whether or not it harmonizes with the true teaching of Christ.

First of all, there is no basis in divine Scriptures to aver that the ancients received the same Holy

227

Spirit and renewal of regeneration as believers in Christ experience now, for the true circumcision of the heart is quite a different matter. God's order must be maintained.

The old covenant is merely a covenant of promise. It is the prediction of God's pointing forward to a new being in Christ Jesus, for in Christ Jesus all things, consciousness, feeling, and the heart of the believing man, have been made new. What was only promised in the Old Testament is fulfilled in the humanity of Christ. All this happened in the fullness of time, and all the creatures of God waited for it. No man received it until this Spirit of the comfort of conscience was given unto remission of sin, until the gifts and the teaching and the guidance into all truth was given unto regeneration. As John says (7:39), no man received it before Christ's ascension: "The Holy Spirit was not yet there, for Christ was not yet glorified." Likewise, Christ the Lord said to His disciples: "If I do not depart, the Comforter who will lead you into all truth cannot come" (Jn. 16:7). Therefore, before the transfiguration of Christ, no one received the Holy Spirit in the same measure as His apostles and all true believers now receive Him. Thus, the true baptism of Christ in water and Spirit is instituted, grounded, and started by Christ. As the Lord said to Nicodemus: "Unless a man be born anew of water and the Spirit, he will never enter the kingdom of God" (Jn. 3:3).

Not a word had been spoken to the ancients concerning such a birth, either through circumcision, sacrifice, or any other ordinance of God. Consequently, baptism can have no comparison with circumcision. Neither can we draw such a comparison on the basis of God's promise to Abraham: "He would be his God and the God of his seed, and

228

G *they would all be His people. And in your seed will I bless all nations" (Gen. 17:7f.) For Christ Jesus built His church upon a different foundation, namely, upon the present confession, which, under the covenant of circumcision, God promised for the future to the ancients. That future was realized by the confession of Peter, and by all believers who confess Christ to be the Lord and the Son of the living God. Whoever, along with Peter, confesses Him, by revelation of the father with his own confession, he is worthy to receive baptism. The Lord asked His disciples, "Who do men think that I am," so that the disciples could say for themselves; neither the Lord, nor those who belonged to Him, took satisfaction from the fact that they were simply confessing Him for the sake of others. Therefore, He says: "But who do you think that I am?" (Mt. 16:15). Then Peter said: "You are the Son of the living God." Upon this basis and upon one's own confession, and not upon a borrowed confession or the confession of someone else, Christ built His church. In order that each person might be incorporated, through baptism, into the fellowship of Christ, that is, His church, he must first confess the three names: God the Father, the Son, and the Holy Spirit. Only then can he be baptized in their name into the fellowship of the church of Christ. Upon this foundation, then, upon their own, and not upon someone else's confession, Christ will build them. When Christ asked him the first time, Peter does not answer, "We believe"; his answer is: "I believe that you are the Son of the Living God." Later, the others, each one for himself, also believed. In this manner, the church came into being. Only then did Peter speak for all of them to the Man Christ, since they were together and were sustained only by the humanity of Christ: "Where shall we go? for we* have believed that you are the Son of the living God" (Jn. 6:68 f.). So, too, the Lord had prayed on their behalf to the Father and they, after His human departure, were committed to the Father as the Holy Spirit. "Holy Father, keep them, whom you have given me, in your name, that they may be one just as you and I are one; while I was with them in the world, I preserved them, whom you have given me, in your name" (Jn. 17: 11 f.). Therefore, Peter first said: "We have believed that you are the Son of the living God." Even today, a believer may say those words on behalf of the church, especially if, prior to uttering them, each one has confessed his own faith before the assembly or the congregation. But before such individual and true confession has been made, no one may truly be called a member of the community of the church of Christ, a member of the church, for upon this foundation, upon the confession of the faith of Peter, the Lord built His church. Thus, baptism is a door, an entrance, into this church. No one may enter through baptism unless he has first come to faith in the Lord, who is the true foundation of the church, laid through the Holy Spirit, and who alone can reveal it to us. He must confess with the mouth that Jesus is the Christ and the Son of the living God upon whom the new church is built. The old church, however, is built upon the promise of God, upon the promised land, given to the physical seed of Abraham, and sealed through circumcision. But the new church of Christ is sealed through baptism in the Holy Spirit. If the church, in the form which was indicated earlier, would have been built and constituted in the same spirit, grace, and knowledge among the ancients, then there would have been no need for Christ to build His church upon the rock and foundation which is Peter's own confession.

229

G ii

227

Indeed, I maintain that, if you could find just one scrap of Scripture, if one speech or word could be found which suggests that in the future Jesus Christ, the Lord Jesus, could be recognized as Christ and the Son of God, then He, the Lord, would not have been rejected by the builders as the true and correct cornerstone of His church. Indeed, the prophets, especially Isaiah and David, did see Him, but only in a figurative way, to be the true man and Son of God; so, too, Abraham also saw His day, and was glad (Jn. 8:56).[51] In the same spirit of his preparatory office, John himself pointed with his finger, and said: "Behold, the Lamb of God, which takes away the sin of the world" (Jn. 1:29).

Christ Himself, through His human physical speech, did not place this revelation into any one's heart without the revelation of the Father. After all, flesh and blood could not reveal the Son of God in truth. Again, in truth, no one knew the Father except the man Jesus Christ, the Son of God, and he to whom the Son revealed Him. This knowledge of the Father first began only in the Son and in the Holy Spirit. For even the physical speech of Christ could not be endured by the apostles until they had been instructed by the Holy Spirit, until the physical sayings of Christ were brought to their remembrance. Therefore, Christ says to Peter: "Flesh and blood did not reveal this to you, but my Father who is in heaven" (Mt. 16:17). Such revelation and confession came to Peter through his perception and realization of Jesus Christ's physical word and work, accomplished by the Father in and through the man Jesus Christ. Thus, it is clear and undeniable that Christ the Lord led and instructed Peter and His other disciples only through His visible miracles, teaching, and powerful physical accomplishments: He kept the disciples with Him when, before the

230

G iii

transfiguration, He says: "Father, I have kept them in Thy name whom Thou hast given me; while I was with them in the world, I kept them in Thy name. Now Father, preserve them in Thy name" (Jn. 17:12). And to Philip and the other disciples, He also said: "Do you not believe that I am in the Father and the Father in Me? If not, then believe Me for the sake of the works which I do" (Jn. 14:11). And, thus, the above-mentioned confession or knowledge came to Peter, not through the Spirit of Christ, which leads into all truth and for which men have longed; even while Christ was physically present, it was not yet there. Contrary to the present situation, the Spirit was not working among all His believers, until the end of the world; as John says, and as Christ Himself said, only after His ascension into heaven would He send the Spirit, and the Spirit would lead into all truth and remind men of the physical words and work of Christ. Only later did this Spirit come when Peter, along with the other disciples, received Him at Pentecost, when Peter had been reminded of his precious confession of the Son of God in truth according to the Lord's Word. For, if Peter would have received that Spirit before the ascension of Jesus Christ, then he would not have sought to restrain his Lord Christ from suffering; nor would Christ have called him a satan, saying: "You do not intend the things of God but rather, the things of men" (Mt. 16:23).

So, too, the ancients adhered only to that which was human and physical, and not to that which is divine, which came only through Christ. As in the case of Peter, the divine, which is both physical faith and faithfulness, came only through Christ. Neither Abraham, nor any other ancient believer, would have conceded, any more than Peter did, that Christ should be hung on the cross;

concerning Abraham, Christ Himself bears witness to this belief when, in John 8:40, He says: "This is not how Abraham acted."

On this testimony of Peter the new church of Christ was built, but it was built only afterward, through the Holy Spirit, which was prophesied ahead of time and which Christ, the Man, achieved through His death. Such a statement is in accordance with the words of Christ when He says: "Upon this rock I will build my church or congregation" (Mt. 16:18). He does not say the church has already been built, nor does He say "I am building it." Rather, He says He "will build" it; further, He says: "To this church I have committed the keys of heaven, which forgives sins and retains them" (Mt. 16:19, 20).

231

G iiii

Where does even one witness or one bit of evidence grant the ancient church[52] such a power? Neither circumcision nor sacrifice conferred such a power; nor did cleansing, promise, commandment, restriction. No matter what the old church may have been built upon, it can in no way be compared with the new church that Christ built. The authority to forgive sins was not committed to them by God, nor did the ancient church have the power to forgive or retain sins as baptism does in the church of Christ. Baptism conferred this power; it is instituted as a witness to the covenant to forgive sins and to retain them. As in the case of circumcision, baptism is a word symbol. And he who does not himself willingly, knowingly, and believingly confess himself to be eagerly believing and accepting of the Word of the Lord, does not allow himself to be baptized unto the forgiveness of sins, his sins shall be retained. Those who believe the contrary may pride themselves with whatever they want, or believe whatever they wish concerning the seed of

Abraham or of those born as Christians according to the flesh. In this form and on this basis, the Holy Spirit rules the external and true Christian church, which is the household of Christ and His church, based on sonship and not upon servitude. This ground stands forever, and the portals of hell will not conquer it.

Those who believe otherwise maintain that, when Scripture says in John 7 that the Holy Spirit is not yet there, because Christ had not yet been glorified, John refers only to the gifts of the Spirit, such as apostolic office, and other services and benefits for the common good, like performing miracles, healing, speaking in tongues, and so on. To them we say that, indeed, you will discover whether this interpretation is true or not, and you will also discover the kind of deceit such teachers practice who want to take the promises of God and tear them apart, dividing them from each other. It is clear from the writings of the apostles and of the New Testament that the Spirit was not there, neither the gifts of the Spirit, nor the Spirit of comfort, nor that Spirit who leads into all truth, to which Christ refers. Also, the Spirit which brings one to faith in the purification of the conscience and the resurrection from sins was not yet there, and came only after the ascension of Christ, through faith in Him. It is only after the ascension that this promised Spirit

232

was realized, the Spirit which deals with forgiveness of sins, comfort, and purification of conscience, as Paul indicates concerning the faith, of those to whom the promise has been given. As is found clearly in Hebrews, among the ancients, conscience

G v

was not yet purified with respect to sins. Only after His death did Christ bring together all men, Jews and Gentiles, whose faith in Him reconciled them with God and robbed the devil of his power; only then were the indivisible spirit of prophecy, the gifts, and purification attained and achieved altogether. Through this Spirit, we first received the sonship of the eternal kingdom and the inheritance of salvation which, according to the words of Paul in Galatians 4:1-3, speaks clearly about this matter, but which the ancients had not achieved nor received before Christ.

If the church of Christ had been built upon the first foundation, laid by God the Father and built according to the standards granted to her time, yes, if even one little spark of grace, achieved only through Christ, would have been present then, neither Christ nor Paul would have had to lay any additional foundation; Christ could have said simply to Peter: "This, my old church, I will renovate and improve, rebuild the temple at Jerusalem and restore it." He would not have said: "This temple, that is my body, I will raise again on the third day." Since, however, His finite body was still mortal and fragile, and had not been raised, how, then, can the old destructible temple at Jerusalem have been the true temple and church?

Here, it can be clearly seen how the Lord has built His church on His body and the body of believers. He built it first through the resurrection, and took His place with His resurrected body at the right hand of the Father. It is only then that the Holy Spirit could build His temple and church in the hearts of the believers. Before that, the material, destructible temple of His body, as the figurative temple, was an entrance and preparation to the indestructible temple of His body, raised up in the resurrection and ascension to heaven, in Himself and in those whom He built up for the church. And that is now the temple of all believers and the Holy Spirit; in Him and through Him, in the temple of *their hearts, He is to be worshiped in spirit and in truth.*

In summary, the ancients had a sketchy, figurative, yet symbolic faith which focused on hope. Such a faith was reckoned as a figurative righteousness which all the ancient believers as followers of Abraham and his righteousness had. Just as a shadow points forward to the light and the figure to the essence, the faith of the ancients pointed forward to Christ and His true believers, and pointed to the regenerate righteousness; it became really essential only in the righteousness of Christ, when He had become justified and when, in His true glorified humanity, He took His seat at the right hand of the Father. Only as a true man from the seed of Abraham did He have preeminent status before the Father. We are speaking here of Abraham's physical seed, not of many seeds, but of one, to whom the promise was given, and in whom and through whom all nations were blessed by the One who occupied heaven. We do not speak here of a difference which took place only in power, might, glory, eternity, or the essence of God the Father and His Word, which were contained in heaven. Rather, we talk about the Word becoming flesh, the humanized Word which came out of, and through, the seed of the woman; about the seed of Abraham in whom the promise was fulfilled. He then occupied heaven after the resurrection and ascension, and seated Himself at the right hand of God the Father.

The providence of God, however, we allow to remain in its place, unperverted in the will of God itself. Yet, it would be a mockery of God, who has given order to all creation, and a contradiction of His divine will and order, to say that it follows that His providence has this form and has no order of time, place, or person of divine will. All creatures are ordered and disposed through the Word. Creatures, time, essence, place, and person must remain, and nothing can come to the fulfillment of the will of God without this means, for He has disclosed His will in His order of the creatures. Thus, it was ordered that Christ, the Son of Man and the seed of Abraham, temporally had to pass on, according to His nature and person as a creature of God. Otherwise, there would be no difference between Creator and creature, and everything would be merely a monkey show, an aping such as the world does when it puts on a play or an act; as it does, for example, in a play about the Passion or ancient history, with its rhymes and costumes, cackling and mimicking. All the work of God would have been rejected had it been used in this way against God in the way preachers and despisers of God teach and speak even about Christ and all creatures. If it had taken place according to the election and providence of God, creation would have been adequate without a process of becoming real essence, and work would be an oversight. The despicable preachers of God can be accused of thus despising election and the providence of God without the order of history or work.

In the case of Esau and Jacob, the purpose of God's order consists, even today, of the providence and election of God, and the order and process of their work, essence, and person. As Paul says, God has ordered His purpose in creaturely matters according to time, place, essence, and person in the process of the work (Rom. 9:11). It does not follow that one should baptize children before their work of faith has manifested itself, for faith is the basis upon which the congregation or the church of Christ is built. Certainly, they should not be baptized before they confess the name of Jesus, and

234

confess that Christ Jesus is the Son of God; Paul says: "Whoever believes in his heart, that one is righteous and confesses with the mouth, that one is saved" (Rom. 10:9 f.). Even though God, according to election, has followers of Esau and Jacob under the same people, loving the good, hating the bad, so it behooves us also as His creatures to look at the order of God, to look at the works and allow God to choose those whom He has ordained.

Nor should one baptize children by reason of circumcision, which is, after all, a token and seal of the future promised Word of God, for faith verifies that which we have already received. The ancients first had to wait and, consequently, there was no difference between a servant and a child, for they were so childish in the covenant of promise that they saw only the physical promises and were, in fact, opposed to the true promise. Similarly, so that His promise might be believed, God in the beginning also gave physical promises and thus stirred the faith of the ancients. Unknown to them, the spiritual was hidden beneath the physical; like young children they did not know what the father will do. In the same way, a servant knows neither the will of his master nor what his master does. Therefore, the ancients made no distinction between children and servants and, therefore, circumcision of their children and servants alike was valid. Even though the practice was quite childish, yet, at that time, through divine patience, it was reckoned to be righteousness. Now, however, since the time of the revelation of the Son of God, this is no longer the case. As Paul says: "But now, quite independently of law [and do not say it used to be the case], God's justice has been brought to light. The Law and the prophets both bear witness to it: it is God's way of righting wrong, effective through *faith in Christ for all who have such faith—all, without distinction. For all alike have sinned, and are deprived of the divine splendour, and all are justified by God's free grace alone, through his act of liberation in the person of Christ Jesus. For God designed him to be the means of expiating sin by his sacrificial death, effective through faith. God meant by this to demonstrate his justice, because in his forbearance he had overlooked the sins of the past—to demonstrate his justice now in the present, showing that he is himself just and also justifies any man who puts his faith in Jesus" (Rom. 3:21-26; NEB).*

235   *Here, it can be clearly understood how the ancients, their legal piety, and their relationship to God were justified before God. Nevertheless, only in the fullness of time and in Christ did they, and we, attain true righteousness.*

Similarly, Abraham's belief is reckoned to be righteousness, which, as Paul speaks of it, is first found in Christ and is the fullness of time in Jesus Christ (Gal. 4:4). At that time, God took pleasure in the ancients, and they in Him. Similarly, the debt of a lost evil debtor is borne patiently until the guarantor himself comes to pay the debt. Christ is a guarantor of a better testament than that of Abraham, Moses, David, and all the ancients, who had merely a physical foretaste. The bread that comes from heaven, which gives the world life, they experienced in faith through figurative, temporal, and physical manifestations and appearances, but not in essence. Abraham begat a physical Isaac and, thus, his faith received a tangible reward.

Again, the people, believing that Abraham and his seed were promised the land, received this physical land as a reward for their faith. The entire eleventh chapter of Hebrews refers to such corporeal, temporal, and visual things in which the ancients placed their faith. As a testimony to their faith, they received physical things. Even though they all died according to this faith (understand by this the faith referred to above), they nevertheless did not receive the promise, but only saw it from a distance, and thereby consoled themselves that God had provided something better (Heb. 11:13-16).

The biblical scholars state that we hope even now for the promise, but we have not received it. To which we answer: In the Holy Spirit we have received pardon and forgiveness of sin and we have found consolation and security for our heart and conscience. Now, unlike the ancients, we, in Christ, never lack the glory of God. Paul bears witness to the same fact. Because of the belief in this hope, and by the grace of God, the promise of the physical and the temporal was attended by so much enjoyment that the face of Moses shone with the brilliance of the Word inscribed in the stone tablets. What kind of brilliance and satisfaction of faith in Christ will those have whose hearts are inscribed by the finger of God (2 Cor. 3:11)? As Jeremiah states in 31:33: "He will not erect a law as had been done with the fathers; rather, He will write a law in the believer's heart." Christ is the end of the law, states Paul, for all who believe in Him (Rom. 10:4). Similarly, Moses is the beginning of law which condemns all who fail to keep it. For we have received from His fullness, grace, and more grace. Law was given by Moses. Grace and truth, however, came into being through Christ (Jn. 1:17).

Don't say that there was grace in the past. He who is a Jew by rote is no Jew. Unlike the circumcision of the heart, which occurs in the spirit, an external circumcision of the heart, done according to the letter, is not grace, a fact supported by the second chapter of Colossians (2:11 ff.). The Lord

237

Jesus Christ is the Head of all kingdoms and rulers. By laying aside your sinful body of the flesh, He is the one in whom you are circumcised. By being baptized, He is the one with whom you are buried, and He is the one in whom you are raised by the faith which God works in you. When you were dead in sin and in the foreskin of your flesh, God, who has raised Him from the dead, has made you alive with Him.

Not one word from these two texts states that baptism can be directly compared with external circumcision. For our baptism into Christ is not commanded to be practiced solely in the flesh nor is it to be given without the Spirit. The Jews were commanded to circumcise servant and child, good and evil, if they desired to live among the children of Israel. Accordingly, since no other physical difference at that time separated them from the heathen, all young children had to be circumcised, whether they believed or not.

H ii

Now, however, in the revealed kingdom of our Lord Jesus, there is no longer any "you must." Rather, whoever wills, let him come and be baptized in the name of Jesus Christ, and find remission and forgiveness of sin; he who is outwardly circumcised is no Jew, and never shall be one. And such circumcision shall no longer be valid. The only true circumcision shall be that of the heart (Rom. 2:29). This circumcision can only occur when man recognizes it himself through his faith in Christ. Only through such faith can the hearts become circumcised. As Paul says, you are circumcised without hands; through the laying aside of the body of sin, you are buried with Him through baptism.

237

Here it is clear to whom Paul is referring. He refers not to the circumcision of young children, which was practiced among the ancients. Rather, he refers to the true circumcision of the heart, performed without hands. If infant baptism, then, constitutes a parallel to the circumcision performed with hands, which Paul rejects here, one would baptize, but without the Spirit, only the flesh of children. How, then, can such a baptism be done according to Paul's word? He draws a parallel between baptism and the circumcision without hands. Baptism without circumcision takes place through a recognized, unconcealed confession of faith in Christ. Baptism is based on this faith, and not upon external circumcision performed on the unknowing flesh; no child can lay aside the body of sin nor can he be questioned as to whether his heart is circumcised through the faith in Christ. If it could happen without this questioning, then let him be baptized. Paul says: "Not all are Israelites who are Israelites according to the flesh, nor are all those who are of Abraham's seed his children. Children born according to the flesh are not the children of Abraham; the children of promise, of God, are considered as seed" (Rom. 9:6-8). These are the children of the eternal inheritance, which is available today in the fullness of the time and in the coming of Christ. These are not the children of the physical as Paul states so that we will receive sonship. This promise takes effect only if you believe God's promise and deeds, for in the deeds the faith becomes effective. Then the circumcision without hands, of which baptism is a covenant witness, begins. Paul draws a parallel, not between baptism and physical circumcision of the flesh, as performed among the physical seed of Abraham, but between baptism and circumcision without hands. This kind of circumcision does not negate God's promise. Even today, descendants of Abraham's physical seed may believe as well as the heathen, since God

H iii

239

has benevolently promised that he desires to be their God as well as the God of the heathen. However, it does not follow that they will all become believers in Christ, who was named as the seed, the true Isaac, the Lord Jesus Christ. Those who baptize their infants because of their faith, because they were born of their flesh and blood in their faith, must assume that faith can be brought or inherited by flesh and blood.

John says that the birth will come for those "who are not of blood, nor of the flesh, nor of the will of man, but are born of God" (Jn. 1:13). The birth, therefore, never issues from the fleshly seed, but from the seed of the Word, which is now the semen that comes from God's nature and impregnates the heart. The children and heirs born into the kingdom of God and His Christ are born of this seed, and rebirth is eternally not based on any other seed. Those children in whom one recognizes and senses the kind of life which comes from yelling and crying because of their sin may be baptized.

Never has a dead infant been circumcised, nor has a child who is still in his mother's womb.[53] If, then, the physical circumcision of the flesh had a parallel (which it does not), one should not baptize a child dead in the spirit, unless it has become alive through faith in Christ through the word of the faith, and is born of the mother, the church. Such shall be baptized in peace, joy, and consolation in the Holy Spirit, and washed in pure water, which is a covenantal witness of a good conscience with God through faith in Christ, for remission and forgiveness of sin in the fellowship of the saints. Only in this way is circumcision a parallel to baptism, for ever. All that God foresaw, promised, and achieved for the ancient believers was accomplished physically. The figures and shadows of the Old

Testament have held up the light. The essence and truth *is now present. After all, we are now no longer* under the Old Testament; we are under the New, in *which God the Father desires to be worshiped in* spirit and truth, and no longer in physical *representations.*

46

Therefore, those who baptize children, and draw a parallel between the physical circumcision *of the physical children of Abraham and external* baptism of the physical children of Christians, do so *without understanding and in gross ignorance.* Until understanding arrives, so that grace might be forthcoming through the Word of God, as through the imperishable seed, Christians do not procreate spiritual children by the seed of the flesh, but procreate only children of the flesh, just as the ancients did under the law of their physical master. This understanding applies only to spiritual children who are to be baptized under grace and blessing, and who are baptized with water and with the Word, which they believe and have witnessed to. If baptism occurs in place of the physical circumcision, then all those who have received infant baptism remain under the curse, and are subject to the entire law.

The other argument which is used to preserve infant baptism is deduced from the Words of Christ: "Permit little children to come to me, and forbid them not, for of such is the kingdom of heaven" (Lk. 18:16).

47

From this statement, they want to prove that one may baptize children, and they do draw that conclusion. After the children were brought to Christ and Christ had drawn them close to Him, received them, and placed His arms around them, He laid His hands on them, and said of them: "Of such is the kingdom of heaven." Thus, why should one not bring the children to Him, and baptize them *with many fancy words?*

Our answer is first: It is undeniable that neither Christ nor anyone else here thinks of baptism. Furthermore, Christ never baptized an infant, or commanded that they should be baptized. Rather, He did what He was asked to do; He laid His hands on the infants, blessed them, and prayed for them. Just as Christ never allowed anyone to leave Him unsatisfied and disheartened, He also accommodated Himself to the parents of these children, and laid His hands on these children and blessed them.

Accordingly, it is merely a *sophist* invention to draw such proof from this verse; a parallel drawn from selfish reason has no connection with Jesus. Children are brought to Christ, and Christ receives them; thus, one could also bring children to the church and baptize them. There is, however, a great difference between "bring to Christ," and "bring to the church" and baptize them. The parents who brought their children to Christ did not bring them to Him for baptism. They brought them to Him as a Savior, and asked that the Lord lay His hands on the children, and bless and protect them against misfortune and mishap, all of which He did. Christian parents should also freely, and with delight, present and commit their children to Christ. For if Christ does not protect the children against misfortune and evil, the parent's concern will also be in vain. *But if Christ protects them, the parents' concern and discipline (which children are to have) will bear fruit and every good thing. The child may also become worthy of baptism, if the recognition and confession of faith in Christ is granted. For faith is a gift of God, and those who believe should be baptized.* He who would bring his child to bap-

H v

48

tism, as to Christ, and thereby intends to make a Christian out of him and thus be saved, denies Christ and places water baptism as an idol in His place. And the same scandal lies hidden in infant baptism, through which the devil blinds and bewitches, snares and imprisons the innocent hearts in an impure conscience. For, if it were the case that there is no abomination of idolatry in infant baptism, and people place or seek no trust or salvation therein, they would certainly have no haste in baptism, *but would patiently allow faith to proceed, which is the true salvation for all who are baptized.* It has frequently happened that children were baptized before they were really born. And if a child dies unbaptized, they believe that it has been deprived of the face of God, and it must be buried in the pagan cemetery.[54]

Now, to return again to our consideration. It has been stated that little children have been brought to Christ, and the conclusion is drawn therefrom that one may baptize infants. This conclusion, however, is not in accordance with baptism. To bring something[55] to Christ is not synonymous with bringing to baptism. If such were the case, we would have an unusual drama unfolding; since we read that all these things, and more like them, were brought to the Lord Christ, stone crockery, tribute money, gold, myrrh, and frankincense would have been brought to be baptized.

Accordingly, the papists would have been correct who, until now, cultivate the practice of baptizing all articles, such as bells, and indulge in other ridiculous actions. The words of Christ, quoted earlier, can in no way justify and substantiate infant baptism. We expect each one, to whom God has granted the insight and who is willing to think through what real baptism is, easily to understand

and accept what we have demonstrated.

Since Christ said, "Of such is the kingdom of heaven," it is further argued that the children should not be denied the lesser right to baptism if God has already granted them the greater right, the kingdom of heaven.

Answer: Christ does not say that the kingdom belongs to the unspeaking child, nor could it be understood to mean all children in general. He says "of such," and not "to them." It can be understood, then, as He Himself expounds in the preceding chapter 13, that those who are heavy-laden and spiritually impoverished, just as children are by nature, to them belongs the kingdom of heaven.[56] Suppose we accept that the kingdom of heaven belongs to the children. What conclusion follows? Should children be baptized, therefore, before receiving education and instruction, before they are inclined or eager for that to happen which is essential to baptism, *and before they are prepared to give public testimony to it?* These questions we have adequately discussed above.

My dear friend, he who desires to be baptized correctly must be baptized according to Christ's instruction and the apostles' practice.

There are some who maintain that the kingdom of heaven belongs, not to all children, but only to the baptized. They claim, therefore, that child baptism was practiced and that Christ referred to it in that saying. Such an opinion, however, cannot be found in, or substantiated by, the writings of the apostles.

The majority of those who propose infant baptism know nothing of the kingdom of heaven; indeed, they know even less than the children do, and don't care to hear about it, much less accept it as theirs or belong to it. All those who have received infant baptism take it for granted that they are then considered Christians, and such an assumption is part of the idolatry which is hidden in infant baptism. Rarely is there further reflection on the subject. To be sure, more is involved in becoming and in being a Christian than to be thrown as a child into water, *or sprinkled* with it, in the name of God. Eventually, by God's grace, we hope to show this fact.

50 Briefly, those who baptize infants mutilate and bend these words of Christ as it best suits them. Yet, in spite of this, or any other quotation or witness in Scripture, their efforts to confirm that the baptism of a speechless and ignorant child is a true Christian baptism are to no avail. Further, they also present all kinds of arguments and replies,[57] which they hope will protect and preserve their opinion.[58] *The pope and his followers baptize their children because baptism is designed for the forgiveness of sins, and all men are conceived and born in sin. Since all are sinners by nature, it follows that the children are also born in original sin. Therefore, they must be freely baptized in the name of Jesus Christ for forgiveness of sin, and must be washed of original sin through the blood of Christ. If they are not baptized, they are denied the presence of God and, in the beyond, a special place without pain. Those who baptize infants use Scripture to support their argument, and refer to David: "I was brought forth in iniquity, and in sin did my mother conceive me" (Ps. 51:5). Now let us examine this quotation to see if, according to Holy Scripture, it can be used or not to validate the baptism of children. As shall be clearly shown, to ascribe original sin to the infants is the invention of the sophist himself, and is without any basis in Scripture.*

First, one should know where sin found its

*origin, and that is in our first father and mother,
Adam and Eve. God forbade Adam and Eve to eat
the fruit of the tree of the knowledge of good and
evil, and he also forbade them to touch it; the same
hour they ate of it, they would die. When Adam and
Eve transgressed this command and ate from the
fruit of the tree of knowledge, sin became their
inheritance and death their wage. And just as Adam
and Eve first inherited sin in the knowledge and
recognition of good and evil, so also do all their pro-
geny first inherit it in the recognition of good and
evil. Thus, in the knowledge and recognition of
good and evil, sin has its beginning, origin, and
heritage; before this, Adam's and Eve's transgression, no sin, hereditary or real, is mentioned by
God. Only after Adam and Eve recognized good
and evil did God accuse them of the sin, and not
before.*

*Thus, the children are born with the purity of
creation, unaware of good and evil. Who, then,
would want to accuse the innocent children of an
inherited sin? Since the origin and basis of sin, the
knowledge of good and evil, does not come with
birth, the inheritance of the sin against God comes
only with the eating of the forbidden fruit. Of its
own volition, the hand has to touch the tree of
knowledge, and not sooner, before man sins against
God and stands accused. For Ezekiel states that
neither will the child carry the father's guilt, nor the
father the child's (Ezek. 18:19, 20). Who, then,
wants to accuse the innocent children of a sin? Not
one letter of Scripture supports this view, any more
than it supports the view that a man should baptize
infants.*

*The psalmist, however, says: "In sin was I
conceived, and my mother brought me forth in
sin." This verse does not point to the children at all;*

rather, it reflects upon mother and father, who create and conceive in sin, as those who know good and evil. Thus, the child does not conceive and create himself, but is conceived and created in his parents', not his own, sin. So much for the summary of this point. It has, we hope, been adequately demonstrated for every understanding person and, just as they have found support for other points of view, so, too, does this view have a basis.

Furthermore, some base the baptism of infants on their belief in the children's inner, hidden, unrevealed, and future faith. For example, writing against the pope in a pamphlet on original sin, Martin Luther rejects original sin in children on the basis of many arguments.[59]

Likewise, Ulrich Zwingli writes against Martin Luther, and denies and rejects the hidden faith of children.[60] Luther's reply to Zwingli is that, if the children possess no inner, hidden faith known only to God, child baptism would be the greatest blasphemy and idolatry ever conceived, for, then, the Word and name of God would be used in vain, and would be used blasphemously upon the child. Luther attempts to prove and uphold this argument with the words of the Lord in Scripture: "He who believes not is damned" (Mk. 16:16). And Paul states that, without faith, it is impossible for anyone to find favor with God (Heb. 11:6).

These, and similar verses, do not provide exceptions for either young or old. This, in brief, is Martin Luther's opinion on infant baptism.

Now, without violating correct teaching, evident throughout all parts of biblical writings, we will also examine whether this position has validity.

First: Taken in its proper context, which, as Paul and the Lord intended, considers to whom they were speaking, no biblical reference substan-

tiates the belief that children possess an invisible faith.[61] *Without a special revelation, should it please God to reveal, baptism cannot be based on a hidden meaning and will of God. No public witness could be called forth, for baptism is a witness to, and testimony of, a faith in Christ for forgiveness of sin. Since children, as yet, have no unbelief and no works of unbelief or sin are manifested in them, they can neither display any work of faith, such as teaching, preaching, or penitential baptism in the name of Jesus Christ for the forgiveness of sin, nor can they receive or comprehend it through the proclaimed Word. Also, they cannot believe the outward teaching which leads to a true witness and an external baptism with water. Thus, the children should not receive an external witness of the faith. If they are given the outward baptism on the basis of a supposed hidden faith, they would similarly receive external communion, on the basis of their supposed inner love, to commemorate the suffering and death of Christ. With respect to faith, it is the same situation in baptism and communion. "He who does not eat my flesh . . . shall not have life (Jn. 6:53).*

If the words "he who believes not" apply to the ignorant and innocent little children, then the words "whoever does not eat or has not love" as stated in John 6, also apply.

244   *What, then, is to be made of the words of Paul dealing with communion: "Let each man examine himself, and so let him eat" (1 Cor. 11:28). How can the uneducated infant examine himself? If you say Christ speaks of the inner nourishment of faith, as is true, then we could say that; if the children have a hidden faith, then they must also have a hidden love. Paul does say, "All is in vain without love" and, though he has a faith that could move moun-*

*tains (1 Cor. 13:2), faith must be preceded by love.
If they have one, they also have the other. If they
have an inner, hidden faith and love, they also have
an inner baptism and communion. If you accept the
one, you must also accept the other.*

I ii   *External baptism is given to the outer church,
and it is given as a witness to the revealed, unhid-
den, uncovered faith before the church of God.
Similarly, communion testifies to the revealed love
of Christ, which the members of the church have
for each other as they proclaim His death. And in
His death, He gives us the new commandment; as a
reminder of Him, we are to give ourselves for each
other unto death and in His name, just as He gave
His life for us out of love. Christ says that "greater
love has no man, than he gives his life for his
friends" (Jn. 15:13). And He asks us to love one
another, just as He has loved us. John also speaks of
this love. We give our lives for our brother, but only
the sword of the Spirit, and not the fleshly sword,
can save him. Unlike those who deny the truth, as
Peter did, we then witness, in all patience, to the
truth of the Word, through which we can save one
another, and continue, in spirit and truth, in an
eternal, and not a temporal, life. These types of
Christians are now many. Yes, the whole world is
full of them, among whom are the papists, Lutherans, and false Anabaptists. Their physical sword
will not suffice and cannot protect them. Under
Christ's rule, such a thing could not happen, unless
one places himself into an unjust state, the greatest
abomination, of which the Lord and Daniel speak.
So their faith in Christ has ended, and they are
destroyed in the rebellion of Korah (Num. 16).*

*But the true participants in Christ offer each
other hope, as did Christ their Lord, who did not
come to destroy. In brief, this, then, is the right and*

249

true communion meal with Christ, which shall endure eternally. More will be said about true communion later. If such inner, hidden faith in infants can be witnessed to by an outer baptism, they may also witness to this supposed love through the outward communion. It is a construct of reason that the unknowing infants, who cannot yet speak, should have a hidden inner faith. Neither their faith nor their baptism will find any basis in Scripture. Nonetheless, let us examine the text already indicated to try and find whether the position can be sustained.

Mark states: "Go forth in all the world and preach the gospel to every creature. He who believes and receives baptism shall be saved; but he who believes not will be damned" (Mk. 16:15, 16).

From the word "damned," it is assumed that, if the child has no faith, it would be damned should it die in childhood. First, the text states they shall preach the gospel to all creatures. It is not to be preached to wood, stone, or the mountains, nor is it to be preached to the dumb animals, nor to the ignorant children, although they are all creatures, each according to its kind. Yes, Christ does not mean that these dumb animals and ignorant children can understand and comprehend the teaching, which would be contrary to God's creaturely order. Nor will they, because they do not believe the gospel, be subject to the damnation of which they are accused. However, according to the design and creation of God, their created nature and their characteristics separate them from those who, according to this quotation, are damned. Those who can be taught, but who will not believe, are the damned ones. Rational man is a creature above all creatures; all creatures are made for the will of man, and man is designed for the will of Christ and

Christ for the will of God (1 Cor. 3:23).

This is the reason why Saint Matthew, in his gospel, does not write of "creatures," but says: "Teach all nations," which is as much as to say that the nations are the creatures above all creatures (Mt. 28:18-20).

Thus, one can also witness to the true gospel and instruct the nations through the creatures over which they have lordship. Moreover, the Lord God rules over them through Jesus Christ. Paul supports this contention when he says that the gospel was preached to all creatures under heaven, for all life exists for the sake of Christ, through whom all things have been created (Col. 1:23).

Just as man acknowledges and rules the creatures for his own personal advantage, so must he acknowledge the one who governs man, as Christ the Lord says. To Him has been given all authority over heaven and over earth. And His apostles have been sent to preach the gospel to all creatures: He alone is the Lord and Christ of God, preeminent over the universe. That means nothing to an ignorant child, since it has, as yet, no mastery of the creatures. Therefore, the infant is unable to witness to any faith and, consequently, cannot be damned.[62]

The words to the Hebrews state, therefore, that it is impossible to find favor with God without faith; he who desires to approach God must believe that God exists (11:6). Such a statement cannot apply to the ignorant children who have, as yet, not laid hands on the forbidden fruit of knowledge of good and evil, and who have no will to know either good or evil. And the Word does state: "He who desires to approach God." How can they want to come to God, since they have not yet been separated from Him by that knowledge of good and evil which is the origin of sin and lack of faith? How can they

I iiii

believe, when they have not attained unbelief, and when they, the good and pure creation of God still exist in their created innocent state? This is the simple state in which God finds favor. God testifies against Jonah that he should have mercy on those who cannot even distinguish between the left hand and the right (4:11), those to whom Jonah did not preach repentance, which could have led them to believe and to repent, and which he had preached to the king and the common people.

God is merciful toward the infants because of their ignorance and genuine innocence; to others, He is merciful because of their faith and repentance. In this way, all Scriptures follow the divine order in their place without error. If, after being instructed through proclamation, the parents do not repent, just as in Lot's time and the flooding of the world in Noah's time, their children, in their innocence, will also be punished in this life, not because of their guilt, but because of the guilt of the parents, who do know good and evil. There, Scripture does not speak of the guilt of the innocent children. Rather, it deals with the roguery, wickedness, and deception of the parents, even though the children were also included in the punishment. No one can declare them damned because of personal guilt. Even today, when those who know good and evil repent and believe, the innocent children receive grace provisionally, and the parents are spared because of the innocence of their children. The children are not condemned because of their parents' knavery. In this way, the whole world quarrels about the salvation of the innocent children, and nobody sees the damnation each one is certain to receive because of personal roguery and wickedness, surely the devil's sport. In short, we have stated the case against those who defend a

supposed, hidden, inner faith in innocent children,
and who thereby retain infant baptism and assume
that they have validated it.

247

50

I v

Those who baptize children also have many
more unfounded reasons and sophistic opinions.
These, however, are so weak and awkward that we
consider it unnecessary to *waste time* with them. It
should be sufficient to note them briefly, and
everyone will easily see for himself that they contribute nothing to the matter, and are in fact useless.[63]

Some also say that the practice of infant baptism has been continuously practiced since the
apostles. Others disagree and deny it. Whichever it
is, even if infant baptism has come to us from the
time of the apostles, it does not follow that it is,
therefore, correct and holy in the manner[64] they say
it, and many other abominations, are. Even the
pope himself and his retinue have endured since the
time of the apostles; similarly, in the apostles' time,
many false teachings crept in, but their existence
does not prove them correct. If it was possible that
the apostles themselves taught and practiced contrary to Scriptures, their teaching would have been
cursed (Gal. 1:8 f.). However, the arguments for
and against infant baptism, and how they harmonize with Scripture, have heretofore been adequately indicated and demonstrated. Many others,
however, contradict these arguments.

Spiritual legal writings, like *Decreto de consec-*
ratione, dist. IIII, state that no one is baptized until
they have been instructed in their faith in the
gospel, confessed it with the laying on of hands by
the bishop, and have renounced the devil.[65]

51

Tertullian's *de Corona Militis* also supports
this position. Therefore, Beatus Rhenanus, who is
an exceptionally experienced historian, shows that,

up to the time of Charlemagne and Kaiser Ludwig, only *the willing and* mature were baptized.[66] It is quite believable, as mentioned above, that the devil applied all his efforts and utilized all his tactics in order to darken baptism, which is a door and entrance into the holy church, so that he can, *through his children,* slip in *to lay waste God's vineyard.*

Martin Luther, in a pamphlet on the councils of the pope, writes that what is confirmed by the pope is doubtful of truth, since the truth is confirmed by Christ and needs no confirmation from any human being.[67]

Thus, Pope Eugenius, who first ratified child baptism, did so because he was in a quandary and doubted the truth.[68] *Otherwise, it would have remained unconfirmed.*

248 We also read in 1 Corinthians 15 that, even during the time of the apostles, baptism was abused because salvation was considered to be dependent on it. Consequently, some were baptized on behalf of the dead in the belief that this baptism would also give the dead salvation, merit, and goodness.

52 *Similarly, today we have in the holy eucharist a sacrificial mass for the dead; one eats and drinks for those who have passed away. This the living do for the sake of the dead, as if this action were to assist the dead, as all papists maintain to be true. In the same way, there was abuse of baptism in the time of Paul.*

Therefore, it is plausible that, since baptism can benefit the dead, it also would do no harm to infants. Such a conclusion has taken hold in time, and has become so firmly entrenched that infant baptism was forced and coerced.

They further try to justify infant baptism by quoting accounts in which the apostles are said to have baptized entire households; they claim that, beyond a doubt, there were children present. Therefore, they say, the apostles baptized children. So, why should we not do so if the apostles did? But this assumption proves nothing. Why? At the time when entire households were baptized, it is just as likely that there were no infants present as it is likely that they were. For there are as many homes in which there are no infants as there are homes with infants. Often, reference is made to an entire land, city, or house without including any children at all. We read that the whole of Judea went out to hear John (Mt. 3:5). Matthew says: "King Herod is afraid and, with him, the whole of Jerusalem" (2:3). It does not follow that the infants went out from their cribs to hear John or that they were afraid. Similar examples can be found in other places in Scripture.

Now, they think of still other arguments, but all quite cold and inept. And after they have understood that baptism can be given to, or received by, no one unless he first sincerely believes, or that he who is performing the baptism must have a clear indication that the one being baptized believes, they nevertheless take great pains, but using a different argument, in trying to prove that the children (as was suggested earlier) do have faith. They state that God can give faith as easily to a child of one day as to someone a hundred years old. But this avowal hardly helps the cause. Even though we have answered this argument frequently enough already, we shall again make short shrift of it. Although God has the power to give faith to an unspeaking child, *even to raise children of Abraham from the stones*, no true Scripture can show that God does so, or that one could come by the faith differently than through the hearing and the revelation of the Word of God which precedes. *For God has sealed His*

249

53

might in the order of the Word; he who attributes other powers to God blasphemes His order and power, and suggests that God has not adequately demonstrated His power and glory in and through the order of His Word.

We freely concede that God certainly has such powers.[69] *We thereby also recognize and know that His might is placed in the order of His Word and will. Otherwise, God would exercise His powers capriciously, according to each man's thought. That would be a nice power of God! Oh, you God-blasphemers, where do you think you are going? Don't you fear that your folly will reveal itself?* Therefore, like the dialecticians say, because a thing is possible, it does not follow that it is or need be so.

We concede even more. It would be possible for God to endow a newborn child with reason, faith, and speech so that it would be proper and beneficial to receive baptism *along with the holy communion.* God certainly has this power, but He does not necessarily exercise it. If God were to bestow such miracles on the infants and they show that they have died by faith to sin and the flesh, they would desire the baptism of their own free will. Then, we would in no way want to deny them baptism nor to oppose it. *Until that happens, we should not act.* As has been stated often enough before now, we have no command to baptize anyone on the basis of a foreign confession and faith.[70]

Finally, those who baptize children have one last defense and refuge and, though they often spar with it, let us get ahead of them and run down this shield.

If one appeals to Scripture and concludes from 54 the Word the nature of those who are to be baptized, and all those qualities are still lacking in the little children, they must remain unbaptized until they have matured in reason and, of their own free will, confess their faith.

Yes, they say, this must be understood only for the adults, and not for the water baptism of children. Answer. Holy Scripture identifies only one kind of baptism with which the believers are to be baptized; only those who have died in sin, and desire to lead a new life, and both must be present, may be baptized. Thus, to suggest that such a statement applies only to the rational and knowing, but not to infants, is a foul excuse and evasion. They thereby create two types of baptism, one for the mature and understanding, and one for the innocent infant. This practice is contrary to Scripture and *according to true understanding* may not be permitted; *Scripture speaks only of one conscious, confessed, and acknowledged baptism based on faith. It does not speak of baptism of unconscious people.*

Of the Child's State and Condition

Concerning the state of the children, *who stand in all created simplicity, knowing neither good nor evil,* Scripture indicates nothing except that they are innocent without guile. Thus, we conclude that we rightly and wisely refrain from *saying anything about it except what is found in Scripture.* Rather, we commit them to the *hidden* verdict of God, *who best knows how to keep them to His praise and honor.*

Since God ordained that they be born in created innocence, God will refrain from accusing this innocence, since sin has its origin in the knowledge of good and evil. The children, therefore, cannot be accused of any sin. What kind of state of salvation such infants have, we will allow God to decide since He has ordered creation in this way. But, we believe we are to recognize, according to the Scriptures, those to whom God grants life and we are to *admonish* them and educate them in all virtue to God's glory. If, then, when they have come of age and come to understanding, they have learned the way of the Lord, and are able to take upon themselves the yoke of the Lord and to learn the will of the Lord, following Him in all righteousness as the Lord gives them grace, *then they shall be baptized if they desire it*. If they do not wish to commit themselves thereto, but would rather pledge themselves to the darkness instead of the light, and if they do not change, we must let them go their way and commit them to the Lord.

K However, the innocent and unknowing who, baptized or not, depart from this earth while still in created innocence must be commended to the orderly will[71] of God, who probably knows best how He should deal with them.

251 Now to abbreviate and conclude this matter: Infant baptism is practiced in two ways, either unnecessarily and in vain, or as idolatry.

Infant baptism is practiced unnecessarily and in vain by those who seek but find no salvation therein, and by those who say that, if it does not help, neither does it harm. They baptize, not out of faith, but out of uncertainty, and use it as a safeguard, certain only that it is God's *wish and* command to baptize in this fashion.*Although well-intentioned,* they use the name of God in vain and thus, *they baptize themselves only for revenge.*[72] Such abuse will not go unpunished by God. To be sure, they say that they baptize in the name of the Lord, but how can they be baptized in His name when He has not commanded it?

Second, these people practice idolatry when they vest their salvation in baptism. As has happened in the past, and still happens, they not only maintain, but also convince themselves that, when a child has been baptized, it is a Christian; should it die, it *would forthwith*[73] ascend to heaven, and be counted among the host of heavenly angels. And they further maintain that, if it dies unbaptized, this poor innocent child, which knows neither good nor evil, is considered to be among *the disbelieving Jews*,[74] and will be confined to eternal darkness.

In the past, many have adhered to this belief concerning infant baptism. Is it not a serious idolatry that baptism has, in this way, been made into an idol?

No one can deny that it has taken place. If this idolatry were not present, people would not be incensed by infant baptism, and the devil also would not rant and rave about it.

This is the meaning and confession of both infant baptism and of true baptism. We have carefully and diligently dealt with the situation at length in order to clarify our understanding for the many whose minds are closed and whose understanding is inexperienced in Scripture. The devils reluctantly admit that the entrance into the holy church is truly opened[75] and bright. But, because they realize what has thus been taken from them, they rant and rave horribly. They know, also, that infant baptism is an introduction *to the realm of the Antichrist, a true and real entrance, beginning, door, and reason for its being, and an instigation to all evil and idolatry which is maintained through his deceptive disguise of Christ, a secure anchor to deceive the people. As soon as infant baptism were to be abolished, the disruption of the realm of the Antichrist would immediately follow. The devil has undermined the true Christian baptism and done away with it. Consequently, the Christian church*

K ii

252

has become desolated and soiled and, because of infant baptism, has, instead, planted the kingdom of the Antichrist. The abolition of infant baptism and the reinstatement of the true baptism, based on faith in Christ, would destroy the kingdom of the 56 *Antichrist,* and would restore the true holy church, purified and cleansed of all unclean animals.

Therefore, we beseech and admonish, by the mercy of God, all true God-fearing lovers of truth to read diligently this, our confession. Judge it by the standard of Holy Scripture, without regard to persons seeking only divine *love,* honor, the salvation of the soul and, *for the betterment of the body of Christ,* the edification of the holy Christian church *in love for God and for the neighbor, on which depend all Scripture, law, and prophets.*

We also request that no one seek his own honor, but seek instead the honor of God and the advancement of the salvation of all men in this writing, and that you consider and judge all things thoroughly. If God reveals something more useful, important, and better to someone, let him not bury his talent, but present it in order that God may grant *that all good-hearted people* may come to a true unity of the holy *and true Christian fellowship* or church.

Furthermore, we humbly submit ourselves to anyone who, openly or privately, asks us to give an account of our faith so that we might refer him to this writing as a witness to our faith. Further, in case we have humanly failed and not directly met the issues, we are also prepared to ask those who have a better answer to share it with us in Christian spirit and temperance, just as we have attempted to K iii do here. Where our conscience is convinced of better things, we will always gladly yield to the truth.

This account of baptism, then, is sufficient for

now. We want to continue by presenting our confession of the Lord's Supper. We eagerly place our confession under the judgment of the holy *Christian* church, which by the Spirit of God tests all things according to the Scriptures.

Here Follows the Confession of the Lord's Supper
Psalm 111:4, 5

57 He hath made His wonderful works to be remembered: the Lord is gracious and full of compassion. He hath given meat unto them that fear Him.

Concerning the Last Supper of Christ

Just as we have until now presented our understanding and definition of holy baptism to be judged by everyone, so we would also like to deal with the communion of Christ, our understanding of which follows.

At present, the scholars have made a major attempt to understand the Word regarding the institution of communion, and they have gone to great pains to interpret the words, "This is my body, this is my blood." Since they could not tolerate each other's opinions on this matter, much dispute, dissension, doubt, and misunderstanding have been created. As a result, the true basis and purpose of the matter has not been adequately considered, if at all, *as to what the Lord's Supper is, and why it was instituted.* Unless someone with puffed-up pride wants to instill animosity, we do not intend to enter into the dispute, nor do we intend to take sides. For the words of Scripture, *of Christ* and Paul express so clearly the meaning of the Lord's Supper that all who are satisfied with Scripture, and whose understandings are guided by the meaning of Scripture, will easily comprehend Christ's intention in His Supper. Thus, since it does not behoove us as Christians, and we are reluctant to engage in disputes and animosity, we want to drop all feuding and animosity, and clearly define our understanding of the Lord's Supper by appealing to Scriptures.

On the Institution of the Lord's Supper and Christ's Instruction

When the hour of suffering of our Lord and Savior Jesus Christ approached, and the Easter celebration (at which time the little lamb was to be sacrificed) was at hand, the Lord sent two of His disciples to prepare for the eating of the Easter lamb with the members of His household in accordance with the law. When the hour arrived, He sat with the twelve apostles at table, and ate the Passover lamb. Upon its completion, He held and instituted His holy communion and, as the evangelists and Paul clearly witness, further instructed His disciples. There is not much to add, since the Evangelists adequately describe the matter. Therefore, let us go straight to the heart of the matter, and discover what is the communion of Christ and show what its function should be.

Concerning the Word "Sacrament"

Earlier, we mentioned that communion can be correctly called a sacrament if the word sacrament is understood in its proper and natural meaning. Nonetheless, since the majority of interpretations of this word differ radically from its natural meaning, and the true meaning of communion is mystified and obscured by the word sacrament, we refrain from using the word, and simply give an account of our understanding of what communion is. Furthermore, nowhere in the Scriptures is communion referred to as a sacrament. Paul calls it the Lord's communion; thus, we shall also not be easily perverted, since we are staying with Scripture, speaking, writing, and maintaining our position according to the evidence in the Scriptures.

Many people regard the holy sacrament of the altar very highly, and regard it as if it is equal to the being and essence of God. But of the communion and its meaning, they possess absolutely no knowledge. Indeed, if you ask them what the sacrament is, they would quickly reply, "it is God." But, if they were asked about communion, they would not know what to reply. The word "sacrament," which does not occur in Scripture, has misled these people into a false superstition. If God wills, everyone could easily understand it, who diligently probes the meaning of communion and, alongside of it, what has been taught and believed until now about the sacrament of the altar, as it is called. Thus, we want to avoid the word sacrament; rather, we will describe the communion and its worth, as God's grace permits, and according to Scripture, and we will describe, interpret, and declare it openly.

A Description of the Lord's Supper

The Last Supper of Christ is a bodily gathering or *assembly* of Christian believers who *partake* of communal food and drink, as Christ instructed them to do, in remembrance of Him. This understanding is supported by the witness of the Evangelists, by Paul, and also by the ancient teachers. They only described how the Last Supper was instituted and commanded by Christ. The Evangelists, and especially John, indicate that the Lord, when He was gathered with His own in the evening meal, proceeded quite corporally and lovingly[76] with both works as well as words. He stopped at nothing to demonstrate His great love (which He had toward His own) through service. It was inadequate for the Lord to address His followers with physical words, consoling and encouraging them, or even to indicate His willingness to give His life for them. Rather, He lowered Himself to washing the feet of His disciples. Thus, John justly and adequately describes the talk of the Last Supper when he says that Christ has loved His own in this world to the end (Jn. 13:1). As you can read in John, Christ strengthens through higher witness. Thus, if we intend to preserve the Lord's Supper correctly, it is vital that we, by loving each other, diligently study and seriously follow the example of our Master. After Christ had washed His disciples' feet, He said, among other things: "I have left you an example, so that you, too, do as I have done to you" (Jn. 13:15).

The meaning of Christ's words, beyond a doubt, is to give all His apostles, who were prepared to die with Him, a clear understanding that they should observe the holy communion in His memory, as a model of love. Let us remember that the Lord's communion can rightly be seen as a physical meeting. When Christians assemble, they are to be girded with love for one another, in the same way as Christ loved them, in order that they might thereby confirm and reveal the love of believers *in Christ*. For this reason, all those who lack faith and love do not belong at the Lord's table, for only those who believe *in Christ* have the true love. Thus, we claim that communion is a physical gathering of those who believe *in Christ*.

Thus, the pope and his camp represent the Antichrist, for they have always made a travesty of Christ and have covered their knavery and deceit by appending to Christ's name. Similarly, the pope has taken communion literally, but has, at all times, made a monkey show of it and has misled the simple hearts. One can still go to the cathedrals on the Thursday before Easter (*also known as Maundy Thursday*), and see this communion play acted out in all seriousness, but without any spirit, *love,* or truth. Then the priests wash each other's feet, read the Scriptures describing the Lord's words at the Last Supper, break the bread, and also pass around the wine. Following this part of the rite, they pick up the host and leave again, all the time uttering the words of Christ: "*Surgite eamus hinc,*" which is, "let us arise and go forth" (Jn. 14:31).

256

The pope has in this fashion brilliantly counterfeited the model of Christ, for all that is lacking is the spirit, *love,* and truth. Therefore, even though they call it communion, it is not the communion of Jesus Christ, but rather a monkeyshine in which Christ's example is thoroughly blasphemed. Christ does not ask us to mimic His works and bearing, for such mimicking would unfortunately reduce His whole suffering to play and ridicule. Rather, Christ asks that we follow Him in constant and sincere love, practicing and proving it to one another in order to achieve a true union *and remembrance,* and asks us to maintain His Last Supper. Therefore, though the Lord's Supper is observed according to His instructions, if love is missing, then Christ's example is completely counterfeited, and the communion cannot be referred to as the Supper of the Lord.

61

This is also the reason why Paul rebuked the Corinthians and said it was not the Lord's Supper they were observing. Undoubtedly, for them to forget the method and external forms, not enough time had elapsed since Paul had instructed them on how to hold communion. They had, however, forgotten the love; their assembly did not remain rich in love for long, they scorned one another, and the rich filled their bellies and let the poor suffer hunger. Paul rebuked them for their lack of love, and said: "Therefore, when you come together in one place, you do not partake of the Lord's Supper, for you take food for yourself first. One remains hungry while the other is full. Have you no homes where you can eat and drink, or do you hold the church of God in contempt and disdain those who have nothing? What shall I say?" (1 Cor. 11:20-22).

We describe the communion of Christ, first, as a physical assembly of believers in Christ who have love. Although it can be considered a supper without love, it would not be a Christian communion even if all other ingredients were present, as Paul vividly and clearly illustrates. The Lord's Supper cannot be eaten without love, which is a requirement for communion. And this true love grows out of a true faith. Therefore, only believers in Christ, and no one else, can hold such a meeting or assembly so rich in love.

We describe communion further, and say that the bread and wine of the Lord shall be eaten and drunk by all true believers as a remembrance of the Lord. Moreover, this eating and drinking is a sign of their participation in His body and blood, and represents a lasting bond of love among Christians, a fact which is articulated and witnessed clearly enough in the words of Christ and Paul.

After He had broken the bread and offered it to His disciples to eat, and after He had asked them to drink of the cup, Christ said: "Do this in re-

257

membrance of me" (Lk. 22:19).

From these words, it is clear that the bread and wine of communion shall be given, eaten, and drunk as a remembrance of Christ.

Paul says the same: "The chalice of blessing which we bless, is it not participation in Christ's blood? And the bread which we break, is not that the participation of Christ's body?" (1 Cor. 10:16 f.). For if it be one bread, then we who are many are one body. We have all taken part in, and nourished ourselves by, one bread.

Are these words of Saint Paul not clear and obvious? The bread we break and the cup we drink in the Lord's Supper is a sharing in the flesh and blood of Jesus Christ. Those who do this communally and in this fashion testify that they have fellowship with Christ, and have become united as one body through one spirit of love. Just as one loaf is made of many kernels ground together so as to become mixed with one another and become one loaf, so do they, who eat this loaf and drink this cup with one another in the Lord's Supper, become one with the body of Christ in love and obedience of the faith.[77] They submit to one another and serve one another *in patience, and not in conflict of the sword of steel; rather, they are willing and ready to do good to friends and enemies.* Just as one member of the body works for another and *is dependent on the others, so also in love we are all members of one body.*

Upon this basis, Paul introduces the Lord's Supper in 1 Corinthians 11. The history of the apostles and the primitive church reveals that the communion was used in this way, as we will discuss later on. Let it suffice for now that we have shown that our concept of communion is grounded in Scripture, even though many people desire something else. We are satisfied with Scripture, and shall not stray from it despite those who speak out against it. Scripture instructs us adequately, and we feel that nothing else may be added. However, should even better evidence be found in Scripture than we think, we will praise God, and always yield to the truth and make room for it.

Why the Lord's Supper Was Decreed and How It Should Be Used and Observed

258

We have stated that the Lord's Supper *or communion* is a physical gathering or assembly of love, and a communal eating and drinking by Christians in remembrance of Christ. It is a fellowship of His body and blood which builds a bond of love among those who *believe in Christ*.

63

Although this description will show any intelligent individual why the Lord's Supper was instituted and how it should be used, nonetheless, for the sake of the less educated, more simple hearts, we intend to present each argument as simply and straightforwardly as possible so that our understanding may be known to everyone. We hope our effort will help the poorly educated find the truth. This topic has been dealt with for a long time with great intelligence and sophistication, but the result has been that many have been enraged. If the instructions of Christ had been examined in their simplicity, and had been duly carried out, quite a lot of ill will and confusion could have been avoided. While cantankerous disputes about words and their artistic subtleties took place, the simple meaning has escaped and has consequently suffered great trouble and misery. We now want to put our efforts, as much as God gives us grace, to the task of presenting the uncomplicated meaning of the insti-

L

tution of the Lord's Supper, how it should be practiced simply, according to Scripture, and omit all altercations which serve no purpose anyway. God help us to find the truth and to obey it. Amen.

The Foremost Consideration in Communion and Why It Has Been Instituted

The foremost question to ask seriously is: why and how should communion be practiced? Such a question must be examined carefully and with great diligence. At the same time, one must keep in mind that a communal eating and drinking is meant here, and it is an evening meal of bread and wine which Christians have been instructed to partake one with the other. One should not dispute or quarrel over the interpretation of the Word as it concerns the nature of the bread and the wine. Certainly, to dispute this aspect of communion has not been commanded. We have been instructed, however, to consider the function of communion. Each individual is to examine diligently his own self before he eats of the bread and drinks of the wine. As Paul clearly shows, when anyone who is not worthy eats of this bread or drinks of this cup, he will eat and drink damnation on himself. Damnation, therefore, is not dependent upon what the bread and the wine are in the Lord's Supper, but rather on the correct use of the bread and the wine, and upon the condition of the heart in which the bread and wine are taken. Whoever is worthy to eat of this bread and drink of this cup experiences a participation in the flesh and blood of Jesus Christ, as Paul testifies. Therefore, he exhorts us so earnestly, saying: Each individual must examine himself and, accordingly, eat of this bread and drink of this cup (1 Cor. 11:28). He does not say that we are to examine the

259

64

L ii

269

bread and the wine, and see what they are. Let each man test himself. This directive means that each individual, if his heart is tuned thereto, should first test himself, and then the bread and wine follow. Are you wholeheartedly fused into the love of Christ and your fellowman? Are you wholeheartedly bent on following the example of Christ, not only for your brethren, *but also for your friends and enemies, according to the words of the Lord Jesus?* Then the breaking of bread and drinking from the cup become a true participation in the body and blood of Christ. If your heart is embittered by evil directed against your neighbor, if it is so deceitful, jealous, and full of ill will that you neglect to repent in true remorse, you will, in the bread and the wine, eat and drink unto damnation. Thus, the entire force and impact depends on the heart of the individual, and not at all on the external, like bread and wine.

The individual is to look in upon himself when he prepares to go to the Lord's Supper, and he should not concern himself with what the external bread and wine signifies. Unfortunately, too much time has been spent in debating, and many have been at their wit's end in their attempt to understand. The bread and the wine of the Lord's Supper have been maliciously examined and disputed at length, and efforts at definition have ended inconclusively. In contrast, the self-examination of the heart proves to be beneficial in the act of eating and drinking the Lord's Supper. By virtue of unity in love and *patience* toward one another, we who eat the bread become one body. Little consideration has been given to the fact that the Lord's Supper is to be a lovely Christian meal, a watchword of the untainted love of the faithful. Instead of love, man has engaged in a war of semantics, finely argu-

65

ing the nature of the bread and the wine, the result of which has been that the Lord's Supper has practically degenerated, and it is frightening to say it, into nothing more than a jealous dog's meal. Had the Lord's Supper been kept as communion, had these hairsplitting and unnecessary disputes been omitted, had each man heeded the wishes of Christ in eating and drinking to His remembrance, and if such were still the case, much garbage would have been discarded and would still be left behind today. Therefore, we ask everyone to heed diligently the testimony of Scriptures, reflect upon the command of Christ, and take it to heart. This command we now want to examine simply, omitting all useless and unnecessary disputes which do nothing to help the matter or to achieve unity.

260

L iii

Christ's Command Regarding the Lord's Supper

Since we have already established the meaning of the Lord's Supper and what should primarily be considered in it, let us now examine what Christ's command is and why He has requested the holy communion of us.

On the night in which Christ was betrayed, He broke the bread and gave it to His disciples; similarly, He passed around the cup. When the disciples had eaten and drunk, Christ, in demanding such a meal or communion of His disciples, said, among other things: "This do, and as often (or frequently) as you do this, do it in remembrance of Me." Upon instituting His holy communion, Christ gave this command to His disciples, entrusting His faithful to instruct others, as Paul adequately testifies, and further explains to the Corinthians (1 Cor. 11:24).

66 At no place can another command be found

which instructs beyond this alone: this do in memory of me. Now for the meaning of the command.

With these words, Christ instructs us to hold a communion, to eat and drink with one another of one bread and cup in His memory. In doing so, we must realize that we are not to recite any particular words following this act, as the apostles, and all believers after them, showed us. The text of Paul and of the Scriptures point this fact out when they state: take and eat, spoke Christ; this is My body. Take and drink, that is the cup of the new testament in My blood. This do you after Me; take bread and wine, break and pour it out, eat and drink and, as often and frequently as you do it, do it in My memory.

Referring to the eating and drinking, Paul expresses himself in a similar way when he states: For whenever, or as frequently as, you eat of the bread or drink of the cup, proclaim the death of the Lord till He comes. For Christ says, this do, that is, take bread and wine, eat and drink in fellowship with one another and do that, as you are doing now and as often as you do it in the future, in memory of Me.

Christ, therefore, states why communion should be observed and why one should engage in it: His memory. Therein lies the power for us to do likewise and to practice the Lord's Supper as commanded here.

He who uses communion differently, and brings in meanings other than those expressed by Christ, eats and drinks damnation unto himself. What do these words, "This do in remembrance of Me," entail for us? What is their true meaning? We must measure this meaning according to our need, as frequently as possible, and we must also articulate it and emphasize it.

The Meaning of the Words: "This Do in Remembrance of Me"

We have heard what Christ has commanded us to do, which is to observe communion. His further comment, that we should do this in remembrance of Him, will here be further expounded. Also to be understood in this matter is that the Lord's Supper is set apart from other communal or evening meals, or eating in general, since these are used to sustain natural life. The Lord's Supper, however, is observed in remembrance of the Lord and for the refreshment, *strengthening, and solace* of the soul, and for no other purpose other than for the Christians mutually to remind one another of the Lord.

Now one might ask: shall one preserve the Lord's Supper and His memory and, if so, why? Answer: There are two reasons, equally important in remembering Christ who is our example.[78] In the holy communion, we should, therefore, remember Him in two ways.

First, we should remember Him for what He has done for our sake. Second, we should bear in mind that which we should do for His sake in grateful return. These two things should be considered at communion, and not only considered, but also brought into reality with profoundest gratitude.

Our first point to examine, that Christ lost His life and His blood for the forgiveness of sin and for our sake, must be looked at and considered with heartfelt reverence and great thankfulness. He spoke to this effect in the Last Supper when He gave His disciples to eat of the bread and drink of the cup: This is My body which is given for you, and my blood which is shed for you.[79] Which remembrance could *console*, renew, *delight*, and *strengthen*, yes, even nourish a true believer *in*

273

Christ as bread and wine might nourish the body? What could be more consoling and delightful than to remember the unutterable, recorded love through which God the Father gave His only Son to us poor sinners? The Word became flesh from the seed of a woman, as if from the seed of a man, and *He whom God gave so lovingly and unbegrudgingly was conceived without human seed or sin.* Not only did God commit Him to an *earthly, natural, physical* life, but He even committed Him, *through patience,* to an *earthly, natural, physical death.*

Thus, Paul emphatically states: For, as often as you eat this bread, and drink this cup, ye do proclaim the Lord's death till He come. That is, eat of the bread and drink of the cup in fellowship one with the other to show and acknowledge thereby the death of the Lord. Show that Christ died for you, giving His body and spilling His blood for you, and show that, in the death of Christ, all your solace and life is directed. *In this* act, too, are seen the works of Christ, which are *love, patience, humility.* Each true believer is called upon to continue them. Otherwise, nobody can take part in the true communion of Christ. And if an unbeliever eats of this bread and drinks of this cup to which only the believers have been consecrated, he eats and drinks damnation unto himself. Thus, Paul says: For he that eats of this bread and drinks of this cup, let him examine himself that he take part with a true heart, that he proclaim with his heart the death of our Lord by which his whole life and consolation stand judged.

This is the first matter to be considered in regard to communion. We believe and proclaim that the Son of God became man, *conceived by the Holy Ghost in the Virgin Mary, conceived and born by the seed of woman as a true, natural, earthly man of the lineage and seed of David.* In death, *He has given* His *earthly, natural* life and body, and shed His blood for the forgiveness of our sins. *Reflection upon this gift is, in short, the first aspect of the memorial in communion.*

The other memorial aspect of communion is our debt of gratitude for Christ's sake. In other words, we should remember to humble ourselves for His sake, and again to be willing, when demanded, to lose our lives for His name. We should be well-disposed in true love, we should love one another as Christ has loved us *and, through patience, we should show our love to all our enemies and also pray for them, even unto death.* This remembrance should put us right with Christ and our neighbor when we approach communion. Thus, we all eat of one bread and drink of one cup, witnessing that we are at one with each other through Christian love. He who has a different attitude, or takes part in the Lord's communion for some other reason, eats and drinks damnation unto himself. If he eats and his heart is dishonest, *if his heart is differently disposed to the meal than his eating indicates,* the eating of the bread and the drinking of the cup of the Lord is an unworthy act, for such a person is impure in heart.

Those who take part without having rebuked, according to the order of the Spirit, any sins or vices dealing with a brother are also unworthy to eat and drink communion, because the body of Christ is not differentiated from the hatred and scorn of the devil, and the innocent participated in other's sins. Therefore, Paul says: "Root out the evildoer from your community" (1 Cor. 5:13), which means that we are to discern the body of Christ. But we are not to be like those who maintain the ban, banning people from the face of the earth, seizing life and

*land, forbidding place and people. Such a ban does
not belong to the Christian church, nor may such a
ban ever be permitted in the kingdom of Christ, according to the words of the Lord and Paul.*

*Christ states they shall be regarded as the
heathen (Mt. 18:17). Paul says they shall be punished, not as enemies, but as friends (2 Thess. 3:15),
for other major vices as well, but only for their
improvement and repentance. The Son of Man is
not come to damn anyone, rather, He has come to
save all of mankind* (Jn. 3:17). And the Lord's communion should be thought of in this way; as stated,
those who wish to participate must possess the
proper attitude. If they do not, they deceive the
holy church; God shall judge them as not discerning
the body of Christ, and find them guilty of . . . [pro-
faning] the body and blood of Christ.

On this basis, Paul deals with the entire issue of
communion in his epistle to the Corinthians. In
speaking with them of unworthy eating and drinking, he rebukes them accordingly. All can be summarized by saying that, when they held communion, they did not possess a true love one for
another. Scriptures, in describing the situation adequately reveal this lack. I hear, he said, that there
be divisions among you, and I partly believe it (1
Cor. 11:18). For in eating, every one takes his own
food, and disgraces the church of God and humil-
iates those who have nothing.

Here one can see that Paul accuses the Corinthians because they had not practiced true
brotherly love; they have scorned one another and,
therefore, he says, they did not observe the Lord's
Supper.

264   Finally, as already stated, when we come
together to eat His supper, we are to observe the
Lord's Supper in remembrance of Him, to remind

ourselves of Christ's sacrifice and to proclaim His death. We also must remember that, just as Christ was filled with true love toward us, so must we also be girded with this love when we come to celebrate communion. If we are to have the proper attitudes, this we must do. Then the outward eating may truly become an inner communion of Christ's body and blood, and may be a testimony of a pure brotherly love. We believe that he who takes this explication to heart and contemplates these points will have no difficulty understanding either the secret of the Lord's Supper or the why and how of Christ's words: "This is My body. This is My blood." It can be understood that, in doing justice to the command of Christ and remembering His righteousness, if we diligently practice only that which has been asked of us, we will have no need for unnecessary hairsplitting arguments. Consequently, we will omit all reason for anger, and easily come to an agreement. And, as far as semantics are concerned, from which most dissension and dispute originate, God will grant the charitable that a true holy solution and a testimony of pure brotherly love will overrule. Thus, let us abandon the unnecessary, and occupy ourselves only with what has been commanded and with what is necessary, as already mentioned, for the appropriate remembrance of our Lord.

70

Since we have now presented our interpretation of the command and function of communion, simply according to Scriptures and to the best of our abilities, we hope it will be not a little useful and acceptable to the unsophisticated. We have presented the ancient and correct use of the communion, as the holy apostles and the first churches practiced it, and it will greatly help matters if it can be seen that the same concept and practice (which we have presented) existed with the early Christians. And, since we cannot elaborate it any more logically and more adeptly than Heinrich Bullinger[80] and Sebastian Franck[81] have done in their writings, we refer each single-minded reader to them. *Not that we recommend that anyone accept the opinions and postulations of Franck or Bullinger (we find them to be erroneous anyway); rather, one should test the good, accept and retain it, and let the rest drop.* We want to present Sebastian Franck's viewpoints, as found in his *Teütschen Chronica*, to the single-minded who are inexperienced in other writings and who have not yet read such chronicles, and other such works, to expand their knowledge to the good.

On the Practice
of the Apostles in Breaking
the Bread
and Their Observance
of the Communion of Christ

Bullinger provides evidence for the practice of the Lord's Supper from the histories of the ancient churches in this manner: People came together first of all, he writes, to pray for God's blessing on every concern of the church. After the prayer, Scripture was read and interpreted according to the order prescribed in 1 Corinthians 14, and following the usage in the ancient synagogue.[82] Thereupon, one considered the failings or deviations of the church, which were then improved. The incurable evil and wickedness would be put away by use of the ban. Each individual would be given what he needed. As indicated in Acts 4, they shared all things in common. *Here we go beyond Bullinger's writings for a better understanding. No coercion or commandment, however, made them share all things com-*

munally. Rather, the sharing was done simply out of a free love which caused the community to be of one heart and soul. Furthermore, nobody laid claim to his own goods, even though each individual could have kept them for himself, nor would he have been excluded from the church of Christ for doing so. As Peter says to Ananias: "Could you not have retained that which was yours?" (Acts 5:4). Among the believers, there is only a free giving of love, and no coercion. Each individual may give or retain. Such a practice is unlike the practice of some who, desiring to have common property more out of greed than of love, coerce others into giving, even though common property is best when it comes

M   *from the freedom of love. But it is only a freedom of love. The Corinthians, Macedonians, and Romans did not share their possessions, as Paul clearly shows in 1 Corinthians 16. Concerning the alms-gathering, Paul says: "Now, concerning the contribution for the saints: As I directed the churches of Galatia, so you are also to do. On the first day of every week, each of you is to put something aside and store it up, as he may prosper, and collect what he has to give at the time" (1 Cor. 16:1-2).*

Here, it can be clearly seen that community of possession was not practiced in all churches. But, even though they control their possessions, such true believers do not say in their hearts that these are theirs; rather, their possessions belong to God and the needy. For this reason, among true Christians who display the freedom of love, all things are communal and are as if they had been offered, since they have been offered by the heart.

Bullinger further writes: this practice was current for some time. Not only was it described by Clement, the Roman bishop, in his epistles, but Augustine also makes it sound as if it was prevalent even in his day. Tertullian, as mentioned above, writes about it in his chronicle of heretics as follows:[83]

266

Tertullian designates the Christian communion an *agape*, that is, a meal for brethren, a banquet of love, in which Scriptures are expounded as the brethren ate together. Thereafter, as Christ did, they broke the bread as[84] a sign of the word that they were all one body in the baked cake[85] and bread, and had all things in common with Christ. Thus, they also broke the Lord's bread as witness to their faith, gave thanks to God, and became incorporated into the body of the church.

Luke, with few words, describes this practice toward the end of the second chapter of Acts, saying: "And they devoted themselves to the apostles' teaching and fellowship, to the breaking of bread and the prayers" (2:42). As they met in fellowship, they seriously practiced these four points when they broke the bread, a practice also interpreted by Erasmus of Rotterdam in his *Advocationibus:*[86] First, he presents the teaching of the gospel and second, the brotherly love, which caused them to have all things in common. Third, the sacred binding of the bread-breaking as an observance of the Christian covenant. Fourth, there was the intercessory prayer for everybody, as found in 1 Timothy 2.

Not only Paul, but also the primitive churches, as seen in Acts 2 (see Erasmus in *Paraphrasibus*)[87] and in *IV Clement*, continued this practice. Here, we see the appearance and structure of the first church and what it has become today, how the bishop and his servants, the deacons, have become the caretakers and stewards of the church, not only spiritually, but in all needs. They dealt out all common goods according to individual needs. *In*

M ii

72

contrast, *see how things have become perverted, how our* bishops have begun to be greedy. They have taken that which belonged to the community, appropriated it, and acquired a great wealth for themselves, thereby misusing what was once an honorable endeavor. Since it is little to the purpose, I consider it unnecessary to bring Scripture to bear here concerning the common possession of all things among Christians. In order to be brief, I will not dwell on it. I intend to deal only with those matters immediately applicable to our topic.

That This Communion Practice Was Kept Pure in the First Church

As the second epistle of Cyprian quite clearly and distinctly indicates, the early church had preserved this practice undamaged up to the time of Arcadius and Honorius.[88] Also, see Pliny's *Letter to Trajan*, chapter 2, as seen in Tertullian *adver. gent.*, ch. 2, etc. These writings cite such ancients as Irenaeus, Eusebius, and Ambrose, and include others up until the time of Augustine; the latter lived around AD 400, and is also considered one of them. Thus, these writings provide substantial testimony. These writings state that, as long as the practice of the Lord's Supper remained unchanged, as mentioned above, it remained a *covenant sign*,[89] and a confirmation of unity and love among the Christians. Also, until now, the mass or its name had not been thought of and was completely foreign. Since the mass has wedged its way into the church, it has been made into an idolatry, and the true function of communion has become completely covered up and repressed, scandalized, and *forgotten*.

For the benefit of the simple and the inexperienced, we have mentioned this matter so that everyone can comprehend to what level humanity has fallen away from the holy state of the Christian church, and see into what kind of abomination the holy city has entered. This we do so that, rather than accepting a long-lasting practice and paying heed to man's law, everyone may open his eyes diligently and seriously and straightway follow God's Word and command diligently and seriously. We have heard enough about the instructions for communion, the how, why, and to what end it is to be practiced, and to what extent it is being abused. In conclusion, we want to summarize our understanding and thus make it more easily comprehended, accepted, and judged by everyone.

Summary of the Lord's Supper

The Lord's Supper is a physical *and loving* gathering or assembly, a communal eating and drinking by Christian believers to proclaim the death of the Lord and to join one another in brotherly love. Christ instituted such a Supper and asked that His disciples might observe it in remembrance of Him and for no other purpose, as commanded: "This do in remembrance of Me. Assemble and come together as one in fellowship, and take bread and pour wine; break, eat and drink with one another. Thereby remember and proclaim that I have given My body for you, and shed My blood for you, for the forgiveness of sin."

The remembrance of Christ in the Lord's Supper or communion requires two things of us: first, that we remember the good deed Christ performed for us and, second, that we remember that we are to love one another as much as Jesus Christ loves us. To this end, the Lord's Supper has been given to us as a sacred trust. Those who receive it shall proclaim the death of Christ with a sincere faith, and shall arm themselves with an unhypocritical love for their fellowman. The breaking of bread and drinking from the cup or chalice then becomes a communion with the body and blood of *our Lord* Jesus Christ. Those who eat and drink, but have not this attitude of heart, eat and drink their own damnation. Similarly, if a soldier accepts a commission from his prince, but is not faithful to him in his heart, he is a traitor. If his lord knew, he would be considered a traitor and judged accordingly.

Thus, whoever attends the Lord's Supper, whoever mingles and becomes part of the believers, whoever eats from one bread and drinks from one cup and partakes of the flesh and blood of Christ, but has an unfaithful and false heart, and does not take to heart the remembrance of Christ, will certainly bring judgment upon himself. Such men will be judged as traitors, for God's eyes, which nobody can escape, look above all into the heart.

The emphasis, therefore, does not lie in what the bread and the wine should be or contain within them in the Lord's Supper but, rather, in the *reasons* for our participation. Saint Paul, for this reason, encourages all individuals to test themselves before eating of the bread and drinking of the cup, since, as already stated earlier, he who unworthily eats and drinks, eats and drinks judgment upon himself. Paul explained only what Christ had commanded and what the early church practiced. We are to proceed with it in this way, as is proper and adequately described.

It is appropriate, timely, and necessary, therefore, to do away with all argument and dispute between enemy and friend. So, too, it is appropriate to drop all false and erroneous opinions, new as well as old, which have wormed and wedged their way into the Lord's Supper and its true apostolic practice. Every *true-hearted* individual himself should excise such dispute, and *become incorporated into the fellowship of the only true, united church of Christ. Those, however, who do not care to join should be regarded as heathen and let go. One should also flee from the false prophets, and the erring spirits with their erroneous opinions for, even though they bear the name of Christ, they are not Christians. In this manner, the body of the Lord is discerned. Everyone who is of a pure heart separates himself from the unclean in this communion with the body of Christ. And he who is of pure heart testifies to the truth, and manifests that, wherever he may be in the world, he has* searched himself with great diligence and earnestness. Thus, we who profess the name of Christ become as one in Jesus Christ. We do make this commitment in order that we may enjoy the Supper of Jesus Christ according to the instructions of Christ. As members of one body, we proclaim the death of Christ and the bodily union attained by untainted *brotherly* love. Thus, we grow together in harmony.

269

The Meaning of the Words: "This Is My Body, This Is My Blood"

M v

Consider that from these words concerning the Lord's Supper so much unnecessary[90] controversy and all kinds of nonsense has arisen, which is highly regrettable, for it serves very little purpose and destroys the true practice of communion. So many unnecessary writings have dealt with the subject that we would gladly refrain from writing about the subject. Thus, if we want to write about it as well, we should be sure that we have something special to say about these words, and not burden simple people with more interpretations of correct usages. Nonetheless, by simply[91] recording Christ's words, along with the main and most noteworthy opinions and interpretations which have been added, we want to present our position on these words so that the simple hearts may also understand us, if they desire to know. We desire everyone to formulate his own conclusions as to what comes closest to the truth and, thereafter, whatever may be our understanding of these words, we will be pleased to receive correction and will allow nothing to silence us.

75

The words of the Last Supper of *our Lord* Christ are these: *The Lord* Christ, *in the night in which He was betrayed*, took the bread and, after having given thanks, He broke it and said: "Take and eat, this is my body which is broken for you: This do in remembrance of me." Likewise, after supper, He took the cup, saying: "This cup is the new testament in my blood: This do, as often as you drink, in remembrance of me."[92]

The interpretations given these words are many, and the bread and wine are also given various names and referred to in various ways by the ancients. Commonly, they call it a sacrament of the body and blood of Christ, a bread and cup of thanksgiving, and also a bread and cup of the fellowship of love. Thus, communion is a sign of commitment, a visible form and shape of an internal dealing which concerns itself in the spirit and in truth.

270

In this and in many other ways, the bread and wine of the Lord's Supper are described by the Fathers, evidenced clearly enough in the summary of the Chronicles of Sebastian Franck; for those who don't have them, or are unable to read them, this summary occurs in the third book. This is the reason why the Fathers spoke in various ways about the bread and wine, and all that is required in the Lord's Supper, for example, the attitude of the heart, and how they thought and acted with respect to the elements; accordingly, they have given them names. Even Paul called the bread a participation in Christ's body, and the cup a participation in Christ's blood. The bread and the wine are not the essential part. Rather, those who eat of it testify thereby that they believe they are also having communion with Christ in the way mentioned above.

As already stated, we intend to present here, as simply as possible, the principal contradictory opinions. Thereafter, we will also present our own, and give justification for our understanding, in order that everyone may judge and test them all, and retain the best.

76   There are three principal beliefs concerning the essence of the bread and wine, and concerning the interpretation of the words, "This is my body, this is my blood." First, some say that the words, "This is my body, this is my blood," mean that the bread and wine in the Lord's Supper are immediately transformed into the actual body and blood of Christ as soon as the words, "This is my body, this is my blood," have been spoken. Thus, no bread and wine remain; under the guise of bread and wine are the true flesh and blood of Christ. This is the Thomist, papist, and Roman belief and understanding, but it cannot be upheld by any Scripture. Contrary to all Scripture and belief, such an interpretation holds that, when a man repeats Christ's words about the bread and wine, "This is my body, this is my blood," from that hour on, wherever and whenever these words are read and spoken, the natural bread and wine become

transformed into the natural body and blood of Christ.

Second, there are those who say that these words, "This is my body, and this is my blood," are not to be understood or interpreted to mean bread and wine specifically. Rather, these become changed in this way: when the words are spoken over the bread and wine, flesh and blood truly are in the bread and wine. By synecdoche, the wheat, together with the sack, and the wine, together with the flask, are called wheat and wine. So, too, the bread is called the body and the wine the blood of Christ. Such is the opinion of Luther and his followers, as can be seen in his writings. They boast that they have the word of Christ on their side, which says of the bread, "This is my body"; therefore, the natural body must also be present. Such an interpretation can never be substantiated by true Scripture. Christ says, "This is my body," and He does not say, as the Lutherans claim, "Therein is my body." They also say that, with these words, man can bring Christ into the bread. But this avowal is also wrong, for Christ will not be brought into anything with those words; He will be brought only through faith into the believing heart. Similarly, the idea that the natural body of Christ is everywhere, and can be received other than spiritually, through faith, is also not in accordance with the Holy Word and the faith.

Third, there are those who believe that these words of Christ were spoken figuratively and thus, must also be understood figuratively, like names. When Christ spoke, "This is my body," He is to be understood to mean, the bread represents My body, or is a memorial to My body; or, as Tertullian states, it is a metaphor for My body, as mentioned above.

Along with many other scholars, particularly

those in the Upland and Friesland,[93] these theories have become particularly associated with the names of Ulrich Zwingli and John Oecolampadius. Their beliefs have caused a powerful, and quite gruesome, split to take place among the people. This split has produced a great scandal among the simple folks, nor has it quieted down, but is still in the air today. He who would like to read and know might obtain their writings and see, but we do not have the time to review and expound both sides of the dreary dispute. Rather, we want to present, as briefly as possible, our views and opinions. In a few short words, we shall straightway put them forward.

Accordingly, we maintain that Oecolampadius and his followers have come closest to the truth and understanding of the Word. We also find that the ancient church came very close to interpreting and expounding these words in the manner already mentioned. *We are not speaking in favor of opinions which we regard as erroneous. Rather, as already mentioned, we desire to retain the good.* With reference to the words, "This is my body," and with reference to bread and wine, and how they are to be understood, we can only interpret them in a figurative manner; that is, we must interpret them, not as they were spoken in reality, but on a different basis, as Christ's words point out. The words, "This is my body which is given for you," can naturally and concretely be interpreted to mean His actual body, which sat at the table and which was also betrayed and truly given for us. But the bread and wine must be understood figuratively to mean the bread we break and the wine we drink, during which we are to remember the body and blood of Christ, and to remember that Christ's body was given for us and His blood was shed for us.

Paul states, "For as often as you eat this bread

and drink from this cup, you proclaim the Lord's death until He comes." The bread and wine are eaten and drunk naturally. But, after Christ has said that His body shall be given for us and His blood spilled, we are to remember and proclaim that act in thankfulness with the bread and wine. The bread and wine, thus, are called the body and blood of Christ in the manner of *riddles and parables. The Lord Himself, after the Supper, said that until now He had talked in proverb and parable, but the time is coming in which He will no longer speak in proverbs* (Jn. 16:25). In essence, bread and wine are not body and blood. Just as the token of remembrance is frequently named, using the name of the matter associated with it, so, too, it is here with the bread and wine. But the symbols, or tokens of remembrance, dare not be the same as that which they represent, or that which one associates with them.

A vivid example in Scripture points to the same understanding, and indicates the way in which these words of Christ should be taken. Since it will enable us to more easily comprehend Christ's words, we will examine it more closely. The example is the *Passover* of the Easter lamb.

We read in Exodus 12: When the Lord wanted to free His people from the bondage of Egypt and when He killed the first-born in Egypt, He commanded His people to cook and eat a little lamb; with the same lamb's blood, they were to paint their door posts, so that the angel of death might see the marked doors, spare that same house, and pass over it. As a remembrance of such a passover, it was commanded that thereafter a lamb be eaten every year. Now, the lamb which was eaten received the name of "Phasach" or "Paschen," which means a passing by or a going over. Such a name does not refer only to the fact that, just then, there was a lamb present which was thus named. Rather, the name implies that he who ate, upon the instruction of God, was passed over by the angel. Since then, this Passover takes place every year. The lamb was prepared and eaten in memory of that event, and the lamb was called a "Pascha Lamb," that is, a passover, for it was instituted as a remembrance to the Passover.

Thus, the bread and wine of the Lord's Supper, which Christ instructed us to eat or drink communally as a remembrance of His body and blood, is in the same way called the body and blood of Christ. Those who carefully think about this concept can easily grasp what the true meaning is of Christ's words, "This is my body, this is my blood."

Now to conclude. Our concept and understanding of the words of the Lord's Supper are as follows:

First, we understand that Christ, by the words, "This is my body which is given for you," and, similarly, "This is my blood which is shed for you," has not meant the natural and actual bread and wine. He spoke of His own physical flesh and blood. These words force us to that conclusion: "which is given for you and which is shed for you." No bread or wine has been given or shed for us, but only the physical body and blood of Christ has been slaughtered and sacrificed for us on the cross. In addition, Christ did not change the bread into the body which was given for us. So, too, with the wine. It did not possess and contain His natural body and blood, because He remained seated at the table with His disciples. He also arose from there, went into the garden, was betrayed and, according to His Word that His body would be given for us and His blood shed for us, delivered over into the hands of the heathen and was sacrificed.

79

Second, we understand these words to mean that the bread and wine serve as the remembrance of Christ and, therefore, the bread and wine could be used figuratively, just as the little lamb also was called the passover. As we eat of the bread and drink of the cup, we shall remember and proclaim that Christ gave His actual body in death for us, and shed His true blood for us for the forgiveness of sins. And those who do this act of remembrance with a true faith and heart participate in the body and blood of Christ.

N ii

Consequently, Paul says: "The bread which we break, is it not the communion of the body of Christ? And the cup which we bless, is it not the communion of Christ's blood?" The bread and wine

274

are nothing more than an external signal. However, the power and the might of that which counts rests alone in the heart of the individual who, girded with genuine faith and love, and thus in the church of Christ, can partake of the bread and wine. If the heart is true, it is in communion with the body of Christ through the breaking of the bread. If the heart is not right in faith and in love, a man eats damnation unto himself, as Paul states, and judgment, as mentioned before. This is, briefly, our concept, understanding, and opinion of the words of the Lord's Supper. Therefore, we exhort and further request that everybody put aside semantic battles concerning the bread and the wine, and search his own heart concerning the matter. Each one must individually fight with himself, and campaign against all evil, malice, and hatred in his own heart and mind, *which are always bracing themselves against the truth and fighting it.* Become diligent in true love that we might achieve a true communion, and be worthy to eat and drink the Lord's bread and cup. As we wholeheartedly search for Him, the peace of God will undoubtedly reward us richly by easing our way graciously to true knowledge.

80   Of the Practice of Communion and to What End Both Baptism and the Lord's Supper Shall Serve. Also, of the Institution and Preservation of the Holy Church. Capped with a Summary of All That Has Been Said Before.

Since we have already dealt with our *understanding, concept,* meaning, and belief concerning baptism and communion, let us now, in closing, present a combined report, dealing in particular with how and why they have been externally instituted and how they are to serve. Jesus Christ wants not only to be recognized internally in His church, but also to be proclaimed externally by the same body, His church, and His holy name made known and praised throughout the world.

Alongside external proclamation of His gospel, Christ has, for this reason, instituted both the external baptism and communion, and has commissioned His external, pure,[94] holy church to carry it out and preserve it. And, when the matter is placed in proper perspective, we can say that, if these three things, the true proclamation of the gospel, correct baptism, and correct communion, are in doubt, there can be no true church of Christ. If one of these parts is missing, it is not possible outwardly to maintain and support a true Christian church.

Our most sincere concern, at all times, especially where the gospel of Christ is proclaimed, is that the church of Christ be holy and properly maintained. So that the pearls may not be dumped

N iii

275

before the sows and swine, we want to present in a logical fashion each individual part, and how it should be used.

To allow the outer church of God to assemble, begin, and be instituted, the first prerequisite is the proclamation of the true and holy gospel. This proclamation is the fishnet for the live catch which is to be thrown over all mankind, for all humanity swims in this world-sea and are as wild animals; they are by nature children of wrath. Those who are caught in this fishnet, that is, with the Word of the gospel (after they have heard it and cling to it with a firm faith), will be brought out of darkness into light, and have the power to be changed from cursed children of wrath to children of God.[95] The temple of God and the church of Christ will be built of these (as Peter testifies), as from living stones (1 Pet. 2:9).

The church of Christ is comprised of true believers and children of God who can praise the name of God. No one else belongs in it except the believers, considering that all people by nature are ignorant of divine matters, and first achieve true faith and knowledge of Christ through the Word. Scripture, also, shows us no other means. Therefore, as much as it is proper for us to judge, the Word, through which all people are gathered, is the initial start for those who are to be brought to a knowledge of God and to God's holy church. Such a process begins with the preaching and the hearing of God's Word, the medium through which their faith is found. They are then counted among the children of God, and may also be considered members of His holy church.

Jesus Christ is the one and true foundation on which the holy church should and *must be founded*, erected, and built. Therefore, this foundation must be laid before a church may be built upon it. If this foundation is to be laid, through the proclamation and witness of the gospel, the holy church must *be armed* and prepared truly to witness to Christ and preach the gospel. Those who accept this faith are to serve *as the stones of believers*, out of which the church of Christ is built, brought together, and constructed. The same shall forthwith be sanctified, as Christ prayed in John 17:17, and the Father will protect, *preserve, and sanctify* them. Why should we spend many words about this matter when all of Scripture is full of evidence that faith comes from hearing the Word, and the holy church is to be built only from the believers? It is undeniable and incontrovertible, therefore, that the true proclamation of Christ's holy gospel is the first thing needed to establish the church.

Holy baptism is the second thing with which the church is built. It is the entrance and the gate to the holy church. According to God's order, nobody is allowed to enter the church except through baptism. This is the common function of baptism in the church, as further explained later on.

We have earlier stated that the holy Christian church is a fellowship of believers in Christ. No one belongs to this church unless he has the holiness of faith and of love, praises the name of God, and is inclined, from the heart, toward serving his fellowman. Baptism shall serve this end, that Christ's church, through baptism, be joined together, *formed*, and united in one body of love. Consequently, anyone given entrance into the holy church, *the community of Christian believers*, must first deny and disown the devil, the world, and all that is a part of it, *as well as die to all vanity, pride, and all lusts of the flesh*. Then, upon verbal confession of the sound of faith which he believes with his heart, he shall be baptized, in God's name, or in Jesus Christ. That is, he shall be baptized, in God's name and in Christ's, when he is cleansed of sin by repentance and faith, and enters into an unblemished, obedient way of life. So shall the holy church be gathered through baptism, and those who do not enter and do not draw near to Christ will also not be reckoned by Christ as belonging to His church, nor will they be accepted. For Christ wants His bride to remain unblemished and pure. In baptism the bride is washed *in faith* and cleansed. Therefore Paul says: "By one Spirit were we all baptized into one body" (1 Cor. 12:13). And further: "Christ loved the church, and gave Himself up for her that He might sanctify her, having cleansed her by the washing of water with the Word; that the church might be presented before Him in splendor, without spot or wrinkle or any such thing; that she might be holy and without blemish" (Eph. 5:25-27).

This, then, is the actual function of baptism, that the believers be joined together visibly and accepted into a holy church.

The third is the Lord's Supper, in which the holy church, which consists of believers brought together by baptism, is to be preserved in single-minded faith and love. For the Lord's Supper is an assembly of the church in love. Among other things, it testifies to, and proclaims with a simple eating and drinking, the unity of faith and love in the remembrance of Christ. This, then, is the function of communion, in which, as mentioned adequately above, the holy church comes together to give thanks to the Lord for His benevolence; thereby, through the unity of faith and love, it maintains fellowship with Jesus Christ. Paul says: "We who are many, are as one body in partaking of the one bread, and those who come together to celebrate the Lord's Supper become one body, in communion, with Christ'' (1 Cor. 10:17). And again, these same persons among themselves and before all mankind, shall lead a pure life in united faith and brotherly love to the glory of God, just as Christ asks that His bride (for whom He has given Himself, and whom He has cleansed and betrothed through the baptism of faith and love) be pure and glorious. The Lord's Supper shall also be used to prevent participation of any unbelievers, of unholy *false teachers, and of idolatrous or other blasphemous people.* Nor will they have any fellowship with *Christ's body, regardless of how eloquently and profusely they appeal to Christ's name and consider themselves one with the name of Christ.* For what fellowship have the believers (states Paul) with the unbelievers? Or what do light and darkness have in common? (2 Cor. 6:14). Also, who of them in their way of life has praised the baptism, and has not truly shown and *proclaimed* it in his actions? Rather, they lead an unclean, *disfigured, deceitful* life which leads to the shame and *chagrin of* Christ and His *holy* church. They move away from the holy, *pure, and true* faith, and again leave the holy commandments. They shall not have communion with Christ's body nor participate in His supper. They shall be cut off and banned so that the church may remain pure and unblemished so that the entire church not become soiled with the foreign sins of a rascal. *Because they do not discern the body of the Lord, those who eat and drink the Lord's Supper with such a one have a share in his wicked, unrighteous deeds. Thus, they also eat damnation, as Paul tells us.*

278   In summary, the function of the Lord's Supper *or communion* in the church is twofold.

The one function is that the holy Christian church shall be held together by it, and be maintained in a united faith and *Christian love.*

The other, that all evil, and all that does not belong to the holy, pure church of *Christ* and is *offensive,* may be cut off and banned.

Summary and Concluding Words of the Entire Article

Finally, now you may understand, dear Christian (we also ask that you pay diligent attention, and take note of it), what should serve the common use of the baptism and the Lord's Supper. Also, in order to preserve a holy, *unblemished essence* and position, three things are of vital significance.

First, the proclamation of God's Word, with which people are to be *brought* to the holy church, and *also prepared* for their membership in it.

Second, the holy baptism, which unifies those who have been prepared by the Word and which admits them to the body of the Christian church. This important matter has already been diligently and adequately mentioned.[96] Thus, baptism and communion are to be used according to Scriptures. Should this happen now, and each part be used as God has commanded, as is proper and correct, we see nothing that could lead to a division developing among the Christians, for the true practice becomes clear to all, and is also experienced in the secret of God's grace.[97] Unfortunately, since the ordinance has been overturned, God's Word has fallen amiss through deceit and dishonesty; baptism becomes child's play, and the Lord's Supper is perverted into a sacrificial mass. *The Antichrist's troops have come, and have grown in the church of Christ.* The holy church has been virtually destroyed and dis-

84

continued by man. *Christ's Word has been fulfilled; He says that few believers will be found on earth upon His return.* The true meaning of the teaching, baptism, and the Lord's Supper have become perverted and obfuscated. But they are not only perverted. Gruesome idolatries, and this fact is quite frightening, have been established on these holy foundations and instructions of Christ because of the devil's cunning and human indifference. These idolatries, unfortunately, are in full swing among *new and old supposed Christians*, which is clearly evident, and has been referred to often enough earlier. But men still do not see *how much sorrow and pain and all* strife *are caused through this* division. *One should examine the question in himself, and cleanse himself of all such misconceptions, strife and quarrels, slander and evil, and all types of idolatries. Without violence, one should eradicate them in oneself through patience.* However, few think of it, yea, almost nobody considers or thinks about how one might again return to a holy church as to a light in the world.[98]

The salt of the earth is also lost, for all salts have lost their sharpness, and the teaching has been spilled and trampled underfoot. Consequently, no longer is it possible to return to a pure church again unless the salt is restored to sharpness and put to use again. The good must be differentiated from the evil by the Word of grace, and the light from the darkness by the proclamation of the Word of truth. If the teaching of Christ is not used with the sharpness of this salt against many, they will consider it deaf and dumb, and it will be trodden underfoot, as it has, unfortunately, been done by almost all mankind. But most teachers pay more heed to the sharpness of the physical sword and its power, even calling attention to the same, than to the sharpness of

279

the Word, which is a sword of the spirit and not of the flesh.

At present, the human, earthly power replaces that of the Word which no longer stands, exercises power, or rules in truth. The dull teachers have lost the sharpness of the Word, and the sword of the Spirit has been stolen from them and given over to human power. Thus, the discipline of the Spirit, the sharpness of the Word, has been discontinued and blasphemed. Even though the literal Word, meaning both testaments in an indiscrete manner, is preached and learned in almost all the world, the vain children of the flesh are drawn under human power and discipline. The Word is dull without the thrust of its edge and the power of the Spirit. So that the people may trample it in scorn, it is dumped out by the satiated, unthankful people. The church and almost all people's hearts, which should be God's temple, have thereby become a dark cave and a den of thieves over which the powers of the world rule freely. Such a perverted church, which does not have the sharpness of the Word and the spiritual sword, does not rule and govern according to the spiritual power of light, but rules according to the human power of darkness over whom this world's authority of darkness should also dominate.

280   If anyone, however, desires to return and come back out of the realm of darkness to the wonderful light of grace, obediently to serve the Word as the sword of the Spirit, and again enter the true church of Christ, which is ruled in the Spirit by the Word of grace, seen to the glory of God outwardly as a light to the world, he must enter in through baptism. He must put to death both the old man (as has been often stated above) and truly be made alive in Christ. The remembrance of Christ, the com-

munion in love, must be observed in fellowship with the body of Christ. All that is evil, be it in himself or in another, must be put away, judged, condemned, and excluded from such a fellowship, which is His body. Only those who are a faithful church, who have fellowship with Christ, who live under the power and sword of the Holy Spirit, that is, all who live by obedience to the Word, are a part of this community. Such a power of the Spirit does not rise up, resist, or assert itself against physical power; it is obedient, and, actively or passively, suffers through patience even to the point of physical death. Whatever is not against God and his conscience he does obediently. If, however, the worldly and temporal powers command something which is against God and conscience, they patiently suffer until death, which is giving God that which is God's and giving to Caesar that which is Caesar's.

O

Therefore, whoever wants to be a member of Christ's church must first enter through baptism, through faith in Christ, and must lead a new life in obedience to the Word, shunning and avoiding all evil through the true ban of Christ. This, summarized, is the true church of Christ, no matter where it is in the world, no matter how many or how few members there are in the world. They lead an external life, that is, in baptism, teaching, the ban, and communion of Christ, and they walk in righteousness and truth.

Where that is in flux, there may be no assembly or church which can be called, or taken to be, a church of Christ, nor will it be recognized and accepted before God.

Although many have preached the gospel for some time (*and God knows the results and order*), know, dear kindhearted people, that we (as God knows) have begun to teach and write on this subject for no other purpose than to encourage the fruit of the gospel to appear and develop. And the fruit should grow out of the instruction of the gospel. This fruit is an unblemished Christian church which

281 man, through God's grace, should now see as a light before the world. *As members of the covenant of the good conscience with God,* we have, for similar reasons, fully presented here our firm belief in order that everybody might understand and evaluate our effort and thinking. And just as we take heed of all lovers of truth, may these not indifferently and unjustly consider our opinion and witness, and may they also not believe those who unjustly slander us.

85 For we know well, though we remain innocent, through God's grace, what terrible and unending slander is dealt out to us by our persecutors and tormentors. Our further endeavor is to hereby awaken each true and pious Christian to pursue and observe the truth more diligently to his betterment and to the glory of God.

Now, therefore, in concluding, our heartfelt and friendly wish is that, as often as we have here attempted to seek and further the truth and all that

O ii which might also serve to foster a true Christian church, a holy way of life (and a true state of well-being), every good-hearted person, upon seriously reading this our confession, and comparing it with the holy Word of God, may also honestly judge and discriminate. And if God reveals something even better to him, may he freely confess it with Christian moderation. *If he recognizes the truth in this our witness, may he acknowledge it as co-witness* to the truth which is in Christ. Thus, we might unitedly praise, honor, and thank God, and also faithfully plead and cry to God that He might let His church, which is still spread and disunited in the world, come together through His eternal almighty Word. (*This Word is also heard from the mouth of the corporeal, earthly man, Jesus Christ, as a physical, earthly, glorious, tangible, visible, perceptible, suffering, mortal, natural Word, which is with the Father eternally, one Word and equal to God for ever).* May it *be gathered and cleansed for His eternal glory, as a shining light shines, and also kept from all evil, from all shame, sin, and offense, in order that His eternal kingdom may come to men, His name may be true here and beyond, blessed and holy, for ever and ever. Amen.*

Those who believe in Christ and are participants in the tribulation which is in Christ.

282   Psalm 112:4

Light rises in the darkness for the upright;
the Lord is gracious, merciful, and righteous.

112:10:

The wicked man sees it and is angry;
he gnashes his teeth and melts away;
the desire of the wicked man comes to nought (RSV).

V

The Letters
of Pilgram Marpeck

Introduction

The letters of Pilgram Marpeck are, in the nature of things, the most interesting of his writings. Altogether, nineteen have been preserved, sixteen of which have been recently discovered in the *Kunstbuch*. These sixteen comprise a total of 282 manuscript pages. While Marpeck's major writings have been known and described during the last fifty years, most of his letters were first made available in 1957. Although their existence had been known to scholars since at least 1950,[1] no one mentioned them or gave them the attention they deserve. Their obvious importance for Anabaptist research is now recognized. The letters have helped fill in the life, activity, and concerns of Marpeck during the 1540s and 1550s; they cover a time span from 1532 to 1555, the year before his death.

No other Anabaptist leader has left behind such a treasure of personal writings. While they are often verbose and repetitive, the letters give us a fuller portrait of the man, his passion for the church of Christ, and his theological views. They provide insights into the life of a group of Anabaptist churches scattered from Alsace to Moravia, churches which are distinct from the Swiss Brethren, the Hutterites, and the Mennonites of the Netherlands and North Germany. This group was characterized by a profounder commitment to the freedom of the gospel than that found among other groups, whose pronounced legalistic tendencies and readiness to use the ban caused much division and acrimony. A church without spot or wrinkle was also Marpeck's concern, and he often discusses that ideal. But, according to him, it can only be achieved by "love working through patience." One must judge, not the flower, but the fruit, and that means allowing room and time for growth and discipleship. Among the Anabaptists, no one emphasizes more than Marpeck that the point of departure is the humanity of Christ. His humanity is the touchstone, and the model for all Christian attitude and action.

Of the nineteen letters translated here, the first is dated around January 12, 1532. It has been published in three different places.[2] It is Marpeck's farewell letter to the Strasbourg Council after it became clear that they would not reverse their decision to banish him from that city. This letter, together with Scharnschlager's letter of June 1534 to the Strasbourg Council, represents one of the most moving documents of the Anabaptist movement.[3] While it acknowledges the authority of the state, it does not recognize the authority of the state to decide on matters of religious belief.

Two letters, written in connection with the publication of the *Admonition* of 1542, are here translated. One is written to Caspar Schwenckfeld, the other to Helena von Streicher. Both were first published by John Loserth in his edition of the *Answer to Caspar Schwenckfeld.*[4]

Along with a collection of other early Anabaptist writings[5], the remaining sixteen letters were found in a handwritten codex known as the *Kunstbuch*. The copyist was Jörg Propst Rothenfelder, also called Maler, a friend and co-worker of Marpeck. The collection is dated 1561. Although Rothenfelder copied the letters, presumably for his own and for others' edification, he does not disappear behind Marpeck; Rothenfelder emerges, especially in his marginal comments, as an independent figure, entirely ready to criticize severely the man whom he evidently respected and held in high esteem.[6]

The translators acknowledge their debt to the transcription of some of the letters made available by Heinold Fast of Emden who prepared them for his own critical edition of the whole

Kunstbuch. The translation is based, however, on the original handwritten text. The introductory notes are by the translators.

Of the four letters taken from the *Kunstbuch,* three have already been published in modern editions, two of which have also been translated into English.[7] In these cases we have followed the modern editions and, on doubtful readings, consulted the manuscript. In the remaining twelve letters, we have worked from Rothenfelder's manuscripts. These nineteen letters represent all of the extant Marpeck correspondence.

The letters are presented here in chronological order with the undated letters at the end. The numbers in brackets, for example, [#8], indicate the numbers given to them in the *Kunstbuch.* Numbers 1, 4, 5, 10, and 15 were translated by W. Klassen. All the other letters were translated by W. Klaassen.

1

To the Strasbourg Council (1532)

Introduction

This short letter was sent to the City Council along with Marpeck's famous Strasbourg Confession. The letter reveals that Marpeck had been expelled from Strasbourg for his refusal to acknowledge that infant baptism had any basis in Scripture[1]. An additional ground for his dismissal, at least as weighty, was Marpeck's refusal to retract his views on the oath and on the defense of the city.[2]

Marpeck had prepared his confession in response to a request from the City Council. Before he finished, he received a further statement from Bucer on infant baptism, to which Marpeck replied with an appendix to the Confession.[3]

The letter reflects Marpeck's determination not to yield on questions of conscience but, at the same time, gives evidence of a deep desire for an understanding with Bucer and the other Reformers inStrasbourg.

The Text

Marpeck's Letter to the Strasbourg Council, January 12, 1532.[4]

Noble, strong, firm, cautious, honorable, wise, gracious, and respectful lords.

The altercation between me and the preachers with respect to the Word of God is known to my gracious lords. You are not authorities over us but are listeners to it, and have had occasion to hear both sides of the question. However, no one can judge in these matters except God alone. Since you have, gracious lords, through the strict Lord Bernard Wurmser and Lord Martin Pötschl, exercised your earthly authority over me and, by means of a written instruction, banned me from this city and ordered me to leave, I shall respond. I accepted your action patiently, but with the humble request that I be given a little additional time, for reasons which I gave. This request my gracious lords granted on two occasions, each time extending my stay here for two weeks. They have, however, let me know your opinion that my gracious lords have some misgivings about my statement on infant baptism; namely, that you do not think that I showed on the basis of Holy Scripture that infant baptism has no ground in Scripture. I affirmed before you, my gracious lords, and testified that, if a single letter of Scripture would be cited in which infant baptism is maintained, I would be willing to give up my life as an Anabaptist. At that time, I was asked, with the concurrence of my gracious lords, to study more carefully the articles which Martin Bucer had graciously made available to me and to pray God for understanding for all of us. This I did with great diligence and seriousness, as is fitting. I recognize that the matter pertains not to me alone, for it would have been easily handled if it dealt only with me, or if we were concerned only with some human matter. Were that the case, I would not have further bothered my gracious lords with the matter. Since, however, we are dealing here with God's honor and His matters which pertain to the salvation of not one man but of all men in these last dangerous times and, since much error originates among people, and no person or opinion is to be given special treatment, I am driven and motivated by my conscience to spare no man, not even myself, as everyone is obligated to do if he looks to God. It is therefore my submissive, serious request and longing that you reflect not upon me but, rather, that each and every one of you (530) reflects with intense seriousness and awe upon the action of God; especially since the Lord has so far been gracious to you in matters of faith and has preserved you from the shedding of blood—not a small grace from God—so that this highly praised city of Strassburg, by the grace of God, has been preserved from that more than all other places in the whole world. This I would pray for you from the bottom of my heart, as my dearly beloved fathers and lords, whose benevolent deeds toward me I will never forget before God. Consequently, gracious lords, please give careful consideration to these matters, not for my sake, but for your own sakes, and for the sake of God's grace. I hope that you completely avoid any persecution of the miserable people who have no place in the world and who flee to you, especially if they are innocent of crimes, to find a haven from their misery without any coercion of their consciences. Not that I desire this on behalf of myself, but rather for your good, for which I call God to witness on my soul. I am prepared to carry out your orders without any protest, until the Lord drives me further. Also, my gracious lords, I wish to keep myself without fault before God in my dealings with you and sincerely pray to God for the salvation of your body and soul. Furthermore, I humbly request that you incline your ears to listen to my confession which I have written for you. It is my prayer that God will, through His fatherly mercy and gracious will, protect us from placing (as happens so often) our foreign fleshly will above the judgments of God. I am also handing over to my gracious lords, an answer, as you will see, to Martin Bucer's arguments and articles regarding infant baptism. I have also prepared my confession and placed it alongside Bucer's articles in order that my gracious lords may see that this is not my will but the will of God, and that my conscience is driving me to be expelled by you. I submit this with submissive requests that I may always pray to God faithfully for all of you, and commend myself herewith to my gracious lords.

Submissive to your graces   Pilgram Marpeck

2

Judgment and Decision

Introduction

This is the first of four letters Marpeck wrote to the Swiss Brethren. Even though this letter is not specifically addressed, the content makes its destination clear. The Swiss tendency of quickly using the ban against erring members had made them fall into legalism. Marpeck desires unity with them but, until they see that their behavior and action is contrary to Christ, he cannot have fellowship with them. He does insist, however, that he is aware of his own weakness and ignorance, and that this ignorance plays a role in the difficulties they are having.

Marpeck begins the description of his understanding with: "Jesus Christ . . . the free Son of God and man, without commandment or prohibition against His own, the faithful." The man who is liberated by Christ is free and subject to no law. He illustrates his point with a short excursus on Sabbath (Sunday) observance. He says that a Christian is lord of time and, therefore, not bound to any legal prescription regarding the day. When Christians then impose laws about observing dress customs and special days, they are still living under the law.

Marpeck defends himself, on the other hand, against the charge that a Christian can do as he pleases, a charge the Swiss had made against him. Nor does he deny that a Christian is commanded to make judgments. He pleads, however, that they be made with true discernment. Christians always judge on the basis of fruit, as Christ commanded, but never on the basis of leaves or blossoms, for leaves and blossoms say little or nothing about the fruit. If a wrong seems to have been committed, it may not immediately become the cause for final judgment. Patience and care are needed. He pleads for recognition that the Christian life involves growth from one stage to another. One is reminded of Augustine's famous statement, "Love and do as you please," when Marpeck says: "[Christians] are free in all things, and are debtors to none except love." The guidance of the Christian is the Spirit of Christ within, and not the literal law from without, the law in this instance meaning any code of law set up by men. He provides a series of cases from holy history where premature judgments would have been very misleading.

A comment on the marginal glosses is called for, especially those on pages 333, 334, 346, 354, 360, 361. Fast and Klassen have commented on them in *ARG*, 47 (1956), p. 241, and "Rothenfelder, Jörg Propst," *ME*, IV, respectively. Both articles point to the fact that Rothenfelder sided with Marpeck in the controversy with the Swiss, a fact which they establish firmly. And yet the marginal glosses are very critical of Marpeck. He objects to Marpeck's spirit and manner of approach to the Swiss, and appears to regard some of Marpeck's protestations of humility and weakness as less than genuine, or at least to suggest that Marpeck was not the only genuine person in the controversy. The gloss on page 354 sounds especially like a thing Sebastian Franck would say: "They are all wrong." Perhaps the fact that these criticisms do not appear to have emerged before Marpeck's death is also evidence of the power and stature of Marpeck within this circle. In any event, Rothenfelder copied the letters and gave them to posterity, an action indicating that he had not disowned Marpeck, but that he was a man who held to his own opinions quite as strongly as Marpeck did.

In this letter, Marpeck also refers to the "gospel of all the creatures," a concept very prominent in the brief writings of Hans Hut, who got it from Müntzer, who in turn derived it from the medieval mystics. The gist of Marpeck's understanding lies in the following statement: "Just as Christ the Lord talked to the people about the kingdom by means of many parables of nature, the creatures must first lead carnal man . . . into a knowledge of God. . . . For him, the creation of God is a true gospel until he knows God the Father in the Son. . . ." Here Marpeck uses only one aspect of the concept found in Bernard of Clairvaux, Tauler, Müntzer, and Hut. In a short treatment of it in No. 16, he goes a little further when he talks of all the creatures who submit "freely and without compulsion to such service and lowliness." That has clear echoes of Hans Hut's treatment of the subject in his *Mystery of Baptism*. Nevertheless, Marpeck does not make it a central pillar in his *theologia crucis* as Hut does.

This is the longest Marpeck letter extant, and it is often repetitive and hard to follow. It also has sections of keen exegesis, telling illustrative materials, and passionate pastoral concern.

Two matters which are dealt with in this epistle have received thorough study in recent literature. The gospel of the creatures has been dealt with by Gordon Rupp in his article, "Thomas Müntzer, Hans Huth, and the Gospel of All Creatures," in *BJRL*, 43 (1961), pp. 492-519. The question of the Sabbath is dealt with by G. F. Hasel in his article, "Capito, Schwenckfeld and Crautwald on Sabbatarian Anabaptist Theology," *MQR*, XLVI (January 1972), pp. 41-57.

The Text

Judgment and Decision

27r This is a copy of an epistle written to those called the Swiss Brethren, and it concerns hasty judgments and decisions in which some may not concur, etc. 1531[1]

Grace and peace from God our Father through Jesus Christ our Lord be with all who fervently love and seek Christ. Amen.

My dear ones, constrained by the love in Jesus Christ, I write this letter because of the schism which, until now, has existed between us, because we have never recognized in our hearts and consciences the acknowledgment and understanding of Christ Jesus in each other, nor have we ever been able to meet. Nevertheless, in my heart, I have always, and even now, consider you to be zealous lovers of God and His Christ, although you lack knowledge and understanding of Christ. Every hour and every moment, I am also concerned about this lack in myself, and I have to be, for eternal life depends on knowing. As Christ the Lord said: "Father, this is eternal life that they may know you, the true God, and Jesus Christ whom you have sent." However, contrary to Christ's words, Paul says: "Whoever thinks he knows, does not yet know what he ought to know," etc. He says further: "Knowledge puffs up, but love improves." For this reason, although he had received his teaching from no man (Gal. 2) [Gal. 1:12], but from the Lord/ / Himself, Paul was still afraid of, and concerned about, mixing his own understanding with revealed teaching, and was traveling to Jerusalem at the behest of a revelation in order to confer with the first apostles that he might not run in vain. It happens easily that we depend more on our own knowledge and understanding than on love, which should be preeminent in all things. All knowledge of God subsists in this love of God and the neighbor. Even the law and all the prophets had this understanding of the love of God, which judges and urges all things for the sake of improvement. It is my fervent request to you, for the sake of Christ, that you will judge and decide this writing according to the true manner of love, which judges only for improvement, and covers many sins. Love has no part in, or fellowship with, sin, but is always merciful to the heart that mourns over its sin. According to that measure, I desire to have this epistle judged. Do not condemn that you may not be condemned!

Jn. 17 [3]
Rom. 12
[Likely
1 Cor. 8:2]
1 Cor. 8 [1]

27v

Do not judge that you may not be judged! That is the commandment and Word of Christ our Healer to His disciples.

Because of your hasty judgments, which are contrary to the words of Christ the Lord, our Master, this way (of Christ) I find to be missing and 28r lacking among you. The Lord says: "If you remain in my words, you will/ / be my true disciples and you will know the truth, and the truth will make you free." As a simple man, I sincerely desire to discuss this freedom with the mature in Christ. I gladly submit my mind to a clear and more lucid understanding, which is given by the Holy Spirit, and I would also gladly submit to the least among Christ's own, and thank my Lord Jesus Christ if I find witness in my conscience. In this freedom of Christ Jesus the Lord, I find comfort, joy, and peace in the Holy Spirit, and nothing else. Everything that commands, forbids, institutes, orders, drives, or produces anything against this freedom brings quarreling, wrong understandings, zeal, strife, and unrest in heart and conscience. Such strife only produces a restless, seared, uncertain conscience without the true peace of God. Now one must not do this, now not do that. Those who make such impositions do not know what they impose. Yet, as 1 Tim. 1 [7] Paul says, they want to be masters of Scripture. More about this matter later.

This is a clear witness and account of my conscience and heart concerning the glorious freedom of Christ and His own. If I am in error, I desire to be taught by God, through His Holy Spirit and the Scriptures. If I testify to the truth (by grace), I desire confirmation of it from those who truly believe. May God the 28v Father give grace through Christ. Amen./ /

313

Difference
between
the true
divinity
and humanity
of Christ

Conceived by the Holy Spirit in Mary, Jesus Christ is the Son as God according to Spirit, Word, and power. The Father has certified God in Him, through the power of His divine essence, with all powers, works, and miracles. He has also shown and certified His true humanity. As the Lord says in John 14 [10]: "Philip, do you not believe that I am in the Father and the Father is in me? If not, why do you not believe for the sake of the works that I do?" Thus, the Father is certified in the Son of true God and the Son in the Father, one God, manner, nature, and divine essence, all in the Son of Man. Brought forth from the seed and line of David, He was shown to be, in His weakness, a natural, earthly, true man. He was born of the race of man, but without the seed of man or sin. He was born of Mary, the spotless virgin in flesh and blood, in the manner of the human race; He grew and was brought up by earthly creatures as a truly earthly man. His physical life was sustained by eating and drinking and He died a natural death. Like those who also died a natural death, or who will yet die, He rose again from among the dead through the nature of God, Spirit, and Word, which is the resurrection and the life (as He said to Martha). He was taken up into heaven, and seated Himself at the right// hand of His heavenly Father. We wait for His return[2] and for our resurrection from the dead, according to the flesh, to be received through Him. Forgiveness and remission of sins come only through the Lord Jesus Christ. That, briefly, is the testimony concerning the true divinity and true humanity of Christ. The divinity is testified to and known through power, and the humanity through weakness in death, for death does not come from heaven. I write on this matter because many Antichrists have now appeared who deny both the di-

Jn. 11 [25]

29r
Heb. 12 [2]
Col. 3 [1]

vinity and humanity of Christ.

This Jesus Christ is the free Son of God and man, and He is without commandment or prohibition against His own, the faithful. For the rebels and transgressors of the commandments, however, the commandments of God are only the commandments of man, and the whole law only the law for damnation. For, where there is no sin or wickedness, no command or prohibition is needed; there is freedom from all law. Where commandment or prohibition rule conscience, heart, and even God's law, one is not free, but is in bondage to sin and wickedness. There no free grace, peace, or joy in the Holy Spirit but, rather, the threat[3] of punishment, fear, sorrowing, and anxiety about the vengeance on sin through the coming wrath of God. Because of this // fear, external works and fruits of sin are at times neglected. Such fear of God is the beginning of true repentance, the hope to become free of the law of sin and to become free, through faith in Jesus Christ, in the word of grace. Such fear is the beginning of wisdom and the knowledge of God in His Son, who is the wisdom of His Father. In this manner, Jesus Christ, the Son of God, sets one free. He alone, through His Holy Spirit, makes godly the heart and the entire disposition of man. He erases the handwriting of the devil so that it is no longer the law that reigns, but grace and freedom in Jesus Christ, according to the nature of the true love of God and neighbor. This love in God is the real freedom. Without any coercion, this love truly fulfills all commands and prohibitions of the whole pleasure of God. That is the true freedom in Christ Jesus. Whomever He thus sets free is truly free, for whoever remains in His words is His true disciple; he will also know the truth that is Christ Jesus, yes, the Word, the truth, and the life. This truth liberates

nota

29v
Prov. 9 [10]
Ecclus. 1 [16]
Ps. 110
[111:10]

Jn. 8 [36]

315

him from all law, command, and prohibition. It is a ruler and sovereign in the Holy Spirit, and a delighted fulfiller of the whole pleasure of God, for it is Christ/ / Jesus Himself who is in the hearts of such liberated people.

Does a father ever command or forbid the son who knows the will of his father and achieves his full pleasure in it? For everyone who believes in Him, Christ is always the end of the law. If we are to please God in Christ, therefore, laws may not rule in the kingdom of Christ. The law and the commandments of God will stand eternally as a means of distinguishing good and evil, and in this knowledge of good and evil is the root and beginning of sin. From thence, the law emerged, along with sin, and was to be a verdict and condemnation of the knowledge and understanding of our devastated reason, which is the head of the serpent. The judgment of Christ acts as the stern righteousness of God, for He has given all judgment to the Son. The head of the serpent, that is, our reason, must be crushed, either through faith, or through vengeance and punishment in unbelief. The law is spiritual, but we are carnal. To be spiritually minded is life; to be carnally minded is death. Similarly, the serpent head/ / of our reason must, and will, be crushed either by the preaching of faith, which takes all reason captive, or by the law in unbelief, which results in eternal destruction. This serpent head must submit to the feet of the seed of the woman, to the natural, earthly, human feet of Christ, who is the seed without the seed of man and without sin.[4] He, whom the serpent deceived, crushes its head. How painful it is for pride to have to submit to, and be humbled by, an earthly creature! But to this our reason, which constantly opposes the good and incites mischief in our mortal

Jn. 5 [22]

Rom. 8 [6]

30 v

2 Cor. 10 [5]

nota

life, must submit in grace or perish. Certainly, the law and the commandments cannot make anyone godly, but only grace through Jesus Christ. The law and commandments of God judge and decide for condemnation, separating the good to the good and the evil to the evil, and creating in our hearts and dispositions nothing but tribulation and sorrowing. No living man who is outside Jesus Christ can be justified before God. Throughout, the epistle to the Romans testifies to this fact, namely, that the law and the commandments work only for death with us, which otherwise is life in Christ Jesus. For, as soon as our devastated / / reason hears the proclamation of the law and the good commandments of God, she finds herself condemned under it, and would gladly keep the law in order to be saved, which, however, is not possible. Because reason presumed to be a god, and to have the power which belongs to God alone, the ability [to keep the law] has been taken away. She imagines that she can be saved or condemned by her own power, and not by God's, who alone has all power. That is why God has likened our reason to the head of the serpent. This old serpent constantly resists God, and now presumes to be saved through its own ability. Oh, how the poison of the serpent works its destruction in all men through presumptuousness![5] For this reason, God the Father has established that His Son, through the weakness, sickness, and infirmity of the nature given to Him by the seed of the woman, should crush this arrogance, this head of the serpent. Born of the seed of David by nature and by the generation of man, but without sin or the seed of man, God the Father has bruised Him and delivered Him to death, the wages of sin, for our iniquities. Indeed, all ability, power, glory, grace, strength, wisdom, understanding, faith, love,

31r

Gen. 3 [15]

Is. 53 [5]

317

hope, yes, all service to the glory of God, all blessedness, virtue, and grace can be taken and received only because of this same weakness, / / this deep suffering of the Lord Jesus Christ, the Son of Man, who was seen by God to be stricken and afflicted, who also cried, "My God, my God, why have you forsaken me?" He is the one to whom all authority is given in heaven and on earth. That is the crushing and eternal destruction of the arrogant serpent that is man's own reason, his assumptions, and his presumption to follow his own wisdom, his own law, his own commandment and prohibition, his own love and pleasure, in short, all arrogance, doctrine, skill, and understanding that proceeds from man's own choice. Christ's victory over all arrogance, spirit and flesh, is to condemn it eternally. How painful for the arrogant serpent before he is condemned with all his heads, his self-will and arrogance! How he snaps about at the heels of Christ and His own! How he pours out his venom, in many ways, in order to destroy the woman and her seed before he is condemned to be a footstool at the feet of Christ, the human feet that were given into death for the sake of our sin! A mortal, fleshly (but now immortal) creature must rule and judge the immortal, indestructible spirit. He [Jesus] was delivered to death / / for our sins and, by this same weakness and sickness, robbed sin, hell, devil, and death of their power. Both today and in eternity, the meekness, humility, and patience of the Lord Jesus Christ has the power to overcome in His own. All that is external, such as baptism, forgiveness of sins, teaching, the Lord's Supper, the laying on of hands, foot washing, and all the external witnesses of faith in Christ, we receive from Christ. And, according to the inner teaching of the Holy Spirit, we receive these external things through those who

Ps. 22 [2]
31v

Mt. 27 [46]
Mt. 28 [18]

Rev. 12 [7-9]

nota
32 r

weakness
of Christ

nota

318

truly believe they are His own and through the love of Christ. How painful for man's reason and arrogance! And whoever is still a prisoner to what possesses him,[6] as indeed the whole world is, that person is no free man in Christ Jesus. For whomever the Son sets free is truly free; he is released from

Eph. 4 [8]
Col. 1 [1]

what possesses him,[6] from sin, death, and hell, which possess[6] all men outside of Christ. In His own body, the Lord Jesus Christ has led this captivity captive because of His disobedience unto death. With no guilt of His own, He has nailed our guilt

Col. 2 [15]

and that which possesses us[6] to the cross in order that He Himself might liberate us from our captivity (2 Cor. 5 [19-21]), and take it unto Himself.

Rom. 8 [1]
Rom. 10 [4]

There is now, therefore, no condemnation for those who are in Christ Jesus,[a] for Christ is the end of all commandment and prohibition, yes, of the whole

32v

law for everyone who believes in Him. / / Here, there is no longer any servitude, but only liberation in God. I am not talking here about the im-

Carnally
minded
1 Pet. 2 [16]
nota

pertinent, self-styled freedoms of the flesh which are used as a cloak for wickedness, and of which the whole world is full. Such freedom is the most dire

Christians
are prisoners
to no one,
nor debtors,
except to love

slavery before God, and leads to destruction. The proper, true liberty is in the Son of God and His own,[7] who are made lords of all law, commandment, and prohibition. They are prisoners to no one, nor debtors to anyone, except to the love in God and God's love in them. They are, and remain, prisoners and subjects and debtors of love,[a] for the proper, true love of God can never repay itself, and always remains a debtor; indeed, together with grace, mercy, and goodness, she holds God captive, and makes Him our debtor continually. And even as love is a debtor to us, so, God the eternal Father, maker of heaven and earth, neither could nor would

a-a emphasized by a wavy line in the margin

319

pay us in cheaper coin[8] than the most costly, deepest, and highest love that He had. We have been paid. The most high Father, God, and Lord showed Himself to be gracious to us in the Son, the Lord Jesus Christ. By Himself, in His Son, He paid for our transgression and guilt. For our sake, He suspended His commandment, law, and prohibition, and transfered it from the first man Adam / / to His Son Jesus Christ; He has established that the love which is Christ should alone be the fulfiller and voluntary keeper of all commandments in Christ and His own. When the Lord drops and cancels out[9] the punishment of, and vengeance upon, sin and the transgression of the commandments, the law and the commandments also fall. They should be fulfilled through the grace which God gives, but He has Himself, for our sake, become the fulfillment of His commandments in His Son and in those who belong to Christ. As Christ the Lord says: "Without me you can do nothing." And Paul likewise: "Whoever boasts, let him boast of the Lord" (1 Cor. 1 [31]; Jer. 9 [23]; 2 Cor. 11 [perhaps 10:17]).

Thus, the true love of the Father, Christ Jesus, the Son of God, is Lord of all commandments and prohibitions. Through the Holy Spirit, even today, He is the fulfiller of the same in His own. All who have, in baptism, died to the law of sin (Col. 3 [3]), and have been buried with Christ (Rom. 6 [4]), do not themselves live. Rather, Christ lives in them, through the law of grace and the voluntary spirit in Christ Jesus.

But it is not the kind of grace the children of the world hope to receive, which allows them to remain in the lasciviousness of flesh and sin. Such can never be grace, nor can it be called so. Rather, it is the wrath, displeasure, vengeance, and punishment of God, as it was when David prayed for

320

vengeance on his enemies in Psalm 68 [most likely 69:23-29], and as (Rom. 11 [9]) it indeed happens to

33v
vengeance

the whole world.// God allows one transgression after another to come over the children of wickedness so that the wrath and displeasure increases more and more. That is the testimony of God's wrath, and not of His grace.

nota

For such children of wickedness no commandment or law is suspended, yes, not even human law, not to speak of God's commandments and laws, of which they[10] are worthy like the heathen. For the

Rom. 2 [17]

world does not even keep its own laws, although she is a law to herself and thereby condemns herself. But the grace from God which man encounters is a complete rebirth from flesh, sin, death, and hell to grace in the peace, joy, and comfort of the Holy Spirit. As the Lord Jesus Christ said to Nicodemus:

Jn. 3 [5 f.]

"Unless a man be born in another way, that is through water and spirit, he cannot come into the kingdom of God. For what is born of the flesh is flesh, and what is born of the Spirit is spirit." Under the curse, the birth of the flesh is a birth to servitude, to the service of the law of sin, under which we are sold and obligated to the life of sin.[11] Thus,

Rom. 7 [25]

Paul says: "With my flesh I serve the law of sin, and with my spirit the Lord Jesus Christ." Flesh and blood, in which no good thing dwells, has to be forcibly protected and preserved from sin under the

34r

free rule // of the Spirit of God. Paul speaks of the desire of the spirit and the action of the flesh when he says: "I do what I do not want and, what I wish to do, I do not do." For flesh and blood always fight against the law of grace, and so they must serve the law of sin, that is, fear of the wrath and the future punishment of God. Thus, Paul does not attribute the compulsion[12] to the free Spirit of Christ, but rather to the disobedient flesh and blood. During

this time, the yoke will not be removed from its
neck. The prayer, "Your kingdom come to us,"
represents the free rule of the Spirit. For whoever
submits to the rule of the free Holy Spirit of the
Lord Jesus Christ keeps his flesh and blood in
obedience, and keeps it so against the will of flesh
and blood until death. Indeed, Christ Jesus the
Lord Himself, although His flesh was weak and His
Spirit willing, prayed the Father to take the cup
from Him. But His Spirit was willing and ready. He
obediently subjected the flesh to death, and said to
the Father: "Not my will, but yours be done."

Thus, when we are baptized, we are born of
His Holy Spirit, who assures us and gladdens our
spirit. Together with flesh and blood, and all its
lusts and appetites, we have been buried in the
death of Christ. As Paul says: "If we / / have died
with Christ, and the lust and will of the flesh is
dead, then it is not flesh and blood that lives in us,
but Jesus Christ. This is the free life as it is found,
through grace, in the free ones, whom the Son sets
free from death to life in free obedience. For to be
carnally minded is death, and to be spiritually
minded is life" (Rom. 8 [6]). Thus, no one is free according to the flesh; rather, he is obligated to obey
the Holy Spirit of the Lord Jesus Christ throughout
all of life. Wherever flesh and blood is free to rule,
the inner man is neither free nor safe, but is made a
servant of sin, and he, who otherwise is the image of
God, is held prisoner for everlasting destruction.
Such are the slaves of sin; they are not free, for they
deny him who can set them free. Although it was
given to us, through grace in Christ, in order that
we might live, the good, spiritual law of God becomes, for them, the cause of everlasting death and
condemnation. Thus, I distinguish between the
freedom of the spirit in Christ, which is life, and the

Lk. 11 [2]

Mt. 26 [39-41]

Rom. 6 [4]

34v
Col. 3 [3]

Gal. 2 [20]
Gal. 5 [12]
Jn. 8 [30]

Jn. 8 [34]
2 Pet. 2 [9 f.]

freedom of the flesh, with its will and desire for death. I do not, as I have been accused, stretch the freedom of Christ too far.[13]

The difference is between the liberty of the Lord Jesus Chrust, and the self-made carnal freedom, which constantly adorns itself with the dead letter as a cover for wickedness. / /

First of all, every individual must possess true and diligent discernment in conscience and heart if he is to have a true and certain judgment and if the self-made freedom of the flesh is not to be taken for the liberty of Jesus Christ. This self-made freedom is, and shall always remain, the most profound slavery, from which release is never possible. To act in accordance with this self-made freedom is to sin, to be led into wickedness and the hardest slavery of sin, for whoever commits sin is the slave of sin. It makes no difference that this self-made carnal freedom always adorns itself with the dead letter and, posing as the true liberty of Christ Jesus the Lord, covers itself with a false, lying appearance. It finally brings forth no fruit but open depravities, sin, and shame. Such is the case with the hypocrites who, because of their choice to live according to human law and its coercion, strut about, and, without knowing anything about it, assume the appearance of the Spirit.

Jn. 8 [34]
Pet. 2 [12-22]

Col. 2 [18]
own choice

Now, the true believers are forbidden to condemn all these people before the right time (1 Cor. 4[5]), that is, until their fruit, which is open vice, appears. Christ says: "By their fruits (He does not say by the blossoms[14] or the foliage) you shall know them." For the day of the Lord will reveal everything. But some vices / / are revealed and clear before that time, for every man expresses that which is within the treasure of his heart. Whether it be before or at the time of the last day, to cover or

Mt. 7 [16]
fruits
Tim. 5 [24]
35v

Ps. 32 [1]

reveal sin is in God's hands.

b For no one may judge the heart until the fruit appears or until the outpouring of the treasure of the heart occurs. Only God, through the Holy Spirit, may judge. He is the true Chastiser and Judge of the heart. He will punish the world, first, for its sin, for they have not believed, and He will judge them because the prince of this world, who has lost his authority, is judged.b Finally, He will punish the world because of His own righteousness, for He, the Lord, goes to the Father. Men, however, again grant and return to him [the prince of this world] the authority which is against the authority and judgment of Christ. Thus, by their own permission, the devil carries out his work and exercises his authority in the children of wickedness. Thus, they also deny the righteousness of Christ in themselves, their words, and their works. But Christ, who alone is acceptable to God, is the righteousness of the children of truth before the Father. This same righteousness does its works in them, and the Holy Spirit witnessses in them through works, power, and deeds. / /[15]

For nothing is valid before God except Christ; the rest, the work in His own before the Father, is only a testimony of righteousness. That is why He speaks "of righteousness: for I go to the Father."

c Whoever, therefore, establishes, commands, prohibits, coerces, drives, punishes, or judges before the time the good or evil fruit is revealed, lays claim to the authority, power, and office of the Holy Spirit of the Lord Jesus Christ and, contrary to love, goodness, and grace, runs ahead of Christ Jesus. For the Son of God Himself has committed this office and work to the Holy Spirit of God, and the office is

_Jn. 16 [8-11]_

1 Cor. 1 [30]
1 Cor. 2 [4 f.]

_36r_

nota

_Jn. 10 [8]_

---

b-b emphasized in the margin with a wavy line
c-c wavy line in the margin

to be carried out after His earthly, human life. With reference to this work, He says: "The Holy Spirit will come and judge because of sin, judgment, and righteousness." This Spirit now does the judging and searches the hearts, for the Holy Spirit has His work and good fruit in the children of light in order to reveal them before men. Similarly, the spirit of wickedness, who often and in many ways disguises himself as a spirit of light, has his work in the children of darkness. These, too, are driven by the Holy Spirit to do their own works in order that by the power and finger of God they may be known and revealed by their fruits.c

Cor. 11 [14]

Therefore, even if one is concerned about a lapse[16] and sees / / the leaves and blossoms of evil appearance, one ought only to warn and admonish, but not judge, before the time of the fruit.

36v

The Lord does not say, "By their blossoms or leaves," but rather, "By their fruits you shall know them." For love also covers a multitude of sins (1 Pet. 4[8]), and judges all things in the best light. Even though it is concerned about evil appearance and evil fruit, it nevertheless always hopes for the best.

1 Cor. 4[5]
Mt. 7 [20]

Cor. 13 [7]

In the same way, Christ covers our sin and shame in the love and grace which leads to improvement.d Whoever presumes to decide and judge, before the revealing of guilt, is a thief and a murderer (Jn. 10:1). He runs ahead of Jesus Christ, who alone is the revealer of good and evil in the heart.d

ning ahead
of Christ

On the other hand, if the sin and wickedness, evident from the revealed fruit, is revealed through wrath in the righteousness of Christ, one must be ready to judge and decide with Christ, the true Judge; otherwise, he too, is a thief and murderer.

d-d wavy line in the margin

running after
Christic

Eph. 6 [17]

Lk. 22 [49]

37r

Lk. 17 [3]

Mt. 6 [5:29, 30]

1 Cor. 6 [3]

Mt. 7 [3-5]
Lk. 6 [41 f.]

nota

Jn. 8 [3-9]
37v

Mt. 21 [31]

He runs behind Jesus Christ and not with Christ. All the elect of God, with Christ, judge in this time with the sword of the Spirit through the Word, and not, as the world does, with the carnal sword. They, too, will decide at the last judgment.

But everywhere the devil selectively[17] uses his weapons against us // through the dead letter. Some do not want to judge at all, and take refuge behind Matthew 7[1]: "Judge not that you be not judged. Do not condemn so that you will not be condemned." They do not see the contrary to this statement, Matthew 18[15]: "If your brother sins, punish him." As long as there are witnesses and they do not listen even to the church, they [sic] should be regarded as heathen. Again, [Jesus says]: "If your eye, hand, foot offends you, tear it out and cut it off." Paul says: "You judge those who are inside" (1 Cor. 5[12]);[18] God will judge those outside; [Paul then asks:] "Do you not know that we are to judge angels? Now, put out what is evil." Many similar Scripture passages enjoin the saints to render judgment.ₑ No one may judge except he who has first judged and sentenced his own life through the grace and mercy of God, whereby he has pulled the beam out of his eye.[19] Then, very properly,[20] in patience, humility, meekness, and love, he may with the greatest care pull the sliver[21] out of his brother's eye without hurting or irritating the eye. That is, after all, how he has been treated by God. And whoever brings someone to Christ in a different way for judgment,ₑ as the Jews brought the adulteress to Him in the temple, // will find himself, together with the hypocritical Jews, running from Christ and the adulteress in the temple. Open sinners will enter the kingdom of God before these do. Christ tolerated them less than the adul-

---

e-e wavy line in the margin

teress. All transgression is adultery before God, to whom man is betrothed.

About the hasty and uncertain judgments

Second, the enemy of truth has another trick, worse than the one referred to above, to lead men astray with hasty and uncertain judgments. By doing so, they are judging and condemning themselves, making sin where there is no sin, setting up laws, commandments, and prohibitions against the authority and sovereignty of the Spirit of the Lord Jesus Christ, who gave His own no law except the law of love (as stated above). They seek

1 Tim. 1 [7]

to establish laws, and would become the masters of Scripture, but they do not know what they establish. Because of this ignorance, the enemy takes hearts and consciences captive. But to those who are in Jesus Christ and who are justified through Christ, no law is given. For to the righteous, says Paul, no law is given, neither commandment nor prohibition; they are given only to the unrighteous. However, wherever men establish, command, or prohibit, the grace of the Holy Spirit does not reign. Rather, the anxiety and fear of unrighteousness

38r

reign. For the true / / love in Christ, indeed the Spirit and God Himself, is a free and willing fulfill-

Cor. 10 [33]
Cor. 13 [5]

ment of all that is good. Love denies herself, and does not seek her own. She pays all debt (Rom. 13[7f]), and she may herself never be paid for. She remains debtor to no one since she is the payment of

nota

all guilt. Therefore in Christ she is free of all law, commandment, and prohibition. Those who have been captured and bound in true bondage of love in God can never be bound with any other bondage in conscience, heart, disposition, or mind. They are free in all things, and are debtors to none except

Cor. 13 [1-3]
Rom. 8 [33]

love. Where there is no love, everything is in vain. Who, then, will accuse God's chosen ones? "For love is stronger than death" (Cant. 8[6]). Love can-

1 Jn. 2 [27]
not be overcome, and no price can be paid for her in all eternity. She is the inner anointing of the heart. Although it is very hot, she feeds among the roses, until the cool evening comes [Cant. 4:5; 6:2, 3], because of her patience of heart, mind, disposition, and all the powers [of the believer]. She teaches everything since she is herself the teaching.

anointing
John speaks about this teaching when he says that the inner anointing will teach us many things. Love is the disciple and truly obedient learner of the Holy Spirit. At the same time, it is the ruler of

38v
heaven and / / earth. In His Son, God the Father has subjected Himself to her, for she is in everything God Himself. There, the true and glorious

The liberty of true love
liberty in Christ dwells and remains. This liberty is given to no one except through the true love in Christ Jesus. Again, the truly free are given no other commandment except to love. This is the bond with

1 Cor. 10 [23]
which the liberty of Christ is bound, although, as Paul says, to this liberty of Christ all things are lawful. Nor did he want to subject his liberty to anyone's judgment or decision (1 Cor. 6 [10:29]), for the believers judge everything, but are themselves judged by no one (1 Cor. 2 [15]). But wherever something does not serve or promote

1 Cor. 8 [9-11]
improvement, the love in Christ acts[22] with all her authority, privileges, and freedom, and never acts against her own nature. Nor does true love suspend liberty; rather, she makes us truly free in all things.

That, briefly, is the true liberty in Christ Jesus

Mt. 12 [1-8]
which all law, Sabbath, commandments, and prohibitions must serve. For they were given for the sake of man, and not man for them, and they were given for the sake of God, who alone is to be

nota
worshiped and served in Christ. That is why true believers are lords of all with Christ. It is not that they serve the letter of the law and the Sabbath, but

rather that the whole law and commandment of God is / / servant of the true liberty in Christ. But the whole law still rules over those who are under condemnation. For cursed is everyone who does not observe all that is written in the book of the law. These are outside of Christ, guilty in all of life, under the rule of the law, and condemned according to the strict justice of God. They are always in fear and anxiety of the agony of hell. Thus, they seek to do the will of God, but, since the law rules over them, in truth they can never accomplish it. They are not free from the law by virtue of the grace which God gives. Rather, they are sold into the slavery of sin to serve the law of sin. They are continually thrown into the fear of damnation without any comfort of conscience.

But the full love of God and the comfort of the Holy Spirit drives out this fear, and releases the imprisoned conscience into the truth and freedom, peace, and joy of the Holy Spirit. John is not speaking in this passage about the fear of the flesh. Otherwise, it would have to follow that even Christ, who is the full love of the Father, did not possess this full love; when He speaks of the baptism with which He has to be baptized, He says: "How anxious I am until it is done." He also prayed the Father / / that, if it were possible, the cup might be taken from Him. He did so because of the fear of the agony of the flesh before Him. The full love of God receives and retains the victory over this bodily fear, but only in death, when physical life ends. The Lord, indeed, cried out: "My God, you have forsaken me!" But then, as He gave up His spirit, He said: "Everything is done!" Love gets the victory over the fear of the body, but this fear is not driven out before death; otherwise, tribulation would not be a cross.

But the fullness of love erases and drives out the fear of sin and punishment by the law to ever-lasting damnation, like the devil's bill of charges, about which Paul writes in Colossians 2 [14]. Paul also says: "We have not received a spirit in which we should again be afraid."

Rom. 8 [15]
2 Tim. 1 [7]

Four kinds
of fear

I discern three varieties of fear. There is also a fourth kind which is without hope, for Judas also had fear.

Fear of the flesh and fear of sin as mentioned above, are profitable for salvation. The third is the pure fear of God, that one does right after the manner of love; in this fear one regards oneself as an unprofitable servant. This / / pure fear of God, which leads to eternal life, can never yield to, nor be driven out by, love. The true way of love fears that, in [doing] all righteousness, she always does too little or too much, but that it is nevertheless pleasing to God.[23] For creatures must tremble before their Creator, however good they may be. Therefore, true fear must be carefully distinguished in order that one does not fall into presumption, tempt God in carnal joy and strength, and forget the Lord Jesus Christ, without whom the flesh is weak and the spirit willing. In Him, the disciple is not above his teacher, nor the servant above his master (Jn. 15 [20]).

Lk. 17 [10]
‾ 40r

nota

Mt. 26 [41]

Wherever one presumes to have this love of God, therewith to drive out the bodily fear of the Lord before bodily death, a fall and denial will soon set in, as it did with Peter who wanted to die with the Lord. For in our weakness, of which we ought to boast, as Paul did, God's power and strength is seen in that the love of God has the victory into eternal life. In this victory, all things are clean to the clean, and unclean to the unclean. ꜰ Moreover, whoever

Mk. 14 [30]

Jer. 9 [23]
2 Cor. 12 [9]
1 Cor. 1 [27]

Tit. 1 [15]

f-f wavy line in the margin

330

2 Pet. 2 [19]
Jn. 8 [34]

40v

boasts that he is free and yet commits sin is a liar. He is not free, but is a servant of sin; he has been sold under sin because of the law / / into eternal death.

nota

Again, whoever presumes to preserve, rule, and lead the kingdom of Christ through law, commandment, and prohibition, yes, through the law of God, not to mention human inventions, no matter how pious it appears, it, too, thrusts the voluntary Spirit of the Lord Jesus Christ, the proper Ruler of

Dan. 9 [26 f.]
Mt. 24 [15]

hearts, out of His place and puts himself in the place where he ought not to be. This is the greatest abomination against Christ. Nothing but sects and popery can come from it, about which Christ the

nota

Lord and Daniel speak. Whoever has the law is not God of the law.[24] If one sins against it, one sins against Him who established and commanded it. Insofar as men order and forbid in the kingdom of Christ and His own, they thrust the Lord out, and make sin where there is no sin.

Jn. 10 [8]

2 Tim. 3 [6]

All such are soul-murderers and robbers. They take prisoner womanish hearts and weak, seared consciences because of commandment and prohibition against themselves. They point to, and seek a different salvation, outside of Jesus Christ. Even though, as does the whole world, they defend everything with the name of Christ, it is all nothing

nota

but deceit and lies against the voluntary Spirit of Christ. Even though they point to Christ here or

Mar. 13
[Mt. 24:26]

there, Christ has forbidden us to believe them or to go out to them. The true saints of God and children

41r

of Christ are those whose ruler_f / / is the Holy Spirit in the Word of truth. Where two or three are

Mt. 18 [20]

gathered in His name, He is among them. He alone rules in faith through patience and love in His own. I pray God my heavenly Father that He will not

nota

allow me to be separated from such a gathering and

331

fellowship of the Holy Spirit, it makes no difference who they are or where they gather in the whole world. I hope to be in their fellowship and to submit myself to the rule of the Holy Spirit of Christ in the obedience of faith.[25]

But I will have nothing to do with any other sect, faction, or gathering, no matter what they are called in the whole world. I will especially avoid those who use the bodily sword, contrary to the patience of Christ, who did not resist any evil and who likewise commands His own not to resist tribulation or evil, in order to rule in the kingdom of Christ. I avoid those who institute, command, and forbid, therewith to lead and rule the kingdom of Christ. I also avoid those who deny the true divinity, Spirit, Word, and power in Jesus Christ. I avoid those who destroy and deny His natural, earthly humanity which was received from man, of the seed of David, born without man's seed and sin, born of Mary the pure virgin; He was crucified and died a natural earthly death, from which He arose again, and has now seated Himself at the right hand / / of God. I also avoid those who, living in open sin and gross evil, want to have fellowship in the kingdom of Christ but without true repentance, and I avoid all those who tolerate such a thing. I avoid all who oppose and fight against the words and the truth of Christ. With all such regardless of what they are called in the world, I will have no part or fellowship in the kingdom of Christ unless they repent.

My salvation depends alone on Christ's, the Lord's, dying and the shedding of His blood. In Him alone have I received the remission and forgiveness of sins from the Holy Spirit in the fellowship of His saints. Into this fellowship I have also been baptized,[26] according to the witness and truth

schism

1.

Mt. 5 [39]
Luke 6 [17-29]

2.

3.

4.

Heb. 12 [24]
Col. 3 [1]

41v   5.

6.

7.

of my heart in the Holy Spirit, on my own testimony and confession of the truth. I also reject all ignorant baptism which happens without true, revealed, personal faith whether in children or adults. For this reason, I also was baptized with external water and external word, in confession of my faith. I was gladly baptized into this fellowship of the Holy Spirit, visibly gathered, for the remission and forgiveness of sins. In it I sincerely desire to remain / / until my end. Amen to all who desire this with me. That is briefly the testimony of my heart in Christ Jesus.

The difference between true and false judgment, and what the divine biblical Scriptures command us to judge and decide according to the example of the Lord Jesus Christ and apostolic teaching.

Men decide and judge in this time for many reasons. First, it is done out of love for the Word and for improvement. This is true and proper decision, and the judgment of the saints made in patience. As said earlier, no other patience[27] has any place in the congregation of Christ.

Second, men judge out of a concern for evil, and they expect to anticipate evil in that way.

gThird, some judge in envy and hate because others do not immediately agree with them. They claim that others resist the truth when, in fact, these others are resisting their own ignorance. These last two kinds of judgment are false and mendaciousg and only create schism and sects.

Fourth, there are a few who do not want to decide or make judgments at all for fear that they would condemn themselves. They have not judged themselves, nor have they submitted to the Word in

g-g wavy line in the margin

Gloss: Every
church desires
to have and
exercise this
power. They
boast about the
Holy Spirit, that
they have Him,
primarily the
Hutterites, the
Swiss, and the
Pilgramites. None
has peace in God
with the other.
They all judge one
another, and all
fall in the
judgment.[28]

Jn. 5 [22], 7 [38],
Jn. 8 [15 f.]

nota

Mt. 7 [20]
Mt. 12 [49]

1 Cor. 4 [5]
43r

obedient faith. / / h The Saints of God have been charged by the Lord to exercise judgment through the Holy Spirit; He says: "Receive the Holy Spirit. If you retain sins, they are retained; if you forgive, they are forgiven" (Jn. 20 [22f.]). For the Holy Spirit of God is the key of heaven, through which sin is retained or forgiven in the community of the saints! For this reason, the apostles wrote to the churches (Acts 15 [28]) and spoke against those who were again introducing the law: "It seemed good to the Holy Spirit and to us." No one is commanded to judge without the Holy Spirit, without whom no certain judgment is possible. That is why the Lord Jesus Christ first gave the Holy Spirit to those whom He empowered to judge so that they should certainly and truly judge, and decide according to the word of grace and truth in order that the witness and fruit, good or evil, may precede and be known in the deed. This is the only way to bind and loose[29] with certainty and, in the external judgment, to judge according to the testimony of the external fruit, and not of the foliage or blossoms which precede the fruit. As mentioned earlier, Christ says: "You shall know them by their fruits." Those who judge in truth may, therefore, not judge before the time, but must wait for the fruit.h / / Otherwise, one meddles with the prerogatives of God's secret and hidden judgment and decision; one judges and punishes before God punishes, as Judas did with Magdalene (sic) and as the Jews did with Christ. This is referred to by the saying of Christ: "Do not judge that you may not be judged; do not condemn that you may not be condemned." In making judgment, one must always distinguish foliage and blossoms from the fruit.

---

h-h wavy line in the margin

The fruits of wickedness, already judged, from which separation is to be made according to the Old and New Testaments, in order to judge with certain judgment.

1. First, unbelief after proclaimed teaching is the greatest sin, that is, if one does not believe the testimony of the gospel. That is the sin against the Holy Spirit, for whoever does not believe is already judged and condemned (Jn. 3 [18], Mk. 16 [16]).

2. Second, whoever falls away from the sweet gift of God and the fellowship of Christ, not because of
Heb. 6 [4-6] fear, care, and anxiety for his bodily life,[30] but with
] Tim. 5 [10] evident malice, has already gone into condemnation and has sinned against the Holy Spirit.

3. Third, there are those with evil intent who contradict the truth, delay it with wickedness and error, and sin against the Holy Spirit stubbornly and with malice. Such have already been delivered
43v to the devil in body and soul. / /

4. Fourth, there are those who deny the truth be-
Mt. 26 [75] cause of the fear of the flesh, as did Peter and others like him; in them the spark of grace remains in the
Gal. 6 [1] heart, which leads them fervently to desire and seek for repentance. It is the same as for all sin and error that so easily overtakes us. But, where the spark of grace and the hope in Christ remains, it leads to hearty repentance, the desire to return to Christ,
Sinning and the desire for the improvement of life. Such sin
against the is only against the Son. They will be forgiven. Al-
Son though they may be judged by Christ and His
1 Cor. 1 church, they are nevertheless not condemned with this world. It is, therefore, dangerous[31] to fall into
nota the stern judgment of God. For no one is assured when he sins whether or not, through grace, he will be given a repentant heart in order that he may
The world's truly repent before sin is complete. For true re-
proverb pentance is not to sin at all.[32] This repentance is a

335

gracious gift of God, and a certain witness of God in the heart for the forgiveness of sins. No one is able to stand by himself, or to become good, without the mighty help of God who alone makes the heart good, and who is goodness Himself. No one is good but God alone. We fall and sin of ourselves, but we do not become good of ourselves. Therefore, whoever sins wantonly / / tempts God, and deliberately falls into His stern judgment. For him, condemnation is certain, and the grace and mercy of God uncertain. However, in saying this, I am not indiscriminately spreading the gracious hand of God out over just anyone.

Although mercy triumphs over judgment, it does not do so over all men and their sin. Let everyone carefully see to it that he does not tempt God. Dear brothers, it is dangerous to fall into the hands of men, but it is much more dangerous to fall into the hands of God.

A parable: The world forbids stealing on pain of hanging, and other wickedness and transgressions on pain of death. If someone transgresses, death is nearer to him than life, even though the world occasionally grants life to someone who has deserved death. These, however, are exceptions, and it is the same with God and sin. It is not that God is not gracious and is not merciful to the sinner. It is, however, far more certain and safe not to sin; then one does not need to be concerned about God's wrath,[33] for God is and remains all grace and goodness.[34] I write about sin because I have been accused by many of using the freedom of Christ as a cloak for wickedness.

Now, the root, ground, and beginning of sin originated with our first parents, Adam and / / Eve, namely the knowledge of good and evil. It is the abandonment of the good, according to our nature

Mt. 19 [17]

44r
Heb. 10 [26]

Jas. 2 [13]

2 Kings 24
= [2 Sam. 24:14]
Eccles. 2 [26?]
Sus. 1 [23]

Parable

1 Pet. 2 [16]

Root of sin
44v

Jn. 3 [6]

nota

Ezek. 38
[Most likely
Chapter 18]
Mt. 19 [14]
Lk. 18 [17]
Mk. 10 [15]

Jn. 3 [3-5]

Reason and
head of the
serpent

Baptism of
innocents

45r

Sin exists
in unbelief

and birth (what is born of flesh is flesh), and doing evil as soon as recognition and knowledge, according to the flesh, begin. All true simplicity of infants is bought with the blood of Christ, but without any law, external teaching, faith, baptism, Lord's Supper, and all other Christian ceremonies, for theirs is the kingdom of heaven without admonition to change. But to those who claim to know good and evil, but in whom knowledge is the root and basis of all sin, which God refers to as the head of the serpent and enmity against God, the Lord says: "You must become as children." He is condemned who is not born again through faith and baptism for the forgiveness of sins, and who is not born again into the obedience of faith, the simplicity and innocence of the child. Before it submits to the simplicity of faith in Christ, reason is the head of the serpent which is crushed by faith in Christ. That is the end of all carnal wisdom.

For this reason, the adversary and prince of pride has invented the baptism of innocents in order that when the proud head of the serpent, which is reason, matures, she refuses to submit to the baptism of faith and to the / / crushing of her head by the feet of Christ. That is why the enemy has his way in the absence of reason. There is the excuse that she is already baptized. Thus, innocence usurps the place of the baptism of faith. Baptism and faith are established to end the knowledge of good and evil, which is carnal reason, and to take it captive so that it may be crushed by the feet of Christ. Where men believe, it leads to salvation; where they do not, it leads to damnation. For reason demands to know, not to believe. Wherever man believes, reason is taken captive under the obedience of Christ. Thus, unbelief is the place of sin. From it comes the fruit of sin; all evil fruit comes from disobedience, from the knowledge of good and evil. Similarly, all good fruit comes from obedience through faith in Christ.

Discussion of the Ten Commandments

First

All false teaching, superstition, idolatry, and self-love are the fruits of sinning against the commandment to believe in God.

Ex. 20 [3]

Deut. 5 [1]
45v

Mt. 7, 19
[likely 22:37-40]

Fearing, honoring, and loving anything above or beside God is idolatry; God alone is to be feared, honored, and loved, in, above, and before all things. Worshiping/ / and serving Him alone is, briefly, the first and foremost commandment. And to love one's neighbor as oneself is equal to it. According to the words of the Lord, these two commandments comprise all that the law and the prophets preach. One may not honor, love, and fear anything besides God. Whenever one acts against the commandment of love, that other fruit emerges which was the reason for establishing the law of the curse. But the Son of God has become our salvation, granting us the freedom of the Spirit so that we willingly do that which pleases God.

2.

The second commandment: You shall not name or use the name of God in vain. No one who transgresses this commandment will be held guiltless. This guilt includes all the blasphemy of self-made, false worship of God, and all ignorant singing and praying done with the mouth but not the heart. The world is full of this.

3.

The third: You shall keep the Sabbath holy, that is, the seventh day. This is a ceremonial law, in force until the human coming of Jesus Christ, the Son of God, into the world. He is the Lord of the Sabbath of God, His heavenly Father, and He completely fulfills it. If, during an entire lifetime, even unto death, a person seeks only work for himself, and thus to find himself only in work, he does not keep the Sabbath of Jesus Christ, the Son of God. // Both those who do no work and those who stand idle also break the Sabbath. The Son of God has established, for all flesh and blood, the celebration and the obedience to death, yes, the death on the cross. Whoever seeks to save himself will find death, and whoever loses life finds life. That is the Sabbath which the children of God observe, and of which they are lords with Christ. For their flesh and blood, with all its lusts and with all its sinful works must in Christ celebrate, even unto death. This is not a reference to the physical work necessary for life; otherwise, we could not eat or drink, nor could we clothe ourselves. Whoever breaks this Sabbath is destroyed from among the people.

However, the literal celebration of the Sabbath can be good, provided it is done in freedom of the Spirit and is not bound by a law to time, state, and person. Otherwise, it is not a celebration for God nor is it done out of love for the neighbor, which is the true celebration.

Rather, one accepts the tyranny of time. But Jesus Christ has already fulfilled time, and thus, we now should rule outside of time. If we bind it to the state, we cause the kingdom of earth to rule over man when in fact, with Christ in patience,[35] // man is lord of the whole earth. If we bind it to a person, for example, to the deceased saints because of their deeds of merit, we bind life to death, for I cannot be saved by the works of someone else.[36] Only Christ, the Son of God and Son of Man, is the time, state, and person of the true celebration of the Sabbath for God, and for the neighbor, in the gloriously free love of God the Father for His own.[37] That, briefly, is the argument against those who

46r

Mt. 16 [25]

nota
Rom. 6
Celebrations
of Christians

nota

46v

Sabbath
sect
Mt. 12 [1-14]

Commands to
Christians

again want to introduce the Sabbath of the body.[38] Jesus Christ is Lord of all ceremonial commandments of both the Old and New Testaments which refer to man's material life.[39]

The new ceremonies of Christ (teaching, baptism, the Lord's Supper, foot washing, laying on of hands) are commanded by Christ, the Lord, to be a testimony and a revealing of every heart to his neighbor; these new ceremonies are to be a witness of true love in order that we all may partake of the same grace, peace, and love.

God only is the knower of hearts. But we are obligated to receive and accept one another on the basis of the Christian testimonies in the love which always believes and hopes the best. And, if someone deceives, he has deceived only himself, and not 47r those who received him believing in true love/ /. Thus far, briefly, concerning all ceremonial laws.

4.
Hutterite sect
Tob. 4 [3-5]

The fourth: You shall honor father and mother so that you may live long and prosper on earth. Whoever transgresses this commandment sins not only against God but also against nature. Therefore, it also has a promise beyond the other command- Ecclus 3 [7]
Eph. 6 [1-3] ments in the nature of a long life. In dumb animals and creatures, nature witnesses to the will and desire of God that every creature loves that which gave it birth. Therefore, God laid heavy penalty, vengeance, and condemnation on such transgressors. Whoever strikes, speaks evil of, or curses father and mother shall die and be destroyed from among the people. He is called cursed, for to curse or to scold means to maledict or speak evil of; to speak well of means to give benediction or to bless.

5. 6.
7.
8.
9. 10

The fifth: You shall not kill. The sixth: You shall not commit adultery. The seventh: You shall not steal. The eighth: You shall not give false witness against your neighbor. The ninth and tenth:

You shall in no way desire or covet the property or wife of your neighbor.

Further, whoever has intercourse with an animal is to be burned/ / and destroyed from among the people.

47v

nota
Ex. 21, 22,
Ex. 23

Following these commandments in Exodus, there are the rights and the judgments of the natural[40] statutes, which are also the commandment and prohibition of God. Through them, man's fallen state is preserved even today, be they Gentiles or Jews. This natural statute, even though it is fallen and evil,[41] nevertheless demands order. In it is expressed God's nature in natural man, but only for man's need, not for God's honor. God is a God of order and not of disorder, and He has firmly united His own omnipotence to His will and order. It is not as the predestinarians[42] and others say, without any discrimination, that God has the right[43] to all salvation and damnation. He has, certainly, but not outside of His order and will, to which His power is subordinated. Otherwise, one may claim His divine power on behalf of all[44] as, indeed, Satan and his prophets are doing. Wherever the omnipotence and might of God serves their purposes, they imperiously and indiscriminately use it, without the will of his[45] Father, as Luther does with the sacrament, child baptism, infant faith, and such like.[46] Whenever they find themselves at their wits' end, they save their theology by appealing to the omnipotence of God. There is no sharper nor more deceitful/ / article of false teaching than to use and preach the power and omnipotence of God outside of the order of God's Word.[47]

'redestinarians

as Luther does

47r

Further, it is the greatest blasphemy against God and the word of His truth, by which He has ordered all things in heaven and on earth, in which order they shall remain in eternity. For God Him-

341

self is the wisest order in and through His Word, that is, Jesus Christ His only begotten from eternity. Whoever manipulates the omnipotence of God outside of this order[48] is a deceiver and seducer. Again, whoever establishes, commands, or prohibits any order outside of the divine order and omnipotence denies God's power and glory. Thus, all the heathen have, by their own violence, become their own law and order. Thereby, they also condemn themselves, according to divine decision, without law, for they are a law to themselves in imitation of God. This imitation as their poets say, they have stolen from God. As Paul says, "Men are God's imitators."[49] Such condemnation and imitation happens as a result of their own order and law, which is outside God's order and law. The consequence is that God's wisdom and order is made into foolishness, and is despised. He who establishes, commands, or prohibits that which has not been established, commanded, or prohibited by the Word of God/ / makes God and His Word into foolishness, as if God did not know or understand, and thus, he makes himself into God. Whoever acts against any statute sins against the Lord of that statute. That is to say, God's honor is stolen, for He alone is sinned against and His place usurped. The whole papacy acts in this fashion. May God save and protect from new man-made statutes those who in our time have been set apart, through the grace of Christ, that they may not experience a new robbery (Col. 2 [20]). The serpent is no less cunning now than he was at the beginning. Indeed, according to the words of Christ: "The latter evil is worse than the former." As Paul also says: "Since we have died with Christ to all man-made statutes, why should we again allow ourselves to be caught and bound by them as though we still lived in the worldly manner of those

nota

denying
God's power

Rom. 2 [15]

Acts 17 [28]

nota

48v

papacy

newly called
evangelicals
and Anabaptists

Mt. 12 [45]

Col. 2:21

342

who say: 'Do not touch this, do not taste that, do
not handle the other'? All of these things only
contribute to man's harm; their misuse comes only
from the commandments and teaching of men.
Such things have the visage[50] and appearance of
wisdom because they do not spare the body. But
they are rooted in a self-chosen spirituality and humility, and one should pay no attention to them,
since it is clear that to do so is to fulfill the appetite
of the flesh."[51]

49r / /   Again, we are to strive for that which is
above, and not for that which is on earth, for we
have died, and our life is hidden with Christ in God.
Here, Paul includes all ethical and human statutes;
all of God's external statutes, commandments, and
prohibitions have ceased and, as Christ says, are being fulfilled and carried out in Christ and in those
who belong to Christ. Throughout the whole of the
Mt. 5, 6, 7   Sermon on the Mount, there is a joyful witness to,
and fulfillment of, the power of the Spirit in the
heart which freely gives love in Christ; we behave
toward others in love and patience, and are ready to
1 Cor. 6 [7]   surrender our own rights in favor of the neighbor
and to suffer injustice.[52] If anyone wants to sue us
for our cloak, we are to give him the coat as well. All
sin is done outside of the love of God and the
neighbor. Love is the New Testament command of
1 Tim. 1 [5]   Christ. All law, in both the Old and New Testaments, consists in love from a pure heart. For all the
vices about which the prophets, Moses, Christ, and
the apostles speak are offenses against the command to love. There is only one sin from which all
the fruit of wickedness begins, namely, disobedience to God's Word. The works of wickedness
are only the fruit and revelation of sin. And the
49v   fruits of sin which grow on the/ / evil tree are those
to which the prophets, Moses, Christ the Lord, and

343

the apostles in the Old and New Testaments witness and testify. Christ commands us to judge by the fruit, and not by the blossoms or the leaves which precede the fruit, for blossom and leaf may become good or evil. Evil fruit, when it appears, can never become good. Then the faithful are obligated to exercise judgment.

The beginning of the disobedience to God's Word consists of arrogance, presumption, pride, self-importance, boasting, and stubbornness about one's own self-will and vainglory. From these follow murderers, those who shed the blood of the innocent, mockers, blasphemers, persecutors of the truth; those who disobey parents, murderers of father and mother, liars, deceivers, and seducers; those who are envious, hateful, and hold grudges, and those who always resist the good, who tend to all wickedness; the blasphemers, those who, because of their malice, are deniers of the truth; playing, eating, drinking, whoring, backbiting, and slandering the neighbor; idolaters, servants of idols, magicians, and venerators of images. All these are delivered over to a perverted mind. They change the way of nature and, against nature, enflame themselves and others with passion, man for man, woman for woman, and for dumb animals; they are seducers of children, brawlers, quarrelers, falsely zealous rioters, rebels, creators of false sects, upon whom the sudden judgment of God will fall before long. Usury, avarice, which is the root of all idolatry, wrath, bad temper, villainy, slanderous talk, disgraceful[53] words, swearers of oaths and perjurers, all of these are the fruit of wickedness, and there can never be any hope that such fruit could become good. These all are separated from the body of Jesus Christ; so, too, are they separated from His holy, external church, by means of which

the fruit of
sin upon which
judgment belongs

Rom. 1 [22, 23]

50r

nota

such fruits are revealed. Whoever has the fellowship of Christ with such a person becomes a partaker in another's sin, shares in his evil works, and crucifies the Son of God afresh in himself. Such fruits of wickedness, which come out of the heart and not from good ground, are subject to the judgment and decision of the children of God whenever they appear in those who call themselves brothers. The believers judge everything, and are themselves judged by no man. Therefore, whatever is evil must be excluded (1 Cor. 5 [13]) from the fellowship of Christ, and not what may become so.

Mt. 15 [19]

Those, briefly, are the wicked actions which Moses also curses.// Therefore, our own wickedness should not make the sin larger than it already is; the law of the curse reveals and preaches to us in our conscience. It follows that many evil blossoms may still turn out good or evil, but do not have fruit by which one could make judgment. Similarly, there are many—all liars, dissemblers, and hypocrites—who pretend to desire to bring good fruit, but who never can bring forth good fruit. But we are forbidden to judge all such individuals before the time of the fruit. We are faithfully warned not to judge prematurely what is hidden, but to commit it to the Lord. This is especially the case with those who appeal to the Lord regarding their evil appearance. Paul commands us to avoid such people, but not to ban. These are to be left to the Lord until the revealing of the fruit, and are not to be separated from the congregation. However, in anyone who, following an evil appearance or blossom, remains arrogant and puffed up in spite of brotherly admonition and warning, good fruit will rarely be found. Pride should be dealt with by discipline and repentance; otherwise, we must wait for the time of the fruit, which will certainly come and not delay.

50v

evil blossoms which. . . .

nota

1 Cor. 4 [5]

2 Thess. 3 [6]
Tit. 2 [10]

Thess. 5 [22]

Thus, one is sure in one's judgment. Certainly, the true shepherds will not drive a patient, humble, meek, / / and loving heart any further than the chief Shepherd, Christ has driven and bound it, but will let it go out and in, find full and sufficient pasture, and be and remain victorious over all temptation in Christ Jesus. Any who act differently are false shephards, liars, and hirelings, who do not own the sheep.[54] If one does not immediately agree with their understanding and concur in their judgment, they do not spare the sheep, but, rather, strike and subject them to a false ban, as the pope does. Now, when Paul commands that one avoid any brother who walks in a disorderly fashion, he does so because of the chaos of the vices mentioned above. Furthermore, when Paul says, "Whoever does not follow the sound teaching," he is not speaking of a salvation that can be achieved by the life or deed of one single work.[55] Not that faith remains without fruit. The fruit, however, is not salvation. Rather, the sound teaching is that Jesus Christ died and rose again for our sins, and He sits at the right hand of God from whence we wait for Him to judge the living and the dead.

In all this, we are to seek that which is above, not that which is on earth. All the rest is merely the fruit of this salvation, for which we must wait until the end. Then, as already/ / indicated, the judgment will be certain and just. All creatures, without exception, were created for good; they become evil for man only because of abuse which comes from man-made rules. Therefore, Paul says such things only to warn, but not to ban and condemn. Paul commands that man's abuse be discontinued, but he does not condemn the creatures which were created for the praise of God and the benefit of man, and not for man's hurt, be they food, drink,

Jn. 10 [11]

Gloss: that for which one has criticized others, one now does oneself.
Rom. 2 [3]
2 Thess. 3 [6]
Eph. 5 [1 ff.]

1 Tim. 6 [3]

Heb. 12 [2]

Col. 3 [1]

51v
1 Tim. 4 [8]

Col. 2 [16 ff.]

1 Cor. 6 [12]
1 Cor. 10 [23]

Rom. 14 [19]
1 Cor. 8 [8]

Gal. 2 [4 f.]
Gal. 5 [7]

1 Cor. 4 [5]
52r
Rev. 3 [16]
1 Cor. 11 [32?]

nota

Mk. [7:18]

Here follow
examples of
evil semblance

Num. 11:[23]

Mt. 7 [16, 20]

clothing, silver, gold, silk, or velvet.[56] Therefore, Paul says he will not allow anyone to judge his liberty, and that all things are lawful for him. But love is always concerned with improvement. Even though all things are lawful, not all things are helpful. Thus, true love uses its liberty for improvement. Nor does true love annul liberty. Again, as Paul says, the liberty of love does not justify the rule of ignorance, to order or forbid, to judge or decide. Everything which is still neither good nor evil, and which may,[57] as already said, become either good or evil, and which occurs frequently, we should not judge or condemn before its time. Nor are we to exclude, nor spew out before their time/ /, the lukewarm and the lame. Rather, the Spirit of God must spew and cast them out through the revealing of the fruit which they finally produce. He does not say that we should cast or spew them out; He does say that He begins to cast them out and spew them out of His mouth, that is, from His kingdom and the word of His grace, that they may be known by their fruits. Thus, one is more certain in one's judgment of them. Otherwise, one usurps the office of the Holy Spirit and condemns oneself. Nothing that is external to man's heart either benefits or harms him. Only what is in the heart and comes out benefits or harms man, and whatever man uses that is external to his heart is blossom and leaf. It may become good or evil; evil fruit in the wicked, and good fruit in the good.

We have examples of those who have had evil semblances, leaves, or blossoms, and in whom all the good was hidden by the secret counsel of God, whose hand, even today, is not so shortened that it cannot help. Therefore, as already said so often, Christ has commanded us to know them by their fruits, not by the leaves or blossoms which precede the fruit. Those who/ / judge by leaves or blossoms, that is, by the appearance of evil (1 Thess. 5 [14]), presume to know God's hidden judgment, just as the Jews did with respect to Christ when He ate with sinners, did not observe food laws, healed the sick on the Sabbath, and much more. From these acts, they judged Him to be a Gentile and demon-possessed.

Then there was Judas with Magdalene (sic). When she poured the costly ointment of pure nard on Christ, Judas called it folly and pointless waste, as though it were overweening arrogance; indeed, with the world, it is pomp and arrogance. Since, however, Magdalene did it out of love for the Lord, the Lord, as the only knower of hearts, said that she had done a good work. For the love in God has power to do anything. Where there is no love, everything is lost and in vain. Had Magdalene done it in arrogance, it would have been a vice before God even if she had done it to Christ a thousand times.

There was also Judith of the city of Bethulia, which was besieged by Holophernes. She was motivated by love of the people and God. She made herself up sumptuously, which could have been interpreted as arrogance before the emergence of the fruit. Nevertheless, she did everything for/ / love of the people and with a humble heart, although the appearance or the blossoms indicated arrogance. It was from a humble heart that, using her beauty and affection, she inflamed the heart of Holophernes, came to him, ate with him, and talked to him in words of betrayal, as though she was planning to betray and surrender the city to him. From all this external show an uncertain heart would have judged, before the time of the fruit, that she was a betrayer and a conceited whore.

Moreover, there was Abraham who, because of the divine command and mystery, was prepared to offer up his son, which was a thing hidden from the understanding of all creatures, even of Abraham himself. If, before the action was carried out, an external, carnal person had seen Abraham when he, with outstretched arm, raised the knife above his son Isaac, but did not carry it out, preserved as he was by the hand of God, that carnal person would have judged Abraham to be a murderer of children, of his own flesh and blood, since it would have been indicated in the appearance or in the blossom. But he would be shown to have been a liar, and would have usurped God's secret judgment and decision. This is what always happens when one does not wait for the fruit, but judges and decides before the time.//

Saul's daughter, Michal, judged before the time when the ark of God was brought into Jerusalem. David was deeply joyful for this in the love of God and completely forgetting himself, and behaving in a manner unseemly for a king, his love and joy compelled him to dance before the ark of God. Love is stronger than wine and makes one more joyful; love is a strong drink, and makes one joyful, even in death, for love is stronger than death. All this joy constrained and drove David. But Michal was ashamed of it, and said in her heart: The king has become a vulgar fellow. She slammed the window shut, and hid her face from him because of shame. Although the blossom of the king's behavior was that of a dissolute drunk, and had the semblance of loutish immorality, rather than the moral behavior of a king, God punished her for this false judgment of her heart. She conceived no fruit from David.

In the same way, the Jews judged the apostles

braham with
Isaac
Gen. 22 [9 f.]

1 Cor. 4 [5]

53v

l's daughter
Michal
2 Kings 6
am. 6:14-16]

Cant. 8 [6]

349

The Jews judged
the apostles
Acts 2 [13]
54r

nota

1 Tim. 1 [13]

to be full of cider or wine when in fact they were full of the Holy Spirit. If the Jews had waited for the fruit in Christ/ / and the apostles, rather than to be offended by the semblance and the blossoms, they would not have sinned against the Holy Spirit. Before the coming of the fruit, they judged Christ and the apostles to be destroyers of God's commandment, ordinance, and statute, a judgment which was partly justified by the semblance of the literal law (Acts 9 [1 f.], 22 [4 f.], 26 [4 ff.]). Because of the same semblance, Paul, a man zealous for the divine law, persecuted the churches of Christ. Because of his untimely judgment, Paul refers to himself as an untimely birth. His judgment was made on the basis of semblance, leaves, and blossoms. Persecution, both spiritual and physical, still happens today because judgment is made on the basis of appearances, and not by the fruit.

The scribes and
Jews acted against
Christ

Similarly, almost throughout the whole New Testament, the learned Jews acted with hasty judgment against Christ and His own before the appearing of evil fruit. This hastiness hardened their hearts to their own destruction. All this is for each one of you to think about carefully.

Even though they had not seen the fruit of wickedness in any work of his, the friends of Job, too, judged Job to be an evildoer. They presumed to meddle with the secret counsels of God. They did so on the basis of Job's own words, who believed God to be so unfailingly just that God would not inflict harm on anyone unless he had first become guilty. Such was their basis of judgment, without the certainty of fruit. In so doing, they acted wrongly against God and Job. Therefore, the wrath of God burned against Job's friends, not because of what they said, for they spoke the truth with Job, according to the witness of Holy Scripture, but only because they meddled in the secret counsel of God without certainty about the guilt of Job. Only because of the apparent punishment of God did they take him for an evildoer; when Job was not aware of any wicked deed, they tried to persuade him to confess his wickedness to God. Thus, God's wrath will happen to all who pursue and burden consciences and hearts without a sure judgment from Rom. 15 [4] God and the fruit of wickedness. What is written is written for our instruction. From these evil appearances and blossoms have come good, just, and 1 Cor. 4 [5] noble fruits. Therefore, one may not judge prematurely, but one must let God be the Judge until the Jer. [37-39] time of the fruit. Another instance will suffice. 55r Jeremiah, the prophet of God, was condemned by / / the people as a traitor, but he only prophesied to Jerusalem what God had commanded him.

Now follows a discussion of good appearance and evil fruit.

There are many blossoms and appearances of good which conceal the most gruesome reality, as is Papists, Lutherans, Zwinglians, and false Anabaptists. true with all hypocrites and liars. By this means, the enemy of truth robs us of the sanctuary;[58] in fact, they have robbed and stolen almost everything. Indeed, the lying dissemblers nowadays do everything so much like the true children of God that true and pious hearts, even if they have all the evidence of good fruit, can only with great difficulty nota be clearly recognized. Thus, by false appearances, the enemy does his work in his own. He suffers the cross, talks about Christ and His kingdom with a concealed mixture of lies, and endures much according to the external semblance. Inside, however, his heart is full of envy, anger, and hate. He also does great deeds of love, but with a dissembling Kiss of Judas heart and a disguised disposition, just as Judas did when he kissed Christ.[59]

351

Thus, every sacred thing is surrendered to the enemy. So, too, did it happen in the time of Antiochus[60] and // Nebuchadnezzar, who robbed the vessels of the temple, stole them for their idols, and used them in all ways as the people of God did. So, too, it happens now in the revealing of the kingdom of Antichrist, which is the fulfillment of the kingdom of Babylon and Antichrist. With all the lying power of wickedness, they portray the sanctuary of truthful hearts, which is the true temple of God, but the appearance of the Son of God, who will reveal everything that is hidden, whether good or evil, will reveal this to be a semblance of truth. Until that time, the life of the truthful is hidden among the hypocrites with Christ in God. They are hidden, not because the fruit of light in the truthful cannot show itself on account of the darkness of the dissembling hearts, but because we have no sure knowledge of who are the righteous, whose light shines warmly because of the light of faith; the lying dissembler acts in the same way until God takes away the power of the enemy. Since now the enemy still has the power to put on a show of good fruit, which is the basis of judgment, the elect can only examine and accept wherever the good appears and // no evil fruit appears, and leave the choice of election to God, who alone knows the hearts.

Gospel of the Creatures

The gospel of the creatures is that the gospel may be preached through discerning the nature of the divine creation by which the Creator is known. Carnal reason, however, has no right to use the witness of the creatures of the gospel; reason errs in its use, an error which has beset all the philosophers in this world. Paul warns us (Col. 2 [4]) not to become

Margin notes:

Antiochus
55v

Kingdom of
Antichrist
2 Thess. 2 [3-12]

1 Cor. 3 [17]

2 Cor. 6 [16]

Mt. 5 [16]
nota

56r

Col. 1 [15 ff., 23]

Philosophers

Col. 2 [8]

their prey. But carnal man, who as yet has no understanding of the law of God, must first, by means of the creatures, be led into a knowledge of God; Christ the Lord talked to the people about the

t. 13 [2-52]
Cor. 2 [14]

kingdom of God by means of many parables of nature. Paul also had to use nature to introduce the Gentiles to the gospel, for natural, carnal man knows nothing of God. For him, the creation of God is a true gospel only until such time as he knows

Jn. 14 [7]

God the Father in the Son, the Lord Jesus Christ, and the Son in the Father. According to the flesh, the Son is a creature of all creatures, since all things

56v

exist for Him. All these things will be fully known beyond this time. For this reason, we all / / have to

Cor. 13 [12]

remain, and work, in partiality and fragmentation until completeness comes, since, as Paul says, all

Cor. 8 [2]
om. 12 [17]

our knowledge is only fragmentary. Paul further says that, if anyone thinks he knows, he does not yet know what he ought to know. But there is nothing lacking in the Spirit. Our schism has sprung only out of the weakness and ignorance of our con-

nota

sciences and understanding. If, by acknowledging ignorance on my part, I could liberate your understanding so that, according to the measure of God's grace, for your sake and mine, an exposition of the gospel of the creatures might bring us together and find each other in our hearts with God in Christ Jesus our Lord, I would gladly do so. It is my earnest prayer to you that you will patiently read, and consider with care, the following parables in Christ. I may be more concerned about you than you are about me.

Christ Jesus the Lord, our Savior, because He

Parable of
the
physician

supernaturally healed natural man, shows nature to be a true physician of body and soul. Since He has helped natural man, Nature also shows that He was

Mt. 9 [12]

able to help the sick. For he who is well, says the

Lord, needs no physician. Thus, I will present Christ Jesus,/ / my healer.

Does not a physician who undertakes to heal someone command those who care for him to have patience with his illness? He does not, however, command them to become ill as well; otherwise, one ill person would poorly serve the other. Thus, it is always the strong who is the servant of him who is ill, in order that his illness may be cured and his weakness become strong while there is breath left in him.

No one buries someone who is still alive, nor does he expel from the house someone in the last stage of illness. Rather, one waits with patience and endurance for him to get better. Nor does one give him strong food which would only make him become weaker. For this reason, Paul commands that overseers and bishops be chosen who will uphold the weak and bear with the wicked. Therefore, I desire to be patient with all who are bought with the costly pearl, the death and shed blood of the Lord Jesus Christ, since God requires patience and long-suffering from us through Christ. I am not speaking here of those who have died a living death, who have separated themselves from Christ, as shown earlier, because of open wickedness, and who have died before death.[62] In such as these, one cannot hope for life, for they have died twice. As both Peter and Paul say, the witness of life in God is to confess Christ in the truth, and to mourn and sorrow for sin.

Wherever this breath of life is found and whenever it is approached with the Word of truth, one is to wait either for death, or for recovery of life, but one is not to thrust others out of the house of God too quickly, to bury them alive and foreshorten life. The true servants of God do not do this, but

2 Tim. 2 [24]

Gloss: It has
not turned out
that way,
although it is
true and ought
to be thus.[61]

Jude [12]

2 Pet. 2 [20]
2 Tim. 3 [?]

Gloss: Paul
says: you
teach others
but not yourself,
Rom. 2 [21-23]

nota

those do who begin to beat their fellow servants, bite one another, and thereby consume one another. Those who deny the kingdom of God in every little matter, regard the precious blood of the Lord Jesus Christ as though it were for sale on the market; they are like those who blaspheme the Son of God and, because of their coarse wickedness, crucify Him again in themselves. One is the same as the other. It is no small matter to burden someone else's conscience and heart. No creature in heaven or on earth can comfort such a one except the Son of God. It costs too much, says David, to redeem one's brother. In eternity, one cannot accomplish it.

I testify before my God, through the Lord Jesus Christ, that whoever charges with sin and burdens the conscience where there is no sin, he accuses // the innocent blood of the Lord Jesus Christ, through which all of us are bought and released from all sin. He makes sin where there is none, which is equivalent to charging someone with murder when in fact he is innocent. And if he thus accused another, he would be guilty of that other's life and innocent death. Much graver is the murder of conscience and soul, both of which belong to God alone. Whoever murders, wounds, and burdens an innocent conscience with his own commands and prohibitions, outside of God's commandment and prohibition, robs God of His honor, murders souls, and tramples the Son of God with his feet. He derides and makes a mockery of the sacrifice of Jesus Christ, with which he is bought.

May God preserve me and every pious heart from participating in a judgment whereby, on the basis of one's own commandment, one accuses an innocent conscience of sin where there is no sin. I know and believe about all of you that you would not take the whole world as payment for sitting in judgment on a known murderer, who in any case deserved death; I also, God willing, would never so participate. But it is far greater and more terrible to

nota

58v

judge those things relating to eternal life, for life and death, eternal salvation and damnation, are at stake. / / Whoever regards this matter as trivial and simple has no authority, nor does he know what the judgment of the saints is. Such a one sits in judgment to his own condemnation. Even the world

no judgment on hearsay

does not judge anyone on the basis of hearsay, suspicion, or appearance, but only on the words of the

Mt. 18 [16]

accused and of reliable witnesses. Christ also commands His own that all testimony must be substantiated by two or three witnesses. Only when evi-

2 Cor. 13 [1]
Gloss: It should be! But where?

dence has been presented before the church, and he will not hear, does the judgment begin with tribulation, anxiety, sorrow. The other members of the body of Christ experience great pain and suffering for at stake is a member of the body of Christ the Lord. They must lose a member in order that the other members, who are well, are not hurt and the whole body destroyed,[63] be it eye, foot, or hand. It

healthy members
Mt. 5 [29 f.]

should be pulled out or cut off according to the commandment of Christ, our Head: "If your eye offends you, or your hand, or foot," etc. The other members of the body of Christ will not be able to do this without great pain and tribulation. If the member is honorable and useful to the body, the

parable

tribulation is so much greater. It cannot possibly happen easily or simply. The natural body cannot

59r

lose a member without / / pain. Nor does it immediately cut it off, even if it is failing and weak; rather it uses all kinds of medicines. As long as it is not dead and is only painful, the body bears it with patience and long-suffering, and delays the penalty

nota

to allow for improvement. If, however, it allows the body no rest, nor does it improve by means of any

Gloss: Every church boasts about this authority

medicine from the Lord Jesus Christ, through suffering and pain, it must be cut off in order that the other members of the body of Christ remain healthy in the fear and love of God and the neighbor, to whom alone the judgment to retain and to forgive sin has been committed (Mt. 16 [19]; 18 [15-19]; John 20 [23]).

Gloss: Neither the Hutterites, the Swiss, nor others believe this.

2 Cor. 12 [5] especially if one acts with such violence, rough-ness, angry spirit, and hurry. Nor is it the true weakness.

59v

My fervent prayer to God and my hope is that no truthful heart should be excluded from the true members of Christ. Indeed it does not happen. My conscience also bears me witness that I am grafted into the body of Christ and, even though I am weak, I hope that God's power and strength will be revealed in my weakness. For I can boast of nothing but my weakness. God must have mercy on our destitution and poverty. By virtue of this poverty, God's glory and // riches are revealed in us through Christ Jesus. So, too, is it revealed in our folly, for, through Him, we become wise. Amen.

Oh, my dear brothers, if our hearts and consciences could only meet on the above-mentioned matter! This is my concern about you. I would hope that, through the grace of God, we would soon be united on the other matters. I am concerned only for you for, as I said earlier, I am more concerned about you than you are about me. God knows my heart, and He will judge it. I pray God to give you and me hearts open to one another

Jn. 17 [3]

so that in Christ Jesus, true Son of God and Man and in whom all knowledge consists, we will recognize each other and be recognized by Jesus Christ. For this is eternal life, that they know you, Father, the true God, and Jesus Christ whom you have sent. May God the Father grant this knowledge to all who desire it through His Jesus Christ. Amen.

Scripture in three ways

Finally, in conclusion, I find that Christ, Moses, the prophets, and the apostles used divine

357

1.

Heb. 6 [1-3]

and biblical Scriptures in three ways. First, for teaching. What is used when one knows nothing of the witness of God and His Word is called teaching by all. The letter to the Hebrews mentions not repeating again those matters belonging to the beginnings of Christian life. If one is ignorant of something, the Scripture serves as guide and teacher.

2.

Second, Scripture is used for admonition and warning to him who is already taught. This is the second function of Scripture, and it is especially important where an evil appearance, the leaves or blossoms which precede the fruit, leads to care or fear that there may in time not be good fruit. But from that no certain judgment of good or evil is possible. That function of Scripture, which is warn-

Deuteronomy

ing and admonition, belongs here. The fifth book of Moses is almost all of this kind. That is why it is called the book of repetition, or in Latin Deuteronomium.[64] The same is true of the admonition and warning of the apostles to the churches throughout the New Testament.

3.

Third, there are commandments and prohibitions. All the writings that announce punishment, the wrath of God and eternal damnation are directed at the transgression of commandments and

60v

prohibitions. Such punitive writings are at times / / used in the hope of repentance. In such punishment

2 Cor. 2 [6-8]

comfort is also offered in order that one does not sink into too much sorrow. But in case of apostasy and denial, they even deliver the sinner to the devil,

1 Tim. 1 [20]
1 Cor. 5 [3-5]

denying him eternal life, as Paul did when he delivered several to the devil in body and soul.

Whoever does not use Holy Scripture with these three differences in mind cannot, with any certainty, handle Holy Scripture. Especially where the Holy Spirit, the true teacher, does not precede in all knowledge of Christ, everything will be misused and wrong when one tries to admonish, where one has not yet learned, or to punish, where there is no certainty of sin, or to make sin, where there is no commandment. All that brings error. Some admonition, advice, and order is certainly used to further godliness and the improvement of the body of Christ. And even if one sins in doing so, certainly one does not punish by banning, but one is patient again and again in hope of improvement.

Testimony of My Understanding of Divine Scripture

Lk. 14 [33]
61r
Cor. 10 [24]

1 Cor. 13 [5]

Mt. 20 [20]

Lk. 18 [28]

. 20 [20-28]

Phil. 2 [19]

The Lord Jesus Christ says: "Whoever does not deny everything he has is not worthy of me." Paul / / also says that no one should seek his own but only that which is good for others. The command of Christ and the apostle, that the true spirit of love never seeks its own, but always that which is of service and of use to others, is a pointed one. Nevertheless, Paul, Christ, and the apostles exercised much patience, as they did, for example, when the mother of the two sons of Zebedee asked that one son sit to the left and the other to the right in the kingdom of Christ; or when Peter asked the Lord what he would get for leaving all for His sake; or when Christ was asked who would be greatest after His departure. There are many similar examples during the time of Christ and the apostles. Paul also wrote to the Philippians, and said that he hoped to send Timothy to them soon, since he had no one who was so much of his mind as Timothy; the others were all self-seekers. But nowhere do we find that Christ or Paul banned or excluded the others from the fellowship of Christ on that ac-

Gloss: This ilgram now es as usury miserliness.

count, even though the true and perfect spirit of the love of God utterly condemns all self-seeking. Nevertheless, Christ and the apostles waited with patience and long-suffering for improvement, and did not judge before the time of the fruits,/ / which take the form of the open vices already mentioned. Thus, in the case of Christ and Judas, and Paul and the fornicator and others, they were delivered to the devil only after the bearing of the fruit (1 Tim. 1 [20]). They were not excluded and banned for minor reasons, even though they were not living in perfect love, as were John with Christ and Timothy with Paul.

61v
1 Cor. 4 [5]
Mt. 26 [23 f.]

1 Cor. 5 [1-5]

nota

The others were borne in patience, because of their gifts of the Holy Spirit. The foot is not as honorable a member as the eye; it becomes much dirtier in the mud than the eye, but the eye watches the foot, and the foot bears the eye. Therefore, one does not say to the other: "You are not a member of the body." It is my fervent prayer that for the sake of Christ, you get your judgments from Christ, and learn long-suffering, forebearance, and meekness from Him. And may the merciful Father forgive me my failures and shortcomings which, through Christ, I daily find in myself, and I also pray for all others who, like me, desire forgiveness. My greatest contention in my conscience with you is that nowhere do I find such precipitate, superficial judgments and verdicts on every little matter in Christ and His apostolic church / / as I find with you. Even if one has thoughtlessly offended God the Father, the highest good, the costly treasure of the death and shed blood is, nevertheless, a reconciliation and an action of the mercy of the Father. Mercy triumphs over judgment. All your precipitate actions make me feel somewhat distant from you; in my conscience I am not sure that I should have any

Rom. 12 [4]
1 Cor. 12 [14-20]

nota

contention

62r

Jas. 2 [13]

Gloss: The same is true in reverse

nota
part or fellowship in such hasty judgments and verdicts.

overseers
There are also very few overseers among you. They have been excluded from you and your gatherings at least once, if not twice. Since God does not repent of His gifts, I do not find in the church of Christ that anyone, having once received the Holy Spirit for the service of the apostolate or the episcopate has ever been excluded from the fellowship of Christ. Therefore, something must be wrong either with your fellowship or with your overseers and, since you are yourselves uncertain about your overseers, it is something that a weak heart like mine, and like those with me, cannot simply ignore.[65] You seem to say that, while these overseers need the discipline and restraint of young children, they yet should be elders in the maturity of Christ, that is, in the understanding of Christ, and feed the flock of God. It is not a question of maturity with Christ according to years, but according to understanding. That the flock should punish the shepherd is always against the Spirit of Christ. The shepherd is to feed the flock. Thus, the younger do not gather treasure for the old, but the old for the young.

Gloss: The ame is true everse and :h disorder.

62v
1 Pet. 5 [2]

Cor. 12 [14]

I have written to you in the hope that God, through His Child Jesus Christ, will grant us the ability to recognize one another in Christ Jesus with a clean conscience. For all schism, discord, and uncertain consciences come, in part, from one's own understanding, flesh, and blood, which mixes itself into the knowledge of God. Every moment, I am conscious of this in myself, for division does not come from the Spirit of Christ. May the Lord Jesus Christ save us from all evil. Amen. I desire the grace of our Lord Jesus Christ to be given to all who long for it. Amen.　　　Pilgram Marpeck

God be gracious to him.

361

3

Another Letter to the Swiss Brethren (1543)

Introduction

This letter is a sequel to Judgment and Decision (#8), and deals more directly with the issue of schism in the church. Marpeck enumerates three causes of schism, but the text itself makes clear that it is the last of the three that afflicts the Swiss, who have once believed, but who have fallen asleep and have grown so careless that the enemy has come in and caused confusion. He insists that they have given him no just cause why they do not consider him and his group a true church. For his part, he refuses to regard them as a true church; he has clearly told them that he does not so regard them because of their "unjustified censoriousness and use of the ban."

Here, the glosses by Rothenfelder are as critical as those in the previous letter. In fact, one could gather from their tone that he was one of the group criticized. He was a member of the Swiss Brethren fellowship and, although he was always in tension with them, he nevertheless seems to have had considerable sympathy for them as well. Unless some new sources are uncovered, the confusion and uncertainty surrounding these glosses will persist. Perhaps Rothenfelder had come to have sentiments not unlike those found in the last statement of Hans Denck, which reflects a disillusionment with the controversy and disagreements of the Reformation era. Or perhaps Rothenfelder wished to offer, on behalf of the Swiss Brethren, a response to some of Marpeck's more severe censures.

The Text

Another letter sent to those called the Swiss Brethren 1543

To the beloved, by virtue of their zeal for God in Appenzell, and wherever they gather, and especially in reply to Uli Scherer[1] and Jörg Maler.

Our fervent desire and prayer for you, and us all, is the pure and true knowledge of Christ. Amen.

Beloved, we write to you again, because of the zeal you have for God and because of the good we hope for in you, which we expect you also hope for in us, to see whether the mercy of God is sufficient for a true unification and fellowship in Christ. May God the Father give and grant us this through His Jesus Christ. Amen.

We have heard from you that you have a serious grievance against us and you consider it unjust that even now we do not regard nor acknowledge you correctly understood as a congregation of God in Christ. It is our hope that, if you will carefully consider these our reasons, you will not bear us ill will, but rather you will praise and thank God for the revelation of His understanding, since eternal life consists alone in the knowledge of God the Father and His / / Christ. Therefore, beloved, accept these reasons diligently and honestly, with humility of heart, and do not slanderously despise them, which only leads to your own bitterness. Remember what injury the enemy may inflict on you and us. No small loss has come to you because, through slandering us, you have become embittered and resentful. Thereby the enemy of truth has prevented you from believing and from being concerned about this so that you are now close to destruction.[2] May God preserve you from this. Amen.

A schism has three causes. The first is the

Jn. 14 [7]

63v

dissembling and hypocrisy of the lying, false prophets who desire that the church and truth of Christ never have unity and fellowship. In them there is no hope of unity nor will the churches of Christ ever desire to unite with such false prophets and churches. Work expended on them is in vain and to no avail.

The second reason is lack of understanding: ignorant, angry, hasty zeal for old customs, for blood relatives, for fellowship based on natural love, for one's own teaching, knowledge, and understanding, which loves to puff itself up and / / which causes communal strife before it has come to self-knowledge. With such characteristics of the flesh nearly all men are burdened. Still the law and fear of God is by nature written on their unclean hearts. Because of this, but still not washed from sin, they accept faith in Christ in baptism, discipline,[3] and the Supper without the accompanying work of the Holy Spirit, presuming in ignorant zeal to be teachers before they have become disciples of Christ. Such persons bring schism into the church of Christ. Nor may they be called a church of God in Christ. But one may be zealous and work for them with hope until they are brought to true understanding. That, briefly, is the second reason of all schism.

The third reason is that men go to sleep in the faith and become careless, even though in baptism they have been washed from sin through the blood of Christ in the Holy Spirit. Since our enemy never sleeps in order to devastate us, they soon fall from the bulwark of faith and true knowledge when they are tempted. If the true believers do not then wake up, especially the watchmen of the people who should give guidance, they misdirect the people / / as well as themselves. They do it in ignorance,

64r

Gloss: Thus
those in Asia
and Corinth
also were not
churches in
Christ

64v

which God brings upon us because of our carelessness. Thus, schism follows in order that the godly
and faithful ones may be revealed. They are the
ones who have remained alert through admonition,
who arouse those who sleep, who direct the sick to
Christ the Physician and portray Him to them in
order that they may come to true knowledge. They
spend their time where God has not in grace sent
someone so that the people to whom they are sent
may not remain in the error of their ignorance
without being admonished. For ignorance is not innocent before God; for, where there is no one,
whom God alone gives and sends with the truth, to
warn, admonish, teach, and preach, there is no
grace, and the wrath of God remains on these as
well as on those who do not believe the truth. We
write this in order that you clearly perceive it and
that you may open your hearts to God, which we
will also properly do with you, otherwise there is
nothing but deception and hypocrisy. Then God
will give us His grace for true union. Amen.

For such zeal without knowledge limits itself of
fellowship and robs itself / / of profit. Even if men
were to regard such zealous people as a congregation, God would not so regard them. For we are
unable to participate with you in the fellowship of
the body and blood of Christ (which all true Christians have eternally in faith and love) when it is
done in impure fear and ignorant zeal—as indeed
you have not participated with us, and still may not
do so, because of a seared conscience. False, unjust
judgments and verdicts follow from such impure
fear, and Christ the Lord denies to His own the
rights to these judgments and verdicts. He warns
them not to judge and condemn in order that they
be not judged and condemned. The Lord does not
forbid just judgments in this present life, and these

65r

nota

Mt. 7 [1 f.]

365

the true believers are commanded to make in the Holy Spirit, since the spiritual man judges all things and is himself judged by no one. But the Lord prohibits judgments made falsely and in ignorance, for thereby one judges and condemns oneself. For wherein one judges another and thereby himself becomes guilty, he judges and condemns himself.

Therefore, dear friends, we must properly wake up and exercise the judgments and ways of God with trembling and fear in just and true knowledge. / / "Judge with right judgment," says the Lord. For, where judgment is perverted, all of God's action, bodily and spiritually, is suspended. Wherever the spirit of justice and truth does not rule in carnal[4] unbelievers (that is: where earthly government is concerned; this is why true believers pray for human government, that God may give it the spirit of true understanding to judge justly), there also just carnal judgments are not possible. How much less in spiritual judgments, which human reason can never reach without the Holy Spirit of Christ who forgives and retains sin, and which are concerned with the eternal and not with the temporal realm. For, says Paul, whoever does not have this Holy Spirit of Christ according to the measure of faith does not belong to Christ. And John says: "Whoever does not abide in the teaching of Christ has no God." For this reason we could not and cannot regard you as a church of Christ, for you have no just accusation against us to which your own conscience will testify. Paul also regarded the Galatians thus (until, with great anxiety, he had given birth to them a second time in the image of Christ). Foolishly and without justification, you also have continued to regard us as not being a church of Christ. Thus, neither of us regards the other as / / a church of Christ. We are much more justified in

65v

Jn. 7 [24]
Glodd: it
follows that
it was sus-
pended for
the Romans, too.
But Paul does not
do that.

Rom. 14 [3 f., 10, 13]

Rom. 8 [9]

2 Jn. [9]

Gal. 4 [19]

66r

Gloss: God
knows who
is innocent

making this accusation of you than you of us, since you have no justification for not regarding us as a church of Christ. Rather, you should look to yourselves, since you have not yet shown us a fault which our conscience confirms. Nevertheless, we do not thereby regard ourselves as justified before God, but only through His grace. But, because of your unjustified censoriousness and use of the ban, we have until the present justifiably denied you fellowship with us in Christ.

Not consider
a church of
Christ

This, then, is your case against us, the reason why you do not consider us a church of Christ: because we exercise the freedom, which we have in Christ, too much, contrary to His Word. If you would prove this to us with a concrete case so that our consciences could be certain, we would gladly accept your not recognizing us as a Christian church. For, it is certainly true that the proper and true fellowship of the body and blood of Christ is unity, and unity in the Holy Spirit is true fellowship. For, there can be no rift in the body of Christ

Eph. 4 [5 f.]

since there is only one faith, one Lord, one Spirit, one God and Father of us all. And this fellowship is without exception, baptized with one Spirit, with water, into one unsundered, undivided body with

67v⁵

united members. / /

Therefore, once more our admonition to you who are guilty (we recognize here that all innocent consciences are excepted and we hold them blameless as always) is that, since you are guilty, bear, in the patience of Christ, the charge of this article, namely, that we did not and do not consider you a church of Christ. Let not your hearts complain against us any longer when you correctly recognize the causes. Cast away your own honor, which cannot stand before God, and tread it into the mud! We continue to hope that you will no longer bear us ill

367

will, but that you will rather praise and thank God with us for His grace and revelation. May you pray that knowledge of Him may be revealed to His honor and praise, and pray also for our need of salvation. May He give us, together with you, the teaching of His Holy Spirit for true knowledge of Him, in which knowledge alone eternal life consists. May we achieve this through God alone. Amen.

Concerning your understanding of the oath on which we have sufficient clarity from you, we cannot bind anyone's conscience nor put a rope around anyone's neck, nor are we able to submit our consciences to your understanding.[6]

4

To Caspar Schwenckfeld (1544)

Introduction

In 1542 Marpeck produced a book on baptism[1] which also came into the hands of Caspar Schwenckfeld.[2] Schwenckfeld was requested by some of his followers to write a reply, which he did.[3] His rebuttal occasioned an exchange of letters between the two men. However, Marpeck's original letter is missing. Schwenckfeld's reply is extant,[4] and it is perhaps to this letter that Marpeck now replies.

The letter accompanied Marpeck's reply to the first half of the *Judicium*.[5] The second half followed years later, to all of which Schwenckfeld did not see fit to reply.

In this letter Marpeck chides Schwenckfeld for lack of that simplicity which Christ said was necessary to receive God's revelation. If Schwenckfeld had it, he would certainly have understood Marpeck. Marpeck evidently knew of Schwenckfeld's view that the Anabaptists were not intellectually capable of convincingly presenting their case.[6]

Here, as elsewhere, Marpeck acknowledges both his fallibility and his readiness to continue the discussion.

The Text

To Caspar Schwenckfeld, 1544[7]

Dear Schwenckfeld: I pray and hope that God through Jesus Christ may grant you understanding of yourself. Self-understanding must precede all other understanding; without it, all other understanding or knowledge is useless and in vain. Also, no true understanding can result, continue, or endure if the scrutinizing and understanding of oneself does not come first. This understanding may be highly developed by knowledge of Scripture and by reason, either your own or another's, but still it will be darkened and blinded by one's own fabricated carnal wisdom, reason, and self-selected spirituality. It will be perverted, and mixed with dishonesty, craftiness, and deceit. Therefore, it will come to shame before God and man. In such a manner, God captures the wisdom of the wise in their treachery; He entrusts His truth to the faithful and truly innocent ones, but conceals it from the highly learned, wise, sly, and obstinately independent ones. He reveals it to the simple, uneducated, coarse, faithful people, who witness to the truth with poor, coarse, simple words and speech, and feel compelled to speak against such *sophists*. When these *sophists* so readily change the truth, inverting the first and the last, how disorderly it frequently becomes. Such wisdom, even today, considers Christ to be an uneducated carpenter's son, on the basis of an artful knowledge of Scripture (p. 56), and with great skill, language, and reason human wisdom itself composed such a lofty Christ. Consequently, the simple people could never understand, comprehend, or attain the true simplicity of faith when confronted by such language, skill, and sophistication.

Thus, such wisdom, with its artistry and mastery, presents itself to the Holy Spirit, as if the Holy Spirit could not instruct anyone except through artistry and wisdom, even though He is a teacher of all truth to all faithful and truly single hearts. Only by means of the Word of truth does the Holy Spirit generate faith, even in all truly believing hearts, no matter how foolish and contemptible they may often seem to man. By faithfulness and true means such believing hearts become a stumbling block to the pedants.

Such wise men cannot understand the language of the simple ones and consequently, consider them as nothing. Thus, they find reasons to despise and ridicule the truth; they pervert the speech, writing, teaching, and words of the simple, interpret

370

it unfaithfully, bend and twist it, as they please, according to their intelligence and skill.

Because of their sophistry, their evil and scheming hearts are then seized by God and made manifest, and they are disgraced before men. Just as God has always begun so will God conclude: with the faithful and simple people. Thus, He will save man by means of true language and teaching. All the more so, because the world in these last days is becoming increasingly more crafty and more cunning, more scribal and more evil. Therefore, God also conceals His true, unadulterated, pure understanding of salvation behind so much deeper, truer simplicity, and brings about the realization of faith in Christ in the simple hearts. I speak here, not of the carnal, but of the true and faithful simplicity, which God uses to blind the eyes of the carnal and worldly-wise, and conceals the divine wisdom. Thus, along with their skill and reason, such carnal, wise men drown in the lowest folly, as they consider it. Even if it were in the small amount of water of baptism, they go under. Just as in the case of the first Flood, they must be disgraced and damned.

Since His resurrection and ascension, the Lord has arrayed Himself against all of man's own intelligence of unbelief (Ps. 29), and sits at the right hand of the Father. From there, He will eventually judge the living and dead, instigate another flood and condemn the world by it. The world was condemned by the first flood, and the counterpart of this first flood has been retained in our time. Even today, in the water of Christ's baptism, all wisdom of the flesh must go under, either to attain grace through Christ, or to suffer the judgment of eternal ruin.

Therefore, to learn the language of the simple, faithful, truly believing hearts is now, in these last dangerous times, when the fullness of the Gentiles has come in, a thousand times more necessary and useful than (p. 57) to learn Latin, Greek, Hebrew, or other languages. Yes, with faithful and humble hearts, the scribes, sages, and highly esteemed men should study this faithful, simple, and honest speech, see what it means, and see how it is to be understood. In this manner, one learns to understand more fully the speech and art of divine wisdom, and surpasses all

371

that the books, skills, and languages of the world have ever been able to hold. I do not suggest that, therefore, we are to reject the Holy Scripture and the gifts of God with which God embellishes nature and endows the man He has created. These gifts, be they languages or other natural skills, are commendable. Such talents should, however, be planted and grown in the true humility of Christ so that, through such true simplicity through God's grace, the learned and the simple people could thereby not only understand each other better, but also better understand divine art and wisdom. Then, even today, no one would become so learned that he would reject such a teacher as the twelve-year-old child, Jesus, who even now teaches in the temple, the hearts of the faithful.

Indeed, even today, God will reveal His art and wisdom only through His Holy Spirit. No matter how highly one's knowledge of Scripture may praise Christ and His Holy Spirit, and if one dares to be a master over the true simplicity of Christ, such mastery will not succeed when they pervert the words of Christ, uttered from the mouths of the simple, and when they interpret these words, according to their kind of skill, in the worst possible way. Even then, they are not satisfied, for they accuse the simple of untruthfulness as well. That is the distinctive manner of the serpent, which constantly desires to achieve its fame at the expense of the true simplicity of Christ. From such serpentine species, the wisdom of Christ and the rule and effect of His Holy Spirit will probably remain concealed eternally. Let such species praise and write as highly of it as they will, they must still be disgraced under the feet of Christ, that is, under the true simplicity of faith. I sincerely hope that you, dear Schwenckfeld, may be freed from such a disgrace, that you will not deceive yourself so badly, together with others, and that, looking after yourself better, you will not fall even deeper into temptation.

However, since you do believe that you are something (Gal. 2:2), you are being deceived in your own mind. I sincerely wish that you might perceive it in yourself; were you to recognize it, you could boast first for yourself, and then boast of the Lord (2

372

Cor. 10:18). I should never have thought it possible that you would first write behind my back, and then accuse me to such an extent without having asked or investigated anything. You have previously discussed so many matters of faith (p. 58) with me, and yet you attribute such things to me, and particularly after my faithful warning and apology, which I sent to you from Ulm in my first writing.[8] However, because you continuously add more untruthful accusations against me, and because you have composed and widely distributed an entire book of accusations against me and have deduced thirty-eight articles from it, which supposedly indicate my beliefs about Christ my Lord, I am attacked by many. Therefore, I am forced to defend myself, even though they already have the confession of my faith according to true sources. You accuse me of untruthfulness, and give evidence for it which I truly do not like to answer. I am sorry for you. I must, however, make an answer, for you have despised my faithful appeal, made to you in my first writing, and it has had no response from you or the others. Thus, I have been forced to justify my simplicity with the truth, but I must do it in accordance with your writing, and toward that person to whom you and Valentin Icelsamer[9] [Valentin Ickelsamer] have written behind my back. Moreover, you have also composed the thirty-eight articles. Furthermore, as if the first untruthful defamation was not enough for you, you have produced even more with your skill and wisdom. I will commend that to God in His judgment, where you will truly find it hard to justify yourself.

If, however, it be God's will, and if you desired as much, you would confess your treachery here, and it might be forgiven you. I, too, heartily desire forgiveness for those times when, for His sake, I did too much against you or others. Insofar as I am unaware of many of my faults, I hope that He might let me realize this excess, and that I might confess it before God and man. Then, through Christ, I might be forgiven. Without this awareness and forgiveness, I do not want to justify myself before God. If you can show me that I falsely accuse you of something, either in this matter or in some other, you and others shall find my heart and mouth, by the grace of God, open to confess and

373

apologize, because we are all fallible and deficient persons.

However, I am not aware of having done you any injury in my whole life. Rather, I have wished you every good thing, and still do. But, if you feel that you would like to continue to press your accusations against me, I will gladly, as I have previously done, concede to you before the world. Indeed, if you wrote the whole world full of books against me and against the truth, I will give no other answer, as far as my conscience gives witness, than to say that what was not true then is not true now. That is the highest joy for me and for all innocent persons, and our justification before God and His judgment.

At the same time, I feel truly sorry for you, and I am also sorry that I have to speak at such length in my defense for the sake of truth, which has been entrusted to me by God, and which is abused and (p. 59) made suspect with such accusations. I am obligated to witness to this truth. No matter how poorly I witness to it, I still know myself to be innocent of your accusation, contained in the many articles; with regard to the others, I say sincerely that you are missing the point.

Herewith, I send you a reply to half of your *Judicium*. In time you shall also receive the other half, if God allows it in His grace and if He should grant you so much grace. I would wish with my whole heart that you might see yourself in it, and also see what kind of shape Christ, whom you profess, has in you. Then, you might see that we are not as fearful of your writing as you believe when you suggest that we do not allow it to appear before our congregation, and thus bar the good-hearted from knowing the truth. You say that we teach in a false way and that you teach in the right way, in Christ. You sharply accuse us, and claim that we do not let our congregation hear anyone but us, for which reason you claim we set aside the freedom of Christ. It can easily be ascertained whether this accusation is true or not.

We are willing to tolerate him who desires a defense of our hope, and we are willing to offer it to him. Anyone who will more fully instruct us, by the witness of truth of the holy, undivided biblical Scripture, will find us open, this being God's will. Nor will we bar or refuse him. Similarly, as this answer to the first part of your *Judicium* testifies, we have shown ourselves to be open to you. God grant that you will publish it unaltered, and that you will publish it as widely as you published the other one, which was almost entirely perverted with dishonest accusations and additions.

We write in order that you may see yourself, together with those who accepted your writing against our truthful witness, and learn to know yourself a little. Where this is not the case, we desire no answer from you, either to this letter or to the previous one. We also shall not give you any further answer, if all of it cannot be valid for you and if you desire only to grasp it in a perverted way in order to cause dispute, and to create schisms and strife among the righteous, contrary to the right way and truth in Christ. Further, we do not desire to test God our Lord with the intrigues, pretenses, plots, and evil deeds in which you find yourselves caught up, but we commend all to His judgment. He will judge those who are outside of the truth. May the will of God be done to you and all of us according to His great mercy. Amen.

[10]Datum New Year's Eve in the year of our Lord Jesus Christ 1544.

A co-witness to the truth and companion in the suffering which is in Christ.

Pilgram Marpeck

5

To Helena von Streicher
(ca.1544)

Introduction

Helena von Streicher was the knowledgeable widow of an Ulm shopkeeper. She and her family were members of the Schwenckfeld conventicle in that city.

It is not clear who initiated the correspondence, but this letter suggests that several exchanges were involved. The correspondence reflects the issues that separated Marpeck and Schwenckfeld in the 1540s. Evidently, Helena von Streicher had faithfully reflected Schwenckfeld's concerns in her letters.

The chief issue was perhaps that Marpeck emphasized the lowliness of Christ and Schwenckfeld His glory. Again, Marpeck's emphasis on the church as the presence of Christ in the world was quite contrary to Schwenckfeld's view of Christ's spiritual presence.

The Text
To Helena von Streicher[2]

Pilgram Marpeck's reply to Mrs. Helena Streicher: If she says that Christ's Word and teaching are Spirit and life, and that, for this reason, one has to raise himself to Him and not make earthly elements, baptism or other elements, a postulate of salvation, he replies: The Christian dare not reject any demand of Christ. If the Lord has enjoined baptism, then the Christian must live by this order. The truly believing person knows of only one command: the baptism of the Lord, the washing away of sins in the blood of Christ, that is, through Spirit, water, and blood, "which are one." In the same way, Marpeck refutes her other views, for example, the view that the Anabaptists have no true understanding of Christ. No date.

Preface

The following epistle has been written to Mrs. Helena Streicher at Ulm. When it reached Schwenckfeld, he became vehement, and wrote against the brother Billgram Marpeck and Miss Magdalena Marschalckin von Bappenhaim. What moved Schwenckfeld is found in the book of the *Judicium*. Thus, the truth has seen the light, and falsehood has yielded to it. Glory to God the Lord in eternity who, by His Holy Spirit, will strengthen His weak people to the end of the world, and who will preserve them against all the cunning of the serpent. Amen.[3]

Marpeck's Letter

From the depth of my heart, my dear Helena, I wish you true understanding of God, the heavenly Father, through Jesus Christ, from whom comes genuine peace (p. 180), joy, consolation, and eternal life. I acknowledge the greeting and wish of our Savior from you, that He may indeed be our glory, as it always has been and always will be, among all true believers in eternity. Yes, just as Saint Paul teaches, he who boasts let him boast of the Lord (1 Cor. 1:31); we live only if Christ lives in us (Gal. 2:20). It is true that Paul instructs us to examine ourselves, to determine whether Christ lives in us (2 Cor. 13:5). If He does not, we are rejected, and whoever does not have the Spirit of Christ is not His. Saint John also says: "He who does not remain in the teaching of Christ, has no God" (2 Jn. 9). And, as witness to his teaching, Saint Paul says that he will not venture to speak of anything except what Christ speaks in him (Rom. 15:18). For this and similar reasons, Christ is truly my boast, and the boast of all true believers. Therefore, I praise God that I may honor such a desire for truth, for I confess, now and always, that all human glory must fall, but the glory and honor of God and His Christ remain eternally.

In reply to your letter, I wrote you that I would not accept what I did not find in Christ, and I adhere to that position as steadfastly as before. Therefore, I am admonished, not only by you, but by Christ Himself, to remain in His teaching and words; only then may we remain His true disciples and recognize the truth. That truth is the Son. As I wrote you earlier, and I remain unchanged despite all your writing, I still confess that he, whom the Lord makes free in the truth, is truly free from sin, and from teaching and deceit of all men. However, as you yourself have written, Christ said that all His teaching, like His Word, is Spirit and life. Therefore, I will raise my spirit to Him increasingly, and have peace, glory, and joy in Him alone, and not in the mortal elements. That is to say, I will not demand that any external thing, be it baptism or anything else, be required for salvation, although it should not be rejected, as you admit. So that it may be entirely confessed in truth, I will insist upon no neglect or omission in one single point or tittle of Christ. This is the reason I am replying to your above-mentioned opinion.

First, I would question whether the physical voice of Christ the Lord can be separated from the Spirit and life. That voice is an outer, physical, magnificent voice, for the same physical voice of Christ enabled the Holy Spirit to have its sovereign movement. Since, however, the Holy Spirit did not move all who heard His physical voice and saw His miracles, therefore, it should follow that there are two doctrines: an outer and an inner one. There is, however, only *one* Spirit and life, and only *one* teaching, by the Lord Himself. But, even though it was, admittedly, an external, human, and audible voice, the physical voice of Christ never simply came from Christ without Spirit and life. Whatever the Son sees the Father doing, the Son of the Father will also do, and He will act both as the Son, who has God and the Spirit in Him, and as the man, who comes from the flesh of the children of man. In Christ, there is, however, only *one* teaching, outer and inner, and not two. Why must the teaching be divided, become a duality, when it still remains one in the Spirit and life? Indeed, this it must do (p. 181) in the person of Christ Himself, because the Father, through the power of the Spirit,

378

committed all things to Him, in His physical humanity, as a created physical man. As long as He dwelt in the flesh, and as long as the physical life lasted, He must by this means lead, guide, and preserve us in the strength of the Spirit.

However, concerning the physical teaching of Christ, Spirit and life were in Him, but Spirit and life are still not in the natural man. Like he distinguishes the wind, the natural man may physically, hear Spirit and life, but only as they are spoken by a physical, understandable, clear, and unequivocal voice. Christ used this elemental voice, together with such an elemental effect, for all miracles, and He commanded His apostles to do likewise. For the sake of the faithful, this voice has not been silenced, nor will it be to the end of the world; it is a witness to all believing and unbelieving peoples. We must use the elemental voice, and other such material things, as long as we dwell in the flesh. Notwithstanding the fact that the Holy Spirit does not move *in* and *over* all men, it must still be witnessed to the world for judgment. But, where the Holy Spirit moves and creates life, there, too, the same physical reality becomes Spirit and life through faith in Christ; it remains elemental for the sake of comprehension, sensitivity, and endurance, which man has according to his nature. Does it not follow that, if one uses the physical elements for the sake of Christ's command, these elements would also be spirit and life, but not merely because of their physical nature? Otherwise, it would have to follow that, although He was the Word, Spirit, and life from eternity, and became flesh, of the seed of David, the physical and earthly, but now heavenly and glorified, Son who is the same as the Father in essence, had not been Spirit and life. Far be it from us that we ourselves should divide the Lord in such a manner that the outer is separated from the inner, and the inner from the outer; we, still being earthly creatures, have been made spirit by God, through the faith in Christ. We are, and remain, human as long as we have not discarded the earthly, which only occurs in physical death.

To shed the earthly element is denied both to the physical Christ and to ourselves; we are not yet what we will be, for it is asserted that, what the Son saw the Father doing, He also did physically among His people. Thus, our use of the physical elements, according to the Word and command of Christ does not deny the inner activity of the Spirit. But, where Spirit and life do not accompany the physical use of the elements, there the elements will remain simply elements, but only among the unbelievers. These elements are merely signs, indicators of outward faith, and these signs can be contradicted. Even Christ Himself is merely a sign for those unbelievers who wish to silence the witness of elements. The elements are conceived thus by Paul in the verse: "Neither he who waters, nor he who plants, is anything; only he who gives the growth" (1 Cor. 3:7). According to your interpretation, it would have to follow that the planting and watering were nothing. But Paul called himself a co-laborer with God and the people, God's field. Paul also says that he, as a wise builder, has laid the foundation, namely Christ, and no other. In our time, this foundation is also laid by the same teaching of Paul. Read 1 Corinthians 3 through to the end, and heed it closely.

(p. 182) You write that, after Christ rules in His heavenly, eternal glory, there will be no more element, neither transitory bread nor water. Instead, there will be totally different bread and water, the water of His spiritual graces, which flows directly from Him, the temple of God. The Lord speaks of it in John 3, 4, 5. You state that the Anabaptists have interpreted this spiritual water to be their external baptismal water, and thus imprison many consciences. To accuse all Baptist brethren, without any distinction, is going too far. But, if it is interpreted to mean water, bread, and wine, but without the participation of the Holy Spirit of Christ, who is the pledge and seal of the true believers, then, I say as before that the elements cannot hold the spiritual reality. No true believer will allow himself to be captured or committed by his own nature without the power of the Holy Spirit, which works in man from above. But where there is no faith and no Holy Spirit, to say that the true believers may be accused does not follow, for all is freely given them by the Father through Christ, as Saint Paul remarks: "If God is for us, who can oppose us? God also did not spare his own Son, but has given Him freely for us all. How, then, shall He not grant us everything with Him?" (Rom. 8:31, 32).

Similarly, because of the participation of the Spirit, the believers do not separate the physical usage of either the water, or the bread and wine, from the spiritual reality. There is only one Lord, one faith, one baptism, one God and Father of us all, who is above us all and in us all. This one Lord can be, and is, divided only by human thoughts and selfish reason that the outer becomes divided from the inner. If someone would speak with angelic understanding on the loftiness of the Godhead and Christ, and speak high spiritual words, but deny the lowliness and the deep humility of Christ, then such a person is not to be trusted. Christ on our behalf became a man, not an angel; He took upon Himself the seed of Abraham and, through the Holy Spirit, received from the inner reality the external form. For this reason, we need both the physical effect, and the spiritual meaning, of Christ's humanity. Then, we can test all emerging spirits by that humanity. Until such time as Christ reveals them, we have to tolerate hypocrites and covert liars who, as we have recently experienced, exist among us as Judas did among the apostles. While he has already gone to his execution, others like him will follow later.

Thus, in light of our confession, your writing opposes the truth; your writing disparages our usage and confession of Christ as if it were against the grace of God. Your creed is easily said and easily written, but it is still far from being true. Those who are weak, uneducated, and young in the faith receive injury to their hearts and consciences. Lofty knowledge makes them arrogant and they are without the means to know that Christ is the truth, who sits at the side of God the Father and His Christ. Such results I have seen, and no better ones emerge from your opinion. May God grant you realization of your understanding.

The plain text itself makes clear that you cannot interpret John and Peter as you do. For this reason, your teaching, understanding, sense, and opinion have become repulsive to me. Nevertheless, I will think about your interpretation some more, and not conceal from you the (p. 183) insight the Lord gives me. Because I consider such teachings as yours to be only a temptation, no matter how high the spirit may acclaim itself in understanding, I also hope that the Lord Jesus Christ, who lives in us and sits at God's right hand, will help me escape (1 Cor. 10:13?) from such and other temptations.

Furthermore, you are offended by my contention that your foundation cannot hold up. In truth, I do not yet admit anything else, for the reason indicated. And I cannot see otherwise, for your argument stands outside of Christ, and is without a true basis in the entire Scripture. As stated before, I confess the inner, just as you do, but I confess much more. You confess the Scriptures, as all sects do, but in your writing you have testified against individuals like the pope, Luther, and Zwingli, and also against groups like the false Anabaptists, who only partially confess the Scriptures. Of this you also accuse us. If you will diligently observe, with humble hearts, you will then find such accusations in yourselves, namely, that you tear out the Scriptures piecemeal, and do not use the whole.

You say you do not belong to the Anabaptists. Nor did Christ command you to do so. He commanded you to belong to Him alone: "Come to me," He says. We, and all those who, with zeal in their hearts, follow Christ in the entire truth and in His profession, also say what Christ said. If, at the invitation of Christ, we follow this command, we also follow Christ. Otherwise, Paul would have wrongly urged the Corinthians to "be my followers, as I am Christ's follower." According to the answer which you have given above, the Corinthians should have simply answered him: "Paul, we want to follow Christ." I know of no true believer who, with a clear conscience, would give such an answer as you do here. You say of Paul that he was not sent to baptize and, although this verse seems to have the meaning that you give it, it really does not. Rather, Paul baptized according to the teaching of the gospel. Paul says one should not baptize without the gospel. If it takes place in the co-witness of the Word in the saints, baptism is the gospel. Without it, all baptism is no baptism just as, without faith, all teaching is no teaching. But, when you appeal to the verse to the Colossians, and avow that, according to this Scripture, Christians have died to all the elements of the world and have been fulfilled, enriched, and blessed in Christ, you present a deceptive intervention. The verse does not say that. It speaks of all the rules of the world, and not of elements. When the Scriptures do speak of the elements of this world, they do not refer to the elements of faith in Christ.

I must also respond to your futile talk about this entire second chapter to the Colossians. Read it diligently, and do not rip out such fictitious fragments. Notice to what the chapter points, and see if it, like a mirror, will not show you and your adherents the condition of your hearts. Before God and man, it is proper to confess Christ, in the witness of truth, through baptism, which was commanded by Christ and taught by Peter: "Let everyone be baptized in the name of Jesus Christ for the forgiveness of sin, and you will receive the gifts of the Holy Spirit" (Acts 2:38). (p. 184) If, as you write, man has "had enough baptism by men" and man was sufficient before man without baptism, then Peter's teaching, in this respect, was doubtless in vain. Baptism was enjoined, not only before God, but also by and before man.

You also say to us: "You are searching for a baptism which is valid before God, but which is different from the baptism we know." We know of one, and only one, baptism, the baptism of the Lord, whereby our sins are washed away in the blood of Christ. Not only are our consciences cleansed, but we are also made one in Christ by virtue of the Spirit, blood, and water served in a single baptism. You, too, write of this baptism. If you do know of two baptisms, then show us the scriptural evidence for this assertion, and interpret it for us so that we should, indeed, have simply an outer baptism of water, without any Spirit. A baptism without Spirit can never be called a baptism of Christ; it is only a useless act which neither can, nor may, have any connection with the name of Christ. For this reason, Paul did not allow the Corinthians to take Christ's communion (1 Cor. 11), even though they used bread and wine, ate and drank, and outwardly practiced it. When they sincerely observed, both outwardly and inwardly, the spiritually enjoined eucharist, their communion was proper and right, just as Paul had commanded and explained it to them. Love, which is the participation of the Spirit in communion, is revealed in the proclamation of Christ's death, and love is then used as a memorial to Him. When this participation of the Spirit was absent, the Corinthians ate their own meal, and not the eucharist of Christ at all. As Paul says, because of the absence of the inner, and not because of the external usage, what they ate was not the Lord's eucharist, but their own.

As has been adequately indicated above, the situation is the same with baptism. Paul speaks of no other baptism: "You are washed" (1 Cor. 6). You accuse us of interpreting such baptism to be the Anabaptist's baptism. We interpret it to be the baptism of the true church of Christ, by whatever name it is called. What difference does it make, to a true Christian, what he is called? The Pharisees and Jews also did not want to grant Christ the honor of calling Him by His right name. Some called Him a Samaritan and, later, His disciples and followers were called *goim*, that is, Nazarenes.[4] They wanted to be the people of God. Even while you boast so loftily of Christ, you do not even want to grant Christ the honor denied Him by the Pharisees and Jews. For this reason, we care little what men call us. If only the truth is among us, we console ourselves with Paul (2 Cor. 6:6) and with the patience of Christ.

When you write that you do not agree with us in our concept of the church, I readily believe that you obviously could not agree with us. According to your boast, you know a proud, lofty, arrogant Christ, for whom poor folk are far too unimportant. Neither you nor your kind could learn humility or gentleness from them, but prefer to invent your own artistry. We have no other consolation but to put forward our poverty with all lowliness. May God let you recognize your riches. Alas, what a difficult thing, what a poor work, it is for you and your kind to recognize that Christ opened the eyes of the man who was born blind; He spat out physical spittle, He made mud, and spread it over the blind man's eyes, and then He sent him to the Pool of

Siloam to wash himself. When such lowly art was reported to the Pharisees, they immediately said that the honor belongs to God, and not to the lowly work. They did not know that the great, marvelous secrets of God lie concealed under such (p. 185) a lowly work. Christ says He came to cause a decision; those who think they can see will become blind, and those who are blind will receive their sight. I am pointing out Christ's words and actions only to those to whom the Lord reveals Himself. May God preserve His own from blindness. Amen over you and over all of us.

You further write that you know of no gathered congregation, or church of Christ, which assembles outwardly in the name of the Lord, in His divine strength and Spirit. You should also say that, while you believe in a holy Christian church, and you truly know it is also on earth, it is dispersed in distress. We agree with you, but add that the church of Christ does not come, nor should it be expected to come, with regard to numbers or persons, as you believe, nor with regard to any place or any time. Christ will be with His own until the end of the world, and will not leave them orphans. And where, on this basis, two or three are gathered in His name, there He is in the midst of them. And whatever they will agree to ask of the heavenly Father in His name and according to His will, that He will do or give.

I would eagerly like to see any Scripture, be it law, prophets, or apostolic writings, which would curtail or render impotent these words of Christ. If one says the Fall would do so, then the Fall has more power than the Word, which is not the case. Indeed, as mentioned before, I do not believe you will find any such writings. If you lower your eyes in humility, you will find Christ in the midst of the spiritual hospital and amongst all offense. Even if you had lived at the time of Christ and the apostles, I truly fear that you, with your haughty countenance, would not have found Christ and His church any more than you do now; then as now, the secret of evil always invites itself along into the churches of Christ. A denier and traitor was even raised at Christ's side, and many who had believed, or were offended by His teaching, turned back on Christ. Later, John says that they ["departed from us because they were not of us" (1 Jn. 2:19)].

There were a number of serious problems in the church. Before the destruction of Jerusalem, the church of Jerusalem already had been scattered and dissolved. The church in Asia defected from Paul. The false apostles sneaked in from the beginning, and taught all churches the coercion of the law rather than the free grace of Christ. They loaded the Sabbath, observance of days and months, circumcision, food and drink, and other burdens upon the disciples' necks. Even Peter and Barnabas, together with others, fell into hypocrisy, and were led astray when Paul met them in Antioch. The Corinthians were accused of incest. By the time the false apostles entered with a false boasting, one wanting to be of Apollos, another of Paul, the third of Cephas, the Corinthians also had wrangled with the heathen about temporal goods, and had left the correct usage of the eucharist. Some said the resurrection had occurred; the sect of the Sadducees said there was no resurrection of the dead. Some said Christ had only a phantom body ["Luftleib"], like the bodies of the three angels who came to Abraham and smote Sodom, whom John called the Antichrist. Some at Thessalonica claimed the judgment day as already at hand. There was conflict at Rome between the Jews (p. 186) and the Gentiles who had come to faith in Christ; each considered himself superior. The Galatians were also misguided by the work of the law. And many similar divisions developed. There was also a great persecution so that, under Emperor Nero and other tyrants, the church had little room, and was dispersed nearly everywhere.

Does it follow from these instances that there was no church at all? Did the church of Christ end immediately at the time of Christ and the apostles? Did it end with baptism, the ban, and eucharist? Such was not the case. Was there no church of Christ just because no greater signs than Christ's were performed by the apostles? The Lord had said that he who believes shall do greater signs than He Himself (Jn. 14:12). To be sure, we find fewer physical signs performed by the apostles than by Christ. According to your interpretation of Christ's words, even the apostles did not have the right faith since they did not perform greater signs, as the Lord said they would. Accordingly, no true churches could be found, either at the time of the apostles or at present. If your opinion were valid, the rest would also follow. Far be it from us to believe that. To say so can be easily imagined, but difficult to prove. More weight must be placed on believing than on sending.

Paul also says that he believed and, therefore, he spoke (2 Cor. 4:13). If his conclusion does follow, and your opinion were to prevail, you would have to show much more reason for your commission to divide and tear apart the inner from the outer: the outer teaching, baptism, ban, and communion from the inner rule of the Holy Spirit. I eagerly desire to have written evidence and an account of your new teaching and commission, just as you demand it of us. Our representatives have a basis in the testimony of Scripture, as has earlier been adequately demonstrated. Even if I do not know all members personally, just as the apostles did not know all members personally, yet all true believers know each other by their co-witness in the Holy Spirit. Where the carcass is, there the eagles gather.

You state that you think the Anabaptists regard Christ only as a creature. May God grant that you do not lack much more in the understanding of Christ than we do. We know well what we think of Christ. Remember, God has also given other people something, even though you may not experience or know it.

You further accuse us of making an idol of the cross, but without true understanding. Such idolatry will not be found among us; rather, we oppose it. But even Paul or other apostles could not prevent it from sneaking in. We accept no such witness without the basis of truth. Nor is it up to us to judge. You also state that you consider the Anabaptists to be outwardly devout, and testify that there are many devout people among them. God grant that you might also see how I confess the honor of my God.

While they were still unrecognized by Christ, many people were of a perverse kind. But they were challenged to the faith, and they testified to the name of Jesus Christ with their blood out of true devotion, which comes out of faith. Such devotion we confess as the only thing valid for our salvation before God; I know personally these people witnessed with their blood to the praise of their God. I testify to this belief so that no one may think we look only to physical and outer devotion. But if the natural, human devotion is joined with the devotion of faith, all is a praise to God. We also confess that natural devotion, according to the flesh only, and without the addition of the devotion of [the] faith, is not adequate to inherit the kingdom of God. Whoever does not believe may be as devout as he wants, Christ says he still is condemned. There is no piety which is an exception. (p. 187)

I want to state further that you have misunderstood me when I assert that the human Christ, even today, serves us, and all men, who desire to be saved. Understand me rightly. According to His Word, Christ did not come into this world in order to be served, but only to serve. For the same reason, He admonishes His followers to serve in the same manner, as members of one body. Thus, He sent them, like the Father sent Him. Similarly, we also confess that Christ serves us through those whom He sent as servants of His Spirit. I confess Christ now, and in eternity, in the clarity of the Father, and the clarity of the Father in the Son. I add that whoever disdains the servitude of His believers disdains not only Christ Himself, but also the Father. I will not defend the fact that many do not know or understand anything of the true knowledge and devotion of Christ. Nor will I slander or judge anyone who does realize it, but bear witness, with discrimination, to the best of my knowledge.

Your remarks on the deficiency of the outward church would undoubtedly point to a deficiency in your own teaching. You consider yourself to be much better, indeed, much loftier, than those with whom you refuse to keep company. However, because you boast that you have the higher insights of the inner person, who possesses much more than the outer (1 Cor. 12), I recognize superiority more in those whom you shun than in you. For that reason, we cannot agree with you. Otherwise, we are well satisfied with the witness of the inner understanding, if it can be revealed and recognized through co-witnessing. We also admit that no life or salvation may be achieved except through the Spirit and the Word, and not through outward activity. But all external things are a service to life and salvation. If we boast of life and salvation, we also freely need the service of salvation.

You alluded to 1 Corinthians 2. I ask you with all my heart to read the chapter thoroughly and correctly. It stands in complete agreement with our testimony. In Christ, neither external teaching, baptism, ban, bread and wine are physical, nor are they prepared by the spirit of this world. They are prepared by the Spirit, and by the teaching of Christ and of the apostles. Thus, the spiritual person judges everything spiritually, be it visible, tangible, or conceivable. The spiritual person conducts that which is then ordained for the service of the Spirit, and it is conducted all to the praise of God and the spiritual welfare of man. The whole chapter does not indicate differently. I am well satisfied with it, for there is no word in it which is contrary to our teaching. But I admit that many people study before they have become good students. May God grant that you would not have placed yourself and yours too highly in the class before you rightly learned to know the school. You must not disdain the invitation and command of Christ, but discern it. I also admit that the inner and the outer have to be kept distinct, but to divide one from the other, to use one and not the other, cannot be substantiated by any Scripture.

I am well satisfied with the opinion expressed in the conclusion of your writing. I should free my heart, and allow it to soar higher and higher to God. If I already include the external in my spiritual instruction, and use it to that end, it will not hinder me, but further me to such an understanding. God grant this understanding to both our hearts and minds. Amen.

May you accept this my writing as my sincere opinion, since I have openly disclosed my reaction to your letter. Just as you have let me know what hinders you from accepting our opinion, so you know that, for the aforementioned reasons, I cannot accept your understanding.

6

The Churches
of Christ and of Hagar
(1544) [#14]

Introduction

Marpeck's passionate devotion to the church repeatedly led him to write about its nature. In this letter to members of his group in Württemberg, written from Chur just before his removal to Augsburg in late 1544, he picks up Paul's typology from Galatians 4. He begins and ends with the already familiar interpretation of the Canticle, which, he says, is a "natural parable of love." By means of this love, "all faithful hearts are led into the real, supernatural love," the mark of the true church. He identifies many who claim to be in the covenant as Ishmaelites, that is, children of Hagar. God is their Father, but they are not children of the true mother, the church of Christ. He charges that they are concerned with, and have, only the letter of Scripture, and not the Spirit. Their faith, then, is a mere external faith which has not permeated and changed all of life, as it has done for the children of promise. He is clearly thinking here of other Christians, perhaps specifically of the Reformed variety found in Strasbourg.

The Text

264r   The Churches of Christ and of Hagar

To all the faithful elect in Christ Jesus in Württemberg and scattered elsewhere, but gathered in faith and spirit, my dear brothers and comrades.

Grace and peace from God our heavenly Father, through Jesus Christ our Lord, be and remain with us eternally. Amen.

390

My dear ones, loved in God the Father through Jesus Christ: This love is the true source from which

all love flows. For this love, which is the one love and the one God, flows from the heavenly Father in Christ and from Christ in the Father. In the Holy Spirit this love brings about the unity of all faithful hearts. She is a bond and an inseparable unity, an eternal beginning stretching from the highest height. She takes to herself the influx of whatever is loved and may in truth be loved. In particular, love, which is God in all, is the observer of that which she

herself has created / / and formed in the likeness of her image. In Him, according to her manner and her nature, which is essence itself, love has an eternal likeness. She is eternally loved again by

man. When she lives in the new heaven and the new earth as a holy city, the new Jerusalem, her form will be fully seen in Him. Prepared as a bride for her husband, she will come down out of heaven from God, Himself the essence of love. A dwelling of God, she will be the most beautiful of all. She shows herself to her bridegroom and husband, and she is the banner above all. She is the seal imprinted on the hearts of all the faithful and she is the pledge for eternal security, victory, and conquest against all hate and enmity. Unmoved, unspotted, and un- changed, she will eternally retain her name against them.

Love's garments, which are the virtues of the Holy Spirit, remain eternally unspotted, untorn, and undamaged. Only love wears the virtues unspotted; for her honor, they were prepared and made in eternity. Whoever does not contemplate or

/ / know love in her finery and adornment knows neither love nor himself. She is the daughter who has left her father's house and who has been brought to the King in her embroidered dress.

Whoever wishes to see her form should behold her in the adornment of her King. Her Christ and King, who is Himself thus dressed and adorned, has dressed her. Whoever, even once, truly sees this loveliest of all brides in her adornment and form will praise her in wonderment. He will exalt her honor, praise, and adornment among the nations. Because he has seen her, he is also able to speak the truth about her apparel and crown from foot to head and because of her beauty and adornment, he has great desire to serve at her feet, and to entice all who gladly hear it to serve love together with him.

I, along with many others who testify to it through faith, have had only a glimpse of her form. This glimpse has created great longing in our hearts to see her again, fully and as she really is. Perhaps we, with all who desire it, may get another glimpse of her, and see her form, so that our hearts may be more eager with desire to seek her / / and see her form. Then, we too, may be clothed with her apparel, and please her with fervent service.

First, I hope that all who, by virtue of the Holy Spirit in true faith, have had a glimpse of her form, will witness with me to her apparel and adornment as the loveliest of all. I hope, too, that they will witness to her King, who has been clothed and crowned by His mother on the day of His joy. This day is the occasion of eternal wonderment in all the creatures.

First, the Holy Spirit witnesses in the Canticle to her beauty and adornment. Similarly, the prophets, patriarchs, evangelists, apostles, and all who have seen and recognized her form, have acknowledged it and testified to it. What they have said and testified I here set down as a seal of our testimony not only to truth, but also to our certain faith. This love testifies to herself. In the Canticle, she says:[1] "He kisses me with the kiss of his mouth, for his breasts are sweeter than wine.[2] They smell of the fragrance of your ointment; your name is like

ointment poured out. That is why the maidens / / love you. Draw me after you, and let us make haste. The king brings me into his chamber. We rejoice and are glad because of you; we will remember your breasts more than the wine. All who are upright love you."

Partly drawn as it is from nature, these brief words show the nature of love. Nearly the whole of the Canticle presents and illustrates the real, supernatural love by means of the natural parable of love. By this means, all faithful hearts are led into the real, supernatural love, into God Himself; yes, into God Himself, and God into them.

First, the Holy Spirit says: "He kisses me with the kiss of his mouth." The eternal Word has gone forth, and continues to go forth, from the mouth of the Father, from God Himself. With [this Word], He kisses the hearts of all the faithful. Thus, the divine nature of the children of God is conceived and born from the love of the Word, the imperishable seed. This seed is the church, bought through the blood of Christ, and the church is His spouse and bride, the loveliest and most beautiful among women.

All who are thus kissed by the mouth of God, and who have conceived a divine nature by the seed of the Word, are brought to this bride and mother,

the church, by the Holy Spirit. / / In her, as the mother, spouse, consort, and church of Christ, are they born. Conceived by the action of the Holy

Spirit, she bears the children of the Word in her body. As stated above, that body is the body of Christ for while Christ is the husband and Head, the two are one flesh. Her children are washed by the blood of Christ for the forgiveness of sins and, washed in the water of the Word, they are cleansed of all filthiness of the flesh, that is, sin. To reveal that the mother has conceived this child through the Holy Spirit and the Word from God [this child], is then included in the covenant of a good conscience with God in Christ. The covenant reveals that God is the child's Father, that it is not illegitimate, but is born out of the marriage with Christ. This child is a true heir of the Father and the eternal kingdom. Their mother, the church, has conceived these legitimate children and they are from the Father, and they are born again through the washing of the water of the Word. Thus, they are the legitimate children of the true Abraham, that is, of God the Father, who is the Father of all such children, and of the true Sara, who is the mother of all such children. As Peter says: "Her daughter you have become." / / Again, as Paul says: "Sing, you who are not pregnant, and bear children you who have not been in childbirth. For she who is left alone will have more children in the eternal kingdom, than she who has a husband." Without this,[3] there is no heir, nor is there any divine birth.

However, practically everyone boasts that they are of Abraham's seed, that they are born of God the Father's Spirit. Nevertheless, their boasts are pretentious and false. They are, and remain, only Ishmaelites; they boast of being born of God, but without a legitimate mother, for their mother is neither promised nor married to God. Their mother is Hagar, the slave woman. Thus, because they are children born of the flesh, theirs is only the first birth. And, although they are of the father Abraham's seed, she and her children serve only in the interests of reward. Their Creator, God, is their

Abraham

Sara

267r
1 Pet. 3 [6]
Is. 54 [1]

Gal. 4 [27]

Hagar the slave

Father, but they are not born, like Isaac, as children of the Holy Spirit's promise, as children of Jesus Christ. Nor are they conceived or born of Christ's espoused bride. Therefore, they cannot feed at the

Sara

breasts of the true, espoused bride, the true Sara. They suck the alien and false milk of the slave woman, and not of the married one. Hagar's breasts are not filled by the Holy Spirit; her breasts are filled by her own cleverness in the dead letter of

267v

Scripture./ /

Because of the fervent love and kiss of the Father, and because she is the bride and spouse of Christ, Sara's breasts are lovelier than wine. Her children suck the pure milk of her breasts, filled as they are by the Holy Spirit. The unadulterated milk flows out of her body. Without deceit or wrong, the mother, the true Sara, bears her children to the Father. And her breasts are loved. The children of the mother are all eager for her milk, and suck from her breasts to their hearts' content. They are raised and nourished, and grow and increase, in the discipline which the mother applies to them. Thus, they live in neither sin nor in the filth of their carnal nature. Rather, when they reach their mature adulthood in Christ their bridegroom, they are taught and instructed in the discipline of the Holy Spirit. Then, possessed with wisdom, understanding, and perception, they are given over to the Father, who receives them as heirs of the eternal inheritance and kingdom with Christ.

Thus, such an inheritance, bequeathed to them only by the Holy Spirit, gives comfort to the Father's heirs. In faith, hope, and true love, they are confident that they are conceived by the Father and that they are born of the spouse and consort of

268r

Christ. / / She is the true and honorable mother, the married one. Through His blood, she is promised and espoused to Christ, the Son of the Father and, because of the washing of water in the Word, her children are born again. Therefore, in order that God may be revealed before the world, the mother bears the Father's children, conceived by Him through the Holy Spirit. Christ's blood then ensures the washing and forgiveness of sins. And this child is of the seed of the Word. Raised, increased, and nourished by the breast of the mother, whose unadulterated milk, the Word of truth, comes from the Holy Spirit, this child and Christ are of one flesh, one bone, one blood. Thus, the sure pledge, the Holy Spirit, instills in this legitimate child the confidence in the inheritance. This child is legitimately born of Father and mother, has the divine nature and manner, and has grown, been nourished, and raised honorably. All these children may with unshakable hope, and without worry of shame, look for the inheritance of the eternal kingdom. Outside of this rebirth, no one will inherit the kingdom of Christ.

For the others, all may boast as they please that they are born only of the Holy Spirit, without the legitimate / / mother, Christ's espoused bride. If they are not conceived by the Father in the legitimate spouse, and if they are not born of her in the washing of water in the Word, they are bastards; they are not heirs. Again, whoever is conceived and born of the slave woman, and not the legitimate spouse, is illegitimate, and no heir.

Hagar does not feed her children with the milk of love, but with lifeless water, kept in a little barrel. The desert destroys the water so that, in the end, neither mother nor child has any nourishment. Then, the mother in despair abandons the child in the wilderness to die of hunger and thirst. Hagar's children boast of being a church and the spouse of

nota

Christ. In fact, they are only Egyptian slaves, and their mothers bear only Ishmaelites, reared on the dead letter and skill in Scripture, and fed on keg water. All these Ishmaelites establish a church on the dead letter, and not on the living water of the eternal source which flows from the Holy Spirit, out of the body of Christ who sits at the right hand of God. This water flows only into the spouse and bride who is one body with Christ: from her body, in turn, flow living / / waters.[4] However, the Hagarish mothers cannot give such water, nor can they give drink to their children. The children of such mothers suck from shriveled[5] breasts to which there is no flow of grace or aid from the Holy Spirit. Thus, Hagar's children drink lifeless, barrel water which has no living source. Nevertheless, they all call themselves mothers and churches of Christ. They claim that they are conceived by Abraham, and that their children are Abraham's seed, God's children. But once their barrel water and their sack lunch[6] are consumed, once the dead letter and their skill in Scritpure come to an end, their faith and hope are also finished, and mothers and children despair in the terrible wilderness of this world.[7]

Therefore, those mothers and children are not to be believed. These mothers have children without God the Father and the Holy Spirit, without the seed of the living Word, they are mothers who produce children as a result of the dead letter, skill in Scripture, and their own cleverness. That is the origin and source of all sects. Nor can any child be believed who claims to be a child of God but who is without a legitimate mother. / / He is a false spirit and a liar who boasts that he lives only as the offspring of the Spirit and Word, that he is born only by virtue of the Holy Spirit, that he is nourished, raised, and taught without a mother.

269r

Nota

269v

397

The Holy Spirit has no child without the legitimate spouse of Christ. The spouse of Christ bears, cares for, and trains the children of God, and the heavenly Father in Christ provides, preserves, and feeds the mother and her children. Whoever despises the birthgiving, care, and training of the mother despises the Father along with her. These are the functions of the paternal and maternal heritage: the father is the eternal promise of that heritage; the mother, because she is His espoused bride, is the mediation of all the grace of the Father, given by the Holy Spirit to the hearts of all the faithful to aid the mother's discipline of her children. All the despised children are disinherited; they are excluded from the heritage, grace, and discipline of the Holy Spirit, and given over to everlasting destruction.

Therefore, Saint Paul faithfully warns us not to forsake the mother, spouse, and consort of Christ, which is the gathering and unity of the church of Christ. In Paul's day, / / some did forsake her and, even though the time is 1,500 years closer than in Paul's day, today we, too, are still in the habit of forsaking her. We have so much more reason to be faithful today. If we are, we may enter into the kingdom of the Father together with our bridegroom Christ, and with all prudent and wise hearts. Unlike the five foolish virgins, against whom the Lord closes the door, nevermore to open it, we will not be without oil. The Lord does not know from whence these others come. They are born, raised, and taught neither by Him nor His spouse. They lack the oil of faith, virtue, and true skill in the knowledge of the Father and of His Christ, wherein is eternal life in the eternal kingdom and heritage. They know neither the Father, Son, or Holy Spirit, nor do they know His espoused bride, which is His

Heb. 10 [25]

270r

Mt. 25 [1-13]

Lk. 13 [25, 27]

Jn. 17 [3]

congregation and church. Nor are they taught by her. How, then, can the Father, Christ, and His congregation know them?

So much concerning the birth of the legitimate and true children of God, who are legitimately born, bred, and nourished by the heavenly Father and the spouse and consort of Christ. The breasts of this Father and mother are lovelier than wine. All the patriarchs, prophets, and apostles have prophesied and / / witnessed to it, and they have affirmed that the name of the bridegroom and the bride is like ointment poured over all peoples for eternal salvation. That is why the maidens of the bride love Him. He draws the bride with her maidens and children after Him, and together they hasten on the upright way to the eternal kingdom. The King leads the bride into His chamber, that is, to His mystery; He shows her all the glory, understanding, and mystery of faith, all of which she, her children, and her maidens will receive from the King and will eternally possess. Thus, they rejoice in the Bridegroom and King, and think of the breasts which they sucked rather than of the wine. They remember His great love, faithfulness, and mercy, shown them in His death, resurrection, and ascension to the right hand of God. His love is the only source of joy and salvation to those born of God, and they rejoice eternally. Therefore, the upright of heart love Him; the unfit, the faithless, and the false cannot love Him. / /

I write to you in the hope that we may earnestly contemplate the birth and beginning of our life. Because of faith, we have received this life out of the seed of the Word, implanted by the Holy Spirit in our legitimate mother, who is the spouse and consort of Christ, the Giver and Creator of life. As true children of God, we are sanctified and consecrated to the eternal kingdom and heritage, to our heavenly Father and His eternal praise, and to the everlasting royal priesthood. We will reign eternally. Together with all the elect of God, we will eternally sacrifice offerings of thanks in the purity of our hearts.

Such is the goodness, grace, and faithfulness with which He has crowned us, and made us worthy for this royal priesthood. As the only High Priest and King, He has made us heirs to this royal priesthood, and we are to take this inheritance. To His eternal thanks and praise, magnification, and exaltation, we are to take away from our heads, dispositions, and consciousness the inheritance He has given us. Similarly, the twenty-four elders took from their heads the crowns with which they had just been crowned, and said: "You, O Lord, are worthy to receive praise, honor, and power; You have made all things and, for Your sake, they / / exist and were created." It behooves all His creatures to give thanks to God, but especially those creatures who have been exalted to His glory. In the purity of their hearts, they should gratefully offer that same glory and honor, with which God has adorned them, to their Creator and bestower. Yes, and that mark of gratitude should be offered with clean, willing hands; it should be offered without any concern for their own honor, even as God, as One who cannot be coerced, has given everything freely to them. Such a heart is the free offering of thanks for everything it has received from its Creator, God, the Lord Jesus Christ, and the Holy Spirit.

Therefore, my loved ones, let us eternally thank God with such hearts. All His gifts are given for the sake of such gratitude; then, all thanksgiving, praise, and honor is, and will remain, His alone. For to Him alone it belongs. It is to Him that I,

Rev. 4 [4]

271v

400

together with all the faithful, gladly and eternally give praise.

Dated at Chur the 15th day of August, anno 1544.

> In the Lord Jesus Christ,
> servant to you all,
>> Pilgram Marpeck.

7

Concerning
the Libertarians
(1544) [#15]

Introduction

Written late in 1544, this is the first letter dated at
Augsburg. Apparently, some members of the Marpeck group in
Moravia and Alsace were more liberal in their interpretation of
the freedom of Christ than Marpeck, who had defended so
strongly this same point against the arguments of the Swiss
Brethren. He appears to have had the same problems here as
Luther did, whose *sola fide* was frequently interpreted as license
for self-indulgence. The point he especially makes here is the
same one he made to the Swiss Brethren; where love is absent,
there is only slavery to sin, no matter how pious the words.

The Text
Concerning the Libertarians

6 r   This is a copy of a letter concerning the libertarians
who want to be free to do everything without any
conscience. It is written to all in Moravia and Alsace
who have true faith.

May the grace and peace of God our heavenly
Father, through Jesus Christ our Lord [Rom. 1:7],
be and remain with us in eternity. Amen.

Dearly beloved in God our Father, and beloved
in Jesus Christ, my fervent sighing, prayer, wish,
and desire is that the Lord will open my way to you
one of these days. I firmly believe that, through the
grace of our Lord Jesus Christ, you, too, desire the
same. May God ordain, to His praise and our salva-

tion, and our comfort, peace, and joy in the Holy Spirit, that you do desire it. Amen.

My dearly beloved in God the Father, through Christ, I also thank my God for you and for all who live, not according to the flesh, but according to the true liberty of the Holy Spirit, and to the true rule and teaching of Christ. I am referring to those who have shed all false judgments and verdicts, who have extricated and freed themselves from all human invention, statutes, bonds, cords, and imprisonment of conscience, and who have become free through the Son of God. He whom the Son sets free is free indeed. I say it, and witness before God and all creatures, that this freedom is turned over and given alone to that love which is in Jesus Christ our Lord. Whoever does not have that love may not boast about his liberty//. Rather, he is, and remains, a slave, sold to serve the law and sin, and always a debtor to the law. Yet they are the ones who do not want to be in debt to anyone for the sake of the love which is in Christ. They boast about their freedom, yet remain servants of destruction. In their invented liberty which, according to the lust of the flesh, they imagine they possess, they live in open offense and scandal to those who have tender consciences. Thus, true liberty and true love itself is missed completely. About this kind of liberty, we know of no instance in Christ's teaching, even as we know nothing about self-invented human statutes, bonds, and cords of the conscience. The free commandment of the love which we have in Christ is a single commandment. The liberty in Christ is one unified liberty. Outside of the love of Christ, there is no liberty.

Therefore, my dearly beloved, it is my fervent prayer, supplication, reminder, and admonition that you take careful note to discern what I am here

Jn. 8 [36]

6 v

Rom. 14 [20 f.]
Cor. 8 [7-13]

403

writing to you. Of what value would it be to escape from the verdicts, bonds, cords, yes, the imprisonment, of conscience and human rules, only to run into the devil's hands because you falsely boast of new insight and indulge in the self-will of carnal liberty? For it is surely true and certain that neither

7 r

flesh or blood, nor any creature / / in heaven or on earth has such power over a free conscience that it can command or forbid those of the true Spirit and character of God. Those who do possess the true Spirit of God are one nature, born again as they are by the Word and Holy Spirit.

Rom. 8 [14]

Those who are driven by God's Spirit are children of God. One can no more order or forbid the children [of God] than one can order or forbid the Holy Spirit of God. Only the Holy Spirit is the commander and prohibitor in those to whom He has given birth. Certainly and truly, all such freely born children do not seek their own advancement,

1 Cor. 10 [24]
1 Cor. 13 [5]

but the growth of all.[1] Like Christ Jesus, who was born like them, they do not seek only what is theirs. Similarly, the apostle Paul, and other children of God, did not seek what was their own. Rather, everything that already was, and could have, become theirs, yes, even themselves, they surrendered, sacrificed and let go to God our Father, through Jesus Christ our Lord, and what they surrendered they considered as dirt and garbage compared to the overwhelming riches of Christ, who is the salvation of those who are to be preserved.

In short, the true liberty of Christ, and the love that belongs to it, is a free surrender, denial, and forgetting of self. The true liberty of Christ fervently desires to serve everyone in that which is good, to the praise of God and the salvation of man.

1 Cor. 10 [23-33]

Yes, even though something is legitimate for them, they surrender it all for the sake of love and growth.

The true liberty of Christ may, according to such love, give evidence of no other spirit, nature, or characteristic. // Whoever uses it differently misses the way of truth, and falls beside the rock on which all truth rests eternally.

Specifically, I write to you in the hope that I might hold the true liberty of Christ before your eyes as a mirror in which you may learn what the image of Christ is. Again, I also put before your eyes the real antichristian, false, blown-up, disobedient, carnal liberty which serves, seeks, magnifies, and raises up only the self. This liberty can in no way deny itself, nor can it ever admit to weakness; it breaks, defies, and criticizes everything. It praises only that which gives room to the lust and greed of the flesh, and yet defends and covers all wantonness and selfishness of the flesh, with the liberty of Christ. Briefly, it desires to be unfettered, unbound, and unrestricted only according to its own pleasure. In its own wantonness and pride, it fights and quarrels incessantly about those things in which the heart is imprisoned and entangled. It seeks redemption and liberty where there are only the eternal imprisonment, bondage, and cords of the devil. And still such libertarians say that they have no conscience about it. They do not want to be under anyone's rule or authority. They use Paul's words to verify that everything is legitimate for them. But they read what Paul says with perverted eyes. // They have no intention of being as beholden to others as Christ and the holy Paul were.[2]

Dear friend, whoever you are that speaks in this manner and uses the words of Paul as a cover-up for your own invented liberty, examine your heart before . . . [you speak], determine whether you, like Christ and Paul, are committed to everyone in all good things. If you are, then you may also say, with a true heart firm in the truth of Christ: "Although everything is permitted, not everything leads to improvement."

My dearly beloved in Christ Jesus, especially you beloved Cornelius,[3] given to me as a son in the faith, and you, my dear brother Paul,[4] together with all the others elect of God, receive this my admonition in the Lord. I have been in fear for you. I had to write in order that we may help one another save our souls from all the cunning deceit of the devil. My dear brother Cornelius, and all the chosen of God, watch diligently over the flock of God. And with respect to liberty, first know your own minds, and then work with the church in order that she may be taught and led by the true rule of Christ. This is what God will demand of me and others.

God grant that, with Paul, we may be able to boast about the day of the Lord, that we may have kept faith, and that we may be found to be of an inoffensive conscience. Amen. Dated in Augsburg anno 1544.

Pilgram Marpeck.

8

Those Dead in Sin (1545) [#4]

Introduction

A scribal note following Marpeck's signature states that this letter was written to Magdalena von Pappenheim,[1] a noble lady, and others who are not identified. It is a response to a letter, presumably from Magdalena who had joined his group a few years before.

Magdalena von Pappenheim was a member of a noble family that maintained a long-standing connection with Anabaptism. At least two others were members, and yet others had close contacts. Magdalena was a former nun of the Benedictine order who was much concerned for her spiritual state. For several years, she served as a link for Marpeck and Schwenckfeld in their correspondence. One other letter in this collection, *The Peasant Aristocracy* (#18), is addressed to her.

It appears from paragraph 2 on page 410 that Magdalena had had some doubts as to whether she was truly raised up and alive in Christ. Marpeck says: "according to the command of Christ, we release you from the fear of death in which you were imprisoned." This is a good example of the binding and loosing which, Marpeck taught, is the duty and prerogative of the church of Christ.

The Text

Those Dead in Sin

3v   This letter concerns those who are dead in sin, what is the work of God and the action of the

Jn. 11 church with respect to them, together with a fine parable of the dead Lazarus.

The grace of our Lord Jesus Christ be with all who fervently desire it. Amen. My loved ones in Christ. First of all, in faith, confidence, and hope in Christ Jesus, our Healer, which is the true work of God, we thank God our heavenly Father for you in whom, through Jesus Christ our Lord, He continues His work with us and you. One has confidence and faith in Him whom the Father has sent, the Lord Lk. 5 [31 f.] Jesus Christ, who alone is the Physician and Healer, who can call into being that which is not, and who can raise up the dead in spirit, soul, and conscience Jn. 11 [17-45] from eternal death. Even today, He raises up the dead Lazarus, who was buried four days, stinking, bound with graveclothes, and He calls him to come forth. Yes, even today, He commands that he be unbound and released from the bonds and cords of eternal death. He commands that the headclothes of anxiety and distress, which are wound around his head, and in which the deceased, in spite of all his 4r reason, is entangled, / / be loosed from his head. [He calls] those whom God makes alive to be released from their graveclothes, from the cords and bonds of death, and to let them go. God, through Christ, yes, Christ Himself, has brought them back to life.

ₐSin kills. Men bury such dead ones in head- and graveclothes. The Lord can revive and raise them up; He can command men to release the head- and graveclothes in which they have bound the dead. Yes, the Lord can command those who live for God, and He can allow . . . [the dead ones] to go and walk before God. He removes the stone from the grave, that is, He removes the hardness of sin which encrusts the heart. Thus, what God raises

---

a-a indented by the copyist.

up and restores to life may come out. That is the work of the church. The life through faith is God's work alone.ₐ

Thus, even today, all the true friends of God in Christ rejoice over those who have been raised from the death of sin, for they witness the wonderful goodness and glory of God in their brother and friend, and can say with Martha and Mary Magdalene (sic): "If the Lord had been with him, he would not have died." Sin which brings forth death has no power where Christ is, for Christ is life. Now, since Christ is the life which remains eternally, death and life cannot be one. Death, however, is the wage of sin, which also remains eternally. Therefore, even though she referred to physical death, Martha spoke the truth. It is indisputable that one does not die in sin where Christ is, for He is life; He is the Physician / / and Healer, who can say even today: "Rise, take your bed and walk; your sins are forgiven." He can restore sight and light to all blindness. Of what use is the light to him who cannot see, or of what use is sight when there is no light? Where the light shines, sight and eyes become useful, and light exercises its blessed power wherever there are eyes and sight.

All this we write to you in order that you may receive perfect comfort in the knowledge of Christ, and may be able to discern the working of God the Father in Christ, yes, the working of Christ Himself in His marriage and the communion of saints. Like the Father, Christ works here even today. It is this way: whoever is found to be dying and dead, because of the deceitfulness of sin, is dead to God, and his face is covered with the headclothes of anxiety, distress, and affliction, for the light is of no use to him. It would be a mockery of light if one were to give light to a dead person. Therefore, he alone has

Jas. 1 [15]

Rom. 6 [23]

4v

409

the headcloth which is anxiety and mourning, for his deluded, dead eyes. Beautiful clothing does not belong to one who is dead, for such beautifying clothing will rot together with him. Similarly, if one adorns the dead // in spirit with the virtues of faith, which are the true garments of the Holy Spirit, it will be of no use; all will rot and spoil in the death of sin, and be a stench before God. Therefore, such a one gets only graveclothes. That is the law of the curse; in sorrow, he is bound for the decay and destruction of the flesh until God, who alone has the power, raises him up from the death of sin through Christ. The friends of God wait in mourning. When, therefore, the dead is awakened and when Christ orders him to come out of the grave of death, and he again comes to life, then the friends and servants properly take the turban from the face, and remove the graveclothes in which, as a dead man, they had bound him. Thus, you may easily understand the work which God does only through and with Christ, and the service and work of the community and friends of Christ.

Thus, my beloved, since you have been raised up in the call and act of Christ, and since Christ calls you to go forth with hearty joy from your mourning and suffering, from death and the graveclothes, according to the command of Christ, we release you from the fear of death in which you were imprisoned.//

ᵇWhen the lost son, who had fled abroad and wasted his inheritance, who was dead and who came to life again, through Christ, recognized his misery and poverty in great lowliness and humility, the father rejoiced and received his lost son. So, too, did the woman, the church, rejoice when she found

---

b-b indented by the copyist.

410

one of the ten coins she had lost. Like the father and the woman, even as it is done in heaven (Lk. 15 [22-24; 9]), all true believers on earth do not rejoice for the ninety-nine just ones who need no repentance. Rather, the true believers rejoice when one sinner repents.b

Beyond this rejoicing, no one has authority but to bury the dead with sorrow,[2] and to release the living from the bonds and cords of death. That is the service of the church and the saints.

This is a hurried reply to all your writing. We fervently greet and comfort you in the peace of Christ in order that we may be comforted with all who have true faith. The grace of our Lord Jesus Christ be with all of you and us. Amen. Pray fervently to God for us, and we will be indebted to do the same for you.

Dated at Augsburg, anno 1545.
In the Lord Jesus Christ
your servant and comrade
in the tribulation of Christ.
Pilgram Marpeck
Written to Magdalena von Pappenheim and others with her.

9

An Epistle
Concerning the Heritage
and Service of Sin

(1545) ^(#13)

Introduction

This letter to Leupold Scharnschlager in Ilanz is one of several personal letters in the collection. It was prompted by a letter which Marpeck had received from members of his group in Moravia who were concerned or confused about the feuding between the various Anabaptist groups in Moravia.

Marpeck again casts his reflections in an allegorical or typological interpretation of Genesis 31:34, 35, the incident of Rachel's hiding the family gods under her skirts, and getting away with it by feigning menstruation. Marpeck draws an analogy between this incident and the sinful state of man. Our embarrassment, he writes, is gone, and we no longer need to deceive others about God, but can confess Him openly without fear.

He then reemphasizes a favorite theme, elaborated at greater length in *The Lowliness of Christ* (#16); since Christ came not to rule but to serve, so His followers are servants and not rulers. Christians will certainly rule with Christ, but only after they have gone through the depth of tribulation with Him. In *The Lowliness of Christ*, Marpeck contrasts this attitude to the judgmental and overbearing attitudes of some individuals among the Swiss Brethren. Perhaps the inclusion of the same theme here in the *Epistle* suggests that a similar problem was in some way plaguing his group in Moravia. Perhaps the reference is to the Hutterites. In any event, he suggests that, if Christians serve as Jesus did, there can be no disunity in the church.

This letter contains a reference to Marpeck's wife, Anna, as well as to a number of other Anabaptists about whom nothing else is known.

The Text
An Epistle Concerning the Heritage and Service of Sin.

238r An epistle concerning the heritage and service, as well as the blood flow,[1] of sin, which was established through Christ, together with other scriptural parables. Finally, also concerning the Christian's service and false messengers.

Grace and peace from God our heavenly Father, through Jesus Christ our Lord, be and remain with us in eternity. Amen.

My dearest brother Leopold![2] Recently, I wrote you and brother Martin[3] [a letter] which I hope you have received. In it, I indicated something about how matters stand with us in the Lord by His grace. We continue to thank God for this and His great mercy; He has given us the privilege to live in His house of peace (yes, in the house of grace and love), not as slaves, strangers, or hirelings, but as friends, children, brothers, and sisters. Unlike Jacob, we are not like those who work for the inheritance (I mean the inheritance of sin) and for wives. Nor do we serve another seven years for the beautiful Rebekah, that is, the church and bride of Christ. Because of blood and death on the cross, we are already given[4] and married to Him, and are as handmaidens to Rebekah, His bride. Nor may we ever steal or make off with the God of our father, or

238v cover / / up and conceal Him with female embarrassment.[5]

In Christ, God our Father has revealed Himself to us in the shape of a man. Yes, Christ Himself is both God and man. From the beginning, God has known of our embarrassment and yet, we have used

413

this embarrassment to deceive. Ashamed of our-selves, we have tried to cover up, hide, and make off with His divinity. He, however, has been lenient with our sin; He did not want to uncover our sick-ness and female embarrassment. Until the time de-termined for the revelation, He will bear with it.

Consequently, we now publicly carry about the God and Father of our Lord Jesus Christ, our spouse of the Father, and, along with all the treasures of Christ, call Him our own.

Everything has been given to us by Him. The wearisome female flow of blood has been staunched and cleansed. Along with our purblind birth, it has been healed and given sight. Yes, like Lazarus, four days dead and stinking, we have been raised to life. Thus, we now participate in the first resurrection, which began with Christ. We are the firstborn from the dead. The second death no longer has power over us because of His liberating power, delivered from above. Moreover, we now rule with Christ by virtue of the power of His Spirit over sin and death, and the working of His Spirit over the devil / / and hell, over all their power, portals, bonds, and cords, and even over ourselves and all creatures under heaven. Death is no longer death for us. Rather, through faith in Christ, we have struggled from death to life.

This love is as strong as death. Thus, neither death nor hell can now overpower us. Previously, deceived as we were by self-love and idolatrous love of the creatures, we loved in spite of God, and ar-rayed ourselves, in confusion and disorder, against God and our neighbor. But the love of God has been shed abroad in our hearts and, for the sake of that love, all else is surrendered to Him, for it is regarded as valueless. For the sake of the love of Christ, we have now achieved this freedom, this

414

release from the slavery of sin under which we were all sold.

However, now that we have this liberty, we no longer serve ourselves and the creatures, nor do we serve for the sake of reward. We serve in the freedom of grace. Christ works in us and gives us His aid. He lives in us and not we in ourselves, and He is our heritage. No slave Himself, the Spirit of the Son, Lord and God is His pledge in us. Whatever we serve in this life, we serve under the sweet yoke of Christ and whatever we suffer in the flesh, we suffer in Christ's stead. Without reward or pay, Christ has / / taken our place, and His service and suffering have reconciled us to the Father. Until we have entered the kingdom and, through His suffering, been endowed with power from on high, we, too, serve. Our service is to Christ's members. In them, we make up whatever is lacking of Christ's sufferings, and we do so in all patience and faith. This service is not only required of our soul, but it is also needful at this time. In no sense do we receive a reward or inheritance for what has already been earned by Christ and given to us. We do overcome, judge, condemn, or acquit. But the sovereignty belongs to Christ, who has, together with the Father, all power over heaven and earth until the time of His appearance. Then, His glory shall glorify our bodies, and His splendor shall raise us into splendor with Him.

Now, Christ did not come to condemn or to destroy men. Nor did He come to be served. He came to offer salvation to man and, through His suffering in all patience, to save and serve them. We have been appointed by Him, not to rule over, judge, condemn, destroy, or inflict any suffering or evil on men. We are to / / serve them, to offer and announce to them His grace and healing, and in His

239v

240r

415

name to proclaim the forgiveness of sin. Men may then be converted to their Creator, God, and Lord, repent for the forgiveness of sins, and believe in and trust God and the Lord Jesus Christ. To proclaim the virtues and grace of Him who called us in our service and appointment at this time. In His name and in His place we now serve, as members of His body. As our Head, we serve under Him. Men need such servants, and may God send many of them in His great mercy.

The opposition is powerful in manifold ways and forms. There are many rulers, many temporal and spiritual tyrants who, while appearing to be Christian, violate, judge, and condemn. They run ahead of Christ, and seize His power like thieves and murderers; they rob Him of His honor and glory, and arrogate it to themselves. They rule before [they have known] patience, distress, and suffering, even though tribulation has to precede glory. They become powerful before they have humbled themselves, they rule and govern before they serve, they condemn and judge before they have judged themselves. The world is full of those who run before they are called. They / / are clouds without water, as Peter says [2 Pet. 2:17], driven by a whirlwind. But perhaps the world does not deserve anything better.

240v

I have written this epistle because the brothers in Moravia have written to me, and because it has been reported to me by a brother, Heinrich Schneider,[6] how those who live there are full of schisms and deceit. May the Lord preserve us. Amen. [I also write to report] that I, my Andle, and the other brothers and sisters are spiritually and physically well through the grace of Christ. We heartily wish you all the same. Greetings from all of us to you. Pray God for our sakes, especially for mine, and we, as debtors to love, will faithfully do the same for you. The grace of our Lord Jesus Christ be and remain with us for ever. Amen.

In the year 1545,
Your comrade and fellow-
contender for the truth in
the tribulation of the Lord
Jesus Christ.

Pilgram Marpeck.

The other Nessling sends faithful greetings to you. He is employed as porter with Franzli's master. (God be merciful to him.) Amen.

10

On the Inner Church
(1545) (#17)

Introduction

The relation of the inner and the outer was of utmost importance to Marpeck and his group. On the one hand, they wished to avoid the error of both the Catholic Church and of those in the magisterial Reformation, who, as they saw it, reduced the outer to a mechanical or magical performance. On the other hand, they also sought to avoid the error of the purely mystical or spiritualistic approach, which stressed only the inner reality, and which either did not see any need for the external manifestations of that inner reality, or even saw the external as a detriment to the internal.

In this letter, Marpeck affirms the central importance of the worship which takes place in the inner man, for the heart is considered to be "the inner and only temple in which God dwells." Into this inner sanctuary only the Holy Spirit can enter, and the church must not enter it and seek to discipline its members until the Holy Spirit has done His work. At this point, the concept of co-witness becomes central to his thought. Christians join with the Holy Spirit in His witness, and do not carry on without Him. When they try to go it alone, they either go ahead of the Spirit or lag behind.

Marpeck does not affirm, however, that man's actions are a complement to that which Christ does. Rather, he begins with John 5:19: "The Son sees what the Father does and, what the Father does the Son does likewise." And Marpeck gives it a distinctive interpretation. He argues that, while the Son works outwardly, the Father works inwardly. Thus, when the church, led by the Spirit, performs external worship, etc., it is really the Son of God at work in their midst. At other places, this interpretation is applied to baptism and other aspects of the life of the church. But the fundamental statement of this position is found in the following letter. In this way, Marpeck recognizes the inner dynamic of the Christian church, but also insists that such a dynamic must have an external expression.

The Text
On the Inner Church[1]

302r   This epistle reports on the inner churches, temple, dwelling place, revelation, inner choir, external work, the order, where and how one should worship, confession of sin, etc., along with other matters.

To the elect, sanctified by God in Christ Jesus, our beloved in Austerlitz and other places, an answer, etc.

Grace and peace from God, our heavenly Father, through the Lord Jesus Christ, abide with you and all of us, who love Christ from the heart. Amen.

Dearly beloved, brethren and sisters in the Lord Jesus Christ. The messengers you sent to us have arrived by the grace of God. Along with your epistle to us, in which we perceived your disposition, mind, and spirit in Christ, we received them and their report with sincere joy in Christ. Through the Lord's grace, we understood everything, and accepted it with sincere joy. On your behalf and ours,

302v   we also praise our God and Father, through Jesus Christ, our Lord, and thank Him for His mercy and grace, which He has shown to us and all the children of men. Our mind sincerely desired to know how the faith of Jesus Christ, its knowledge and confession, stands with you, because eternal life consists in the knowledge of the truth of Christ

419

Jn. 17
302v

alone. As the Lord Jesus Christ, the true Son of God and of man, says: "This is life eternal, that they know you, Father, true God, and Jesus Christ whom you have sent." / / Human salvation and eternal life consists only in the knowledge of God the Father and His Christ, and it remains so in eternity. To hear that we are of one mind in the truth of Christ and the Father is a joyous thing. And what more joyous thing can we experience than to confess to one another that we know that Christ Jesus is in the Father and God the Father is in Christ, and remains so eternally. Indeed, we know, recognize, and also feel that Christ is in us and we in Christ, and remain so eternally. Moreover, we know and recognize that the dwelling of God the Father and His Christ is built in our hearts. Now, in this time, they have made a dwelling, and dwell in us. Indeed, we also know and recognize the fruit and work of the Son, which the Father works in the Son and the Son in us, whereby we remain in His Word. The fruit is perfect love. We recognize therein that the Father and the Son have made their dwelling in us, and live in us.

Dwelling
of God and
Christ

Jn. 14

These are the ones who love the Father and the Son, and keep the words in unity. But those who do not love Him do not keep His words. Furthermore, we must also recognize that we love one another, as He loved us; thus, we are perceived as His true disciples. Whoever has this command, and keeps it, loves Him. He, too, will be loved by the Father. And Christ will also love him, and reveal Himself to him. / / The true revelation of Christ Jesus is to feel and recognize that the will, work, and good pleasure of the Father is, through Christ, performed in us. Thus, God the Father dwells in Christ, Christ dwells with God the Father in us, and we dwell in Christ with God. This place and dwelling was first

1 Jn. 3

Revelation
of Christ,
etc.
303r

Jn. 14

prepared for us through Christ. Before Christ's ascension, such a place and dwelling was not ready for anyone. But this dwelling means that we have the presence of God the Father and the Son in us, and thereby keep His Word and His commands, which are not heavy but light.

Place of worship
Jn. 4

Consequently, we also dwell in God, in God the Father and in Christ, in the Jerusalem which is above, and now here below upon the earth. The only place of worship is above. There the true worshipers worship in spirit and in truth, and in the fellowship of the saints. Eternal life consists of such true and similar knowledge. To achieve it, we must truly learn to know God the Father and Christ, who was sent by God. If we received it by grace and prayer, such knowledge in Christ is also life eternal. Hence, our joy toward one another is complete in God and thus, we rejoice in you, and hope that you are also rejoicing with us in the truth.

The heart
is a temple

303v

Inner choir,
heart of man

Jer. 17

Inner
church, etc.

Because the Jerusalem, which is above, is only built by Jesus Christ in the Spirit, the heart is the inner and only temple. In this Jerusalem is the place of worship, namely, in Spirit/ / and in truth. The hearts of men, the hearts of the true believers, are also the inner choir and sanctuary, into which no one can enter except our High Priest; to Him alone the choir and the sanctuary have been dedicated by God the Father, who is able to search the heart, thoughts, and soul. This choir and sanctuary is known only by the High Priest, Christ; in it He prays to the Father for the sins of men. Only this High Priest, Christ Jesus, can see how the inner choir and the sanctuary are shepherded and formed. This church is seen only by the Spirit, and only in the Spirit, through the High Priest Christ, is there forgiveness and remission of sins. That is the inner church of Christ.

Eternal life means that man now shall and must know for himself whether Christ dwells in him or not. Also, through Christ, God alone knows how it stands in the heart of man, whether it is right before God or not. This inner church will only be revealed by the coming of the Lord Jesus Christ, at which time He will transfigure and reveal the hearts with Him. However, when Christ, our life, is revealed in the glory which He had before that time, we, too, will be revealed with Him. His glory is revealed to no creature in heaven or on earth, yea, not even to the angels, because liars and hypocrites can also do the external work Christ already commanded/ / and ordained to His church, and they can change their external appearance to angels of light.

In collaboration with the Holy Spirit, this inner church of the Holy Spirit is also directed to perform external works, to be a light before the world. It witnesses inwardly between God and man, but it is also formed externally, and testifies in love shown toward the neighbor. According to the measure of the internal working of the Holy Spirit, which leads to the external forgiveness of sin and the improvement of the external man, teaching, baptism, and the Lord's Supper show love toward all men. In this manner, the Spirit, mind, and will of the Father are revealed by the external man, Jesus Christ; they are revealed bodily, by word and work, in the same form as the internal working of God the Father [Jn. 5:19]. Unless the Father draws him, no one comes to the Son, and no one knows the Father except the Son. The Son reveals him to the Father. Therefore today, as long as it is today, the full knowledge of the Father and of His Christ consists in the internal and the external workings of the Holy Spirit. Saint Paul also says: "In Him dwells the fullness of the

2 Cor. 13

nota

304r
2 Cor. 11

Inner is
not without
the outer.

nota

Jn. 6

Mt. 11

422

Col. 2

304v

Eph. 4

Jn. 6

Jn. 3

2 Cor. 6

nota

305r

Jn. 6 & 17

Heb. 3, 4

Godhead bodily." And ye are full of the same, one // faith, one baptism, one teaching, one Lord's Supper, one God, Father of us all, who rules over the one church, inner and outer, in eternity. Amen.

What the Father does, as Spirit and God, the Son immediately does likewise, but He does it as an external man who performs outward works. The Father loves the Son, and has given all things into His hand. Those who are born anew in Christ, according to the inner working of the Holy Spirit, are those who are baptized with fire, who are aglow with love. Moreover, these children, born of the Spirit, see what the Father, working through Christ, does for the inner man; they, too, by co-witnessing in the Holy Spirit, immediately do likewise for the external man. Thus, the body of Christ is also built inwardly through the Holy Spirit, and externally through the co-witness of works. His church or communion is His bride, internally in the Spirit and truth, externally with praise to God, and to be a light before the world. But this church is separated from the world, for it is a witness over it. Similarly, through word and work, the gospel must be preached before the coming of the Son of Man.

I do not mean to suggest that the cities of Israel should be accomplished by anyone other than the commissioned apostles, nor should it be carried out before the day of the Lord./ / I write merely to ensure that those whom God the Father draws and gives to the Son will be fulfilled, and will have salvation proclaimed to them. These He will keep, and He will only lose the children of perdition. The children who are kept will often, because of the children of perdition, suffer great loss. It may even seem that they come to destruction and fall victims to it. Yet, not one of them will be cast aside. I refer to those in whom hope remains for, as God pleases,

423

hope is a spring from which one may again receive grace for the future. Those who do not lack hope, and who do not, as a consequence, harden their hearts, may all be brought again to Christ while today is still today. His body, which is at the present moment still upon the earth, will assist them. The communion of the saints means that, through Jesus Christ, remission of sins is available.

Discerning
and punishing
sin

nota

1 Cor. 5 & 11

The Holy Spirit punishes a committed sin and, before His saints carry out any external punishment, He alone first punishes. If, however, the Holy Spirit reveals this sin, then the church of Christ first punishes through the co-witness[2] of the Holy Spirit, which means that He reveals sin. Thus, the saints co-witness[2] that sins may not be tolerated on the body of Christ, and they distinguish these sins from the body of Christ. Wherever the Holy Spirit punishes inwardly in a hidden way, from grace to grace, with the comfort of forgiveness, no creature, either in heaven or on earth, is authorized to inflict punishment,/ / which some do out of a false concern. They judge the hearts, and desire to reveal them before the time.

Not to
judge the
hidden

305v

1 Cor. 4

As the psalmist says: "Blessed is he whose transgression is forgiven, whose sin is covered, and in whose spirit there is no guile." Whoever does not confess his sin before God, who knows and sees all things, him the Holy Spirit punishes with the manifestation of the sin. If he then refuses to recognize or confess it either to God or man, if the sin is openly known and seen on him, and if he still refuses in spite of admonition and punishment to confess his transgression, then he belongs to the world, and the Holy Spirit will punish him for the sin of unbelief. If, however, the Holy Spirit punishes unto grace, the hope the sinner has received remains with his remorse for the sin, as it

Ps. 32

1 Cor. 5

nota

often takes a long time before this sin is forgiven by the Holy Spirit, and the erring one is blessed with inward comfort. Such forgiveness and comfort naturally precede all forgiveness and comfort in man as a spark of grace,[3] through which divine fire (out of the fullness of Christ to give grace for grace) the inner is fed further with admonition and intercession of saints. So, until a man confesses his sin before God and the fellowship of His saints in Christ, and until he confesses against himself and judges himself, to that time only belongs the prayer of the saints for such sinners. All sin must be atoned with prayer through the death of Christ. Only when there is no deceit in / / confessing sin, and only when the prayer of the saints is pure does the Holy Spirit put comfort into the heart of the sinner, and forgive the sin. Only then may the saints forgive him through Christ and the Holy Spirit, all of which is only one forgiveness. Whoever grieves God has also grieved His saints, and whoever grieves His saints, has also grieved God.

Sin atoned by prayer

306r

nota

I write this letter to you, my beloved, so that we in nothing, neither with ban or forgiveness of sin, nor command or restriction, nor order or custom, may outrun the Holy Spirit. Indeed, there are many law-makers and ban-ers today who capture the conscience and burn through the cheek. Also, there are many deceivers who completely despise, and seek to discontinue admonition, prayer, ban, punishment, teaching, baptism, the Lord's Supper, and the forgiveness of sins in the fellowship of the saints. Therefore, my beloved, let us in nothing allow the grace given to us to be taken away or robbed. Rather, let us hold on to our unwavering hope in Christ, which I desire from the heart and ask on your behalf and ours, and all elect of God in Christ. Amen.

Order suspended

425

Since both brother Leopold[4] and the brethren from Strasbourg have written you, and revealed my heart and mind along with theirs, to write more, and in greater detail, I consider to be unnecessary. You will be orally informed / / by the brethren, and it will be like the living epistle from us to you. I pray God, if it be His pleasure and serve His honor, that He will allow us to read orally the letters written in our hearts by the finger of God, which I hope will

Col. 1 undoubtedly take place. Pray God the Father through Christ that we all may fulfill and complete the suffering of Christ, which is left over in His body, that each, as faithful fellow witnesses to the suffering of Christ, do so, even unto death, according to the manner of love, and that we also suffer one for another, as Christ has suffered for us unto the end. Amen.

Jörg Stadler[5] and his matrimonial sister [wife] Anna, both unknown to you by face, send greetings. So do my matrimonial sister[6] [wife], Anna, along with me and all those who are personally known to us and we to them; God knows all of our names. Pray God fervently and earnestly, according to the need, on our behalf. As debtors for you, we, and all who desire it and are obligated by love, shall do likewise. The grace of our Lord Jesus Christ abide with us, and with all who love and seek Christ from the heart. Amen.

> In the Lord Jesus Christ
> your (and all true believers')
> servant and comrade in the
> tribulation of Christ.
> Pilgram Marpeck.

11

Concerning
the Lowliness of Christ
(1547) [#16]

Introduction

In 1542 Marpeck had begun attempts to achieve union with
the Swiss Brethren, and had tried to clarify the issues as he saw
them, but without success. In February 1547, he again returned
to the matter in a long letter. It went to the Swiss as well as to
some in Alsace.

He began his letter by stressing the humanity of Christ. In
this instance, he uses the analogy of an ark. Everything that God
had to give men was "locked up" in Jesus the man, just as things
are "locked up" in an ark. The cross represented the opening of
the ark to all those who believe. That happened, however, because Christ was willing to accept complete and utter humiliation, even to the *descensus ad infernos*, which Marpeck specifically states was not a triumphant descent, but the nadir of His
humiliation: "He went into the depths of hell in His human
poverty with our sin." Such a belief, then, is a direct link to Marpeck's concern for the Swiss Brethren. Christ's saints do not rule
or exercise power. They first follow Christ in His humiliation.
Indeed, "there is no possibility of salvation except through the
deep humility of Christ." Men like to begin with the height, the
glory of Christ, since that makes no demand on them.

God has given His gifts to men in earthly vessels which
easily break. Therefore, they must be handled with care, and
with patience and love. Patience is, in fact, the ark which
preserves all that God has to give His own. If patience is forsaken
for impatience and precipitate action, everything is destroyed.
Indeed, Marpeck insists that there is a close relationship between
hasty judgments and actions against fellow saints, and the vio-

lence practiced by Catholics and Protestants in their religious intolerance. Faith cannot be coerced in any form, and to justify coercion on allegedly Christian grounds does not make it any less the devil's work. He emphasizes that all such violence brings only ruin in its train. In a marginal gloss, Rothenfelder provides the examples of Zwingli's war with the Catholics, and the Schmalkald War between Catholics and Protestants.

It is important to note that this letter was written early in 1547. Augsburg had surrendered to the emperor in late 1546 and in April 1547 the last of the Protestant forces had been defeated in battle. That, Marpeck reminds his readers, happens when men do not abandon all claims to power and submit to the lowliness of Christ.

If, then, a Christian lives in absolute liberty in Christ, how is he guided in his actions? To those who long for such guidance, the Holy Spirit brings to remembrance the words and life of the man Jesus. If they follow the book He writes in their hearts, the faithful will reap only blessing, never curse. They need not fear, then, to stray onto false paths, and they will constantly preserve the proper balance between the inner and the outer.

Of special interest here is Marpeck's description of the church which stands in marked contrast to the Catholic and Protestant definitions. The church has a special name and a special location only if there are those who are faithful, for the dwelling of God is in men. It is not associated with a church building, or with the performance of external rites in and of themselves. It is an eloquent description of the pilgrim church.

The Text
Concerning the Lowliness of Christ
Together with Other Fine Expositions, etc. [Also Concerning]
the New Year

278r   To all the elect and saints of God in the Grisons, Appenzell, St. Gall, in Alsace, and wherever they are scattered hither and yon, my dearest ones in Christ.

Grace and peace from God our Father, and our Lord Jesus Christ, be and remain with us for ever. Amen.

My dearly beloved in God the Father and the Lord Jesus Christ. Especially in this critical time of great danger, my fervent prayer, wish, and desire, now and always, is that one of these days, before my end, God might open the way to [come to] you all. There, together, we might rejoice in the way, truth, and life which is Jesus Christ, discuss His will, mind, and Spirit which are given in word, deed, and act, and share our delight in the love and truth of the gospel of Christ.

This is the message which Christ in His grace has given, commanded, and delivered to us. It is the costliest and most esteemed treasure, for it is Christ the Lord Himself. In this treasure are hidden all the treasures of the secret will and pleasure of the Father, for no one has seen the Father, much less known Him, except the Son who is in the bosom of the Father. Similarly, no one has known the Son except the Father who sent Him. The Son reveals [His Father] in His holy, external[1] teaching. And the miracle and power of His works on earth are the Father's testimony to His teaching. He to whom the Father has not been revealed cannot, and may not, know the Father of lights. Similarly, no one can know that Jesus Christ is the Son of the living God unless the Father reveals it to him. Thus, the Son is glorified through the Father and the Father through the Son.

278v

He was born to the Father from the race of man, for the sake of man. He was born to liberate man from the power of the devil, sin, death, and hell, that is, from the guilt of Adam into which all men have come. [They have come into it] because of the guilt of sin, and because of the pains of hell

429

and death which were laid on men. Men have been given over to the devil, who has the power of death and torment as well as of sin. And it is sin which causes the wrath of God so that, even among men who possess the salvation given by the Son of God, there can be no cessation of sin. Thus, the wrath of God delivers to sin, death, hell, pain, and the devil. Because of the one sin of disobedience, man in all eternity is no longer able to know his God, Father, and Creator. Even today, man is utterly under the wrath of God and because of sin, man is outside of Christ, the / / Lord and Savior.

279r

However, because of our sin, the Father did not spare the Son. He has given Him for the sake of man, and delivered Him into the suffering and pain of death, even to condemnation, as a salvation for men. Thus, Christ's sufferings enable men to regain the original purity and innocence in which they were created and to be prepared for their God, Father, Creator, and Maker. The Holy Spirit, who cannot be where sin is, can again find a place and gain a dwelling in men, and then [transfer them] from the earthly to the heavenly. Thus, man is created an earthly creature but, through the incarnation of Christ, the earthly may become heavenly. Had Adam not fallen, there would be no need for suffering. But, because of sin, suffering and death came upon Christ. And, unlike man who experiences suffering and death because of guilt, Christ is without guilt. Grace, and the justification which leads to true devotion and which proceeds from faith, transfers man from the earthly to the eternal, heavenly state. Therefore, all earthly creatures are made subject to man in order that man might be made subject to the Lord Jesus Christ in His heavenly state and glory. Similarly, in true manhood, the Son is subject to the Father.

Rom. [?] 1

By the will of the Father, He was born of a virgin from the generation of the fathers. He was born the true Son of God, full of grace and truth and according to the Spirit. He is the eternal Word,

279v

and the only born / / Son of the Father. He is filled with every counsel and knowledge, wisdom, understanding, and perception of the Father's will. As announced in Isaiah 9[6]: "For to us a child is born, a

1 Reg. 2
Sam. 8:11-18]

son is given, and the kingship will be upon his shoulder." As Samuel told the people of Israel when, like the Gentiles, they desired a king, the kings of this world rest their kingship as a heavy burden upon the shoulders of the people. Such a king had the right to expect that his kingship should rest on the shoulders of the people, that they should bear the burden of the king. However, this King, the Lord Jesus Christ, has liberated His people from their eternal burden; He has put it on His own shoulders and has fastened it to the cross. Can we

1 Pet. 2

conceive of a more glorious kingdom, priesthood, kingship, or king? Isaiah further says that His name is Wonderful Counselor, the mighty God, the everlasting Father, the Prince of Peace. His kingdom shall have no end, and peace will be multiplied [Is. 9:7]. This child has been given to us by the Father with all His treasures and gifts. That same Lord, King, and true God has given Himself with all His treasures and gifts, and He will be the acceptable

New Year

new year [Lk. 4:19].

These treasures were hidden and locked in the trunk of His body, the ark of the covenant. This ark He destroyed on the cross, and then He pried it

280r

open, which was the finishing of His work. / / The child fulfilled the Father's promise to us. The suffering and death on the cross completed His work on earth. Then, He made the descent into hell, and dwelt with the condemned, with those imprisoned

431

in perdition, and with those held by death. As Christ Himself said: "My God, why have you forsaken me?" [Mk. 15:24]. However, both on earth and in the Pit,[2] Christ was proclaimed. In the depth of death and in the abyss of hell, the Lord of both life and death proclaimed the Word to the dead. Here, the soul of Christ preached the gospel. On earth, Christ's physical suffering and death proclaimed the Word to men living in the body. Just as it was on earth, among the dead in the prison of hell all faith and hope had disappeared. Because of the guilt of the first Adam, death and hell had seized, and held captive, Him who had brought and accomplished salvation on earth, and who had also brought salvation to the prisoners of death and hell in the Pit. Then, all faith and hope disappeared from the earth and from the dead in the Pit.

Jon. 2 [1-6]

The parable and prediction of the Prophet Jonah was fulfilled in Christ. Even as Jonah was swallowed by the actual leviathan in the real depth of the sea, so, too, was the Lord, together with the rest of the dead, swallowed and made captive by the spiritual leviathan, the lord of the spiritual sea, of

280v

torment and // death, who has power eternally. Contrary to the view held by some erring spirits,

Schwenckfeld

Christ did not descend in triumph to the dead. Such a fabrication contradicts the true teaching of Christ. Even as Jonah sang a song of triumph in the whale, Christ triumphed in hell and death. And just as

Mt. 12 [39]

Jonah was in the belly of the whale three days and three nights, even so, the Son of Man will be in the middle of the earth three days and three nights. And just as Jonah was in the whale only a short while, Christ remained in death and hell until He had completely paid, for our sake, the guilt of sin.

Rom. 8 [32]
Jn. 3 [15]

Thus, the Father did not spare the Son, but gave Him up so that all who believe in Him may have eternal life. The Father sealed the guilt of sin in death and in the prison of hell forever. In His human poverty, the payer of the debt, the true warrantor, went Himself into the depths of hell with our sins, and yet without any sin of His own, through His torment on earth in order to make payment. Moreover, He took the power away from Heb. 2 [14] death and from him who has the dominion over 281r pain and / / death. The whale could not hold Jonah, nor could the Pit hold Him there. Life broke through in its power, which the Lord had had in Himself against all the power of hell. By means of the glory, dominion, and power of life He took life back again out of the midst of death, together with all who have hoped for the Lord and His salvation.[3] Their hope, and also the hope of the apostles on earth,[4] was gone. For their very sakes, the joy, splendor, and glory of Christ has ascended to the heights, not only with all the imprisoned, but with the prison itself. Paul's question is appropriate here: "Death, hell, devil, and sin, where is your power 1 Cor. 15 [55] and dominion?"

Thus, death has been swallowed up in victory, and Christ has emerged from death to life with all His chosen ones. To do so, He had both to descend and ascend, for His soul did not remain in hell. Death could not possibly keep the life of all life imprisoned, and darkness could not put out or comprehend the light, even though the light had come into the darkness of hell. Since the light Himself was imprisoned and held by darkness, there were three hours of darkness over the whole earth, not from some natural cause, but from the irruption of the Pit, which is the source of all darkness. The true light, which had the most right to shine, did not assert His power and, since He Himself had commanded all other lights to shine, the natural lights then had to surrender their brilliance. But the Lord, as the true light, has broken out of the darkness of the devil, death, sin, and hell, through the brilliance of His light and clarity and returned alive from death. In His own power He took life back; He ascended, and seated Himself to the right of the majesty of God the Father and in the glorification of the Father, with that eternal, preexistent glory which He had with the Father before the foundations of the world were laid.

Is. 53 [12]

The Son conquered the sin of many precisely by this descent into the depths[5], this greatest humility with which He humbled Himself before the Father, and by which the Father afflicted and humbled the Son. All the saints of God must learn the depths of Christ, these same depths of humility and damnation, into which the leaven of our sin brought Christ. [They must learn] the consequences of sin. Provided the devil completes[6] sin's work in man, sin brings man into death. Here, only the deep humility of Christ brings any possibility of salvation. Whoever does not grasp that he must be condemned with and in Christ in the depths can never understand nor achieve the height of Christ. Indeed, the whole world does not want to grasp this depth of Christ; it does not want to be condemned, / / to recognize its lostness, and so be saved.

282r
Mt. 16 [24-26]
Lk. 19 [24, 25]

However, almost everyone babbles and boasts deceitfully about the height and divinity of Christ, and uses reason and scriptural subtleties,[7] to find a false sufficiency of joy in themselves. Yet, no one is prepared to go down with Christ into death and be buried with Him. They begin with the height [of Christ], in order to deceive themselves and others. Thus, they must go down to destruction and suffer eternal exclusion from the height of Christ.

Rom. 6 [3, 4]

Baptism is a secret, severe water which drives all reason down into the depth to die with Christ and be buried in His death. Only then can the soul rise with Christ and become a partaker of His gifts and the treasures of His kingdom, which He distributes to all His chosen ones and gives to His own. Thus, the Son makes the Father known, and the Father makes known and reveals the Son. The elect are glorified in them, just as the Father and Son are glorified in and with themselves.

But all this has been revealed and learned first through His holy humanity. His power and miracles proved that men might believe what He said, did, and accomplished on / / earth. And He has received His power from the Father. To His honor and glory, He has opened it to us. Thus, our lives are renewed in order that we should eternally honor, praise, and thank the heavenly Father through His beloved Son.

282v

To the honor and glory of the Father, He has sealed us with the Holy Spirit. As the true Prince of Peace, He, through the Holy Spirit, has established eternal, perpetual peace with us in our hearts and consciences. He never ceases to increase the kingdom of His peace, not in the world's manner, but eternally and without end. [He gives], not only peace, but also joy and comfort. Hence, no disaster may come eternally near the dwelling which is God and man eternally, Jesus Christ Himself, in whom all believers dwell and He in them.

Gloss

The faithful have their dwelling and safety in the temple of Christ's body. Thus, the Father and Son, after the manner of deity, have their dwelling in the hearts of all the faithful through the action of the Spirit.

After this temple or tabernacle of His body had been broken, He raised it up again on the third day.

435

The hearts of all the faithful ascended with Him, and their hearts were made temples and dwellings of God, in which God, Father, Son, and Holy Spirit live, govern, and reign in righteousness, godliness, faithfulness, and truth, from now until eternity. Thus, all the faithful live and dwell in the risen temple of the body of Christ, / / which is built, raised, and erected to the right of the majesty of God, the almighty, heavenly Father. The Father Himself has prepared and erected this temple for Himself, for in it the one God, the Father, Word, and Holy Spirit, dwells eternally. He dwells nowhere else, and God cannot be found, nor comprehended, at any other place or location eternally; nor can He be known, seen, or heard anywhere else.[8]

In[9] this eternal, sublime, and holiest place, God allows Himself to be apprehended, seen, and heard. As the true mercy seat, the place of worship in the Spirit and in truth is now this sole temple. Because of the sharp sword of the Word, which proceeds out of the mouth of Him who sits on the throne, nothing unclean can approach. In this temple all the faithful find pardon and rest for their souls, yes, all that is needful for their life, and all the treasures, glory, and pleasure of the temple, in which God Himself is the highest adornment, treasure, and glory eternally. For this reason, all the faithful, like David, properly demand what they have prayed for: that they may remain in the house of God their whole life and behold the pleasure of His temple. They would rather be doorkeepers than live in the dwellings of the godless.

For your soul, and for my own, I fervently desire an acceptable year, which all the faithful ought properly to explore.

I wish to discuss briefly this acceptable year,

/ / in which everything, including the treasures given us, has become new in Christ. We should see and observe the pleasure of the temple of His body and thus comfort and make glad our souls. Indeed, we should fall into wonderment, and thank our God and Father for it. We should frequently contemplate the gifts, for we should pay more attention to the giver than to the gifts. Such is the giver's intention. He who does not contemplate the gifts cannot understand either the gift or the giver. Nor may he love either of them properly, nor can he truly thank the giver.

All gifts are given us by God, and they are given for two reasons. First, in them we can learn to know our Creator, God, and Father and thus, with a pure heart, we may glorify, praise, and thank Him. Second, we are to use the gifts to serve each other, and not to lord it over each other. And, if we accomplish something to the praise of the Lord and the benefit of the neighbor, we do not rejoice over it. Our highest joy shall be that, in heaven, our names are written in the book of life (Lk. 10:20). To show, with unwavering faith and certain hope, love toward our neighbor, and thus prove our love of God, is and shall be our highest joy. Not the work, but love itself, to serve and to be a guardian / / of the salvation of all the elect of God, is heavenly joy.

284r

Therefore, we are obligated to contemplate, and pay attention to, the treasures and most precious gems of Christ; we are obligated to explore, to fathom, and to observe them diligently, and in the shrine of our hearts to protect them carefully from thieves and murderers. Thus, one may discover what a wonderful, acceptable new year the heavenly Father has given and committed to us to proclaim through His child Jesus Christ. Isaiah 61 speaks about the child and Lord, and His kingdom;

observe treasures

he also speaks of the Lord's servants, messengers, and ambassadors and their office, and what they are to accomplish in the power of the Spirit. Therefore, the Lord has also given the Holy Spirit to His ambassadors and servants for this office. Isaiah says: "The Spirit of the Lord is upon me, for the Lord has anointed me and sent me to announce good news to the poor, to bind up wounded hearts, to announce deliverance to the captives, and to open the prison-house of those in bondage. I am to announce the year of the Lord's favor and the vengeance of our God, comfort all who mourn and give beauty instead of ashes to those who lament in Zion. I am to give them a happy anointing instead of a stench, a beautiful garment instead of a heavy heart. They will be called gods of righteousness, a planting of the Lord in which he will exult."

Gloss
284v

Christ's garment of innocence for sin. The prisoners and sick and wounded in spirit. / /

This text describes the service of the Lord Himself and the office of His ambassadors in this time of our mortal life which all ambassadors still have. We should take care that we do not speak evil of this precious treasure. Paul says: "That we may comprehend, together with all the saints of God, the depth and the height, the length and the breadth of Christ, yes, the love which surpasses all understanding and knowledge." To this end, all the chosen of God must strive to follow the pattern and example given to us by the Lord Himself. The servant is not, nor ever will be, above his Lord, nor will the disciple be above his master, or the apostle above Him who sent him. The Lord Himself has tested this principle; so, too, will it also be tested in His servants.

Eph. 3 [18]

The Lord has opened, given, and revealed His priceless treasure and gift without price. Through

His divine skill, He has unlocked and released the Scriptures, the most sublime and learned old and new treasure, written for Himself by the Holy Spirit. All the patriarchs, law, and prophets point to Himself. Then, according to the fullness of understanding and knowledge of the Father, the fullness of Godhead appeared bodily in Christ Himself.[10]

This is the conclusion / / concerning the old and new treasure.

Moses gives the law, and the prophets have predicted the future grace until as the one who prepared the way of the Lord, John baptized unto repentance and fasting. The old treasure was given because of sin, and it was to point them and to lead them, in faith and hope, to the future grace, accomplished by the Spirit of Christ in the law, the prophets, and John, who pointed with his finger to the Lord as the true Lamb of God that takes away the sin of the world. Through the Lamb, the Lord Jesus Christ, grace and truth have appeared. On the cross, His death and blood, offered up for the remission and forgiveness of sins, fulfilled grace and truth. There, on the cross, the old was completed and there, the new treasure, the grace and truth which Christ brought with Him, was offered. Thus, our greatest scribe and treasurer gave everyone in his time his due.

Similarly, it behooves all the apostles and evangelists, who are the scribes of the Holy Spirit, to give to each in his time his due out of the old and new treasure. The old treasure, the law and the prophets, still minister to the old Adam. / / They live in his sin and under his sin, for they live only according to the flesh. As His first grace, Christ in His fullness gives to them the old treasure. God's stern wrath, His penalty and vengeance, are proclaimed against him and against all ungodliness. He is shown that he must repent, forsake sin, and show regret and remorse for his sin. A genuine sorrowing is begun in their hearts by which they are bruised, and made captive and ill in their consciences. Thus, they are prepared for the Lord, the true Physician. The old treasure applies solely to the children of the first Adamic birth, and their repentance from sin rightly comes from the old treasure.

Thus, through His preceding Holy Spirit, the Lord Jesus Christ worked in John and the prophets.

In the same way, according to the measure of His will, He fills His servants with His skill, wisdom, and understanding in order that they may administer in the right manner, according to time, measure, and apportionment, His treasures and wealth. The true treasure is Christ Himself. He is the fulfillment of all in all, be it skill, wisdom, under-standing or knowledge. His body and true hu-manity are, moreover, the genuine temple and treasure-house, the true dwelling and abode of God. As the true dwellings, treasure-houses, and temples of God, in which Father and Son themselves, the most sublime treasures, / / live and remain in the power of the Spirit, the hearts of all the faithful are prepared and built up by Him for [the enjoyment of] these treasures. He adorns and consecrates this temple with all its utensils and glorious gems, the gifts and virtues of the Holy Spirit, and anoints them with the oil of gladness with which the Lord Himself has been anointed by the Father above all His fellows. Thus, He is the High Priest before the Father, and He accomplishes the priestly office in the hearts of the faithful. He establishes His own as fellow priests to rule and reign with Him forever. That is the length and the breadth of Christ, the highest treasure, who is from eternity and who spreads Himself out in the hearts of all the faithful.

In this new and acceptable year, He has been given to us in our earthen vessels. These vessels are easily broken or damaged if we do not take care of ourselves, or if we speak evil of the treasure. If struck, these earthen vessels will break. One must also diligently watch that his own earthen vessel, in which the treasure is given, is not exposed to offense; one should not easily become offended by Christ and His own, and thus sustain damage. Moreover, it behooves us not to give offense or scandal to others, or to take it ourselves. Rather, we should cling firmly and immovably to the truth, and preserve from offense the earthen vessel into which the treasure of Christ is laid by God the Father, Son, and Holy Spirit.

/ / Thus, we should allow ourselves neither to be offended nor scandalized by anything. Also, we are to watch diligently that our earthen vessel does not cause offense to anyone else. Otherwise, our own or our neighbor's vessel might be broken. If we carnally attack one another, or fight one another in the spirit of the flesh, in arrogance and conceit, such breakage will occur. It also happens if we give room and place to the lust of the flesh. To do so, under the guise of the liberty of Christ, is to assume that one is free to do anything; such an assumption is contrary to the manner of Christ, and defiles the treasure of the love which is in Christ. In whatever form offense happens and manifests itself, the earthen vessels and containers are easily shattered and destroyed, and the treasures, along with all the gifts of Christ, are defiled and slandered. Yes, in us, Christ Himself is shamed, despised, blasphemed, and crucified anew. What is even worse is if someone is injured by deception and cunning, and polluted by abominable vices. Even in the law of Moses, such vices were condemned; much less may

not to give
or take
offense

2 Cor. 4 [7]

286v

441

they have room under the grace of Christ.

Therefore, my beloved ones, let us be aware of the High Priest Christ in our hearts, and of His anointment of us, with the oil of gladness, comfort, and peace. This anointing gives us all learning, wisdom, understanding, and comprehension, / / and then we may understand what is best and most pleasing to the Father of our Lord Jesus Christ.

287r

We should often take the treasures out in one place, and diligently discern what God the heavenly Father has conferred upon and given to each for the service of building up the body of Christ. The gifts in every single member must be heard and seen. There can be no unendowed member who has not been given something of the treasures of Christ, such as virtues and the fruits of the Holy Spirit on the body of Christ. Everything has been given to us by the Father of lights with and in Christ. Always, the gifts of the Father are only good gifts, which He gives to His children who ask Him. There are no stones for bread, nor scorpions for eggs, nor serpents for fish. Thus, the Father does not regret that He gives the gifts to His children. Nor does He give His gifts and treasures to unclean wild animals, for He never throws the pearls before swine nor what is holy to the dogs; the Lord Himself forbade His own to do it. His holiness is the pearls, treasures, precious stones, and gems with which He has sanctified Himself for His own. And these treasures which He gives are given only to the sanctified. Thus, with such sacred treasures, yes, with Christ Himself, His own may cleanse one another and, to the pleasure of their God and Father, sanctify one another with all the virtues and gifts, and with the Holy / / Spirit's adornment and finery.

Rom. 12 [6-8]
1 Cor. 12

Eph. 4 [11, 12]

Jas. 1 [17]

Lk. 11 [11-13]

Mt. 7 [6]

1 Pet. 1 [22]

287v

The Father of our Lord Jesus Christ desires

442

and expects the mother, the bride of Christ and sanctified by Christ, to nourish, raise, and preserve the children for the Father in all sanctification, adornment, and ornament. Isaiah says: "[Such children] will be the Father's boast, His honor, glory, and majesty, and the mother with her children will express and give eternal praise, laud, honor, and thanks to the heavenly Father forever." Such housekeeping is demanded not only of the mother and the bride of Christ herself, but also of her servants, the highest angels of God, who freely serve. Indeed, the angels desired to see this housekeeping of Christ and His bride. And, unlike Christ's bride and her children, those angels who, because of their willful pride, did not freely surrender themselves to this service, the deep humility of Christ, were eternally cast out and bound in hell. Christ's bride and her children did serve Him and, as He did in the time of His human life, they humbled themselves.

Gloss

Jacob was deceived with his first wife, but he served again for the beautiful Rachel. These two wives represent the old and new marriage.

288r

Whoever, therefore, serves from pride or, because of pride, refuses to serve, relates to this housekeeping of Christ and His / / espoused bride as the whole world does, which wants to rule and not serve, and what it serves it serves from pride. They are all like their ruler, the devil, and the outcast angels.

Therefore, the precious gems, pearls, and sacred things are to be given to all who are washed, cleansed, and redeemed through the blood of the Lamb. They are children of and fellow-heirs to all the treasures of Christ's grace. They are to be adorned and beautified to the honor of their God

443

and Father, and the Lord Jesus Christ. Only for the others are Christ, His riches[11] and treasures a mockery and a derision.

Therefore, my dear ones, let us be aware of our calling. Let us rightly look to our High Priest and forerunner. Let us see the treasure, gems, and ornaments, the fullness of grace and truth, with which He Himself has adorned the temple of His body, and see the glorious, beautiful, and priestly garments, all the virtues and gifts of the Holy Spirit, with which He, as the true God, was clad by His heavenly Father. His faithful ones should learn from His example, and be amazed by it. Just as the whole of the true and chosen ones, the royal priestly generation and God's own people, / / are clad with the virtues and gifts of the Holy Spirit, so should the faithful ones long to be similarly clad. They are all fellow-priests. Through Jesus Christ and the Holy Spirit, their God and heavenly Father clothes them with the same gifts and virtues.

Moses prepared the figurative temple and the Aaronic or Levitical priesthood. God had showed him the design on Mount Sinai. The temple was to be adorned with glorious ornament and lavishly decorated with gold, silver, copper, bronze, and iron, and all kinds of precious wood and stone. Everything was washed, anointed, sanctified, consecrated, and cleansed. Thus, God was worshiped and honored with great external pomp and splendor. The high priest used no unclean or unconsecrated vessels in his high priestly function.

Much more glorious, however, is the most exalted form, the real manner and way, which is not according to any model, but according to the glory of the true Priest, the Son of God Himself. More glorious is He Himself who came down from the highest eternal God and Father in the Son, and pro-

288v

[1] Pet. 1[13]
[1] Pet. 2[9]

Yesterday and the figurative temple

2 Cor. 3 [3]

444

claimed the will, pleasure, and commandment of the heavenly Father. That commandment was no longer written in stone tablets, that is, in hardened hearts; it was written by the finger of God in broken hearts of flesh. It is not adorned with earthly gold, but with spiritual gold; it is fired, purified, and

289r cleansed, and made steadfast / / in all tribulation in the power of faith. This gold is love, that is, God Himself, and it does not pass away, but endures forever.

Similarly, all the other sacred gems of the temple, and of the royal High Priest Christ and His own, are not of earthly production, of elemental or creaturely birth. Given to the Son Himself, to His fellow-priests and the spiritual temple, the Father gives these treasures in the power and working of the Spirit. This compactly built temple is not cleansed, nor is it consecrated with the blood of animals. It is consecrated with the precious blood of Christ Jesus. The washing, cleansing and purifying in baptism are the basis of faith in the forgiveness of sins. They are a co-witness to the belief in the Holy Spirit and the truth of the Father. This temple and its priesthood receive the treasures, gems, and gifts, which are not of silver, gold, or precious stones, nor apparel of silk. Rather, such treasures, gems, ornaments, and honor are spiritual gifts, produced and prepared by the Holy Spirit, of which Saint Paul (Gal. 5 [22, 23]) and John wrote: "The virtues of the Holy Spirit are love, faith, hope, patience, joy, peace, long-suffering, goodness, kindness, gentleness, purity," etc.

Our apparel is justification and chastisement; it is the grace of our heavenly Father, who does not

289v allow His own to appear in the shame of nakedness.

nota Therefore, / / it behooves us to keep our priestly garments unsullied, unspotted, and clean so that

445

they may not be taken from us, and we be found unclothed in the shame of nakedness. All belongs to our priestly office and priesthood, and to our hearts, the temples of God. In them, God dwells. They are the most precious treasures and gems, given to us by our Father God and Lord with Christ. With them, we may eternally offer thanksgiving, laud, and sacrifices of praise.

No high priest, serving in the temple and spiritual house of God, may ever use an unholy, unclean or unconsecrated utensil. Every utensil must be sprinkled with the blood and the grace of Jesus Christ in the forgiveness of sins. Whenever so-called Christians do use unclean utensils, and it happens today, God's anger flares. The gifts of the Holy Spirit are withdrawn, and the hearts of the faithful destroyed and desecrated. So it happened with the figurative treasures, temple, and priests. The same happens daily before our eyes through deceit. But, in the house and temple of God, no vessel is used in dishonor. In and for His wrath, God uses such unclean and unholy vessels outside of the house.[12] But in the house and temple of the Father, our High Priest uses only pure, holy vessels in all holiness. / / He has Himself hallowed them in His holiness. In them, and in the hiddenness and patience of their hearts, He conceals His treasure and gems according to the mystery of His will.

Yes, they are hidden from the whole world and all unclean animals. The ark or coffer of the new covenant or testament is the Christ and the patience of faithful saints, who are prepared for the Father's praise in all patience. In this coffer, all the household furnishings of God, the treasures, virtues, and gifts of the Holy Spirit, are safely kept and locked away from all enemies of God and His own. Neither the violence, aggression, pride, and pomp

2 Tim. 2 [20 f.]

God uses un-
clean vessels
outside the
house
290r

The ark of
the new
covenant is
patience.

of the world, nor anything else that may rise up against it, will be able to open, destroy or shatter this ark or coffer, which is the patience of Christ itself, bound, mounted, and locked away with the band of love, humility, and surrender. Without this ark or coffer, our treasure, the virtues and gifts of the Holy Spirit, which are placed in our hearts as temples of God, cannot be locked, protected, or preserved. Therefore, as the Lord says, we must arm and prepare our souls with patience, for we will need patience if we wish to preserve the treasures and the true rod of our high priest Aaron which, together with the golden bucket, blossomed in our souls.

b. 10 [35-37]

290v

In the loving hearts of the faithful is the true / / bread from heaven, which the father gave us from heaven and which has given us life, kept for a perpetual remembrance. This bread [is] His broken or prepared[13] flesh and blood, given up for our life.[14] The pure flesh and blood of the virgin Mary prepared this flesh and blood for us, and this heavenly bread, which the Word made flesh, raises us from death to life. It is the true food and drink, given for our life; it nourishes and preserves our souls. The true bread of remembrance belongs in the golden bucket, and this bread is kept locked in the ark of the New Testament. In all patience, united with gentleness, humility, and surrender, our High Priest has locked the treasures in the ark. Thus, the temple of His body is preserved in the ark of the covenant of the New Testament so that we have a perpetual remembrance of Him. Had our High Priest not so carefully locked His treasure for us, every covenant and witness of the eternal covenant would be pillaged by the enemy, who steals all divine treasure. Wherever impatience breaks the ark of the covenant, all the treasures of

bread of remembrance

nota

Heb. 5 [1-10]

impatience destroys the ark of the covenant

447

our temple, that is, of our hearts, are lost, pillaged, and stolen, and the temple of God is destroyed and broken down. / / Therefore, if, indeed, we wish to preserve the treasures of our temples in this new and acceptable year, in this time of grace, and if we wish to save these gems from the Philistines, we need patience.

The ark of the New Testament is not compatible with the Philistines, I mean with the world. The impatience of the Philistines opposes the true patience of Christ. Were they to possess it, and were they to decide to use it, patience would only cause them disaster. If, indeed, it is the ark of the New Testament, and it is truly called patience, tribulation always accompanies the ark. And when tribulation comes, they impatiently send it away again. Ignorant and unbridled animals, soldiers armed with weapons, accomplish for them what patience cannot. In their secret parts, the tribulation of Christ is a plague and a shame to them. Thus along with an offering, which God refuses, they send the ark back to its place. They endure their suffering and death to death in every impatience. If one wishes to, one can see that such is the case these days. There are those who have adopted the gospel, but they only appear to adopt the patience of Christ; the Philistines now send the ark back home again. Are these not truly the unspiritual Philistines who, together with their Goliath, trust only in human power? Such a trust is contrary to the true manner of the patience of Christ; it contradicts the / / genuine and true David. Armor and sword do not fit Him. He kills all His enemies with their own sword. Under the new David, their own impatience consumes them. As the Lord says: "Whoever fights with the sword will be destroyed by it." Human coercion will destroy all who [support] a human,

291r

[1] Sam. 6[3]

That is
the way
it was
in the
Schmalkald
War and in
Switzerland
with Zwingli

291v

1 Sam. 17 [51]

Mt. 26 [52]

448

forcibly imposed faith and all who claim the Word
of faith, but who trust and depend upon human
protection and power; like Peter, they will be
nota driven to a denial. Peter also thought that Christ
would be a temporal and earthly Redeemer who
would save them with carnal weapons. Thus, Peter
pledged that he was prepared to give his life for the
Lord. However, he received no help from the Lord
. 18[10, 11] in his carnal fighting; Jesus, for example, helped the
one whose ear Peter had cut off. Then, Peter denied
the Lord three times, and swore that he had never
known the Man.

So it happens to all who know Christ only after
the flesh, who know Him only in terms of temporal
aid and the saving of temporal life and property.
They know nothing of the Holy Spirit's heavenly
treasures and gifts, which are given to all faithful
believers in Christ. God grant that they fall into no
292r worse denial, or into a / / betrayal like Judas did, or
that they have become thus toward each other.[15]
Rather, God grant that they should later confess
their sin and repent like Peter, who in his ignorance
and fear denied the Lord. Nevertheless, he risked
his life and entered the fray with no thought about
what might happen to him. He did not, like Judas,
like Judas betray the Lord for the price of shame.

Would to God, for their sake, that it were not
true that today there are worse and even more evil
merchants than the Jewish Pharisees, who bought
the Lord from Judas out of envy and hate. [But, to-
day], whole lands, armies, and peoples (many
hundreds of thousands of people, even though they
are not good people)[16] are betrayed, sold, and
bought by their loans, finance, and usury. It is done
out of avarice, envy, and hate, an attempt to
preserve their earthly pomp, pride, and vain honor.
Moreover, all the actions, of both the old and new[17]

449

forcers of faith, are done in the semblance of Christ
and His gospel. I am concerned that, shortly, the
words of James, "Howl and weep, you rich," etc.,
will be fulfilled in them.

Those who hold a faith which has been forced
on them cannot bring forth better fruit. Whatever is
preached from the dead letter of Scripture or
ancient, idolatrous custom, and whatever is taught
under human power, protection, and patronage will

also by / / human coercion and power be destroyed
and scattered again in mutual denial and betrayal.
Even though all creatures are clean, the riches,

treasures, gold and silver, precious stones, pearls,
velvet and silk garments can produce no better fruit
in the heart than eternal condemnation. I do not
intend to judge or condemn the world. The world,
along with her prince, the devil, has already been
judged before God. Rather, I write this letter as a
testimony to Christ that their works are evil. Just as
the light is distinguished from darkness, or the
riches and treasures of Christ from the treasures of
this world, I distinguish them from good works. The
children of light always bring forth good from the

treasures of their hearts, and the evil bring forth evil
from their evil treasures. Where the treasure is,
there the heart is also.

Therefore, it behooves us to look again to our

calling and to Him who called us from the horrible
darkness of this world to His marvelous light. For
He called us from the world, not we Him. He has
revealed to us the will of His heavenly Father. He
has taught and instructed us with full understanding. He has also sent us the teacher in the heart, and
the Comforter to comfort, and to teach us with
Jesus' own words and teaching. He equips and em-
powers us with the heavenly, inner, hidden power

from above; He leads, / / instructs, and guides us,

and He anoints us, as the Father of lights anointed the Lord Himself, with the oil of gladness.

Our life is hidden with Christ in God; it is not we who live, but Christ who lives in us. We are not taught by the human voice, by the literal, external teaching of Christ and the apostolic preaching of the gospel. We are taught, not by man, but by God, the Holy Spirit Himself. The Spirit takes the treasures and good things of the Father and the Son, and has poured into our hearts the love which is the mind of Christ and the true and only understanding. Only what Christ Himself has said and taught, and no other word, does the Spirit of wisdom bring to remembrance in His own.

Therefore, no matter how holy they may appear, all those who take away and add to this word and teaching are false priests. Nor does God teach those who only hear the Word from the mouth of Christ, the apostles and other saintly people, nor does He teach those who read their writings only according to the letter, without the reminder of truth and teaching of the Holy Spirit. They are thieves and murderers who run before, and lag behind, Christ. With their own inventions and sophistries[18]in Scripture, they either run ahead of the Holy Spirit of Christ, before they have been driven by Him, or else they lag behind Christ, and presume to teach those who are under God's judgment.[19] Thus, without being called, and without any discrimination / / about who is drawn or sent by the Father, they throw the pearls before the swine and what is sacred only to the dogs. They pay no regard to the admonition the Lord gave to His own to distinguish between people. Instead, these others, without discrimination, dump their teachers and teaching, like the useless salt, in front of all men, so that men trample it underfoot and, as one

Jn. 10[1]
before and
ehind Christ

293v

451

2 Pet. 2[17]

Jn. 14[16:13]
Rom. 8[14]

2 Tim. 4[3]
2 Cor. 2[?]

Ezek. 13[12]

can now see, mock it. Men, like swine and ravenous dogs, turn around and rend them. These are the clouds without water which are driven by the whirlwind; they are not driven, taught, or reminded by the Holy Spirit, nor are they led by Him in the truth. Those whom the Spirit of God drives, they are the children of God. All these teachers, self-appointed or reestablished by the violence of men, who teach for the sake of carnal gain and self-indulgence under the protection of men, who have not drunk at the streams of living water but have stolen their human sophistry of Scripture from stagnant cisterns, all these, as the prophet says, build with crumbling mortar.

Therefore, their building immediately collapses, and they perish along with it. They are destroyed by the human violence and protection under which they build their edifice. Through the deceit and error of man's teaching, they fall and are overcome by the debris.

Let him who has ears to hear, hear, and him who has eyes to see, see. / / See what has happened everywhere to these so-called Christians, who have only the semblance of the gospel. Such righteous judgments by the almighty righteous God, our heavenly Father of the Lord Jesus Christ, rightly follow. It is the judgment of the Holy Spirit who now, because of sin, judges the world, together with her prince. With the justice of Christ, the Potentate of heaven and earth, who now sits at the right hand of the majesty of God, the Holy Spirit judges the sin of the unbelief into which they are rejected and thrown. His is the true righteousness. He went to the Father for the sake of exercising this righteousness and judgment of the Holy Spirit. From above, He now creates and effects the same righteousness, which alone is valid before God, and which exists

294r

452

and remains eternally before the Father in His saints.

Prior to this ascension of Christ and access to the Father, no man was justified in the justification of grace. Before His departure to the Father, even the earthly teaching, power, and miracles of Christ could not justify the apostles, nor any other man, to this eternal justification. For this reason, even though the earthly teaching of Christ, the Son / / of Man, was testified to by His miracles and the divine power which the Father had in Him and He in the Father, the apostles could not bear, understand, nor comprehend the teaching of Christ so that they might have remained steadfast in it. Thus, since only God could do the works He did, the apostles were led to believe and to confess Him as the Lord Jesus Christ, the true God, the Son of the Father. This faith, however, was received from the earthly teachings and miracles. Without the true teacher and reminder, the Holy Spirit who comforts and leads into the truth, and whom Christ promised to send, such faith was not valid. After His resurrection from the dead, He sent Him and made the promise, which still stands, that He would eternally be with all the faithful believers who have been taught, reminded, and led into truth by His Holy Spirit. He comforts man in his repentance and sorrow for sin, and forgives.

Therefore, all external service of Christ, and of those who belong to Him in the time of this mortal life, serves and prepares the way for the Holy Spirit. [This external service consists] of the external preaching, teaching, miracles, baptism, foot washing, the Lord's Supper, discipline, chastisement, and admonition. Such service also includes the ban of exclusion and separation from the fellowship of the body of Christ. In order to preserve the true fellowship of all the faithful, we are commanded to keep the ban, together with the Lord's Supper, in remembrance of the true love of Christ and His gracious deed in His death. In the time of His mortal life, Christ did not rule; / / He served. Thus, He sent His own to serve, not to rule. Man is to be served by Christ and His own, and man is to be prepared for the Holy Spirit. Some spirits either regard such preparation as unnecessary, or else they regard it too highly. But wherever this service of Christ is not carried out in all its provisions, there the Holy Spirit cannot do His work. To believe, like Peter, that such a Lord should not wash one's feet, and to refuse to have the act performed on the basis of such carnal reasoning, is to rely on private invention rather than the Holy Spirit. Even today, Christ says to these individuals that they can have no part in His kingdom. For the Holy Spirit may not, and cannot, function, nor can it find an abiding place without the preparatory teaching. Service is commanded by Christ, and it is the means by which, according to the command of Christ, men are prepared. Moreover, the Key of David is also a means, for it is the key of understanding with which man's earthly mind is opened. Then, the Holy Spirit, as true God with Father and Son, can move where He will, namely, in those whom the Father draws to Christ, to / / the same apostolic church and bodily service, preaching and teaching, baptism, foot washing, and the Lord's Supper. Men submit to this service in the obedience of faith in Christ and under the discipline of the Spirit.

When we as men are renewed, and born again of the Holy Spirit, the Holy Spirit becomes the pledge and the third witness of salvation. The apostolic service of the church is properly carried out, in accordance with the commands of Christ, when it

295r
Jn. 13[13-15]

nota
Jn. 13[8]
Jn. 6[44]
295v

1 Cor. 3[6-9]

prepares, cultivates, fertilizes and, as God's helper, breaks again[20] the hearts of men. When this new breaking occurs, the church seeds and plants, in the heart, the word of truth, which is to be believed, and it waters the heart with the baptism of water. But even if all external service is done according to the command of Christ, the earthly Man, the Spirit still moves in glorious liberty wherever He will, and He gives the increase and the growth to whomever He will. Such is the prerogative, in eternity, of the Godhead, and it belongs to the Father and the Son.

order of
Christ
16 [15, 16]

Gloss:

Antichrist has destroyed the apostolic service and therefore, Christ moves wherever He is prayed for.

It is sheer fabrication and deception when some insist that the Holy Spirit moves apart from the apostolic service of the church, that such service, / / commanded by Christ, is unnecessary.

296r

On which Holy Spirit, then, did the Lord base His teaching, Word, and work? If not the actual spoken words, commands, and laws of Christ, reminded and taught by the Spirit, what[21] other teaching words or work can, or may, the Holy Spirit teach, remind, and lead us into as the truth? For the Lord Himself promised that the Holy Spirit would remind us of all that Jesus said or commanded. Certainly, a spirit who teaches contrary to the Son of Man, who taught men with a human voice, is a deceiving spirit.

Jn. 14[26]

1.

deceptive
spirit
nota

2.

Again, they deceive themselves who think that, when they serve, teach, and baptize, simply because the apostolic service is performed, it follows that the Holy Spirit also moves and teaches. Nor is the church of Christ merely where the external service is properly done. *Not so!* If the inner, through the Holy Spirit, does not witness to the external, through faith, everything is in vain for,

Mt. 24[28]

where the carcass is, the eagles gather. The true community and gathering of Christ cannot be identified with a place, nor can it be called a human name. Wherever such a gathering is, according to the Word of the Lord, there Christ is with the Father and the eternally abiding Holy Spirit. They love Him who keep His Word and commandment. To them, He and the Father will come and dwell.

Therefore, / / whoever says that Christ is anywhere else than living on earth, as in heaven, in the power and clarity of the Spirit and in the heart of each faithful believer, he is a deceiver. Whoever does not find Christ dwelling in his own heart, eternally, will not find Him elsewhere.

However, where such hearts as temples and dwellings of God, are built into a spiritual dwelling for the Lord, these places are named and identified only so long as the faithful live there.[22] Thus, that place is holy for the sake of the saints, even as God sanctified the figurative temple. When it was destroyed, its place was profaned. The same is true of a place without saints. Where they do not dwell, it is a curse and malediction; it is desecrated, destroyed, and profaned before God. At this time, we see it clearly in the whole world.

Because of their sectarian, external, coerced religion, by which they deceive themselves, the whole world imagines that it has Christ living here or there. Since the earthly and true service of Christ did not come into force in the hearts of the apostles without the moving of the Holy Spirit, how can the forced and coerced faith, or the faith based on old custom, stand before God? This forced, coerced faith, based as it is on sophistic interpretation of Scripture or on ancient custom, is not from God, nor is it taught by the Holy Spirit and His manner, birth, artistry[23] and / / wisdom; [it is unrelated to

Jn. 14[21]

296v

nota

yesterday
today

Christ here
or there

1.

2.

297r

the Spirit's] reminding and leading us into truth. Rather, it is from the generation and will of the flesh of man (Jn. 1[12]), who is steeped in his earthly, fallen nature and human reason, sophistry, and wisdom.

Thus, even if, in the power of the Spirit before man, one should preach the apostolic service and teach the teaching of Christ which flows out of the inmost being of believers as a fountain flowing into eternal life, still, the teaching of the Spirit, which alone reminds and leads us into truth, and which teaches the divine artistry of wisdom, must always accompany it. Those who are thus taught are not taught by any man, but by God.

Tim. 3 [6, 7] All the others continually learn from, and are taught by, men. But these others never come to the knowledge of the truth, which is eternal life (Jn. 17 [3]). They never know God the Father as the true God, and Jesus Christ as the One whom the Father Mt. 7 [21] has sent. Therefore, the Lord says that not everyone who cries "Lord, Lord" will enter the kingdom of heaven. Only he will enter who does the will of the heavenly Father. Since no one knows the Father but the Son and him to whom the Son reveals the Father (Mt. 11[27]), no one but the Son could do the will and pleasure of the heavenly Father. Thus, 297v no one but the Father knows the Son. / /

Therefore, Paul writes in 1 Corinthians 12[3] that no one can call Christ Lord except by the Holy Spirit. Thus, no one can do the will of the Father without the Son. It follows that those who are in Christ do not themselves live, but Christ lives in them (Gal. 2[20]). Moreover, whatever they ask the Father, Christ Himself will do and perform in the hearts of all the faithful. Such is the true righteousness, the reason why Christ went to the Father (Jn. 14[13]). Thus, Saint Paul says that everyone should examine to see whether Christ dwells in his heart (2 Cor. 13[5]). If He does not, that individual is cast off. Therefore, whoever calls Jesus "Lord" and God "Father" without the Holy Spirit does not for that reason enter the kingdom of heaven. To such, God says: "You call me Father, but where is my honor? You call me Lord, but where is my fear?" (Mal. 1[6]).

1 Cor. 13

Without the artistry and teaching of the Holy Spirit, who pours out the love, which is God, into the hearts of all the faithful, and which surpasses all reason and understanding, everything is in vain. The Holy Spirit proceeds from the Father and Son, and He witnesses to the Father and Son in the hearts of all the faithful; He copies and repeats the perfect law of the liberty of Christ. The faithful look into this law of liberty in order that they may fervently do what Christ spoke and commanded. They have a blessing, but not a temporal or temporary one as Moses did, who engraved the written literal law through twelve witnesses from the twelve tribes of Israel with earthly blessings and maledictions (Deut. 27:11-13). The Father, as true / / God, Himself witnesses to the Son and the Son to the Father. Hence, all who believe in the Son have an eternal blessing.

12 witnesses
yesterday
298r

12 witnesses
today

Thus, twelve witnesses are established from the twelve tribes of Israel; they are the twelve apostles of which the Lord speaks in Acts 1[8], where He says that they should be His witnesses to the ends of the earth. They had been with Him from the beginning and, for witness, He gave them the Holy Spirit so that they should announce to all nations repentance and forgiveness of sins through His death and blood. "Whoever believes and is baptized for the forgiveness of sins shall be saved. Whoever does not believe is condemned." The

Mk. 16[16]

Holy Spirit is the true, complete copier of the law of Christ in the appointed messengers and witnesses of Christ. The Holy Spirit renews and copies Christ's law in the hearts of believers so that all things are rightly understood, recognized, and known, even as the Lord spoke, taught, and intended what He knew and received from the Father. Without this copier of the law of Christ, I mean the Holy Spirit, the apostles could neither understand nor bear the teaching of their Master. He repeated in them again what Christ had said, taught, and commanded. He is the true pledge of our salvation, and the true witness to our faith; He is the true repeater, Teacher, and reminder of our perfect law, no longer written on stone tablets, but in the hearts of the faithful. The Holy Spirit Himself no longer takes from the image[24] or the mediation of angels, nor does he take it in fire, clouds / / or darkness, as Moses received it and took it from God. He takes it from the Father and the Son, and gives it to the hearts of all the faithful. In them are the laws and new commandments of Christ the Lord written by the finger of God.

That is the true book of replication,[25] for all the faithful, written by the three heavenly witnesses and affirmed by the Father, the Word, and the Holy Spirit. Physical action, the power displayed with signs and wonders, testify to it on earth before men. The Father performed it in the Son, and the Son in the Father. As the Lord says in John 5[17]: "My Father works hitherto and I work also." The Father, the Spirit, and the Word are the three witnesses who witness in the incomprehensible, invisible, heavenly Being, and these three witnesses have also witnessed before actual men on earth in visible, tangible, and bodily form. The bodily miracles of the Son showed the Father. The Son taught the

Jn. 16[14]

2 Cor. 3[3]

298v

Heb. 8[5]

1 Jn. 5[7, 8]

Father 1

459

external words, which He Himself was as the Word of the Father, and revealed the Father. Thus, He was glorified before man as true God. The Holy Spirit, in visible form as a dove, testified to the Son that God, the Creator of heaven and earth, was His Father. He also appeared as tongues of fire to the apostles. Although God is, and remains, a Spirit in three persons, Father, Word, and Spirit, and is, eternally, invisible heavenly unity, nevertheless, Father, Son, and Holy Spirit witnessed before men on earth in bodily, visible form (as / / stated above) as one unitary Spirit, God, Father, and Son.

Thus, with water and blood (1 Jn. 5[7, 8]), the Holy Spirit also witnesses on earth to the Lord Jesus Christ as true man on earth. But there is blood as well as water so that all three serve in the one Lord, Jesus Christ, on earth [and] in heaven. If, with integrity of heart and with the co-witness of the three names and persons, God the Father, Son, and Holy Spirit, one is baptized in exact copy of Christ's command, and if that baptism is witnessed to in heaven as on earth, this witness is the subject of a fine new book of replication written in the hearts of all the faithful. This law and book of replication cause no curse, but only blessing for men. It has not only human witnesses on earth, but also divine witnesses in heaven, for it is witnessed to by Father, Son, and Holy Spirit, along with the co-witnesses of the apostles and servants of Christ. As the Lord said to the Twelve: "You are my witnesses because you have been with me from the beginning." So, too, have the apostles patiently witnessed to the spiritual law of complete liberty and to the book of replication. As the true ark of the covenant of the New Testament, they preserve in patience together with all the other gems of the temple of Christ's body. Their deaths and their lives preserved it from all

460

enemies. To our heavenly Father's eternal praise, they possessed the power of the love that was poured out so that, in this ark of / / patience, we could bring home the treasures and vessels, and all the gems of our temple, to the heavenly Jerusalem, to the true temple of the body of Christ.

This temple was erected for perpetual worship, and it is [served by] a royal priesthood that is not perishable or destructible, but remains forever. Thus, the Lord Himself, in all gentleness, humility, and patience, determined and has preserved it from all the enemies whom He has overcome in the depth. As they travel through the wilderness of this world, it behooves all faithful believers to exercise the greatest care for this ark of the new covenant, and ensure that it may not be broken and seized by the enemy, and the treasures of Christ robbed. In this ark of patience, if indeed we want to be glorified with Christ and share His joy, all the treasures and gifts of Christ are kept until the last enemy is overcome.

Christ has overcome His enemies in the depth

Misery always precedes honor. In the Lord's case, tribulation, sorrowing, and grief were followed by joy, blessing, and glory. Our treasures will then no longer be mocked, nor will they be seized by any enemy. Indeed, the ark is no longer necessary, for all the treasures and gems, as well as the garments of honor, are in discipline and virtue, taken out of the ark of patience to the praise and glory of the heavenly Father, and to the eternal honor and glory of the Lord Jesus Christ. / / We, in the Holy Spirit, return and offer again [to them] these gifts and virtues. There, before the eternal glory and only majesty of God, they will be used without any fear or care in eternal worship. Only there, with all the angels, will the hallelujah be truly sung and understood. Finally, it will be revealed that the sufferings

300r

Rom. 8[18]

461

of this world are not worthy to be compared with the future glory, and that all the tribulation and poverty is worthless by comparison with the unsurpassed riches and glories of the treasures of Christ.

A new year

This acceptable new year has been prepared for all the faithful in order that we may fervently rejoice over it and in it, and thank and praise our heavenly Father. We invite all creatures to rejoice with us and to sing praise to our God. Together with David, let us heartily sing the song of praises:

Ps. 145

"I will extol you, O King, and praise your name forever and ever. Every day I will bless you and praise your name forever and ever. Great is the Lord and worthy of all praise; His greatness is unfathomable. Children's children will praise your deeds and speak of your power. I will speak of the glory of your praise and of your wonders so that others will speak of the power of your deeds and extol your glory. They shall tell the story of your great goodness, and praise your justice. Gracious 300v and merciful is the / / Lord, forbearing and of great goodness. The Lord is good to all, and His mercy is over all His works. All your works thank you, and all your saints praise you. They talk of the glory of your kingdom and of your power so that all the children of men know your power and the glorious gifts of your kingdom. Your kingdom endures for all time, and to your dominion there is no end. The Lord preserves all those who fall, and raises up those who have been beaten down. All eyes are lifted up to you, and you give them their food when it is time. You open your hand and fill everything that lives with what is good. The Lord is just in all His ways and holy in all His deeds. The Lord is near to all who call on Him. He does His pleasure to those who fear Him; He hears their cry and helps them. The Lord protects all who love Him, and will exterminate the wicked. My mouth shall announce the praise of the Lord, and all flesh shall praise His name forever and ever." Amen.

For all of you, as for my own soul, I wish fervently that you may sing this song of praise. Pray the Lord faithfully for us, and all the faithful with me, and send to all who are in the Lord from me, and all the faithful, the greeting of peace and love in Christ Jesus our Lord. Amen. / /

301r

The grace of our Lord Jesus Christ be and remain with us all forever. Amen. Dated at Augsburg, the first day of February, anno domini 1547.

Your servant and comrade in
the tribulation which is in
Christ.
Pilgram Marpeck.

12

Men in Judgment and the Peasant Aristocracy (1547) [#18]

Introduction

This is Marpeck's second extant letter to Magdalena von Pappenheim. But, since it was also addressed to several others, it has the character of a circular letter. The title of the letter is somewhat misleading. Marpeck actually deals with five different types of men in judgment. Evidently, he began writing and found as he proceeded that there were not three but five kinds of men under the judgment of Christ. However, he did not return to revise his introductory sentences. The copyist apparently did not wish to take the liberty and make the revisions himself.

Marpeck deals in this letter with the problem summarized in Luther's *simul justus et peccator*, that is, that Christians are at the same time justified and sinners. While he does not adopt perfectionism, he does insist that those who claim Christ as Savior but continue in sin, even if reluctantly, are still under judgment. He does grant them the status of believers: "they are sinners under Christ, but they are not yet in the kingdom of Christ." When he says that "there are no sinners in the kingdom of Christ," he is not saying that Christians do not sin. Rather, he asserts that they are to be distinguished from those who have not committed themselves to the freedom of Christ. Living in the freedom of Christ is living in liberation from sin; sin no longer rules over them.

Marpeck's allegory of the peasant aristocracy has no parallel in Anabaptist writings. Perhaps it suggested itself to him because the recipient of this letter belonged to the nobility. It may also be that he remembered the jingle used by peasants in Germany long after the Peasant's Revolt: *Als Adam hackt und Eva span,*

464

wer war dann der Edelman? (When Adam delved and Eve span, who was then the gentleman?)

God appointed Adam a lord. Equipped with all that goes with such nobility, Adam was to rule over creation. But all his dominion was lost when Adam disobeyed God. In consequence, he and his descendants became boorish peasants, doomed to live "in the great village of this bleak world's wilderness." But Christ came, and brought with Him the power to once again confer nobility on those who unite themselves with Him. To those who do unite themselves with Him, He also gave the virtues and the treasures that go with nobility. Although Marpeck's theology echoes the patristic recapitulation theory, his fertile mind, always searching for new analogies, may have seen new possibilities in such a familiar jingle.

Marpeck also applies this allegory to the church. Just as a noble house cannot tolerate a member who brings disgrace and shame to its escutcheon, so the church of Christ cannot allow open sinners to remain, for they dishonor Christ the Lord and His name. Marpeck calls for church discipline, especially among the Protestant communions which, because of their doctrine of the church, could not make the distinctions Marpeck calls for.

When he analyses the reasons why men lay claim to Christ, in spite of their unwillingness to take on themselves the consequences of true discipleship, Marpeck gives evidence of considerable psychological insight. Some men act like peasants, but insist that, because they are sinners, they cannot act differently. They boast about being sinners even while they claim to be redeemed. Others adopt self-righteous attitudes. By comparing themselves to sinners, these self-righteous ones assert their own moral superiority, but their assertion is based solely on their own estimation. Then there are those who take a humble, perverse pride in their sinfulness, contrasting it with the claims of the pious who would be saved by their works. Finally, there are those who blame others for their sinfulness, and will assume no responsibility for it themselves. Marpeck knew what was going on around him, and he tries to steer a straight course through all the error and deceit he saw.

465

The Text

Concerning three kinds of men in judgment and also
concerning the peasant aristocracy

307r   To all the elect of God, but especially to my
beloved in Christ, Magdalena von Pappenheim,
and also to all other brothers and sisters and beloved
in the Lord who are scattered here and there; to all
my dear ones in Christ.

Grace and peace from God our heavenly
Father and the Lord Jesus Christ our Savior be and
remain with us forever. Amen.

This is a treatise concerning three kinds
of people who find themselves in judgment;
also concerning the peasant aristocracy, etc.

Those who are beloved in God the Father are
loved in Jesus Christ after the manner of true faith,
the true understanding and knowledge of Jesus
Jn. 17[3]   Christ. According to the words of the Lord, in such
knowledge is eternal life: "Father, this is eternal
life: that they know you the only true God and Jesus
Christ whom you have sent."

And what is now the true understanding and
perception of the eternal and blessed life of Christ?
Mt. 4 [18-22]   God is perceived only in the teaching and instruction of the Holy Spirit. As the Lord Himself said to
His disciples, whom He had Himself chosen and
called, and who had surrendered themselves wholeheartedly to His school and discipline in order that
they might follow Him in the new birth of the
Jn. 18 [31 f.]   Word: "If you remain in my words, you will be my
true disciples. You will know the truth, and the
truth will set you free." Thus, only those who
Jn. 1   remain in the teaching of Christ are the true dis-
likely 2 Jn. 9   ciples. The others have no God, says John in his
307v   epistle. To have true / / knowledge of salvation is

466

to recognize the truth in Christ's teaching, which is the right word of truth. For this purpose, Christ, the Son of God, was sent by the Father, that He might give His people knowledge of salvation; bind up hearts by the deceit of sin and by the devil, the enemy of truth; open the prison for the captives and proclaim liberty to them; and proclaim the acceptable year of the Lord and the day of vengeance of our God.

Is. 61 [1 f.]

Lk. 4 [15 f.]

In this sending of Jesus Christ is the Spirit of the Father. He is the Spirit of glory Himself, the One whom the Lord promised to send to His apostles, and upon whom, as true man, He rested. The Lord Himself is the Spirit of the Father, one God and one essence. Thus, He will also rest today upon all true disciples of Jesus; He will dwell in them, be the legitimate teacher of the true understanding and knowledge of salvation, and remind and teach them everything that Christ, the true ambassador from the Father, said, taught, and commanded. He is rightly acknowledged as eternal life, as true God and as true Man of the generation of man. Born of the chaste, virginal, pure Mary and conceived by the Holy Spirit, He is born of God. He is the eternal Word of the Father. He who is of the nature of God, who is one God with the Father and God the Word, became flesh of and in Mary, and was born a true Man from her faithful pure flesh as of the seed of Abraham. His speech, teaching, and life are the truth and eternal life, the healing of all the wounded, the / / redemption and liberation of all prisoners, the faithfulness, love, and goodness of all believers, and it is this goodness which leads them out of the wickedness and deceit of sin into all truth, faithfulness, and love. He reminds and teaches them nothing but what He Himself is, namely love, faithfulness, truth, and goodness, all

nota

308r

467

of which come from true faith in Jesus Christ.

That is the true knowledge of salvation and that knowledge is eternal life. All other knowledge, knowledge which is falsely acclaimed and foreign, is death and not life before God. Such knowledge is condemnation, not salvation; it is lies and sin, not goodness or truth. From this enmity, anger, even hate against God, one wickedness follows after another in the children of unbelief. Thus, they persist in their sins.

As Isaiah said about the Israelites [Is. 10:22], I say about all so-called Christians, who in their numbers are like the sand of the sea, that only a few (the remainder of the Gentiles) have remained true to the Lord, and only they will be saved. Like the Jews at the time of Christ, the time of the Gentiles is almost over. The fulfillment of their time is at hand. Therefore, everything which speaks and teaches against the knowledge of the teaching, Word, life, and walk of Christ is falsely acclaimed knowledge; it teaches and persists in sin.

All true believers have died with Christ, and thus have risen from sin and death. Yet, boasting of a grace and forgiveness that bears only vice, the whole world falsely believes the claim that Christ established before God a grace and mercy which demands no repentance, no forsaking of sin. God has

only to forgive and remit / / sin. Such deceit assumes that Christ did not redeem His own from

sin, death, and hell, and from all the power of the

Gloss: The highest power and might of the devil, which is sin, wherewith he overpowers men and holds them prisoner.

devil. Whoever commits sin, the cause of death, is the slave of sin, and he serves the devil and the power of the devil. Whoever truly believes serves Christ in all goodness, love, faithfulness, and truth. Through Christ, we are justified to love, faithfulness, and truth. The power of the devil, which is his deceit and our imprisonment in sin, makes us the imprisoned servants of the devil. But, through Christ, the devil never will rule over us.

However, these so-called Christians deny and slander the Lord Jesus Christ. When they claim that sin needs no repentance, they deny that Christ took away the devil's power. Thus, the devil's power continues to manifest itself in the children of unbelief and wickedness, who in turn contaminate those who truly believe in Christ Jesus, the children of faith and light. They slander God and His dwelling in heaven. Darkness and light, goodness and wickedness, Christ and Belial can never be compared nor can they have fellowship one with the other. Therefore, it is a terrible slandering of God and His dwelling, that is, of His saints in whom God dwells, to say that the devil and his power of sin should live alongside of God. Such an assertion denies that Christ robbed the devil of his power, that Christ overcame and judged him, and drove him out of the faithful. I insist that to speak in this manner is to speak where it is improper,[1] and to slander God and His dwelling.

It behooves man therefore, diligently to search, to investigate, / / and to test himself, according to the words of Paul, whether Christ dwells in him. If Christ lives in him with the action of His grace, that man is no longer a sinner. But if he is still a sinner, he is cast off. He has time to repent, to forsake sin, and to confess his sin to God. If God extends His grace and again liberates him from the bonds, cords, and power of the devil, and if Christ lives in him again through His Holy Spirit, he is justified through Christ and no longer a sinner. His sins and the stain of his wickedness have been washed away and cleansed through the blood of Christ, and God does not hold sin against him (Ps. 32 [2]). The true discernment is that those who are in Christ and in

309r
2 Cor. 13 [5]

469

whom Christ dwells are not sinners. If they do sin, however, they cannot claim to be in grace until their sins have again been cleansed and, through confession, remorse, and sorrow for their sins, they return to true goodness. Therefore, whoever is in grace, let him boast of the grace of Christ; whoever has sinned, let him fear the wrath of God, for He punishes sin eternally. If God's goodness leads him to repentance, let him diligently perform the deeds of repentance so that he may receive mercy. If he receives mercy and grace, let him boast of Christ and not that he is a sinner. But if he remains under the wrath and displeasure of God, let him confess himself a sinner and repent in the hope of receiving grace. I do not refer here to the hardened, deliberate knaves who will neither be shamed, nor will they fear any sin or will they repent / / of any. I refer to two kinds of believers.

I mean, first of all, the believers who believe according to the law of malediction, who sin against God and His Christ, and who know that Christ is the Savior and that God is the avenger and punisher of sin. Nevertheless, they hope that their sin will be forgiven through Christ, who will make them one with God His Father. Such individuals possess faith, but it is a faith under judgment, not under grace, until the time when Christ will pardon them. They are sinners under Christ who are not yet in the kingdom of Christ, that is, in the community of saints, which is the sole fellowship of the body of Christ in remission and forgiveness of sin. There alone, in the community of saints, is the conscience cleansed of sin, and the heart vindicated and made good. In that community there are no sinners, only those made good, through Christ, by faith in Him. Those are the acquitted who are free from sin purchased by the blood of Christ. The Spirit of

Gloss: Such boasting of the truth is a credit to me.

309v

470

grace justifies them to be heirs of Christ's eternal kingdom. Thus, there are no sinners in the kingdom of Christ and the community of saints. Those, however, who believe that they are damned by sin and that Christ might redeem them are in the judgment of Christ. As said earlier, these individuals repent and repent, and they do believe in Christ. Even more are they sinners who do not belong in Christ's kingdom of grace, those who continually lie and remain in sin.

My intention is to indicate the real differences between the true knowledge of Christ and the falsely acclaimed knowledge, and the differences

310r

between sinners and those justified / / in faith. Therefore, whoever sins should acknowledge himself a sinner so that he may receive grace. Those who have received grace are not sinners; they are

Jn. 8 [36]

the redeemed, those who have been acquitted of sin. Those whom the Son sets free are free indeed. How, then, can they be indentured prisoners of sin?

There are three kinds of persons in the judgment and kingdom of Christ.

1. Sinners: Coarse Generation of Peasants[2]

In the judgment of acquittal, there are first of all sinners. "If we say we have no sin," says John, "we deceive ourselves and the truth is not in us. If

1 Jn. 1 [10]

we confess our sins, He is faithful and just, and He will forgive our sins and cleanse us from all unrighteousness. If we say we have not sinned, we make Him a liar and His Word is not in us." This text clearly shows that there are sinners and penitents in the judgment of grace. If someone has

Gloss: For such a one we are not to pray.

sinned and does not confess it, he makes God a liar, and His Word is not in that man. Nor does he desire any intercession to give him life again. He thinks he lives. Really, he is dead. But those who confess their sins, in the hope that Christ will cleanse them from all stain, are penitents and forsake sin. If Christ the Savior cleanses such a person, he is acquitted and no longer a sinner; he is born anew of God. A part of that new birth is that he no longer sins. Therefore, the judgment of grace is committed to the saints of God. / / Each should diligently test and judge those who have been cleansed by grace and washed from sin in the blood of Christ.

Such may eat the bread of the Lord and drink His cup, not as sinners, but as those cleansed from all stain of sin. That is the true communion of saints in Jesus Christ, our Lord. Yes, the chosen people and royal priesthood, even the people of the manner and nature of God, are born through the word of truth, cleansed from sin in the blood of the Lord Jesus Christ and washed by the water of grace. To be washed from sin is the baptism into the communion of saints. As co-witness, the Holy Spirit testifies that they are born of water and Spirit, that they are like newborn children in the Spirit and nature of the Lord Jesus Christ; they are filled with grace, love, faithfulness, truth, goodness, and righteousness. These are the fruits of the Holy Spirit, against which there is no law. These newborn children are not imprisoned but free children, peaceable and free in conscience and heart.

In Holy Scripture, David the psalmist, the prophets, the evangelists, and the apostles witness to the kingdom, people, and generation of Christ. It is the highest and most noble lineage, and the virtues, treasures, riches, honor, and property have from ancient times belonged to this royal and most noble house[3] of Christ. These virtues, these priceless noble gems, are not / / worn externally on

nota

311r

physical throats, arms, hands, or fingers; these gems
are the power of the Holy Spirit in spirit and soul.
The Father of lights, from whom all good gifts
come, gives and presents these gems to the most noble house of Christ. Through the Holy Spirit, they
are given to the honor of the bridegroom Christ,
and they are to be worn on throats, arms, and hands
in the real power of the virtue of the noble gems.
Man does not need elemental gems, which only signify virtue, but which have no unchanging,
eternally enduring power. In honor of its king, the
royal family wears this power and virtue of the no-
blest, eternally enduring gem on their throats, arms,
hands, and fingers. That is, they surrender all their
powers and members to the power and effect of that
noble gem given by the Father. With all diligence,
they see to it that, before the Father and His Christ,
the power and effect of this virtue remains unspotted in them. Particularly in the Revelation of John,
the Holy Scripture says much about these noble
gems, especially about their virtues, which only the
nobility of Christ may wear.

Gloss: Figura-
tively, the
physical Israel
e the stone on
unhallowed
garments

Rev. [21:9-23]

Gloss: I do
not speak
here of the
fleshly nobility
or succession
n which one is
raised or in
which one
raises
elf above 311v

another.
In their fallen
nature, no one
better before
God than
another.

The ornament of these precious gems and garments does not belong to those whose sin and whose
deceit of wickedness before God have made them
into wretched peasants. Since the fall of Adam, all
men have been so. To them, only the earth and
earthly things have been given. They make their
living with labor and the sweat / / of their brows.
Since the fall of Adam, they have not yet been ennobled by Christ, for whose sake all things are, to
rule and reign over heaven and earth. Rather, because of sin, with the deceit of sin and in all wickedness, they still build the cursed and not the blessed
earth. Christ has not ennobled them to wear these
gems and ornaments. Neither are they disciplined
or instructed; they are coarse, knavish laborers be-

473

cause of the original curse. Therefore, they cannot handle the gems. The natural, earthly man knows and understands nothing about God.

Therefore, whoever lays claims to natural nobility must be gifted with natural virtues if they are to wear with justification the elemental gems, which are only a sign of natural virtues. In the natural nobility, it is a scandal to wear much gold, chains, gems, and noble garments, and to lack withal the natural honors and virtues. A nobility without virtue is like a sow bedecked with gold and gems. She immediately drags it all through the dirt, rather than wearing it honorably. Now, if one were to inscribe virtue on the coat of arms[4] of the fleshly nobility, one would find few true nobles. For their sake, I would gladly be made a liar, and I readily grant them their natural honor.[5]

312r

I write what I do, not because I am concerned with the comings and goings of the natural nobility, or presume / / to scold them, but for this reason: an ancient, honorable, noble line does not gladly tolerate dishonorable persons who disgrace and dishonor their name and ancestry. We who claim to belong to the ancient, eternal name and lineage of the birth of the Lord Jesus Christ, we who have been taken from the world and adorned with virtue and grace, gifted and acquitted by the Father of lights, should be a hundred thousand times more concerned that there be no one among us who would dishonor and blaspheme the noble name and line of the most noble house of Jesus Christ!

Gloss: No one should call anyone a Christian unless he is given testimony to birth from the Father.

Similarly, no one should be allowed to bear the noble name who is not nobly born in this family, that is, born and conceived of the Holy Spirit and of the honorable bride of Christ. She conceives in her body children born to the Father of Jesus Christ; her body is the body of Christ, which is His holy church, and she raises them in her discipline. Christ and His church are one flesh. She is espoused by Christ in the word of truth and married with the ring of love which has no end. Through the washing of water in the Word, which they believe for the remission of sins, she is the legitimate spouse who bears the children conceived by the Father. She tends her children by the Father, and with her breasts, which are filled with the pure milk of the Holy Spirit, she nourishes her children. According to the words of Peter, these children, born of God, // are by nature eager to suck this milk for their own growth and increase. For that is the nature of God. Whoever is born of God hears God's Word. Whoever is not so born is not to be included in the house and lineage of Christ. And even if someone boasts of the Father and is not born of the legitimate mother, he is a bastard. He does not inherit, nor may he bear the name of the line, nor may he be included in the high nobility of Christ.

The first unfallen, creaturely Adam was the first fleshly nobleman,[6] ennobled and created in the image of God from whom all nobility and virtue derives. He was the first earthly nobleman and ruler under heaven. His wife was created from his flesh and of the same lineage to help him; they were to plant the garden of God without effort and work, not as peasants but as nobles, in obedience to their Creator. Functionally, they were lord and god to the creatures, for they had been thus appointed under heaven not to work in wretchedness as a peasant does in the sweat of his brow. If Adam and his wife had not sinned against their Creator, they and all their line, their descendants of earthly lords and nobility, would be without toil and labor. Nor would there be shame, disgrace, death, sickness, toil, or labor, nor would any suffering have come on

Eph. 5 [26]

nota

1 Pet. 2:[2]

312v

them. Rather, all other creatures would have obeyed them as their divinely appointed lords and

313r

nobles, and they, along with their descendants, would have been accepted as such by all creatures // under heaven until the appearance of the heavenly man, also of Adam's line, Jesus Christ.

He ennobled Adam and his family even more, that is, in soul and spirit, and raised them into the heavenly realm. He established and made Adam a lord with the Lord Jesus Christ, who has all power in heaven and on earth. Even the angels, who were subject to Him and His obedient servants, desired and were eager to see this ennobling of Adam.

This freedom to become heavenly lords

nota

without tribulation, pain, death, and suffering Christ brought with Him for the whole human race. Through His own tribulation, suffering, and death, He brought it; to make heavenly men out of earthly ones, raised up with Christ through suffering with Him into eternal liberty and glory. Therefore, as

1 Cor. 3:[22, 23]

Paul says: "All creatures are for the sake of man, man for the sake of Christ, and Christ for the sake of God." That is the true, highly gifted, and liberated noble ancient house which has its origin from eternity. We may boast that we belong to this noble house, that we may partake in such glory with Christ, and that we have the right to wear the golden chains with all the gems, necklaces, bracelets, and rings as well as the elegant garments with which Christ honors His bride and wedding guests. As the legitimate and true nobility we may

313v

use the glory and the liberty // of the most precious gems and virtues which belong to Christians as the true nobility. Much could be written of it as the Scriptures make clear.

When, however, Adam and Eve despised the noble title given them by God, fell into shame and disgrace through the deceit of sin, and trespassed the command of their Lord and Creator, all their freedom and glory and their dominion over the other creatures was taken from them, and they were expelled from the garden of pleasure. The garden was closed along with the heavenly city and the fiery sword of the wrath of God upon men was placed before it. Adam and his wife were made into peasants of the earth in the great village of this bleak world's wilderness in order to make his living in the sweat of his brow. With wretchedness and toil he and all his descendants were to make a living on it, and the wives were to bear children in suffering. There the primeval divine nobility and the true freedom of man with all the glory of it came to its end. The noble, divine house died off through death which came from sin, and the glory of man faded. They all became wretched, coarse peasants and unfaithful workers, working the earth in

314r falsehood and deceit, in all wickedness, shame, / / and licentiousness, sold under sin, and made into coarse, undisciplined slaves of sin.

That is the origin of that coarse generation of peasants which knows neither discipline nor virtuous custom before God. Since the time of Adam it has grown in coarseness, licentiousness, undiscipline, and wickedness, raised up by the father of lies, the enemy of all virtue and truth, and remained till the time of Christ coarse, undisciplined peasants. Even though in a heathen manner they have presumed to be noble on the model of the pure nobility of creation mentioned above, it was only a theft before Christ and His noble virtue.

Gloss Earthly emperors and rulers create nobles with shield, gems, and helmets. The virtures, however, which belong to nobility, they have no power to give. But those who are ennobled by Christ are also gifted with the virtues by Christ.

Jn. 10 [8]

Therefore all who came before and lag behind Christ—but are not with Him—are thieves and murderers, nor are they of the highborn lineage or nobility of Christ, but a wild, undisciplined, coarse, bucolic lot, full of all vice, lacking goodness, unlovely, unfriendly, wanton, proud, boastful, full of envy and hate, bloodthirsty, whoring, gluttonous, quaffers, greedy for vain honor, not desirous of the good, cunning / / and malicious, ready for all wickedness, financiers, liars, deceivers, miserly, thieving, murderous, unbelieving, idolatrous, sorcerers, contentious, quarrelers and brawlers, disobedient to parents, perjurers, faithless and deniers of the truth. In short, they do whatever they feel like, regardless of all natural honor, not to speak of any divine virtue. They are beastly people like swine and dogs before whom the precious pearls should not be cast; rather they should be kept and hidden from them. They are the coarsest of all people, to whom not even the earthly is commanded and entrusted, let alone the divine, any more than it would be given to beastly, unreasoning, raging animals which are inclined only to kill and destroy. All of that and one transgression after another follows from the curse of sin.

314v

2. The Peasants under the Natural Law

Second, there are the legalistic, law and order[7] people who hold to a human, legalistic, honor and goodness for the sake of physical need and vain honor. It is rooted and written in their created nature. Thus they make themselves a law on the basis of which they love honesty and natural virtue, as the devout heathen have done, but know little or nothing about any God. They invent all manner of idolatry and create it in them by their fallen reason / / so that they learn to believe and love it. For everything that is loved or feared above or alongside of God the Creator of heaven and earth is an idol no matter what its appearance. Whatever is done with it is a rustic, earthly, coarse effort. Its essence is transitory and perishable and is loved and feared only for earthly reasons. These are the coarse, earthly workers and peasants who as yet know nothing of the nobility and virtue of Christ. However, through the understanding and knowledge of Christ they may come to a mature faith in Christ and be gifted and ennobled with the virtue and goodness which comes through faith.

3. The Peasants under God's Law

Third, there are people who are captive to the law of God, who believe and hold that all things are of God who has made them and all creatures, but who, because of their rough, earthly, fallen, peasant ways cannot receive or follow the noble law of God. That is why they will endure condemnation and more heavy blows on their backs because they know the will of the Lord, but do not do it. They proclaim it to be beyond their capacity and do not do it. Rather, although they should do the good and inherit the blessing, they do evil and wickedness and inherit the malediction and the curse, and sin takes over in them / / against their wills to such a degree that they do not know where to turn to escape the stern anger of God. For regardless of what they try to cultivate in their earthly, fallen nature, only thistles and thorns grow. In spite of all their ef-

315r

315v

479

fort and work the weeds, that is sin, take over, and all their work leads only to tribulation and grief. Wherever sin thus takes over, there also grace can take over if there is repentance in true remorse and sorrow over sin, and a hearty dissatisfaction of self; then one can receive grace upon grace. Even though one finds oneself condemned under the law given by Moses, which is good and given for man's salvation, one nevertheless receives grace and truth which comes from Christ, by which one is freed from sin and ennobled and graced with the virtues of faith in Christ.

Jn. 1[16 f.]

Gloss: for them Christ hallows Himself.

4. The Hypocrites

Fourth, there are the hypocrites and dissemblers who in all their coming and going seek to justify and hallow themselves and regard themselves as devout and well. All the sects in the world are full of them. Even today they sit with the hypocrites in the temple, grandly thanking God that they are not like so and so. Those who thus justify and heal themselves need no physician. Their health remains an eternal illness and death, their sight eternal blindness and darkness. Since they cannot produce anything to excuse / / their sin, it remains on them.

Lk. 18 [11 f.]

Lk. 5 [31]

316r

Here one also finds the opposite, namely hypocritical sinners. These are they, who in confessing that they are sinners imagine themselves to be better than the hypocrites [mentioned above], even as the hypocrites think themselves better than the sinners. But they are all the same. These sinners, in their villainy, wickedness, and sin presume to despise the righteous who are justified by Christ and made good through faith, and to turn the devotion and truth of Christ in the righteous into hypocrisy. They regard and cherish their knavery as

better than the true devotion of Christ which comes
from faith and not from the works about which the
hypocrite boasts. They presume by such confession
of their sin to sanctify their wicked, sinful lives, and
by so doing make the faithful and devout appear to
be hypocrites who expect to be justified by their
works. They expect, therefore, to go from the
temple justified with all the sin and wickedness in
which they lie (without any remorse and repentance
or decision to forsake it). In so doing they slander
the righteous and those acquitted by Christ as
dissemblers and hypocrites although they
themselves are the real mockers of Christ who expect to sneak in under the parable of Christ and say
with a false heart: God be merciful to me a sinner;
but have no intention, desire, nor petition to
abstain from sin. / / They are worse than any other
dissemblers on earth.

316v

5. *Those Who Appear to Have Faith*

Fifth, and finally, there are those who have the
appearance of faith in Christ but who seek their
goodness only in the hearts of other people. They
accuse everyone of wickedness and sin as though
the sin of others were the reason for their own sin
and wickedness and as though they cannot get rid
of their sin because of other people. They presume
to judge and justify everyone. One is said to have
done first this, then that, and they seem to assume
that they sin only because of the wickedness and sin
of others. Otherwise they would be devout and upright. Such usually go from one sect and error to
another, of which the world is as full as the raging
sea is full of terrible and marvelous beasts. They run
around to find the gospel and peace of Christ and
never find it. All they have in themselves is a stone

and so die of hunger, ever lacking the word of truth, the true Bread of God, because they do not look for it in that place where the Lord and His true nourishment alone is to be found, namely in their own hearts. Whoever does not find the Lord and His Word as food of the soul there, will find it in no other place eternally. To such people the false prophets usually come and say: Come, I will show you Christ in our gathering, company, or church, and you will find Christ. You will see there the true life in Spirit and grace, and God dwelling in our hearts as chamber and temple. You will see the true light and salt which belongs to the true food / / and with which it must be salted. Therefore such people hear the falsely acclaimed [Christians] rather than those who truly know Christ and are led into strange hearts unknown to Christ, away from their own hearts in which alone they can and should find Christ. Thus they are imprisoned and deceived, evermore lost and undone in their consciences. They are clouds without water (that is, without the water of grace) driven by the whirlwind (that is, with mere, inflated, vain, empty words without the accompanying work of the Holy Spirit who alone can bring it into the heart of the faithful).

May the Lord protect and preserve us from such prophets about whom He Himself warned us, as well as from all other evil and errors, that we seek the goodness of Christ in His Word and truth in no other place than our own hearts. There He reveals Himself to us and with the Father dwells in us if we truly love and keep His commandments which are not difficult. Those are the true signs by which each may judge whether Christ dwells in him. Such a heart will soon find the true gathering and fellowship of Christ's saints. For where the carcass is, the eagles will gather. There also the gathering and true

Mt. 24 [5]

317r

Jude 1 [12 f.]

2 Cor. 13 [5]

Mt. 24 [28]

482

fellowship of the saints will soon be found. May He allow us to be found in His fellowship which is His body. Amen.

317v The grace / / of our Lord Jesus Christ be with us all. Amen.

My sister Anna and I thank you kindly for your gifts and contribution. This indication and proof of the spirit of your hearts is dearer to me in Christ than the gift, even if it were worth the whole world. I thank the Lord for you, also you. The church here as well as I and my Anna greet you fervently in the Lord. Brother Veit[8] himself writes his greeting. Pray the Lord faithfully for us, and we will, by God's grace, do the same. Dated at Augsburg on December 9, anno 1547.

In the Lord Jesus Christ, servant to you and all the faithful, and comrade in the tribulation in Christ.
Pilgram Marpeck.

13

Five Fruits of Repentance[1] (1550) [#12]

Introduction

This letter provides no clue as to who the recipients were; thus one may perhaps assume that they were members of Marpeck's own circle. The specific issue here is the chief difference between the Anabaptist understanding of the order of the church and that of the Catholics and Protestants. They all claim the name of Christ, talk much of repentance, confession of sin, and even the ban. But their understanding and use of them is perverted so that men are brought by them to destruction. For Anabaptists the issue was of the greatest importance, for it had to do with the integrity and the visibility of the church.

The first fruit of repentance Marpeck identifies as the recognition that a man can get no help from the creatures, that is, the solitary experience of the descent into hell, of the complete forsakenness of guilt. The second fruit is the recognition that one must wait for God's grace and that one cannot seize it with superficial words about repentance. The third fruit is that the sinner is in sorrow for his sins and not for the consequences which he must suffer. He wants only to be remembered by God. The fourth fruit is the determination no longer to commit sin. Without this everything is in vain and a sham. The fifth fruit is the full acceptance of responsibility for one's own sin and the refusal to blame anyone or anything else. To do this is ultimately to blame God.

This little letter is perhaps the most unified and concise statement of a subject in Marpeck's correspondence.

In his introduction Fast writes: "The epistle concerning five fruits of repentance makes it apparent that Marpeck comes from another tradition than the Zürich Anabaptists. Compare the presentation of the process of repentance in Hubmaier (*Der Linke Flügel*, pp. 35 ff.)! How much more profoundly Marpeck, the lay theologian, uncovers what true repentance is than does the learned theologian! In the first place one suspects the influence of Hans Hut. For both suffering is one stage on the road to true faith. While Hut, however, sees suffering as an ascetic means, for Marpeck it is the just punishment for our sin. The acceptance of this punishment is an essential step toward true repentance. In so doing Marpeck picks up a theme central to the reformation. Precisely in this way Luther in his ninety-five theses developed his view of repentance in opposition to Catholic teaching. Just like the young Luther, Marpeck uses the concepts and presuppositions of the mystics in order to express his understanding of the gospel. Most striking is the thought of a *resignatio ad infernum,* an acceptance of the punishment of hell itself. Related to this Marpeck develops his own theology of Christ's descent into hell at another place.

"Other writings of Marpeck emphasize the specifically Anabaptist ideas more. This present writing betrays its Anabaptist origin in the introduction especially through its identification of the Holy Spirit and the fellowship of the saints. Apart from both there is no salvation! Concerning such an exclusive claim it must not be forgotten that Marpeck expressly took a free attitude among his brethren on such matters as discipline, the oath, and community of goods. Some have even concluded that the South German Anabaptists took a distinctive position over against the Swiss Brethren. Research on this matter has not yet however brought forth a consensus".[2]

The Text

171r   Five Fruits of True Repentance

The grace of our Lord Jesus Christ and His compassion be with you and all who are poor in spirit. Amen.

We have reason to thank God our heavenly

Father when someone grieves because of his sins, when there are men who come to true repentance through grace, and appear before Christ, the throne of grace, with remorse and regret, confess their sins to Him, recognizing them, through the law of grace, by which they receive grace and more grace. For the law of vengeance was given through Moses. Grace and truth have become ours through Christ. This grace and truth in turn lead on into the true comfort, peace, and joy of the Holy Spirit. In this Holy Spirit alone there is forgiveness of sin through the sacrifice of death on the cross and the shedding of the blood of Christ. Such forgiveness, however, takes place only in the fellowship of saints, which alone received such power from Christ.

Therefore Paul says: "The bread which we bless (which means: to speak well of, to praise and thank our God) is the fellowship of the body of Christ, and the cup with which we give thanks (meaning: to thank our God for the forgiveness of sin), is the fellowship of the blood of Christ" (1 Cor. 171v 10 [16 f.]). / / For this reason there is no forgiveness of sin outside of the fellowship of Christ, however much the whole world may claim for itself grace and forgiveness of sin with false boasting. I write you this so that you may be in possession of genuine and true evidence for your hope for pardon and the forgiveness of sins, and produce the honest fruit of repentance in order to escape the coming wrath of God, and that we may not be found among the generation of vipers (Mt. 3:7; 12:34; 23:33; Lk. 3:7).

This generation and kind belongs under the law of the curse and is eternally condemned and exiled. Even if this generation feigns repentance with its confession of sin and acceptance of the ban of Christ a thousand times the poison of vipers still remains in it in order to poison others as well as itself with the future wickedness and to become an offense. In spite of it they fall from one sin into another. However much warning, scolding, reproof, and admonition is attempted, it does no good, for their whole performance has the one aim of leading astray and deceiving themselves and others. Concerning this generation John, the baptizer to repentance, spoke gravely and terribly / / and said: "You generation of vipers, who told you to flee from the coming wrath of God? Do not say: we are Abraham's children, for God can make children for Abraham out of these stones" (Mt. 3:7 ff.). That means: do not boast that you are the generation of Christ (of the seed of the Word). For even today the axe is laid to the root of such barren, unfruitful, and twice dead trees (although according to the appearance of the Word they are green) to cut them down, especially when no work, digging, or cultivation will any longer benefit them. Christ may come to them whenever He pleases: He will find only His name, that is to say, only green leaves which, although they correspond to the name of Christ, certainly do not serve for the healing of the nations (Rev. 22 [2]), and no fruit.

The curse of Christ applies to such as to the fig tree (Mt. 21 [19]). For when Christ arrives hungry, desiring and seeking fruit, but finds no fruit, nothing can follow but the curse, as with the fig tree, so that it dries up and, as those who do not bear fruit are cut off the vine which is Christ, is prepared for the fire.

I write this so that we may take careful note of the witness within our hearts / / so that when we sin we may perform and complete the true fruit of repentance, in order that the wrath of God and the curse of Christ may not come over us to our destruc-

487

tion, as they will certainly come upon all the enemies of God so that the last evil is worse than the first (Lk. 11:26). With regard to such the psalmist David also pleads for vengeance when he says: "Lord, let one evil after another come upon them; turn their table into a trap" (Ps. 68 [61:23]) etc. For no greater punishment nor vengeance can be found than to fall from one transgression and sin into another and still assume that one participates in the table fellowship of Christ, although they are and remain only at their own table which has become a trap for them and from which they eat judgment to themselves, and not from the Lord's table. Al-

Mt. 22 [11-13]

though they have been invited (Mt. 22:22 ff.; Lk. 14:16 ff.) or else appear at the wedding banquet with soiled garments, they will nevertheless not taste the Lord's Supper eternally, but rather they will eat their own meal from their table perverted into a trap and will be judged so that they will depart exiled and condemned. For they cannot stand in the judgment as the psalmist says and prays: "Let them be condemned when they are judged" (109:7) etc. The Lord commands such dishonest people to be bound hands and feet and to be thrown

173r

// into outer darkness (Mt. 22:13).

Those are all terrible and hard sayings which cause consternation and fright when one seriously considers them. Happy are those who thus allow themselves to be alarmed by the Word of God and who are earnestly shocked because of it. Salvation draws near to them. For they are prepared for and led to the Lord Christ through the genuine fruits of repentance so that He bestows His grace upon them. This fruit of repentance proves itself true in suffering, sorrowing, fear, and pain of conscience, in deep affliction and in true fruits of repentance.

The First Fruit of True Repentance

This is the first fruit: that the sinner confesses himself guilty of eternal death under the stern, serious righteousness and wrathful vengeance of God; that he becomes ashamed and completely battered and broken in his own eyes, and with fear and trembling appears before the face of God helpless, without comfort, and completely forsaken of all creatures in heaven and on earth; that he has and knows, seeks and recognizes no help in himself or in anything else. He recognizes only his sin and guilt which condemns him with the devil and his following to hell. / / That is the first and most bitter fruit of a true repentance in order that prior to all other fruits we test and experience what kind of fruits sin, which we have committed, produces, and that we taste and eat this fruit. Yes, prior to all other fruit a true penitent must taste what he himself (through the deceit of sin) has done and sown.

173v

Gloss

> It is not enough that one merely says: I would gladly repent and confess my sins. A part of it is to recognize what kind of fruit sin brings.

For what each man sows, he will and must reap or harvest (Gal. 6 [8]). For all pains, anxiety, and distress, and suffering together with eternal death, are the true fruits and reward, yes, the true wages of sin, which is given to all sinners who have not received grace, and by which they are condemned to eternal destruction. Whoever does not find Christ in this depth (that is, in this true baptism for the remission of sin) will not find Him in the height in joy and glory eternally. For He who descended is the one who has ascended (Eph. 4, 10). Whoever desires to eat this paschal Lamb must eat bitter herbs with it (Ex. 12 [8]). Nevertheless, it still depends on God's free grace, even when man has tried the in-

	nocent bitterness, whether or not He will grant / / him to partake of the Lamb of God which takes away the sin of the world. Even if we drink the cup of the suffering of guilt, we are not for that reason given the kingdom of God.
174r	

Gloss

We are not to boast of suffering but of grace, since all suffering proceeds from sin and guilt. For Cain, Esau, Saul, Judas, and others have (Heb. 11:1 ff.), as all sinners, felt that bitterness, but the enjoyment of the Lamb was eternally denied them. Whoever therefore would contemplate the goodness of God must first contemplate the severity (Rom. 11:22). Thus far briefly concerning the first fruit of repentance.

The Second Fruit of Repentance

The second fruit is that God allows a small light of the hope of His grace to shine along with His condemnation in order that the sinner may anticipate that grace with patience and become aware that he cannot rob God of His grace or seize it. In the meantime he regards the divine hesitation and withholding of the grace of the comfort and peace in the Holy Spirit as his blessedness, until the light— the day of grace at the pool of the water of grace— appears in brightness and [the water] be moved for the hope of recovery—or else until Christ, in such hope and patience, finds him in the Portico of Solomon after thirty-eight years of illness / / in order to take pity on him. Then He bids him rise, takes the agony of sin, the anxiety and distress of conscience, as well as sin itself away, and freely gives him peace and joy in the Holy Spirit. Oh God, how utterly impatient we are to await your comfort! We like to assume that You would prostrate Yourself at our feet with Your comfort and

Jn. 5 [1 ff].

174v

490

mercy, and that all we need to do is to confess our sin and to devise a sorrow and fictitious remorse, in order to be received into the fellowship of Christ, and then the whole matter is made right. Whoever thinks thus will go far off the mark, and be a victim of self-deceit.

The Third Fruit of True Repentance

The third fruit of repentance is that the sinner is more in sorrow about what he has done against God than about what he must suffer in consequence. Thus he desires from God (in the hope of His grace) that he not be delivered from cross and suffering until God's will has been satisfied in him and until (like the evildoer on the cross) he desires to be remembered by God. For the thief on the cross had no thought of being delivered from his cross of death. Rather it was the unrepentant evildoer on the left (whom the other admonished for not fearing God, while he committed his own guilt to the care of the innocence of Christ) / / who said: "If you are the Son of God deliver us and yourself from the cross" (Lk. 23:39 f.). Thus the viperish penitents still do today who are only sorry that they must suffer because of sin but have no sorrow for the sin itself which is the cause of their suffering. True penitents, however, do not desire to be rid of their deserved suffering but of the sin. They commit their guilt to the intercession of the innocence of Christ, confess that they suffer justifiably by their own guilt, and that the Lord Jesus Christ suffered innocently for our sins, and await patiently the release from their suffering through Him who has delivered them from their sins, never again to carry out sin, in order that henceforth they may live completely so as to please their God. Thus far concerning the third fruit of repentance.

175r

491

The Fourth Fruit of Repentance

Although sin is lodged within us (according to the first Adamic birth of the flesh), a true penitent does not allow it to rule since he is still suffering on the cross with the innocence of Christ because of sin. For what evildoer still desires or does the evil deed when he is imprisoned and suffers tortures because of his evil deed, / / unless indeed he be in blasphemous despair? Even less do these sinners allow sin to rule because they are true prisoners of God and suffer agony of conscience because of sin and still have no certain comfort, but merely hope to be rid of sin. It would needs be a monstrous wickedness and impertinence against God to commit sin while one repents, is captive in conscience, and has hope for deliverance. For this reason a true penitent does not allow sin to rule, but along with his repentance, insofar as it is true persevering repentance, accepts the command of Christ, that he should no longer commit sin, lest the latter evil be worse than the first (Lk. 11 [24-26]). For that is the highest, greatest, and more beneficial repentance that henceforth one lives in the will of God and not in wickedness. Without this all repentance is in vain and the Son of God is crucified and trodden under foot (Heb. 6:6; 10:26).

The Fifth Fruit of Repentance

The fifth fruit is that I do not blame any creature in heaven or on earth for my sin or point to it as the cause of my sin, somewhat as follows: If this or that had not been so, I would have been pious enough not to have done it. For original wickedness has its source only in itself. It takes its beginning in and through itself / / as though it were eternal as a

175v

176r

492

lying false god who of himself creates an eternity out of identical, true divine honors; a thief and a murderer, who robs the true God of all honor, and murders those who yield all honor to the true God. Thus he is the beginning of wickedness, a father of murderers, of lies, and of all malice and wickedness, a hater of all good and lover of all evil. Consequently he is lord, god, and potentate of all the pain which, because of the guilt of wickedness, he bears in himself. Sin, death, and hell follow their god. For deception and all wickedness is, as was already mentioned, a veritable god, uncreated, who (like the eternal and true God) created himself out of nothing, as though wickedness (along with its god) were from all eternity. Thus this god (as ruler of the world) remains eternally in his own domain. Hell, death, and sin with all their agony follow him as their god. Whoever therefore points to any creature in heaven and on earth as the cause of his sin, deceptiveness, and wickedness in order to excuse himself, he accuses his own God, Creator and Maker of all creatures, even though these creatures have been created for all good.

176v

That is the same as blaspheming God, and as though I / / said: if it were not for God I would not have sinned. The opposite is true: if it were not for the wicked god (his and all my own wickedness) no sin would occur. However, anyone who attempts to excuse himself with some other cause of sin really wishes that instead [of the wicked god] the true God with His creatures were the liar and doer of wickedness. This, however, is a fruit of true repentance that God together with His creatures is regarded as true and good, as indeed He is true and good. Indeed, it is better that all men are liars and that God be true, as Paul says. But the viperish kind and its poison is full of such pretenses in order to conceal

Ps. 115:1
Rom. 3 [4]

itself and plunge others into guilt. Wherever there is such hidden poison no genuine fruit of repentance can ever follow, rather one is compelled to confess with David and say: "Lord, I, I, I myself am the transgressor. Therefore, my God, do not accuse or punish any other work of your hands because of my sins." All the guilt with its torment and penalty comes justly upon me, me, me. For I have constantly followed that monarch, namely the god of all // wickedness and given consent to him by my own impertinence. For You are always my God, Lord, and Deliverer. You have reconquered the power and capability to withstand all wickedness for me and all men, and freely bestowed and given it to us. But I have again wantonly surrendered this power, this judgment, and this righteousness which You achieved, and with which You have judged, fettered, and overcome the rulers of this world; of my own free will I returned it to the enemy of my salvation, and have permitted him to rule over me with his wickedness and perversity. He has again taken me prisoner and taken the power from me. Thus I have again lost the might, Your judgment, Your truth, and Your righteousness which You conquered, and surrendered it to him whom You have bound with Your power, and from whom You had wrested all his weapons, his power, and also all the riches which he had stolen from the human race, and given them to us all again as spoils, distributing his plunder, and giving back to us the might, power, and strength (Mt. 12:29). I should have held on to them and should have watched better over the welfare of my soul. Carelessly I slept until the enemy, thief, and murderer dug into my house, and through deceit of sin sowed weeds in my heart, so that the fall of my house // was very great (Mt. 24:43; 13:25). Nor will it be built up again, and my

2 Sam. 12 [12]

177r

177v

494

heart and my soul will not recover. But then, Lord Jesus Christ, You stand surety for the fall and the breach. This I hope for from Your mercy and grace, that You will again save and deliver me from the hand of my enemy, rebuild my house, root out once again the weeds of sin, that You will have compassion on my distress and great poverty, and be merciful to me a poor sinner.

Moreover, as I desired that God should cover my sin, not hold me accountable for the greatness of my guilt but forgive my transgression, even so one is prepared to do the same in true repentance to all creatures and not to reveal or to receive confession of the sin of any other person if God has not first uncovered, witnessed, brought forth, and revealed it to them by a public deed. The person who confesses and reveals his sin to others only after they have disclosed or revealed it to him, although (according to the command of Christ) he could have done it first, but did not submit to this discipline—he acts as the whole world acts and says: At any rate, I am not the only one nor the first one; another has also done this and that, one thing and another, or still does it. He uncovers his sins and brings them out / / against the whole order of God, since according to God's command he could have done it first, prior to the revealing of his sin and shame. But he does it only after God has brought out and revealed his sin and shamed him. Thus the viperish kind intrudes itself into the mystery of God and the Holy Spirit and reveals its shame and sin in order to appear in a better light.

Much more could be discerned concerning true and false repentance for our instruction and cleansing of our conscience. God our heavenly Father grant us grace, and the Lord Jesus Christ, that we be truly humble before the great majesty

178r

and goodness of our Father and that we present and reveal ourselves and confess honestly and truly without any falseness of spirit. We can never humble ourselves sufficiently before our God against whom we have sinned. Wherever such remorse, which is true sorrow and suffering, is found in sinners, it produces a repentance which no one will 2 Cor. [10] regret, and wherever sin so abounds in sorrow (not the works of wickedness), there grace also abounds. Without this eternal regret, pain and agony of 179v conscience remain / / together with eternal torment and wherever man forsakes the right and the good and again commits the lie, sin, wickedness together with all unrighteousness remain.

Receive this admonition and reminder therefore together with other Holy Scripture,which directs us, not against the discipline and obedience of the Word of truth, but leads us into it and shows us what serves the praise of God and the salvation of our souls. And even if it makes for remorse, suffering, and sorrowing, no one sustains any harm, except those who deliberately persist in stubbornness and despair and who begrudge God His glory. For all discipline, penalty, threatening of conscience, as well as all suffering in spirit, soul, and body, in short everything that contributes to cleansing and sanctification is regarded as a melancholy thing, and, if one is stuck in it, as a heavy anxiety. Afterward, however, says Saint Paul, it yields the peaceable fruit of eternal blessedness (2 Cor. 4:17).

Please accept this writing also to your and our improvement and in all things look forward to the strength of comfort, peace, grace, and love in and with true hope and patience. For this I pray God 179r our heavenly Father and the Lord Jesus/ / Christ that He would grant and give you and us the working and moving of His Holy Spirit, to expect such things from Him. Amen. Amen. Amen. (117)

The grace of our Lord Jesus Christ be your comfort and that of all of us. In Him we can rejoice in the truth with you, and be comforted and brought joy in our sorrows. Amen.

Dated at Augsburg, August 24, Anno 1550.
In the Lord Jesus Christ
Servant to you and all true believers
and companion in the
affliction which is in Christ.
Pilgram Marpeck.

14

To the Church in
St Gallen and Appenzell
(1551) (#34)

Introduction

In 1551 Marpeck tried once again to reach the Swiss Brethren. This letter is one of a series written at this time by both parties. Marpeck had written at least once, had received a reply, but was unsatisfied and mystified by their response. What the "demand" of the Swiss Brethren is to which he refers is not clear, but it may well be that they resented his long, admonitory letters which, like Paul's, are sometimes "hard to understand," and that they had suggested that if he would only stop, things would right themselves. In any event, he felt their attitude as a bellicose attack on himself. He counters with a sustained warning against Christians exposing themselves to the wiles of the devil by being censorious and quarrelsome. He laments the divided state of the Anabaptist fellowship, and emphasizes that the Holy Spirit works in His own way and not necessarily according to human rules and regulations. The Holy Spirit can do His uniting work only if Christians will talk with each other, or in his case, write.

While it is not hard to see how his letter could further antagonize the Swiss—since he charges them with unwillingness to listen to the Holy Spirit—the letter is testimony to his concern for the unity and peace of Christ's church.

The Text

To the Church in St. Gallen and Appenzell

272r This letter was carried to the churches at St. Gallen and in Appenzell by old Thomas Schuhmacher for reasons that you will understand.

498

Grace and peace from God, our heavenly Father through and from the Lord Jesus Christ be and remain with us to eternity. Amen.

Dearly beloved, loved in Jesus Christ, our Healer. We, and especially I, Pilgram, have received your letter at the hand of the carrier, your and our dear brother. However, neither through the oral nor the written account am I even now able to discover or understand any reason for your demand and desire from which not a human or carnal but a godly impulse or movement, caused by the grace of God, might follow. Thus I also recently wrote you requesting information and anything else that was pertinent, but you did not acknowledge [our letter] nor indicate where it had reached you and how you thought and felt about it. Similarly your messenger was unable to report to us. Nor did he know whether our letter had been brought before the congregation./ /

272v

Because of this we are gravely concerned, especially I, Pilgram. Your whole demand is shrouded in uncertainty. Consequently I also find in me no urging of the Holy Spirit without whom all striving and intention is in vain. I am ready, however, to take the blame myself rather than to blame you. Perhaps God does not consider me worthy to serve you in your grave concern about which you wrote and complained in your letters, twice before and again now. Nevertheless, I would have to do it even if I would rather not, and even if a whale, that is, any human power, regime, or temporal service or business—which I trust to God would not hinder me— had swallowed me, I would still have to come out, as frequently occurred, and carry out and accomplish the bidding for which God sent and urged me. In such matters and situations (please understand me right that I mean that strife, error, disunity, and

499

antipathy which flows from fleshly acclaimed wisdom and self-chosen feigned spirituality) I would rather have God urge, drive, press, and thrust me out by force / / than that I (not to speak of an unknown cause) should act myself.

273r

More yet, I might even be justifiably censured without discernment by spiritual people if I had a strong driving of the Holy Spirit in me to engage in the strife, error, and attacks referred to above. Then I would slowly and sadly submit and desist. It is not that I desire to resist the prompting of the Holy Spirit! God forbid! Rather, my reason is to test the prompting carefully, not because of the Holy Spirit, but because of my own human inability, weakness, ignorance, lack of understanding, folly, inconstancy, and fickleness.

Gloss

> The Holy Spirit often drives the guilty to their own fall because of their presumptuousness in order that they acquire self-knowledge.

The following must be included in testing the urging of the Holy Spirit: whether I have been clothed with the power from above to cover my weakness; that I feel enablement against my inability; that I sense and recognize true knowledge, wisdom, and understanding of God against / / my ignorance and folly in order to know wisdom; that I have laid hold of steadfastness on the firm foundation of truth against my fickleness, and only then to accept the urging of the Holy Spirit with fear, anxiety, and trembling, in order that one acts with certainty and not in uncertainty. However, no one should hide behind the sense of the above with a false appearance, or deliberately to obstruct, but to persevere in good faith in the fear of God. For the enemy of our salvation does not slumber nor take a nap[1] with his cunning and deception, everywhere to lead men astray. He stirs up much discord and

273v

fighting in man—who does not know why—and all with a persuasive appearance of godly zeal, although he is concerned only for himself and not for divine honor and truth. Thus he mortally wounds men and brings them to the verge of destruction from which they are saved, won, and healed again only with great difficulty. Whoever meddles to separate men without a specific urging and command of God sustains great harm, indeed destruction, which has overtaken many as examples for us.

274r I am not writing this to show that you are forsaken by God/ / but to admonish you earnestly not to enter into quarreling and strife with one another, but to bear with one another in sincere love and to confess your sins to each other in trust, to bring about true repentance. For we are not ignorant of the designs of our enemy, for he is the greatest envier and hater of man's salvation. Therefore it behooves us to watch over our souls, our own and each other's, especially to observe and search out whether the enemy has secretly started a fire in our innermost heart, conscience, and soul in order to consume soul, conscience, and heart in the wrath of God. There is among you a hidden fire which has an evil, stinking smoke and taste of fire, which the enemy of truth is seeking to conceal in order that he may ignite, destroy, and burn to ashes many hearts before it is discovered, as the means of the wrath of God which burns brightly everywhere.[2] Thus he also kindles his strife with deceit, lies, cunning, false suspicion, evil, faultfinding, mistrust, gossip, blandishment, flattery, greed for personal honor, scolding, slandering, anger, envy, hate, antipathy, unfriendliness, stubbornness, boastfulness, and pride. From this it follows that no one will yield to anyone else. These are the weapons of his knighthood with which he conducts his campaign to sneak

274v

501

up on and slay men. Now when the fire in the houses (that is, human hearts in which God should dwell) burns most fiercely so that fire and sword, hunger after the truth and famine meet, then he looks about for help lest it be too late.

The fire must be understood to mean the wrath of God; the sword the deceit and cunning of the enemies; on the other hand the sharp sword of God's Word that slays those who resist; famine: the withdrawal of the Word of grace and the faithful builders, workers, and servants.

When it is all but burned down, then is the time to rescue and defend with haste; to intervene and to obstruct the cunning, deadly strokes of the enemy with the sharpness of the Word of truth after one has already been fatally wounded. Only then the hungry must be given bread to eat, and good wine to the thirsty (that is, the comfort of the Holy Spirit) so that the heart may be made glad, since the enemy has ravaged and consumed it, scattered and slain the builders and workers, and devastated/ / the earth (that is, the earthly man).

275r

What can one workman do in such a situation? He really ought also to burn, be killed, or die of hunger, since the earth has been cursed, laid waste, and execrated. I do not write this to point at someone specifically but only for our mutual warning so that we put out the fire and save, apply the greatest earnestness, care, and diligence to get each other out of the fire before we perish, and learn to fight with the sword of the Spirit before we are attacked, wounded, and killed by the enemy with the weapons described above. [It is a warning] not to allow our land and soil to be wasted and to bear thorns and thistles (which, if it happens, means that the curse is near) and so to surrender it to the destruction of the enemy, but rather to build up our earthly body and to root out the weeds which grow from the evil seed of the enemy in order that the blessing of God may follow our labor, so that the fruit may prosper. If there are faithful builders and laborers, they should be loved and respected. If by the blessing of God fruit is produced, they should be supported, cared for, and given diligent attention; that we do not leave the bread lying under men's feet nor carelessly throw out the wine which gladdens our hearts. Thus when hunger/ / and thirst come we can be comforted by them, made glad, satisfied, and guided.

275v

I say it before God, that great gifts and the fruits of God's blessing could have come in our time through many faithful workers if we had only been more careful of the fruit, if we had stored and kept it in the cupboard of our hearts, since it came to our doors so utterly without cost. Had we truly cared for and gathered them and thanked God for them, it would surely not have been possible for us to go to someone else for bread and run around and beg. We would have our fill, and enough for all other peoples.

Still, my God, we can only lament before you about ourselves, for the fault is ours and not yours. You have richly given to us, but we have not given thanks, nor listened diligently. That is why we are in dire need in all places and in many ways, so that we must now search for that which we did not care for and have lost, and now have to call on you with ashamed face. And even if you continually turn us away,[3] refusing to hear or advise us, you would do no wrong. For first you recompense us for our carelessness and idleness in order to rouse our sleepy spirits and to warm/ / our lukewarm hearts with the fire of poverty. Thus, my God, you have ample right

276r

to tell us that we ought to be ashamed of our request because we have regarded as trifling your gift and grace. Nevertheless, we will continue shamelessly and importunately to beg with hope that you will listen to us for the sake of your own peace. And we will not be surprised nor deterred from our urgent prayer by your delay, in the hope that you will grant us assistance to fill our needs. No one who has not felt it knows how hot the fire of God's wrath is. Nor does anyone know the strategy of the enemy and the injuries he can inflict with his poisoned weapons who has not often gained salvation and victory in the battle. Again only he who has been thirsty and hungry knows what true hunger and thirst is. In these experiences God teaches his own to care for, protect, and watch over their souls for His sake, and to pray earnestly not to be led into and be destroyed by the temptation which will come.

Truly, my dear brothers, in a variety of ways the Lord sends a concise, direct word to those people to save their souls. Regardless of the form, whether it be in writing or in speech, it behooves 276v us// to accept (as Christ Himself) whatever in them is the testimony and the truth. Even though because of our carnal mind many things are difficult to understand and incomprehensible, and even though because of guilt and human weakness we may not immediately be able to understand or grasp, the time does come when we grasp and receive it with thanksgiving and when, in tribulation under the rod in the school of Christ we truly learn to understand, and become wise with the wise. Thus Saint Paul says: "Test everything, keep 1 Thess. 5:20, 21 the good, and discard the evil". He has written many things in great wisdom and divine earnestness, some of which are hard to understand. Peter

504

also testifies to this when he says: "About which our dear brother Paul writes much (notice, much), of which some things are hard to understand, and which the ignorant twist—as also they do other Scriptures—to their own destruction."

Thus it behooves us that we carefully examine and test all things, and that we do not judge, reject, misinterpret, nor falsify what we do not understand, in order that in so doing we do not condemn ourselves and be plunged into error. For the gifts of the Holy Spirit are weighty.[4] He moves as, when, and/ / where He wills, giving them to whomever He desires, through Scriptures, speech, discipline, fear, tribulation, and judgment as He desires and pleases. He gives through profound and mediocre understanding, in length and breadth, in height and depth. Everything is His. He is Lord and Sovereign over all, over written and spoken Scriptures which men test, learn, experience, witness to, and judge to the praise of God and their own salvation, and from them judge themselves and others.

Therefore whoever despises and scorns the written and spoken aid of the Holy Spirit as though it would do more harm than good, and it were better not to write or speak so much and things would thus be better all round, accuses the Holy Spirit and the aid of His gifts. He scorns and mocks what he has never known and what serves his salvation. He expects to learn about the Holy Spirit and His gifts by putting himself in the place which belongs to God the Holy Spirit alone.

Thus it were well for every person to take care what he says against the spoken and written gifts of the Holy Spirit, against whom he complains[5] and speaks, and whether it is man or God that he mocks and scorns. All good gifts/ / come from God except evil. Therefore one must hold on to what God loves

277r

277v

505

and let go of evil which God hates. May God save us from such judgments, despising, scorn, and accusation. For it would be an abominable error to despise the written and spoken gifts of the Holy Spirit. That be far from us! I write this because you have never given me a testimony in the Holy Spirit nor gratitude to God about my repeated writing which are our due because of His gifts. Fear and worry have seized me and have caused me to write you in my faithful care for you, to save and shield our souls from the deceit and cunning of the enemy of our salvation.

May our heavenly Father grant this through Jesus Christ our Lord from now on to eternity, Amen.

Fervent greetings in Jesus Christ to each of you by name from me and all of us. Let us pray God earnestly to save us from this and all our temptations. Amen.

Dated at Augsburg, the 9th day of August anno 1551.

> In the Lord Jesus Christ,
> Servant to you and all the
> faithful, and comrade in the
> tribulation in Christ.
> Pilgram Marpeck

15

Concerning
the Humanity of Christ
(1555) (#15)

Introduction

Although Marpeck never developed a comprehensive theological system, it is generally agreed that Christology formed the center of his concern. In respect to his doctrine of Christ he laid emphasis on the humanity of Christ and its implications for church order. For him Christ was true God and true man and the implications of the latter for the Christian life and for the corporate body of Christ attracted him like a magnetic field.

The present letter was written close to the end of Marpeck's life and may indicate that he was an active participant in the Christological discussions which were in full swing around Strasbourg at that time. The letter was written from Augsburg and is addressed to his followers in Langnau, near Schopfheim in the Kinzig valley. At the end of the theological treatise Marpeck dispenses some medical advice to various members of the community. Apparently he was very well acquainted with this group.

Despite the fact that the tract carries the title it does its most important section deals with the difference between servile and filial obedience and gives some indications on how to discern whether we are being led by the Spirit. It is thus a prime example of the way in which theory becomes a part of the practical life of the church for Marpeck.

The Text

Concerning the Humanity of Christ[1]

This epistle deals with the humanity of Christ and the Son of Man, etc., also with the Christian life and calling, etc., and the difference between servants and children, etc.

Grace and peace from God, our heavenly Father, and from the Lord Jesus Christ His beloved Son, abide with us and all who love and seek Christ with a pure heart. Amen.

Dearly beloved, loved in God the Father and in Christ. First we thank God for the bestowal of all His graces, which He, through Jesus Christ, and for the sake of Christ, indeed, the Lord Jesus Christ Himself working in us, does and accomplishes, ruling, directing, and leading us through His Holy Spirit in all truth of His divine will and good pleasure; namely, in all who love and seek Christ Jesus with pure heart, in them He accomplishes the good pleasure of our heavenly Father. Therefore no one (indeed no creature, in heaven or on earth) is accounted as anything before the Father, but alone the Son of man, who was born of Him of the virgin of the tribe of Judah, and of the seed of David. This Son of Man (I say "Son of Man") is appointed a Lord and Ruler of all things; yes indeed humanity is taken up into God the Father and God the Father into the Son, who from eternity has been one essence, / / Spirit, and God. Indeed, He has been the true way, the truth, and the life in true humanity by nature and kind, born of the generation of men in and of Mary, the pure virgin, a true, pure, immutable Man. In Him alone the fullness of the Godhead dwells bodily. From the fullness of the Son of God, all true believers are filled with the Holy Spirit, so that they may not speak anything unless Christ (the Son of God and of man) works, completes, acts, and rules in them Himself (Rom. 15:18). This is written so that the actions of all men (however lofty they may seem), however often the Lord is called Lord by men, indeed, even recog-

158v

nized as the Son of God, as even the devil has confessed and acknowledges Him, may truly confess Christ. It does not please the Father unless the Lord confess Himself through His Holy Spirit in faith, through the physical mind of the believing man, and likewise no man can call the Son of Man "Lord" without the Holy Spirit. Even the unclean spirits can call Him a Son of God, indeed, even a Lord. However, to ascribe honor to the Son of Man as a true man of the race of men and to confess Him as their Lord and God, this no unclean spirit can do. Either they consider Him (the Lord) as purely human to whom they / / do not want to ascribe the honor that He is also Lord and God, etc., or else they confess Him as purely the Son of God also according to the flesh, thereby failing to ascribe to Him the honor of being a Son of Man, of the race of men, flesh, blood, and human.

The flesh is of a creaturely nature that is taken up into and entered into the Godhead and the Godhead is united and one essence in the flesh as the true Word which became flesh which is then the truth and the life itself. To the flesh, body, and blood, I ascribe all the honors which the Father has ascribed to Him that I reasonably honor Him as much as the Father. Yes, I also grant Him all judgment which was committed to Him by the Father. For the very reason that He is the Son of Man He will be a Judge and not for the reason that He is also the Son of God, one essence with the Father. The Spirit of the Father and the Son are judges apart from and prior to that. The transfer [of power] which took place, took place for the sake of the humanity of Christ, that it might be honored like the Father as essentially true Son of God and of man. He, the Man Jesus Christ (who alone accomplishes in the believers the good pleasure of the Father),

He, the Lord, a true Son of Man, is Lord, Ruler, Leader, and Director of His saints.

They know also through the Holy Spirit that all their actions are governed and led in and through 159v Christ, so that / / they do not live (understand unto the good pleasure of the Father) but Christ lives in them and does and accomplishes the good pleasure of the Father. Thus Saint Paul says that he dares to speak nothing but what Christ works in him, etc., further, those whom the Spirit of God impels are children of God. And at another place: test whether Christ is in you; if not, you are cast aside, etc. That is testified in order that we may be reminded and shall know wherein (I mean the believers, in matters of faith) our committing and omitting consists, viz., in Christ, that nothing else shall impel, lead, and guide the believers than Christ, the Word of truth. Our words shall be so, that we do not speak, read, write, run, gather, or assemble unless the Lord Himself work it and do it. Without that truly all is in vain and not pleasing to God the Father, whatever may be its appearance. / / Therefore, it does not depend on our willing or running, but rather on the mercy of God and on His grace in and with Christ. He gives the will, He can also do and accomplish it in His own. We must simply in all of our actions stand idle ourselves, as dead in ourselves, if Christ is to live in us, which life and walk alone are pleasing to the Father. For human wisdom can dis-160r guise itself / / as an angel of light, especially the human wisdom of the scribal kind, indeed also it is often coarse, carnal simplicity that it [human wisdom] deems its simplicity to be a self-chosen spirituality from which it runs, impels itself, and erects outward sensual sects (which have no spirit), and indeed have neither natural nor divine understanding. These the apostle calls clouds without water (understand the water of the graces of Christ, His Holy Spirit) driven about by the whirlwind, etc. Ah, my brethren, how diligently and carefully we have to take heed that we do not consider our own impulse the impulse of the Holy Spirit, our own course the course and walk of Christ.

I must differentiate it a little and show how it can be tested and recognized, first of all in me, after that also in others, whether our actions are impelled by the Holy Spirit, or flow from a carnal mind. To make the test: first, it often happens, and I have experienced that in myself, also through many narratives of biblical writings, that natural piety hates the evil, and is zealous about the good, even after divine nature, which men have in them by nature, that they eagerly further the good, and hinder the evil as they are able; that they are overpowered

160v therein and driven with zeal, / / exerting themselves considerably. That is not therefore the compulsion of the Holy Spirit of Christ, nor do they become children through it; it is only a servile compulsion and no fatherly compulsion nor childlike progress. This happened to Paul, who persecuted the church of God out of the compulsion of his zeal, and Peter also was driven to cut off Malchus' ear. Even today this happens through zeal for the sake of Christ, for the good against the evil, as the false apostles in the semblance of Christ were driven out of zeal for themselves, some also driven by true faithfulness, who thought one ought to keep the Sabbath, refrain from foods, be circumcised, etc., and other things by which they were driven. / / Similarly even today, and even unto the end of the world, many men act because of zeal concerning the good, who do not know or suppose otherwise than that they are driven by the Holy Spirit. In part, it is probably true, that it is often of God, but not under the office of the true Holy Spirit of Christ, but driven by a servile service. God also uses such servants now, often as a provisional forerunner and preparer of the way for those who are rightly driven of the Holy Spirit of Christ, that they may make the path and the road, clear it, and weed it. They are however only / / servants, and not friends or children, who do not know what their Master is doing, nor what He has in mind.[2] Such a servile compulsion has frequently taken place in our time for quite a while now and contributed to all divisions and sects, in order that the righteous who are driven by the Holy Spirit of Christ may become manifest.

161r

Gloss: Luther, Zwingli, M. Hofman, C. Schwenckfeld, S. Frank, and others have been only servants who did not know what their lord would do.

I write all this in order that each one may well perceive for himself, what drives him, from what source it flows, from what source his drive stems. This the servants do not know. The friends and children however know what their Lord does and why the compulsion of the Holy Spirit is in them. Paul knew that he must be led to Rome to preach the gospel to the Gentiles. Peter was driven by revelation to speak the gospel to the centurion, Cornelius. Philip also was driven to the eunuch in the carriage. Paul had no peace until he came again to Jerusalem, to converse again with the leading apostles. Peter was driven to arise and preach to all the nations. Thus the apostles and their followers each were driven according to the measure of his faith. / / So also they are driven even today through the Holy Spirit as children and not as servants, who with good and true knowledge, know what their Father and Lord has in mind, viz. in such a way that they always know and are certain of the basic reason

161v

of their compulsion through the Holy Spirit. This certainty and guarantee consists principally in four things, or reasons.

First is love for God and granting my neighbor that which God has granted and given to me for His praise, and the salvation of my soul. Second, is a devaluation and giving up of life unto death to suffer for the sake of Christ and the gospel in all patience. Third, to realize when God unlocks or opens a door that one enter the same with the teaching of the gospel. No one shall open a door which God has not opened, in order that the office of the Holy Spirit remain His own and free. For it is He who opens, and no one closes, He closes and no one opens, in order that the pearls be not cast before swine nor the holy things before the dogs, lest they turn about and a mangling result. Fourth, that one be free and sound in teaching and judgments and in truth, / / in order that none speak unless Christ work through His Holy Spirit. By this one can recognize if the listeners are eager, thirsty, and hungry, weak, sick, tired and fatigued; to them belongs the nourishment, the bread and the drink of the physician, and the salve. For the healthy and the despisers need no physician, nor salve, which salve is the Word of truth that serves for the health of the nations. These four parts are the true proof that the compulsion is of the Holy Spirit; also that it brings forth fruit at each season. Where Christ does not find fruit through the proclaimed Word there the curse and barrenness soon fall as over the fig tree. All trees are to have fruit, wherever and whenever Christ arrives, be it in season or out of season.

Therefore it behooves us to give diligent heed that we distinguish sharply, diligently, and well our own drives from the drives of the Holy Spirit. I do not write this to weaken, detain, or set aside any one's progress or compulsion, but rather only that it may be well and truly discerned, through the pure fear of God, which fear is the beginning, root, and ground of all wisdom, / / understanding, and knowledge of God. May the Lord grant us this to His praise and our salvation in eternity. Amen.

Concerning the brethren from Langnau, we thank God, who always bears with our weakness and gives us a way of escape in all temptations. Nevertheless it seems to us, as also I said to them here, that they should try to return there. Perhaps God would grant them a sojourn there for a while, especially the old brother and the very old sister. We do not think that their councillor's (lord's) command would be so strict that they would be expelled [from the canton]. Rather a threat often occurs that one should be quiet and not give the authorities occasion to persecute if one meets together unnecessarily. That one should exercise moderation and discretion in such a case, to this end a government often presses out of respect for its own punishment, since they do not like to persecute us. Hence it behooves us to spare it [the government] in order that it may not wrongly seize the believers. This I write also to you beloved brother Abraham, that you will for your sake and the sake of other brethren and sisters use discretion and moderation / / in order that we do not through lack of moderation lose the place which God has granted us. If the old sister does not want to remain, try to have her cared for by one of her friends so that she can leave you. It would bring upon you and her a special persecution unto death, hence one should proceed with moderation and wisdom. However, if God's honor and truth are at stake, then we are obligated to give up all and to endure all persecution unto death. So much concerning the brethren.[3]

Among you at Langnau, for the sake of the wife of Lawrence in Lebertal it is my advice, dearly beloved brother Lawrence, that you let her continually drink of the valerian herb and drink no other liquid so that it might be strong from the herb. Do not boil it but only place one, three, or four herbs in one batch and then let it stand three or four days always adding fresh. At the same time a dry healing salve can be used for the injury. The quiet brother Lienhart Schuhmacher used it; he had serious wounds but was healed. She should have no strong herbs,[4] pork, and no liquid food and drink like strong wine. Bathing is harmful, unless the trouble / / is not in the head. All this, as said, only draws the rheumatism into the head. Food which is not cured [or does not smell?] is beneficial to her. For this time I have no further advice.[5] May the Lord grant us that we may bear all things with patience, since as pertains to the flesh we are oppressed under all infirmities and weakness.

163v

Bartle will himself report to you how we dealt with him out of grace. Every other report he has given to us according to your writing. We thank God for all grace. May the Lord grant us all to continue to the end. Amen. The grace of our Lord Jesus be with you and us all, who desire it from a pure heart. Amen. All of you, each one of you especially by name, are heartily greeted with the peace and love in Jesus Christ. Pray God earnestly for us. The same we desire out of the grace to do also for you. When you have read the letter among you (if it pleases you in the Holy Spirit) allow it to get to Lebertal and other places. Dated in Augsburg on the twenty-second day of January, 1555.

In the Lord Jesus Christ, the servant and fellow comrade of you all in the tribulation which is in Christ, Pilgram Marpeck.

16

Concerning Love

Introduction

This little letter is undated and has no specific address. It is perhaps safe to assume that it was sent to one or more of the Marpeck groups around Strasbourg or in Moravia.

Marpeck returns in this little treatise to the theme of love which is the *sine qua non* of being a Christian. He resorts to the allegory of love in the Canticle. The treatment here is more pronouncedly allegorical than in no. 5, for he identifies individual details such as the little foxes who are the cunning people of this world. He ends by announcing that the victory over these and all others who resist the gospel will be won by "love through patience, by overcoming them with the truth even as Christ overcame the world."

The Text

8v

1 Cor. 13 [3-7]

Concerning love, to serve one another in it according to the measure of faith, all of which follows from true love. Otherwise everything is in vain.

My dearly beloved, let us faithfully serve each other for improvement in service according to the spirit of love and the measure and gift of faith given to each one. For it is certain that no useless member will be found on the true body, and truly, every member exercises his gift according to the measure of love in rendering service to the body.

In this concern, beloved, remember us, for I

desire it fervently for the sake of the whole body which through the Word of grace and the gifts of the Holy Spirit through love which was prepared in Christ, is fused together for mutual service in love. She [love] is a true servant and fulfiller of all the works of grace without urging, compulsion, force, or worry. Yes, love is never commanded, for she is the commandment herself. She is God Himself, sole holder of sovereignty in all things, a monarch and ruler, yet still a free servant in all. She fulfills everything in all things for him with whom she dwells; wherever she is absent there is weakness, tribulation, mourning, and want. She cannot live with him who does not know her. She is always ready for him who longs fervently for her and makes herself known to him [sic.] and to him who

9r truly/ / learns to know her she also makes herself known. She lives with her whole heart with him who embraces her and surrenders enthusiastically[1] to him with everything she is and has. She gives herself to him who has been given to her. She is the honored daughter of God. God lives in him to whom she is promised and he in God. Knowledge [of God] is her mother, faith her brother, hope her sister, for through knowledge [of God] love is born. If a thing is not known, it is impossible to receive love from it, and if no love is received, none can be born. Therefore knowledge is the mother of love.

Faith is the brother of love. For where there is

nota no faith, love can have no brother. And where there is no hope, love has no sister. For love and faith cannot exist without hope. Experience is the mother of

Rom. 5 [4 f.] hope, for experience gives birth to hope, and hope will not disappoint. Everything comes from one Father who is God, and faith, love, and hope will also be born with him who is born of God, to live with him in this world. Beyond this time faith and

517

hope cease, but love remains eternally in the knowledge of God and of His Christ, for she remains in God and God in her.

Beloved brothers and sisters, I write to you out of a foretaste of love to the extent to which God extends His love to us. Nevertheless, our knowledge of what the love of God is, is only / / fragmentary, one knowing it more completely than another. Dearest brothers and sisters in God, the desire of my heart, my prayer, and my sighing to God for you and us is for that self-same love which fulfills everything in all. Yes, we may well say and pray with the Spirit in the Canticle: Draw me after you, and we will follow. For truly, my dear ones, where love does not draw, our path is dangerous and hard. If love has not been placed over the vineyard of God to protect it, and if the vineyard does not bear the fruit of love, she does not protect it and allows it to be devastated. However, where love is the protector of God's vineyard and brings fruit, and the friend lives behind us constantly, is behind all our actions, and looks for the fruit in the vineyard under the care of the keeper, the friend looks through the lattice, our flesh and blood, in which we are now imprisoned into the heart. He replies to us and says to love who is our protectress:

Arise, my friend, my fair one, and come to me. For behold, the winter is past, the rain is over and gone. That is, the previous destruction has been removed from us, so that now the flowers appear in the land. They appear in his community through the protectress, which is love. Spring[2] has arrived, the time to bring fruit to our God. The turtledove, that is, the Holy Spirit acting / / through His Word and work in the hearts of the believers, is heard in our land. The fig tree has developed buds, that is, the sweetness of the graciousness of God breaks out

1 Cor. 13 [12]

9v

nota

Exposition
of Canticle
2 [10-13]

10r

518

in His own. The vines have sprouted blossoms[3] and exude fragrance, that is, the planting of the heavenly Father which He has planted as the true Gardner in Christ Jesus, the true vine. The shoots from the vine which are planted are the true believers in Christ Jesus. Through the sap of grace from Christ the vine, they develop blossoms[3] that they may see God's working in them through His plantings in Christ and give God praise, in Christ Jesus. As the Spirit says: They give forth fragrance, and again the Spirit says in another passage: Arise, My friend, My fair one, and come to Me. Only that love is commanded which is the protectress of the vineyard and who brings the fruit of the vineyard of God with her as a sweet aroma. The Spirit speaks further: My dove, in the clefts of the rock. This is only that love which is in Christ Jesus, the rock in whose clefts true love dwells. These clefts are his suffering, wounds, bloodshed, and dying in which the believers in love have free security and rest from birds of prey, that is the devil and his seed which are enemies of love. Again the Spirit says: Let Me hear your voice, for your voice is sweet and your form is lovely. Here God demands the fruit as well

10v

as the voice from / / love, so that word and work agree. This voice is beautiful to God, and this form is lovely and pleasing. When He commands the Spirit to catch the little foxes that spoil the vineyard, He means the cunning people of this world, the small ones, who have no worth in God's

Lk. 13 [32]

eyes. For Christ also called Herod a fox when He said: Go, and tell that fox, etc. These foxes are caught only in love through patience by overcoming them with the truth even as Christ overcame the

Jn. 16 [33]

world. He has promised us the same comfort of victory. As Paul says: "Our preaching of faith takes all

2 Cor. 10 [5]

reason and all fortresses captive to destroy

519

everything that opposes the knowledge of God." It is this kind of capture of which the Holy Spirit of God speaks here in the Canticle. All this I have written to you in order to bring it to our mutual remembrance and that we may partake of the same gifts. Is the gift a costly one? Praise God as the Giver and love Him more than the gift. For the gift is given only in order that it may be used for the honor of the Giver. No one should grasp this honor for himself lest he incur the wrath of the Giver who is God. He alone merits all honor, and to Him may it be given from now on into eternity. Amen.

In the Lord Jesus Christ
your servant and brother in the
kingdom and the tribulation
which is in Christ.
P.M.

17

The Unity of the Bride of Christ

Introduction

This is the first of Marpeck's letters concerned with the unity of the church. He employs the analogy of marriage to Christ and the church here, as in many other letters. He loved especially the allegorical interpretation of the Canticle which has a long history going back through the mystic tradition to Jewish and Christian interpretations in the Hellenistic era. Jerome, Augustine, Bernard of Clairvaux, and Luther all interpreted the Canticle as an allegory of Christ and the church.[1]

Nevertheless, Marpeck gives it his own peculiar cast. He emphasizes the unique qualities of love as being humility, endurance, patience, and long-suffering. These are the wedding gifts without which the unity of the church cannot continue. Thus he does not simply borrow, but integrates an ancient interpretation into his own very concrete flesh and blood Christianity, thus enriching the Anabaptist heritage.

It is addressed to groups belonging to his circle in the area where he had worked as Strasbourg city engineer in the years 1528-1532.

The Text

Concerning the Unity of the Bride of Christ

Law: winter, gospel: summer.

This epistle concerns the unity of the bride of Christ, her adornment, and fruit. It is taken from the Canticle. It also tells how the winter, rain, and storm is past, and the summer has come, etc.

To the chosen, God's saints in Jesus Christ, our

521

beloved ones about Strassburg, Alsace, the Kinzig and Leber valleys[2] scattered here and there.

Grace and peace from God our heavenly Father through Jesus Christ our Lord remain among us and all who seek and love Christ sincerely. Amen.

Dearly beloved, loved in God the Father and in His Jesus Christ.

We have received and accepted the epistle you sent by the dear brother Ludwig Hafner[3] together with the oral report of your well-being in our holy faith, with affectionate love, peace, and joy, as well as with comfort of the Holy Spirit and your supporting comfort.

We therefore thank God on your behalf, as you do on ours for the redemption from sins through His blood, our first cleansing, which we should never forget, with unceasing thanksgiving to our Father God through His Son Jesus Christ. Amen.

For the Holy Spirit also gives thanks in us on our behalf in the eucharist of the blessing of the bread of His body and the cup in His blood, through which He has united us into one body in His body (with the sacrifice of His body), and has reconciled us with God the Father and Himself, that we should be one in Him, as He is one in the Father and the Father is one / / in Him. Such unity of the Holy Spirit Christ begged of the Father for His own, to be one in Him, as He is one in the Father, the Father in Him, and He in us, provided we keep the unity in Him one with another in the Holy Spirit. Thus we also may be a sacrifice for one another before God the Father as Christ for us, for such a sacrifice of unity and reconciliation pleases the Father. That is the true worship of God by which we may repay God for everything; it is the

2 Pet. 1:9

Rom. 8:26, 27

1 Cor. 10; 11

Jn. 17 [21]
11v

Eph. 4 [3]

true blessing, laud, praise, and honor of our Father in His Jesus Christ. Amen.

It is further the proper and true remembrance of His death, by which we do not forget the cleansing from our first sin which we experienced through the blood of Christ out of the pure love of the Father in His Jesus Christ. For in Christ God is one and not divided or separated. How then can those who are born of Him in His manner and nature be separated? For unity is the bond of love according to the nature of the Father and the Son. No one can live in Jesus Christ without this unity of love, nor can anyone find, see, or recognize the Father in Jesus Christ without it. Even the man Jesus Christ cannot reveal the Father in Himself to anyone outside of this reconciliation and unity in the Holy Spirit.

I write this to you that you may truly awaken, and that you may not lose the glorious treasure, // the true necklace, bracelet, wreath, and crown. For the Father has decorated His Son and His bride, love, the dearest of all, which is the communion of Christ, and which the Father Himself has given in marriage to Christ His Son, with this treasure of unity. For Christ prayed to the Father for this treasure (and the shelter of love), in order to beautify His bride with it, which is love and the most beautiful of all. For unity is the highest adornment of love. This treasure, unity, brings with it all other virtues and treasures, namely peace, joy, comfort in the Holy Spirit, as well as humility, meekness, temperance, modesty, knowledge, friendliness, endurance, patience, wisdom, perseverance, courage, and much else, in order that the bride of Christ be clothed, adorned, and beautified. Because of this adornment even the angels desire and long to see the Bridegroom in His glory together with His

12r

2 Pet. 1 [5-7]
Gal. 5 [22, 23]

Fruit of
the Spirit

bride. Love appears and shows herself in this same adornment and beautification with a happy countenance and in fair form to the pleasure of her Bridegroom. He invites His bride in her adornment and glory and says: "Arise, My love, My fair one, come here and see; the winter has passed, the rain is gone, the flowers have come forth in the land, the fig tree // is in bud, the vines have developed blossoms and give forth fragrance. Arise, My love, My fair one, come here and show Me yourself and let Me hear your voice. For your voice is sweet and your appearance is lovely."

My dearest ones, observe this text carefully with spiritual eyes. Although the words are brief, their understanding and meaning in the Holy Spirit are great. Flesh and blood can and will never attain to it. For the Lord will call His bride in no other form than in the adornment of the virtue of Christ, since the storm, winter, and rain, that is, the time of sin and sleeping, are past and gone; their affliction and tribulation is over. For we had nowhere to flee in the storm of our sin until Christ came down, the true summer, in which alone all the flowers can bloom.

These flowers are the people who, before the advent of Christ, remained stuck with their root in the earth through sin without blossom or fruit. Indeed, although they were sweet, friendly, and happy people, like the fig tree and the vine they had neither buds nor blossoms before the summer, that is, before the advent of the Man Jesus Christ, who is the true day, light, and summer of the world, yes, not until this true sun left the lowliness of the winter of our sin and again appeared in the presence of the Father in the heights in glory and power. // Before that the sun of the Father shone on men as on arid ground with the righteousness of

Canticle
2 [10-14]

12v

Interpretation

Christ the
true summer

nota

13r

the law through wrath, but no fruit was found in men because of the heat of the Father's wrath. But

Christ the Sun

when the sun Christ Jesus appeared on earth in weakness as true Man, from the seed of the woman and the race of man, then only men began to bloom, fig tree and vine developed buds and blossoms, but without fruit before the setting of this sun, Jesus Christ. Through this setting the heat of the day, the Father's wrath, has cooled. Until the time of the resurrection and ascension of Christ the Bridegroom reveled with His bride under flowers, buds, blossoms, and roses as a foretaste and shadow until the brightness or the spring should come.

The Holy Spirit, the Turtledove

When the turtledove, that is the Holy Spirit, was heard, then only the first and earliest fruits were borne. The blossoms ceased with the appearance of the fruit, the shadow shrank away through the sun of union and reconciliation to bring fruits to God through the beautiful dawn. This is also the sealing of the Holy Spirit in the forgiveness of sins with the cool dew of grace. My dearest ones, the highest ornament and adornment of love is therefore the preserving of the unity in the Holy Spirit, for without this unity there is no sincere love.

My dearest ones / /, brothers and sisters in the Lord, behold the created man in nature. A young

13v

Parable

woman, married or promised to a man, will eagerly seek and desire such carnal, temporal, earthy treasures and attire, to receive from her bridegroom and parents such adornment for her marriage as gold, silver, pearls, and other precious stones, as well as silk, velvet, embroidered dresses with gold thread, etc. But these treasures are only a picture of the treasures of the Holy Spirit, and according to their nature an image of the supernatural and eternal. Human bridegrooms, according to their means, commonly give their brides coronets, lockets, necklaces, bracelets, dresses, and other things for their pleasure. Suppose now the bride were careless and inattentive, and a thief stole her best coronet in the presence of all her maidens, who were given to the bride for her honor, to serve her and take good care of her, would not the bridegroom punish the bride with her maidens for such folly? And how would the bride and the maidens be able to excuse themselves? Would they not rather be sorrowful, weep, and mourn because of the loss, and confess their folly? And if the bridegroom recovered the treasure from the thief and through grace presented it again to the bride and her

14r maidens, would she not rejoice with / / them and be much more careful and diligent to protect her treasures from thieves?

I do not write this to accuse you but to entice you to emulate the true and proper humility of

nota Christ, that the innocent may not rise up against the guilty to insist on their rights, but rather to act like the Lord who in His innocence gave Himself for us the guilty, accepted our guilt, and suffered, the just one for us the unjust.

Still less should we become conceited since no one can excuse himself before God or man. If you truly contemplate these things you will honor this

2 Pet. 1: [9?] great treasure of the bride (love), which is unity in the Holy Spirit, and preserve it in your midst without laziness and carelessness. For this treasure

Jn. 17 [21] alone the Bridegroom prayed to the Father on behalf of the bride, that is, to keep the unity with one another as the Father and Son are one in Spirit and truth. This is the true and chief treasure of our most holy Bridegroom, Christ. This calls for watchfulness, prayer, wisdom to act and to guard it from dogs and foxes which destroy the vineyard of God, and that the thief and robber may not dig under our house. For we know that our enemy and antagonist never closes his eyes toward us.

14v   My dearest ones, for your own improvement diligently / / read Hebrews Chapter 12. This is the true admonition of Paul that you tolerate nothing unclean among you. For the whole world would have to be judged and destroyed before God would tolerate evil in His church. For this we have ample analogies in Exodus. Pay diligent attention so that the tempter does not surprise you through human temptation since we have been rescued and kept from all powerful errors through the grace of Christ. May the Lord rescue and redeem us together with you from all temptations as He has done until now.

The grace of our Lord Jesus Christ be and remain with you and us all. Amen.

All the saints of God with us salute you with greeting and unity in Christ. Pray fervently to God for us, and we, as debtors, will do the same for you in the love of Christ.

Given on St. Thomas Day[4] anno 1540 at Probin in the Grisons.[5]

In the Lord Jesus Christ, servant to you and all true believers, members of the body of Christ, gathered and united in the Union and the Confederacy in the tribulation of Christ, which according to the flesh destroys, and in His Spirit.

Pilgram Marpeck.

18
Concerning
the Love of God in Christ
(#10)

Introduction

This letter, like number 4, is undated and unaddressed. It deals with one of Marpeck's favorite subjects which he pursues in a long argument and which touches on a number of points in his theology.

He begins with an orthodox statement concerning the Trinity. The Son was taken into the Trinity and therefore He had a beginning, but He is nevertheless one in and with God. Marpeck also reiterates the two-nature theory of orthodox Christianity.

Christ Himself in His humanity is complete love "since He sought and accepted no benefit for Himself which could have caused or initiated love." Love in the creatures—that includes man—is weak, and therefore in them love is full of patience. It is ready to wait and suffer for its own triumph. These statements lead Marpeck into a canticle of his own in praise of love. The psychological insight into the nature and ways of love is perhaps evidence that the writing comes from his later years.

As so frequently in his writings, Marpeck appeals to the humanity of Christ as the model for the Christians. He did not use the power he could have used, but rather submitted himself to all authority in patience. He is especially critical of all who claim to believe in God but who believe that they will be saved by violence and coercion. He mentions especially Jews, Catholics, Protestants, and certain sects. But such salvation is temporal and does not last since it has no relation at all to love which is rooted through Christ in the eternal God and which works in time through patience.

The whole letter is as powerful a statement on the power of love and nonviolence as one can find in Anabaptist literature.

The Text

Concerning the Love of God in Christ

There is some solid stuff in this epistle. Read it with understanding.[1]

129r The following deals with the love of God in Christ and the love which has been poured out by God upon men and the creatures, together with other clarifications, and in conclusion concerning the sacred cross of Christ and the guilt of the believers as well as the condemning cross of the condemned, etc.

Grace and peace from God our heavenly father through and from the Lord Jesus Christ abide with us eternally. Amen.

My dear ones, loved in and by Jesus Christ our Healer, Lord and God with an eternal love which is God Himself eternally through and in everything that is called divine love and which is loved by God in Christ.

Gloss The difference between what is from eternity and in eternity. They are separated by the time in between which has a beginning and an end.

For whoever abides in love abides in God and God in him. He is and remains eternally with God. For God Himself is the eternal in him, about him, and with him. He cannot pass away or diminish; he cannot come to an end or be changed, for He is self-subsistent for ever.

Gloss By the power of the love which is God, and is in those who according to the measure of faith by
129v faith enter into God and He into them. / /

Love is all power, authority, strength, might, wisdom, reason, skill, understanding, truth, righteousness, mercy, forbearance, patience, meekness in all humility and lowliness. She is fully God in all, in, with, and through her summation Jesus Christ our Healer. He is the complete, whole, eternally coming true love of the Father, and the Father Himself is the true love of the Son, one Spirit, God, and Lord forever, not mixed but One from eternity to eternity, not separated into two or three but three in One eternally.

Only what God Himself is from eternity in and of Himself is everlasting (understand: not "in" but "from" eternity), and nothing can be added to Him. For the eternal is one from eternity and remains eternally, God the Word and Spirit. The incarnate Word is taken into the unity, and, according to the measure of time, one in and with God. He is two natures, one Man, two natures, one God, divine and human in one. But whatever is taken in has a beginning, a middle, and also eternity to eternity (understand: "in" eternity not "from" eternity). Those are the / / creatures which have eternal existence with God and in God and from God. They are, for example, the angelic creatures as well as human spirits and souls. These, even though they did not desire it, must be and exist and remain in eternity. The charm of the creaturely species and characteristics which must exist and remain eternally is still not the blessed, blissful, and joyful eternity. Rather, the blissful eternity occurs when the creaturely exists in the creaturely love in which she was created in dependence upon the Creator and is taken unperverted into God, Word and Spirit, who is blissful and everlasting love.

For this love, for the sake of Christ, man was created. That is, grace and more grace, love and more love, faithfulness and more faithfulness, truth and more truth, the unity of God and the creature and love eternal. But those who fall away from this

130r

first creaturely love, be they angels or men, will exist and remain in eternity against their will. As a recompense for the works which they have committed against the ways and the nature of the creature in which they were created in love and for love, it may thus be revealed to them by the stern righteousness [of God] that they have wantonly / / [forsaken] the proper way and their Creator and embraced wickedness. This stands and must stand eternally, that [they] must endure eternal agony because they have of their own will become evil. When time ends (after which the grace in Christ and the time of repentance ends and eternity begins) they can never again become good, for agony and sin must remain eternally evil, eternally surrounded by death, pain, and hell. Thus the creatures of the divine nature are taken into and come into everlastingness (understand: "taken into" is grace and more grace, "Coming into" is guilt and more guilt, evil and more evil, agony for sin) into which they come through their fault. Those who are taken in, however, through grace and more grace, in love and more love remain in everlasting love and glory with Christ Jesus, for whose sake all things are, for through Him and to Him and in Him are all things and everything exists in Him. It is not that they are absorbed in God or will no longer be what they were before the creation, as some erring spirits desire, and that God should remain alone and everything be absorbed in Him. Such error be far from us![2]

Thus the elect, who have been justified and who live in love in / / God and God in them, enter into the one eternal real love which remains eternally and is God Himself. But it is impossible to have or come by the power of love, which God has and Himself is eternally (as stated earlier), wholly in this time of grace. [It is available only] up to the measure of the power man is given and he receives, and not in his own powers.

Gloss   The difference between the love which is God and Christ Himself and the love which is poured out by God on man and the creatures and which works in and reigns over that which is incomplete.

I speak here about that complete power which is in its fullness and without measure only in Christ, and not about the measure of love that is poured out into man. For in Christ the fullness of Godhead dwells bodily; in us, in this time, it is only in part. Love is our teacher through the Holy Spirit that only in this time we should be led and directed by Lk. 7 [37 f.] her, and learn of her. We remain seated at the feet of Christ with Magdalene, who loved much and therefore received much forgiveness and remission according to the Word of the Lord. But that is love only for our benefit and salvation. But in Christ love is complete since He sought and accepted no benefit for Himself which could have caused or 131v initiated love. He / / is the fullness of everything eternally. In the creatures love is awakened and 1 Cor. 13 [4-7] given for the benefit [of the creature] to the praise of God. For complete love has no defect. But men, in whom she already dwells, are full of weakness; there she is full of patience. They are and know themselves to fail constantly under the governance nota of love, but love replaces all failure and shortcoming. They are often unwilling, but love is willing. They are idle, but love acts. They are unfriendly, but love is friendly. They are arrogant, but love is humble. They are quarrelsome, but love is conciliatory. Love suffers all things, endures all things, and bears all things. Thus, true love often dwells even today in a believing soul and spirit in order that she alone may assert her sovereignty against the ill-mannered, contrary flesh. Such evil obstructionism was not found in the humanity of Christ, for He is the fullness of love, and God Himself. This obstructionism should not lead us to make excuses but awaken fear and shame. For in this time we cannot lay claim to the fullness of love with its power to convince. But [we can] follow her path with sincere

132r desire, / / and mark her footprints and tracks with earnestness, as love pleads with and speaks to love in the Canticle: "Draw me after you and let us make haste" [Song of Sol. 1:4], and never to lose sight of her until we completely possess her in that day with Christ. For he who possesses her to the fullest degree possible in this time is merely given a greater desire for her, but can never see her form clearly nor embrace her as she has embraced him. She is like a stag or deer, which, when they see someone, quickly dash out of sight. Thus, her return is swift to human eyes to grant man his desire to see her form and to prove with power why it is that she

nota is called love. She is not to be bought. She cannot be coerced, driven, nor urged. Even if one gave his wealth for her, he will not gain her, for she is priceless and unconquerable. With her beauty and ornament she is beyond price, and her praise is unspeakable. Even the Holy Spirit Himself has not found a perfect expression for love in all the creatures to show or reveal her transfiguration[3] of all

132v virtue, beauty, ornament, / / or form. He seeks to show her form and to bear witness to it, to demonstrate with sufficient power and deeds, to search out and seek to fathom the depth of her patience, to show her sympathy, the means and abundance of her friendliness, the conversation of beauty with which she is adorned, and to make visible her form. Her mildness no one can tell, nor can

533

anyone fully receive what she bestows, distributes, and gives in abundance. For the overflowing of her mildness is fullness and sufficiency, indeed the granting of hope. Whatever and however much there is to be hoped for, blushes in shame in the presence of her mildness and generosity, for in her all hope and faith must come to an end and vanish.

Only love, who is most beloved, remains eternally independent. This self-subsistence and immovability of love no one can achieve nor comprehend. For this reason she is compared to a rock, a wall, and a strong tower, upon which creatures and men (who have been set ablaze by her flames and heat) build silver bastions that will survive the terror of the night because of her dependability and strength. Those are the temptations / / by which men are afflicted until her brightness, light, and dawn fully breaks forth, and her morningstar rises, taking away the darkness of the night, and all darkness passes away by her perpetual light, as it must.

Love is patient in time; who can recount her patience, or declare her end or her measure? For her patience and forbearance is the blessedness of man. The delay of love is, in its time, the highest reward of waiting. For even the angels wait with longing to see what fulfillment her patience will accomplish. For the patience of love's delay is the blessedness of man.

The difference between the transfiguration of the Word from eternity and the transfiguration of the incarnate Word to eternity.

No creature has been found to express, teach, and to witness and state with power what love is, along with its virtues and powers except the Man Jesus, Jesus, Jesus Christ, the Son of God. The same was brought forth, glorified, and revealed by the

133r

Gloss

534

Father with that glory which He as the incarnate Word had before the Father from eternity, as He 133v also with love declares Himself to be the true Son of God / / commissioned even to the condemnation of death, and has achieved the fullest, greatest, and Jn. 14, 15[13] exalted love in that He gives His life for His friends. For no one has greater love than he who gives his life for his friends.

To this Christ has witnessed and in love declared Himself, with the incarnate Word, deed, Rev. 5[5] and power. This is the Lamb that was found worthy to open the sealed and closed book, that is the hiddenness of all virtue, power, and effulgence of love and Himself to reveal before the Father the glory of love in Himself, according to His holy Manhood. He declares that the Father Himself has glorified Him with that glory which He had with the Father before the foundation of the world was laid. And as He was glorified in love in and before the Father before the beginning of the world, so He also glorified Himself before men and angels, and so the Father will glorify Him again. In Him virtue, such as the power of love, is completed and revealed before time, in the time of His flesh, as well as after this time to eternity. As this [power of love] is declared and witnessed to in that manner before the Father, so the Father will fully glorify the Son in the 134r fulfillment of / / time in all of Christ's elect, and they will be as He is and He as His own in God and God in them eternally. It is not as though He had just become love, but this shows that He is from nota eternity. Thus, the incarnate Word is God and Man, Man and God, two natures, one God, and also two natures, one Man, the beginning of time, the center, and end of all things, A and O. For His sake are all things. He is the breaking in of time out of eternity and into eternity.

Thus for the sake of love the Lamb of God, which has taken away the sin of the world, was slain in love from the foundation of the world (Apoc. 13: [8]). He, without guilt and sin, was sacrificed in history for the guilt and sin of man in order to restore the fall of man from the original love and raise him up into the blissful, joyful, eternally enduring love out of grace and more grace and be made worthy to be to the glory, praise, and honor of God as an eternal thanksgiving.

Rev. 1 [8]

Gloss

Paul says that all creatures are for the sake of man, man for the sake of Christ, and Christ for the sake of God.

All that is written so that one may be able to distinguish what is from eternity (for example, three in one) from what will be and remain in eternity, and perceive inbreaking time (between what is from eternity and what remains into eternity), and that the incarnate Word is beginning, center, and end, for [4] the sake of all creatures.

Gloss

The difference between the creatures which pass away and end with time and the creatures which are and remain eternally.

Time will cease to be. Sun, moon, stars, and everything that exists in time and for the sake of man (not created to remain eternally) must cease to be for the sake of that which is and must remain eternally (such as men and angels which are taken up into God and God into them). For there will no longer be any need for time nor the creatures of time such as animals, birds, fish, light, nor day. For in eternity time ceases, and God Himself is day and light. Darkness and night will [depart] from the light, the incarnate Word and Spirit, and go to its eternal place where no grace or creaturely light will ever again be seen. Only the hellish and eternally deadly fire is the revelation and illumination of

Rev. 22 [5]

everlasting torment.[5] They will suffer eternally, be
and remain eternally / / in the darkness of God's
wrath, yea, in eternal envy, hate, anger, murder,
and in agonized crying because of the fire which
will never depart from them.

135r

Gloss

The difference between eternal bliss and
eternal damnation.

For all their sin and guilt along with their wickedness remains eternally in them and with them.
For salvation and mediation are no longer available
so that they do not have even the smallest particle
of comfort.

Gloss

God has ordained the governing power for this
time and for the sake of godly men; as a protection, arbiter, and punishment; and as inter-
mediate gods[6] between the evil and the good.

The fallen angels and men are delivered over
to each other as the greatest enemies with never-
ending enmity, envy, and hate, in order completely
to fulfill in one another their hellishly incorporated
wantonness and their envious, hateful, and wrathful
manner without the means of any adjudication,
judgment, or restraint. Whatever in their greed
and lustful wrath they invent and scheme to torment, insult, and to hurt each other they completely
carry out. Beyond that all the evil they do to each
other / / will be most bitterly salted with fire when
the torment and great pain of eternal fire will be
their arbiter. Thus the great pain of eternal fire
together with everlasting despair will by far exceed
their own torment, and all this in immortality. It
would be as though a mortal man had many deadly
pains in his body, each pain far exceeding the other,
with no surcease. Thus the lesser pains would be a
small relief compared to the greater torment, but
added to the greatest torment, be even unto death.
Thus not a single remedy will be available for all

135v

Parable

537

those condemned, each according to their deserts.

[7]For all authorities are in this time gods and mediators between goodness and evil, between the just and the unjust, established to provide physical rest and peace and to restrain evil and protect the good. For evil and good now exist together in this physical life undifferentiated and [un]separated[8] until the day when judgment takes place and good and evil are separated. This will take place when the last person to be saved is brought in.[9] Then all worldly authority will be dissolved, one house will

136r

fall upon the other, there will be war and / / the cry of war without any means of peace or rescue, and all piety, faithfulness, love, truth, faith, and confidence will cease. For the pious and the godly, for whose sake the world with its wickedness is spared, will be

Mt. 24[6]
Lk. 21[28]

saved. They will be separated from all wickedness and gain rest and eternal joy as Christ said: When you hear war and the cry of war lift your heads, for your salvation approaches.

Only then goodness and wickedness are sep-

nota

arated one from the other, love and truth from envy, hate, and lying, hope from despair, belief from unbelief, peace from strife, patience from vengeance, joy and comfort from mourning and discouragement, mildness from greed, mercy from mercilessness, humility from arrogance, meekness from pride and haughtiness, and truth from lying.

That will be the salvation and final decision for all the godly, who in themselves and among the wicked are now attacked, prone to fall, and imprisoned, afflicted, sorrowful, anxious, tormented, and molested daily against their will by evil, abom-

136v

inable behavior. / / Thus they will be redeemed and led out of all temptation. Because the kingdom of Christ is not of this world, and because the kingdoms of the world and the kingdom of Christ

Jn. 16[33]

are the complete opposite of each other, Christ says: In the world you are afraid, but in Me you have peace. Be glad for I have overcome the world (that is, in patience, hope, and faith). You will be in need

1 Pet. 3:[9-11]
Rom. 12:[21]

of patience (that is, patience in time of evil tribulation). And do not resist evil with evil, but overcome evil with good. Thus and in no other way has Christ overcome the world that we may be joyful in hope and so to overcome and to await our Savior, according to His promise, who will be our victory and our overcoming.

Gloss

The distinction between the redemption of Christ and man's redemption.

Far be it from us that we should seek to be redeemed like the Jews and these present alleged Christians who comfort themselves and hope to be redeemed by human power and the arm of man. The Jews, contrary to Christ and His own, claim to expect a Messiah or Christ who will redeem them from all power of the Gentiles by means of the arm

137v

of man and carnal weapons and / / lead them into the promised land. Thus also the alleged Christians are now blinded by this Jewish error (contrary to the

nota

bright light and Word which they claim to have and of which they boast), [and assume that] with the carnal sword and the arm of man Christ will release and redeem them from those who justifiably coerce and frighten them through the appearance of His coming. The old Latin Roman Church, which is ruled by imperial power, also hopes that the emperor will achieve the victory in the semblance and

nota

name of Christ against all those who resist her, and rigidly insists that this will happen. [It will happen] in order that all those will be punished who, in the semblance of Christ, suppose that they will decide with the carnal sword. . . .

The Lord says the Holy Spirit would come and judge the world for sin. But now the human authority presumes to do what belongs alone to the Holy Spirit and to punish unbelief,

. . . themselves become coercers of faith, and persecute with the carnal sword those who do not agree with them, and insist on maintaining violence against violence with the carnal sword in the semblance of Christ.

[10]Christ Himself, in His holy Manhood, submitted to every authority in patience, who Himself had and has all authority in heaven and on earth. // For whoever takes the sword to make decisions about Christ and himself in the semblance of the Word, takes and uses it like Peter, who cut off Malchus' ear, which Christ put back on and healed. If someone today takes and uses the sword thus and fights for Christ the same person must and will, according to the words of the Lord, perish by the sword. The guilt rests on their heads as long as they boast of Christ and do not believe His words. The Jews boasted that they were children of God and Abraham and did not believe the words of His Christ but crucified Him under the authority of Caesar. They set themselves against the imperial authority deliberately and with a perverted mind. Into [this perverted state] God delivered them and has to this day abandoned them. Because of this they were coerced by the authority of Caesar with great persecution, interrogation, and destruction.

137v

Mt. 26:[51f.]
Jn. 18:[10f.]

Gloss
The distinction between the consolation of redemption in Christ and the deceptive consolation of redemption by men.

1
Everyone is confident in a false hope and illusion concerning his healer and savior. The Jews console themselves with the Turk [that he will help them] against the emperor and all sects of the

138r
2

Christian name.[11] / / The old Roman, Latin, apparently [Christian] church with the renown of its age and traditions under all the Roman emperors, is confident in the emperor as its protector and savior from all the opposing sects of Christian name and

3

also from the power of the Turk. Thus also the self-styled evangelicals are confident about all those who set themselves against the Roman authority and church as though they were all means of their salvation from the Roman authority and church. Wherever an insurrection against the emperor as the Roman authority occurs, be it Turk, Frenchman, the cities,[12] or other rulers, lords, and people,

4

they regard it joyfully as a hope of their own salvation. There are also alleged sects and Christians rejoicing in false hope and consolation of salvation not by the arm of man or human authority but by miracles. They believe that God will exercise

nota

vengeance on all who oppose them, and wait for newly sent prophets and miracles with vengeance in their hearts.[13] They are enemies of their enemies (and not friends and benefactors according to the teaching of Christ), and think that because of their supposed sanctity they should be saved from bodily tribulation and the cross of Christ, and hope in this time to achieve what will no doubt happen, a human and bodily rest.[14]

138r

That joy, however, is not for Christians, / / but rather the sorrow of human corruption. It is proper for the believer, however, to rejoice in the righteous judgments of God to which is added the sorrow over human corruption. Abraham interceded for Sodom

Gen. 18[22-32]

because he was sorry for the destruction of those souls, but he nevertheless rejoiced in the righteousness of God and the salvation of the godly. Thus we are to rejoice and in no other way. But all those described above know Christ (like the Jews) only according to the flesh and not in spirit and in truth. They seek rest, peace, and joy where none can ever be found in eternity. For this is the rest and redemption of Christ, that we are redeemed from sin to renounce wickedness (never to fulfill it) and from henceforth to live for Christ. That is peace, joy, and comfort in the Holy Spirit and our true salvation. I know of no other salvation in Christ in this time. Whoever hopes in any other salvation is truly imprisoned in his own vengeance, builds on the sand of this passing life, and is in the company of all the false hopes described above with war and the cry of war.

Whatever waits for temporal salvation and is already temporally saved will again / / pass away and come to an end because of the nature of time. For death takes everything again into its power. Such a salvation cannot be imputed to Christ, for He is an eternal Redeemer.

All these can never rejoice at the approach of [their] salvation for it brings forth only fear, misery, and distress, and never accomplishes any redemption. For temporal and eternal death takes everything into bondage again. Whoever imputes such a salvation to Christ, imputes all bondage to Him and makes of Him a servant [who] traps and ensnares for death, in the bonds of which man is kept against His will. From this imprisonment Christ alone is the Savior. For such temporal consolation and hope can never be called the consolation or hope of Christ. Those who trust in it suffer not for the sacred, innocent cross of Christ, but for the cross of their own guilt.

The distinction between the holy, innocent cross of Christ, the guilty cross of believers, and the damnable cross of the condemned.

For there is a great difference between the light burden and the sweet yoke of Christ, which is the sin-

forgiving cross of Christ washed, cleansed, and
hallowed in the innocent blood of Christ, / / and the
cross of guilt. For the cross of guilt can never be called
the sacred cross of Christ. Not that I am including the
cleansing from sin done in unbelief [before their
cleansing] by those who were born again through
faith in Christ, in the original guilt. Never! But those
who sin again after faith in Christ, [they bear] the
cross of guilt, even though they gain forgiveness
through grace under chastisement and punishment.
Nor is it a cross of guilt because according to the
words of Christ no evil goes unpunished and no good
unrewarded. As Saint Paul writes to the Corinthians,
charging them with disorderly living: "For this
reason many of you are weak and ill, and a number
have fallen asleep." Certainly he means the sickness
and sleep of the spirit in unbelief in which one becomes ill and even goes to sleep. But he definitely also
means the believers whose guilt and sin has been forgiven under chastisement and punishment, but who
are often caught in the plagues and vengeance of the
world such as pestilence, hunger, war, and destruction, which are the greatest plagues and penalties of
vengeance in this mortal time. / / The psalmist witnesses to the same thing—one should read it!—saying
that [God] does not allow faith to fail but punishes
transgression with a rod. Thus believers retain the sin
they commit in the cross of guilt. That cannot be the
hallowed cross of Christ, but may be called the cross of
guilt of the grace of Christ, a rod of discipline, a humble submission with the folly wherein they have
transgressed. Stupidity and folly must be humbled in
man because of their transgression. Whoever is thus
humbled will be made great in Christ. However, we
may never say of anyone that he bears the cross of
guilt, but [it is known] only as everyone finds it
himself in his own conscience before God. If a man has

139v

1 Cor. 11:[30]

140r
Ps. 107:[10-16]

543

a clear conscience, let him endure torment, revenge, punishment, or sickness in faith, such torments, no matter how great they are, will not make him guilty any more than Job. For all men must suffer physical death no matter what form it takes.

Cross of guilt

140v
Lk.23[33, 39-42]

The guilty cross of the world is greatly to be distinguished from the guilty cross of the believers. For this we have a clear, plain story, history, and figure in the two thieves who were crucified with Christ, / / one to the right and one to the left. The one on the right confessed his sin and guilt to the innocence of Christ, who in innocence, was crucified and tortured beside him on the most hallowed and purest cross in torment and suffering. The thief did not desire [to be rescued] from the cross of guilt but that he might receive grace, and begged the Lord to remember him when He should come into His kingdom. Moreover, he chastised the other thief for blaspheming God and not fearing Him when he said: "If you are the Son of God help us and yourself down from the cross." Thus the world does with its cross of guilt; it desires constantly to be released from it. And yet because of its guilt, it must hang and remain on the eternal cross of guilt, namely its own condemnation, without grace, in everlasting torment. For the world and its children like the thief on the left, are sorry only for the suffering and not at all for the sin. Thus those who have received grace have sorrow under the weight of their cross of guilt only for their sin and not at all for the suffering. Although it terrifies even to the death of condemnation, they confess that death and all suffering is the result of sin. Therefore they desire to be released from sin which is the actual root of all suffering.

141r
So great is the difference between the believers' cross of guilt and that / / of the world. Although in this time they are punished with the same torments,

but the manners and ways of those who have received grace are far removed from those of the damned.

Gloss The believer's cross of guilt has not the fullness of patience of the sacred, innocent cross of Christ. The cross of guilt is bitter.

The sacred, easy, light, sweet, and innocent cross of Christ is as greatly to be distinguished from the believers' cross of guilt, not to speak of the world's, as heaven and earth are to be distinguished. The innocent cross of Christ can never be taken up and carried in this time by any believer. For it has its source and beginning in the word of promise to restore the fall of Adam. This is the source of the hate and enmity of the serpent against men, that to them [Adam and Eve] was given the promise of restoration for the sake of the humanized word, and to the serpent no restoration, but the crushing of his head through the seed of the woman, the humanized word.

The head of the serpent must be understood to mean that all his intention, cunning, and plotting against the humanized word will be destroyed and crushed with the feet of Christ, and, together with his 141v seed, made an open shame. / / Nevertheless, the serpent will bite the heel of the humanized word and the seed of the woman, which is born through the generation[15] of the Word (that is of the mother, the church), and who still walk in the flesh as members of the body of Christ. This [biting of the heel] is the affliction of flesh and blood with much cross, tribulation, and torment. On this point one should read Psalm 56:[6, 7]: "They band themselves together, they lurk and watch my heel, how they may seize my soul. Deliver him because of wickedness." This means the seed of the serpent. Flesh and blood, led in obedience to the Spirit in the word of truth, is the very heel and lowest part of the inner man who is fashioned after God. The Holy Spirit walks and makes his foot-

545

prints on such a man against all the plots of the serpent and the gates of hell. Whatever of pain and torment the serpent (as the source of all agony) inflicts on the flesh and blood of believers, and thus bites the heel of Christ, his head is nevertheless crushed, overcome, and executed by the heel. The heel is all the weakness

of the flesh and blood of Christ in all patience in His saints. This holy cross / / of Christ is the occasion of the enmity between the seed of the serpent and the woman, so that no peace or harmony can ever be between these two. The serpent, together with his seed and children of his innate wickedness, envy, and hate, desires to destroy the seed of the woman through every cunning, lie, and the deceit of sin, death, suffering, and torment. That is the enmity between the seed of the woman and the serpent and his seed. The former hates and opposes the wickedness, deviousness, deceit, and cunning of the serpent and his seed, and resists it with all power by the word of truth, and carried out the strife and battle against all pain, death, sin, and hell, of which the serpent is the ruler and head, with true and proper patience, and thus will overcome eternally with Christ (the Lamb of patience) and achieve the victory. Thus the lamb was killed by Cain in Abel according to the flesh (meaning not the physical killing but because of patience), but it was victorious in the spirit according to creaturely love and faithfulness through patience which he showed to his brother.

The same was true of the seed of the woman, Sarah's son Isaac, against Ishmael. Rebecca bore Isaac two antagonistic sons, Esau and Jacob, who began their hate, cross, and struggle in the womb.

That the children were contrary to each other through the enmity of the[16] seed of the serpent and the woman by nature and from the time of conception and birth, shows that the wicked one hated the godly one and that the godly one overcame the wicked one with patience. Jacob was the father of Joseph who also through patience overcame the brothers who hated him (repaying them good for evil), and, although he was innocent, sold him into Egypt. Thus many of the ancients (Job and others) overcame evil by means of good deeds through patience in tribulation, who afterward overcame everything in and through[17] patience and waited for the redemption of Christ.

With gentle patience, love, and truth He overcame evil with all goodness, love, faithfulness, truth, and mercy, and [for evil] returned passionate intercession for His enemies, and surrendered His human life and eternal bliss on the cross in unbroken patience, a submissive and silent Lamb of sacrifice for the sins of man and his salvation. This is the universally hallowed cross of Christ—and no cross of guilt—by which in the innocence of Christ all the followers of Christ overcome, and through which they have free access in and to God, provided their hearts do not accuse them in guilt.

For they are washed from their sins through the innocence of Christ to be a pure and sanctified / / co-sacrifice pleasing and acceptable to God, as Paul says which is the reasonable service of God. In it the highest joy can be expected and had, namely that one does not have to suffer as a debtor or an evildoer, but may praise God in the matter according to the words of Peter: "Let no one among you suffer as a murderer, thief, evildoer, or a covetous one." If someone suffers as a Christian, however, he should not be ashamed; let him praise God in the matter. For it is time that judgment begins on the house of God (1 Pet. 4:16 ff.). Furthermore, those who suffer, commit their souls to the faithful Creator with good works. Thus the cross of Christ is a holy, innocent cross if one suffers innocently as a

143r
Rom. 12[1]

547

witness of God in the truth and for the truth to the praise of God. To this holy cross of Christ, our highest shelter and shield, we have surrendered with holy patience (not obliged or forced patience) to overcome all our enemies in the victory of Christ.

May the heavenly Father and the Lord Jesus Christ establish, strengthen, and keep us in this patience to His praise and our salvation to life's end. Amen. All the chosen of God greet you by name in the peace and grace of Christ. Pray to God for us and all of the concerns of the union and fellowship of the saints in Christ, and we desire to do the same for you as your debtors. The grace of our Lord Jesus Christ be and remain with us eternally. Amen.

> In the Lord Jesus Christ
> servant to you and the rest in true faith,
> and companion in the tribulation of Christ.
> Pilgram Marpeck.

19

The Servants and Service of the Church

Introduction

(#11)

The Marpeck circle was widely dispersed geographically. The saints in Moravia, to whom this letter is addressed, were apparently not the Hutterites, but seven churches (located at Austerlitz, Poppitz, Eibenschütz, Jamnitz, Znaim, Vienna, and one referred to as, am Wald), brought into being through the work and inspiration of Marpeck himself. The letter was carried to Moravia by Jörg Maler (Rothenfelder) and a shoemaker Jacob Schultz, both members of the Augsburg fellowship.

The letter is a pastoral admonition concerning the nature of Christian service. Again Jesus is the model. He served man even to the loss of His life, and all creatures are now expected to serve similarly. Followers of Jesus are under obligation thus to serve, and not to fall into pride and destruction like the fallen angels, who wanted to serve in pride and power.

There is specific reference at the end to two other letters by Marpeck which have not survived so far as is known. They dealt with *Gelassenheit*, an important Anabaptist concept meaning the state of surrender, and with the Lord's Supper. Both were carried to Moravia by Maler and Schultz and were second copies since they had already been sent earlier by another carrier. There was some doubt as to whether they had arrived the first time. The answer to this letter is No. 17 in the *Kunstbuch* which testifies to the fraternal love between the Augsburg and the Moravia churches.

164r **The Text**

This letter concerns the service and servants of the church.

To God's elect, the holy ones, our beloved in Christ in the Margraviate of Moravia, gathered at Au-

549

sterlitz[1] and Eibenschütz[2] and in other places.

Grace and peace from God our heavenly Father and from the Lord Jesus Christ be and remain with us and you and all who love and seek Christ with a pure heart through voluntary patience under the acquittal of Christ. Amen.

Dearly beloved in Jesus Christ, loved in the witness to the truth! Our dear brothers Jörg Maler and Jacob Schultz[3] the shoemaker have decided voluntarily to journey to you in order to become acquainted with your way of living and the knowledge of God our Father and His Christ (in whom is our salvation) among you, and also that you may receive from them both a spoken and a written testimony to the truth of the state of our life in order that all of us may have received the same comfort, peace, and joy and bear the same compassion in the tribulation of Christ in the fellowship of His body.

In this body the gifts of the Holy Spirit are manifest in each member according to the measure of faith in Jesus Christ for service in the growth of the body of Christ. By this service the weakest, least, and

164v

smallest / / members are strengthened, comforted, led, guided, and pastured by the strong, leading, and most able members. Thus they are trained, preserved, increased, and nourished until they reach the full maturity of Christ. For whoever would be the greatest must be the vassal and servant and not the ruler of all

Mt. 20:26
Lk. 22:45-47
Mk. 10:20,21

1 Pet. 5:2

the others, says the Lord. Their service is not compelled or forced not for the sake of shameful gain; rather it flows voluntarily from an affectionate disposition. They do not rule over the heritage of God but become an example to the flock, says Peter. For it is certain that the highest good treasure, which is the Son of the Father, was not (in this time) sent to rule in order that He should be served, but rather, that He voluntarily presented Himself to us all to serve our salvation, and never desired that He should be served. In this the Lord is a true example for all who are His disciples and servants.

Thus the eternal Father subjected the angels as the highest of the creatures to the Son for Christ's sake because He served man as the least of the creatures (although He is the image and likeness of God), in order that they (the angels) should properly and voluntarily serve (as the Son of the Father), without compulsion or urging. Those angels who did not present themselves to the Son voluntarily in all hu-

165r mility / / and lowliness for service with Him on behalf of men, were thrown into the abyss and eternally rejected. This is the just judgment of God, since they had received knowledge of it from the Son (in the divine intention that it was so to happen) through the preaching of the everlasting gospel.[4]

Rev. 14[6 f.] This intention of God was proclaimed in the midst of heaven by an angel and is eternally so proclaimed, that all creatures of God should, like the Son of the Father, submit freely and without compulsion to such service and lowliness. Any creature that has not thus voluntarily served man with and in Christ prior to the revelation of the mighty glory of the Son is cursed and eternally damned. The fall of the angels on account of man took place in immediate response to the intention of God in the eternal gospel, preached from eternity to eternity, through which the envy and hate of the serpent, the fallen angel, has come upon man. In this [same envy and hate] he also turned man away from service together with the Son, from the law and obedience of God. Even today he continues to turn men away from believing the eternal gospel and giving free obedience and fellow-service in and to all,

165v with / / and in Christ.

For this reason man too comes under condemnation together with the enemy of all truth and obedience. The true servanthood of the Son even to the loss of His life which He has shown as Man has become our salvation through faith in Him. Thus we again serve men together with all the holy angels of God until the glorious appearance of the Son of God from heaven together with His holy angels and men. The Son Himself did not come into this time of His servanthood that He should desire or allow Himself to be served, or to enjoy even the smallest honor or benefit from any creature. Instead He regarded as nothing all the service He rendered to the honor of God and the salvation of man, even to the loss of His life, as though He had done or deserved nothing when in fact He earned, achieved, won, and conquered all alone without any assistance or fellow-service from angels or men or any creature. The [presumed] assistance of all other creatures is only the hopeless, unpayable debt of unworthy servants who cannot earn anything. Whatever is given to them is given from pure, unsullied / / goodness, faithfulness, grace, and mercy, alone through the merit of Christ. Whoever does not serve in the voluntary spirit of Christ even to the loss of his life or from fear and threat of condemnation, the same seeks his own satisfaction and the shameful benefit of a vain, proud, purloined reward and honor. His reward is destruction.

Now if someone neglects to serve man in and through Christ with the gift God has given him, because of scorn, fear, idleness, laziness, carelessness, or any other cause, let him beware that he does not receive the same judgment along with the angels whom God did not spare even though they were the highest and most honored creation. To all his true servants God promises the reward and the heritage with Christ. The true childlike servants do not look to the reward as though they could earn it with their service; they look alone to the rewarder and the Giver

Mt. 20 [25-28]

Lk. 17[10]

166r

and not to the gift or the reward. Nor do they measure their services according to the size of the reward. God does not measure or weigh the reward or gift, but He constantly gives an overflowing measure of His kindness and goodness freely. Similarly all our conduct will be judged regardless of how good it may be. (In any event it has all been given to us by God in the first place.) Therefore everything has been given to us for service in order that we should not wantonly waste it

166v

as though it belonged to us and regard it as of no account in opposition to the inexpressible goodness and grace of God.[5] In truth, it does not flow from our

2 Cor. 3[5 f.]

ability and conduct. It is only that God in His love takes pleasure in us His children, and we receive everything from the Father in Christ. It is this love alone which motivates us to perform the services of Christ to one another by grace. Thus the angels too, who were created holy and pure, rejoice to serve men (those who are justified in Christ and washed and cleansed from their sins). Since even the Lord Himself desired and rejoiced to serve men for their salvation, although He was Lord and Master, how many hundred thousand times more should we perform our service to one another eagerly, joyfully, and freely? We do not serve ourselves but rather serve to the praise of God and our own salvation, because the Lord Himself has served us. The angels also continue to serve us to this day without any pleasure of their own.

O dearest friends of God, if we really reflect on it, let us not become lazy, dull, nor careless. It will cheer up our hearts, regardless of all the offense, frustration, and affliction of the enemy and our own flesh and blood and what we must endure and suffer because of it, None of this compares to the inex-

Rom. 8[18]

pressible glory which we have through the knowledge of Christ. What therefore should prevent, vex, and hinder us in our godly life, conduct, and service in the love which is in Christ? May the Lord Jesus Christ give us the gifts and aid of His Holy Spirit. Indeed, may the Holy Spirit Himself as the mind, will, and pleasure of the Father and the Son be in us the Giver and Doer, Ruler and Accomplisher, Teacher and Leader, Reminder and Urger, that we may be found to be free servants of one another in Christ until our end. Amen.

May the heavenly Father grant this to you and us all who desire it from a pure heart. Amen.

Further we send you twenty Bundtzeug-knussen[6] and two epistles. The one about true surrender[7] and poverty of spirit we had already sent earlier by an older brother from Silesia by the name of Thoma.[8] Can it be that you have not received it? The other deals with our latest thinking on the Lord's Supper. We hope you will receive everything as servants without merit[9] to the comfort of our salvation in Christ. The Lord Jesus Christ make it fruitful to grow and increase in all things. Amen. The grace of our Lord Jesus Christ be and remain with us eternally. Amen.

In the Lord Jesus Christ,
Your servant of all the
faithful and participant
in the tribulation which is in Christ
Pilgram Marpeck

VI

Preface to the "Explanation of the Testaments"

Introduction

The *Testamentserleutterung*[1] is a biblical concordance of about 800 pages dealing with the relationship of the New Testament to the Old. The preface to this work printed below briefly describes the work, its intentions, and the reasons for its production.

The *Testamentserleutterung* was prepared by Marpeck and several co-workers[2] no earlier than 1544 for it is not cited in the first part of the *Verantwortung*. It would appear then that the author felt the necessity for preparing this concordance of biblical passages which would illustrate the relation of the two Testaments before they proceeded to the second part of the *Verantwortung*. The work must have been completed before 1550.[3]

The work was clearly aimed at Schwenckfeld as several references in the Preface made clear. That so much effort and expense was invested indicates that the Schwenckfeldian position must have continued its appeal to some Anabaptists.

The Text

Preface to "Explanation of the Testaments"

For some time now, and even at present, there has been dissension over the difference between the Old and New Testaments, between the old Mosaic and the new Christian church. For some say: Christ's suffering was retroactive to the Old Testament.[4] They also say that there was actual forgiveness of sin in the Old Testament leading to eternal life, just as in the New. Furthermore that there was also actual[5] atonement, sacrifice, salvation, healing, comfort, cleansing, sanctification, justification, righteousness, goodness, peace, joy, rest, grace, mediator, hope, faith, love, Spirit, anointing, knowledge, light, life, covenant, Testament, law, kingdom, congregation, people, sonship, food, drink, blessing, and the like in the Old as well as in the New Testaments. Although all these were somewhat less bright, less free, more childish and incomplete, nevertheless the people of the Old Testament were, like us, Christians. Since moreover, among them as Christians the sword was used it is quite as proper to use the worldly sword in the new church, that is to-day's[6] Christian church as it was in the Old, that is, in the Mosaic church.

There are however, those who believe that there is a difference. They say that in the Old Testament it was all only fleshly, figurative,[7] shadowy, and temporal, but not actual.[8] Nor did they have the spirit of divine promise which leads to eternal life. Nor did they have other actual things spoken of in this book for they were not then given but only promised. The believers of the Old Testament hoped to receive them only when Christ became Man.

To begin with, the first opinion listed above would be a denial of the common Christian article of faith which says "Descended into hell." For why would Christ (this is the other opinion) have descended to preach the gospel to the dead and to the spirits in prison according to the Scriptures if yesterday[9] those in the Old Testament were Christians, that is, if their sins had been forgiven unto eternal life? It would be calling the Scriptures lies which testify that there were under the Old Testament unforgiven and uncanceled sins. For how could the sins have remained if they had already been Christians, that is if they had actually been saved from sin, for all Christians are actually saved from sin through the blood of Christ? And what would happen to the saying in Acts 2: "You did not leave his soul in hell" (v. 27) if Christ had not descended to hell? Indeed, what would happen to the faith of the ancient teachers and many others with them who on their understanding of the witness of holy apostolic Scripture have believed and still believe the article about the descent of Christ to hell and that actual redemption took place through Him today? Such an opinion would become an error and become known as a special sect.

Second, the suffering, death, resurrection, and ascension of Christ would be greatly slandered and insulted by this view. Yes, it would be trampled underfoot and subject to suspicion and derision as will be shown in the second section of the last chapter of this book.

Third, all holy, clear biblical Scripture, especially of the New Testament, which shows clearly that the aforementioned actual salvation and other things were not present yesterday but came only today would be made a lie according to all the articles about today found in this book.

Fourth, according to the first opinion the worldly power as servant of God (to whom everyone should be subject according to Paul's teaching in Romans 13) would be removed from its true God-ordained service and station contrary to God, and put into the holy place (Dan. 9, Mt. 24) by a false certainty that it ought to stand there. Thus it has led to a grave violation and into the wrath and the punishment of God involving many people. Rather it ought to have been allowed to remain in the station and honor in which it was placed by God (according to the words of Paul in Romans 13) and its assigned service clearly recognized. It should also clearly be recognized whom Paul meant when he said "servant of God." He meant all worldly and pagan[10] power which in its own time had been and still is everywhere in the world whether they are believing or unbelieving. If one asks whether it is called a servant of God because of the spiritual or the external sword, one will easily recognize this power with its service ordained by God. Moreover the government too will recognize it and stay unmovably in its station. For if it should be right, according to the first opinion, to put it in the holy place then the pope is justified in clinging to the power of the figurative priesthood since the priests yesterday held the highest power to judge according to Dueteronomy 17 [9] 21 [5]. Accordingly he should not be reproached for being the abomination of desolation in the holy place. If however the pope is in the wrong and is the abomination of desolation in that place, how much less ought worldly magistrates to be put into the holy place!

Rather, as stated above, they should be allowed to remain in their proper service of God to fulfill it according to God's will through the fear of God and that wisdom which is necessary and requisite for all worldly pagan authority (whom Paul calls the servants of God regardless of faith in Christ as stated above) as wisdom herself says in Proverbs 8:15: "By me kings reign and councillors establish justice, by me princes deal rightly and all the judges on earth rule." Wisdom 6 also admonishes rulers concerning this wisdom. This is described further in the 108th chapter of this book. But Saint Paul distinguishes this wisdom of the worldly magistrates from the wisdom of Christ when he says: It is not the wisdom of the rulers of this world 1 Corinthians 2:6. It is thus clear that worldly rulers have a special wisdom for their service. For Christian wisdom is not suited to their office nor will it serve them since it brings about only grace, mercy, love for the enemy, spiritual supernatural things, cross, tribulation, patience and faith in Christ without coercion, killing of the body and the external sword, but only through the Word of God. The wisdom of the office of the worldly rulers is designed to work through the external sword in vindictiveness, mercilessness, hatred of the enemy, physical vengeance, killing of evildoers, worldly natural governments, judgments, and similar things. It is therefore without foundation to say that no one can exercise worldly government better than a Christian. That would imply that he needed the wisdom of Christ for it or that Christ's wisdom is his wisdom of office. Christ's wisdom is merciful and will not serve him in his office because he is not merciful in his office but rather an avenger.

These are the arguments which have moved the workers to produce such a book. Everyone who hungers and thirsts after the truth but has been caught in the bondage of incomprehension[11] may through the grace of God draw and find unchangeable and certain judgment, understanding and discernment from the pure clear text.

For love of such hungry and imprisoned ones and to their praise and growth there follows now an excerpt concerning the subjects mentioned above. They include forgiveness of sin, atonement, sacrifice, redemption, salvation, comfort, cleansing, sanctification, justification, righteousness, goodness, peace, joy, rest, grace, mediator, hope, faith, love, spirit, anointing, knowledge, light, life, covenant, testament, law, kingdom, congregation, people, sonship, food, drink, blessing, and the like from the holy Scriptures both of the Old and the New Testaments. They have been placed in separate columns, the writings of the Old first and those of the New following, through brief introduction to and indication of the verses and their location. Thus everyone who has a taste for it may take wholehearted delight, joy, and pleasure as in a rose garden or a meadow with a variety of colorful flowers.

The time of the Old Testament before Christ became Man is called yesterday, and the time of the New Testament after the incarnation of Christ, His death, resurrection, and ascension is called today. The passages are taken from the German Bible printed in Zürich.[12] Therefore whenever the text is found to be wrongly translated the writer will be without fault. And even if there should be faulty translation he who is hungry after the truth will find sufficient to satisfy him in those many passages correctly translated since one passage aids and interprets the other. And where at times the Worms edition[13] is used it is so indicated at the proper place next to the Zürich edition.

Since the arguments and proofs of the first opinion regarding each excerpted article (namely that yesterday was even as it is today) are not new but are known to everyone since they have been frequently printed they have been omitted for the sake of brevity. Thus only the other opinion has been briefly presented since it is not yet so well known. That is also why there is more about it in this preface. That is, in fact, why this preface is written so that you can become aware of the author's position and be able the more certainly to go on and act. In the book this is always referred to as the second opinion. . . .[14] And if it is presented differently than the first opinion thinks and has been changed at one or two points this was done deliberately by the author. The other articles which are not dealt with in the first part will be done by another faithful worker. The author of this book has had his fill of work.[15]

This book is arranged in chapters, each chapter having two main articles (except for the additions to the one part). First comes the biblical text concerning yesterday, then the biblical text concerning today usually accompanied by yesterday's promises of today's reality. Finally there are several other chapters as one will see from chapter 113 to the end. The reader is admonished that if in one chapter or article he is not satisfied he should not judge too hastily but rather wait until he finds it elsewhere. For what cannot be found in one chapter and discussion will be found in the other. Frequently one chapter or article will refer to another.

When the author uses the word "actual" he means the things unto eternal life which were prefigured yesterday and became reality today. Yesterday they were not available but had to be awaited in the future. Saint Paul himself uses this name in Colosians 2:17 when he says: "These are only a shadow of what is to come; but the substance is Christ." Heb. 19[16] says: "The law has but a shadow of the good things to come, not the true form of the things themselves." The use of this word is justified in the article, "Truth Today," in chapter 93 in two places.

Whoever does not understand the little word *ut supra* should know that it indicates that the matter which precedes it was treated at greater length above in the same chapter.

It should also be noticed in the following work that whenever today's actuality is promised yesterday one pays close attention to the words which clearly refer to today and do not concern themselves with the figure itself. That way one will not misunderstand and suppose that the word refers to the figure or to the Babylonian exile and the physical redemption therefrom

560

with no further meaning. For this reason all those references to the promise of today's actuality are supported by several passages and appendices so that the reader will the more easily understand which passages clearly refer to today. Although (as the other opinion asserts) all those passages which refer to the figurative salvation of Israel can be understood as referring to today's actuality and salvation, there are some passages which refer very clearly to today's actuality. (A thing is called a figure when its meaning goes beyond itself and penetrates to the present).

Therefore wherever the prophets speak figuratively about the salvation from Egypt or the Babylonian Exile they also express at the same time by means of clear words the promises of today's actuality. Even if it appears to be only figurative it nevertheless refers to and means the actuality. Thus also the apostolic word in Acts 3:18 says that all prophets have spoken about it, for all the prophets richly proclaimed the promise of today's actuality which saves.

It is important to know further that some passages in the law and the prophets and particularly the Scriptures of the New Testament speak not only of today as the time of Christ's incarnation, death, and ascension, but they speak as well of the promise of tomorrow, that is Christ's return from heaven. That means that the Scriptures of the Old and New Testaments speak in three ways. First there is the figure of yesterday, the first degree. Then there is the actuality that has come today which is the redemption from sin, death, and the legal servile yoke into the freedom of Christ. Third it speaks about the actuality that will come tomorrow of which the coming of Christ from heaven is an example. First, the salvation of yesterday, Deuteronomy 7, Judges 6. Second, the salvation of today, Luke 1, Romans 1, Isaiah 59. Third, tomorrow's salvation and actuality Luke 21, Romans 8, 1 Corinthians 15, Philippians 3, 1 Thessalonians 4.

At the same time the cited Scriptures of the Old and New Testaments speak of other things and actualities, of yesterday, today, and tomorrow such as kingdom, life, comfort, and joy, but in this work we will cite only those concerning yesterday and today. The controversy concerns only the difference between yesterday and today, the Old and New Testaments. If however someone insists that in some passage matters concerning tomorrow are also mixed in, the author does not deny it. Frequently a passage speaks of today and tomorrow as one. And it really is one since it begins today and remains in eternity. Examples are the continuing Holy Spirit in John 14, Isaiah 59, continuing truth 2 John 1, the continuing covenant, Jeremiah 32, the continuing sacrifice, Hebrews 10, and the never-ending kingdom, Daniel 2. If, moreover, during the many labors, passages of today have been misplaced in yesterday and passages of yesterday have been misplaced in today's things and actualities, may the reader not hold it against the author who has done his best. Let him simply allow those passages that he thinks are misplaced and not clear enough stand where they are, and give attention to the most certain passages and witnesses of which he will find more than enough. These matters the reader should understand so that he does not despise the whole book and its substance because of the misplacement of several passages. Also the reader should not confuse yesterday's with today's or today's for tomorrow's or tomorrow's for today's as some do. They turn today's actualities into tomorrow's and say that we have received redemption and salvation and other things for which they waited yesterday and about which the prophets spoke and promised as little as those of yesterday and that we are still waiting along with them. Thereby they ungratefully deny all the grace and salvation which has come today according to this work.

Moreover one must consider the manner in which the prophets prophesy about future things as though they were today's since from their words it often appears as though it were already present, had already happened, or were already fulfilled although it was still to come. The reader should understand that these passages did not deal with yesterday nor were they fulfilled then. He should note how the prophets were used in the New Testament and then he will understand. For example Isaiah says in the 61st chapter: "The spirit of the Lord is upon me, for the Lord has anointed me and sent me." Item, Psalm 2: "You are my Son; today I have begotten you." Item, Psalm 22: "They divide

my garments among them, and for my raiment they cast lots."
Item, Psalm 68: "You ascended on high and led captivity captive, and received gifts for men." These passages give the appearance of having happened yesterday although the witness of the New Testament (Lk. 4, Acts 13, Mt. 17, Eph. 4) is that they concern today and have only today been fulfilled. This is shown in the article The Dwelling of God Today in chapter 64.

It would also be proper (says the author) to give God praise and thanks for this excerpt composed by the grace of God. For it is no mean work and nothing like it has appeared before. It will be useful for the clarification and understanding of the Scriptures of the Old and New Testaments and for the making of a proper judgment about them. May this excerpt be accepted as of more value than a collection of earthly gems, for the matter is and will be of great importance. Those who are serious about the truth will be able to form a judgment by reading these passages which interpret one another together without having to read much further. This judgment is of the greatest urgency so that the differences between the Testaments and which opinion is right or wrong may emerge brightly, clearly, and openly. But whoever is more concerned for his temporal life, food, and other things than for the truth, and who therefore attempts to judge and master the Scriptures with his reason and understanding, will not be satisfied with this excerpt and will to his own hurt look for powerless, idle fabrications and glosses. From that may God graciously protect His own through Jesus Christ our Lord. Amen.

Many people who want to buy or read a book ask more about the person who wrote it than about the truth. They ask whether he is of high[17] or low[18] estate or what his faith or opinions are. Thus they will not buy or read a book because of the person or name since they think he belongs to a party, or take offense at it because it is too exalted or too lowly, too erudite or too ignorant.[19] Actually there is some justification for this attitude since these last and dangerous times are full of errors, sects, schisms, and opinions concerning faith. However to their own hurt, they also at the same time often deny themselves glorious and useful knowledge of the truth. In order to prevent this and to point the reader solely to the truth of God's Word the name of the author of this book is omitted. It is omitted further because he did not prepare this book by himself. Moreover the biblical texts need no other name than its own, especially since the author did not write it or translate it into German. The two parts referred to above will be recognized in their passages and uses. Thus everyone who really desires it may read only the plain texts of biblical Scripture, omit the additional notes, and thus make his judgement. The text itself can stand for the name of the author.

Further, A Preface Concerning Our Intentions[20]

Further the one group says that this book is necessary because heretofore some have acted and opposed the other party concerning the difference between the Old and the New Testaments thus showing the foundation of truth and faithfully presented it. Among them the Scriptures dealing with the forgiveness, redemption, comfort, cleansing, righteousness, piety, grace, faith, spirit, covenant, people, and other concepts of yesterday which are contained herein have never been fully elucidated, nor could because of lack of time, and the erroneous passages to which the other party appeals in particular, although written before their eyes, are still to a large extent unresolved and misunderstood. Thus they remain in captivity and some cannot free themselves and still think that yesterday there was also forgiveness, redemption, grace, comfort, cleansing, grace, faith, covenant, etc., because these words appear in the Old Testament as well as in the New.

Therefore we are at pains in this book to show that what the Scriptures say about yesterday's forgiveness, redemption, grace, faith, etc., are in contrast with these realities today and in order to resolve the errors of the passages which are often erroneously understood insofar as God gives grace.

No less benefit will come to people when they read this book as they know how it is to be understood when they read in

564

the Old Testament about forgiveness, redemption, piety, etc. Is it meant to be taken as temporal or eternal, symbol or essence, natural or supernatural? Many who read the Bible do not discriminate in their reading between yesterday's forgiveness, etc., and thus identify the two. Because they do not recognize a difference they are unable to recognize the goodness of today's grace and other matters which have come through Jesus Christ the Man nor be grateful for it. Such a book would further be useful for many things to all who fear and seek God, and to believers. For a large mass of biblical Scriptures, Old and New Testaments are garnered here and Christ can be clearly recognized according to Today as eternal salvation and essence, along with His body or community without confusion. In part the reader will also be reminded here what are the gifts of the Spirit (1 Cor. 12) what is wisdom, knowledge, faith, and the discerning of the spirits.

Our side is also prepared in case it has missed the correct interpretation to yield its position without controversy, when a better understanding or exposition of Holy Scripture is offered. In such instances we will not cling in error to our view, for we know that the more thoroughly Holy Scriptures are interpreted the more clearly the meaning will agree with it, for the Holy Scriptures cannot contradict each other as long as they are correctly compared and interpreted. For in the main matters in which the Scriptures and this book agree and in the appended sections this writer is aware of no errors. He begs the reader that where he disagrees with my interpretation not to lose sight of the main point by being offended. Above all the text of Holy Scriptures is innocent of errors and should not be discarded or despised but only look at the main point, at the summary, and hold to those passages where we have reached indisputable conclusions. There is sufficient abundance of such passages and he can safely build his conclusions on them.

The author, in what was said above, beseeches the one party to put away all possible offense so that this book may be free and its main purpose may be achieved: to establish through common massive witness that only today the essence of eternal salvation has come and did not exist yesterday. He also admonishes those who read this book or hear it and cannot on basis of truth find anything against the main point or its massive contents and appendices, that they do not oppose the truth or deny it, or use force to try to halt or detour its pouring stream and thus act against God. Ecclus. 4, [26][21]

Notes

Introduction: The Life and Thought of Pilgram Marpeck

1. The name Marpeck has also been spelled Marbeck, especially by European scholars. The signatures transcribed by Maler which appear in this volume are always spelled Marpeckh but since the "h" is silent it is dropped in the present volume. J. C. Wenger preferred the spelling Marpeck since this coincided with the autograph. Grete Mecenseffy also prefers this spelling (QGT, *Österreich*, II, 1972, p. 32).

2. Two sources are followed here: W. Klassen, *Covenant and Community*, pp. 15-56, and H. S. Bender, "Pilgram Marpeck," *MQR*, 38 (1964), pp. 231-265.

3. See Otto Stolz, "Zur Geschichte des Bergbaues im Elsass im 15. und 16. Jahrhundert," *Elsass-Lothringisches Jahrbuch*, XVIII (1939), pp. 116-171, esp. pp. 125-126. See also E. Gothein, "Beiträge zur Geschichte des Bergbaus im Schwarzwald," *Zeitschrift für die Geschichte des Oberrheins*, N.F. II (1887), p. 436.

4. See H. S. Bender, "Pilgram Marpeck," *MQR*, 38 (July 1964), p. 232.

5. In a government communication dated December 14, 1527, from Innsbruck written to the provincial official (Richter) in Rattenberg certain directions are given with reference to Leonhard Schiemer and a certain Seiler. It goes on: "We enclose also an order for our mining magistrate in Rattenberg to assist you from now on in the capture of the Anabaptists and their relations. We would not withhold such support from you. Dated December 14, 1527.

"Accordingly we direct the mining magistrate at Rattenberg to assist and faithfully support the city and provincial official there in his apprehending and punishment of the Anabaptists (33), their adherents and relatives in order that the sect may be rooted out, so that the unrest and insurrection which comes from it may be avoided for the maintenance of peace and unity in the land." (Mecenseffy, *op. cit.*, pp. 32, 33). Although the magistrate is not named, Loserth, Widmoser, and Klassen (*Covenant and Community*, p. 24) have identified the unnamed magistrate in the edict as Marpeck.

6. Mecenseffy, *op. cit.*, p. 2.

7. Bender, *op. cit.*, p. 236. The figures given by Claus-Peter Clasen in his book, *Anabaptism* (1972), are 413+ martyrs from 1525 to 1610 (p. 437) with about 2,012 Anabaptist converts from 1525 to 1618 in the Tirol (p. 21). Bender, *op. cit.*, follows Widmoser who came to the conclusion there were 20,000 Anabaptists in the Tirol with about 600 executions (see article "Tirol," *ME*, IV, p. 726).

8. Mecenseffy, *op. cit.*, p. 48.

9. Mecenseffy, *op. cit.*, pp. 51, 52.

10. *Ibid.*, p. 66.

11. *Ibid.*

12. See letter of government to the Rattenberg magistrate of February 23, 1528 (Mecenseffy, p. 83). Bender claims that Schiemer's execution "did not shock him into flight" (p. 239) but provides no evidence.

13. Mecenseffy, *op. cit.*, pp. 99-103.

14. *Ibid.*, p. 77.

15. *Op. cit.*, p. 237.

16. Krebs-Rott, I, p. 352.

17. Bender, *op. cit.*, p. 239.

18. Klassen, *op. cit.*, pp. 25 ff.

19. Krebs-Rott, I, p. 232; pp. 6, 7.

20. Krebs-Rott, I, p. 185.

21. *Ibid.*

22. *Op. cit.*, pp. 21.

23. Bender, *op. cit.*, p. 241. Whether in fact this means that Marpeck was, according to their standards, an elder or bishop is debatable. It is doubtful that the early Anabaptists defined a minister or elder as one authorized to baptize. Harold Bender has however shown convincingly that Marpeck did baptize and supports this with at least three references in the Strassburg records.

24. Bender, *op. cit.*, p. 242.

25. *Op. cit.*, p. 243.

26. Identified by W. Klassen and presented here on pp. 43-67.

27. Bergsten, *op. cit.*, pp. 44 ff.

28. Klassen, *op. cit.*, pp. 61 ff.

29. Located and identified by W. Klassen and presented here on pp. 69-106 Bergsten, *op. cit.*, Klassen, *op. cit.*, pp. 165 ff.

30. Otto Stolz, *op. cit.*, p. 171.

31. Krebs-Rott, I, p. 258 (letter dated August 19, 1531).

32. Krebs-Rott, I, p. 184.

33. Krebs-Rott, I, p. 277.

34. In a letter to Margaret Blaurer ca. November 24-29, 1531. See Krebs-Rott, I, p. 275.

35. Krebs-Rott, I, p. 231.

36. Krebs-Rott, I, pp. 359 ff.

37. Krebs-Rott, I, p. 529.

38. See below pp. 107-157.

39. Pp. 306-308.

40. Krebs-Rott, I, p. 531.

41. Krebs-Rott, I, p. 306.

42. V, 149:37.

43. *CS*, IV, p. 254.

44. Klassen, *op. cit.*, p.32.

45. Klassen, *op. cit.*, pp. 32-34. See Nos. 7, 9, 11, 15, 16, 17 in this vol.

46. Klassen, *op. cit.*, p. 33.

47. The account of this episode by Claus-Peter Clasen (*op. cit.*, pp. 43)

goes beyond the sources. See the text in Klassen, *op. cit.,* p. 15.

48. Klassen, *op. cit.,* p. 33 where the date of the letter is wrong.

49. *CS,* VII, p. 675.

50. Wenger, *op. cit.,* p. 160. When Bender (*op. cit.,* p. 252 f.) says, "The warning of July 1545 . . . came only a month after he had been engaged permanently as engineer," there is an obvious discrepancy between him and Wenger. According to Wenger the first warning came two days before he was hired.

51. Klassen, *op. cit.,* pp. 35, 36.

I. A Clear Refutation

1. By Camill Gerbert, *Geschichte der Strassburger Sectenbewegung* (Strassburg, 1889), p. 96; A. Nicoladoni, *Johannes Bünderlin* (Berlin, 1893), p. 126; G. H. Williams, *Spiritual and Anabaptist Writers* (Philadelphia, 1957), p. 156; Ernst Crous (RGG,[3] I, 1496) describes it as Bünderlin's last writing against which Marpeck replied in the *Klarer unterricht!*

2. Hillerbrand first referred to it in "An Early Treatise on the Christian and the State," *MQR,* XXXII (1958), p. 29, footnote 5, and called it to Klassen's attention. Klassen then identified it as Marpeck's work in the article, "Pilgram Marpeck's Two Books of 1531," *MQR,* XXXIII (1959), pp. 18-30. See also Klassen, *Covenant and Community,* pp. 36-45; and *ME,* IV, pp. 808-809. Prior to its discovery by Hillerbrand and its identification by Klassen it was considered lost. It was neither discovered by William Klassen nor edited by him, as stated by G. H. Williams in *The Radical Reformation* (Philadelphia, 1962), p. 274. As far as is known, the only copy extant is the one found in the Stuttgart library.

3. Torsten Bergsten's "Pilgram Marpeck," pp. 130 ff., is still the best treatment of this subject, although he sees the episode at Münster as decisive.

4. Although the name is not attached to the book, the reasons for attributing it to Marpeck are given in the introduction.

5. This verse is also referred to in *KU* Aii.

6. The basic principle of voluntarism is supported here by a number of scriptural references. It is particularly strong in this period of Marpeck's writing.

7. For *masen,* although the translation is uncertain. Reference could be made here to the sixteenth-century translations of Deuteronomy 32:5 which is obviously in his thoughts.

8. Marpeck's use of the Old Testament is dealt with in Klassen, *Covenant and Community,* pp. 101-148. The present work represents Marpeck's most intensive use of the Old Testament.

9. The original *Uebersprung* is a term used also by Bünderlin. Thus, in his *Ein Gemayn Einleittung* (1529), he often refers to *der rechte Uebersprung* and states as one of his intentions *einen Vbersprung auff das geystlich thun* (p. 84).

10. The Anabaptist understanding of the Great Commission was first dealt with by F. H. Littell in his *Anabaptist View of the Church* (American Society of Church History, 1952), ch. V. See also W. Schäufele, *Das missionarische Bewusstsein und Wirken der Täufer* (Neukirchener Verlag, 1966).

11. Basic to Anabaptist theology is the conviction that true proclamation also takes place through sufferings, martyrdom, and sacrifice. It was first

studied in detail by E. Stauffer in his article, "Märtyrertheologie und Täuferbewegung," *ZKG*, 52 (1933), pp. 545-598.

12. A term used frequently by writers in the Reformation period. It is also a favorite term for Marpeck; even though he never did believe in setting dates, he believed in the imminence of the Parousia. The last days were for him essentially the time between the Ascension and the Parousia.

13. *The Martyrs Mirror* gives many instances of this.

14. An interesting case in which an implicit negative in the text is made explicit by Marpeck's misquotation of it.

15. "Sophistic" is a favorite term found frequently in Marpeck's writings, e.g., TB, 197:6; 203:1; 225:15; 239:17; 241:40; 247:2.

16. The strange and elaborate theology of the creatures developed by the Anabaptists is treated by G. Rupp in *Bulletin of John Rylands Library*, 43 (1961), pp. 492-519.

17. "*Sie wollen den brunnen dess geistes auss der glaubigen hertzen fliessent / Joh. vii. ii Corinth. iiii. Ac. ii. Ro. x. Psalm. cxv. Verschieben / mit ihren grienen / aber von erd genomen wasen / dz ist / jrdischer weisshait.*" The meaning of *grien* is a sandy place (see *Grimm*) and *wasen* is equivalent to *Rasenfläche*, thus, the meaning may be that they are trying to stop up the well of the Spirit with sandy or rocky soil and pieces of sod. I am indebted to Marie Luise Linn, Konstanz University, for assistance here.

18. On the concept here discussed, see Klassen, *Covenant and Community*, pp. 83 ff.

19. Clarence Bauman has shown just how central loving the enemy is to the Anabaptist view of discipleship, *Gewaltlosigkeit im Täufertum* (Leiden, 1968), pp. 174 ff.

20. For *an* I read *on [ohn]*, for the meaning "without" is the only one that makes sense here.

II. A Clear and Useful Instruction

1. For the censor's report see Krebs-Rott, I, p. 335 (July 1531), and I, pp. 298 ff. See also Klassen, *Covenant*, pp. 36-43.

2. *CS*, IV, 259:25f.

3. Krebs-Rott, I, p. 301.

4. The assistance in the translation of this work of Henry Klaassen and Claude R. Foster is gratefully acknowledged. The editors, however, assume full responsibility for the translation.

5. *Nit was, sonder das* is a formula which most likely goes back to Seneca's *Non quis, sed quid dicatur, attende,* and may have come to Marpeck via Schwenckfeld. See *Corpus Schwenckfeldianorum*, XVI, p. 283. Possibly it means, "Listen not to who is speaking, but to what is being said." It appears also in the Preface to the *Kunstbuch*.

6. The case for the argument that this book was directed toward Schwenckfeld rests in part on the frequency with which the term *Stillstand* or its cognate appears in this book. For Schwenckfeld's view, see *CS*, II, p. 332; III, pp. 383, 384; IV, pp. 819, 820; XVII, pp. 729-734.

7. On the place of *kunst* in Marpeck's thought see W. Klassen, *Covenant and Community*, pp. 58, 70.

8. The point seems to be that, notwithstanding the fact that John was sent by God, he was less than the least of the believers who are in the covenant. Accepting the Word of Christ and faith in Him is given greater precedence than a special commission under the old covenant.

9. *Still zu steen.*

10. The allusion is apparently to John 13:7.

11. The original text is as obscure as the English. It would seem that we are dealing here with a *non sequitur*, although it is clear from Marpeck's total position that one cannot really say which is the highest, Christ's humanity or His divinity.

12. The words *Anfang eines Christlichen Lebens* appear in the title of one of Hans Hut's writings. See Herbert C. Klassen, "The Life and Theology of Hans Hut," *MQR*, 33 (1959), pp. 171-205; 267-304; and also the article, "Hans Hut" in *ME*, II, pp. 846-850.

13. Marpeck uses the diminutive, *Lämmlein*—"Lamblet"?

14. *Gelassenheit.*

15. *Still stehen.*

16. This statement agrees with the report of the censors that, in one of the booklets of 1531, Marpeck admits to having been baptized himself.

17. The translation from the Greek is very loose here, and it may be that Marpeck is following a version unknown to us.

18. Literally "cooked clay." But the word *gekocht* can also mean prepared.

19. The reference to *bank* is obscure. The gospel reference is to the marketplace, but here the reference is maybe even to a yoke. Or did children have an aid in learning to walk?

III. Pilgram Marpeck's Confession of 1532

1. The text is taken from M. Krebs and H. G. Rott, *Elsass, I Teil: Strassburg*, 1522-1532 (Quellen zur Geschichte der Täufer, vol. VII, Gütersloh: Gerd Mohn, 1959). The numbers on the left-hand column indicate their pagination; the numbers in the text designate the folio signatures of the original.

2. If Marpeck has 2 Corinthians 2:16 in mind, he finds something in the text which does not appear to be there.

3. Along with J. C. Wenger (*op. cit.*, p. 196), we read *on=ohn* instead of *an*. Cf. above, p. 570, note 20.

4. *kein christliche obrigkhait.*

5. The articles by Bucer were likely his statement on infant baptism which Marpeck had suggested on December 29. See J. C. Wenger, "Pilgram Marpeck's Confession of Faith Composed at Strassburg December 1531-January 1532," *MQR*, XII (July 1938), p. 167, and W. Klassen, *Covenant*, pp. 28, 29.

IV. The Admonition of 1542

1. Schwenckfeld remarks in a letter to Helene von Freyberg (May 27, 1543) about "*das büchlin von Pilgram, welchs er wider uns geschriben . . .*"

(*CS*, VIII, p. 618). The editors of the *Corpus Schwenckfeldianorum* mistakenly identify the book as the *Verantwortung* (*CS*, VIII, p. 617) which, however, was not written until January 1, 1544, at the earliest.

2. As demonstrated first by Frank Wray, "The 'Vermanung' of 1542 and Rothmann's 'Bekentnisse' " in *ARG*, 47(1956), pp. 243-251. The edition of the *Bekentnisse* used for comparison with the *Vermanung* in the present translation is edited by H. Detmer and R. Krumbholtz, *Zwei Schriften des Münsterschen Wiedertäufers Bernhard Rothmann* (Dortmund, 1904), pp. 1-85. Rothmann's writings have recently been edited and published by R. Stupperich, *Die Schriften B. Rothmanns*, 2 vols (Münster, 1971).

3. By Christian Hege in *Gedenkschrift zum 400 Jährigen Jubiläum der Mennoniten* (Ludwigshafen, 1925), pp. 185-282. Since it has remarkably few errors, this text was used as our base in the translation. According to Wray, differences in folio signatures between the two copies we have, indicate two separate printings (*op. cit.*, p. 243). Page references on the margin are given in the following order: original, Hege's edition, and then the *Bekentnisse* text.

4. See Klassen, *Covenant*, pp. 45-47.

5. The Marpeck additions are in italics. For a precise and accurate summary of the aspects which the Marpeck group added see Wray, *op. cit.*, pp. 246-251.

6. The word *Vermanung* is close to the modern German word *Ermahnung*, and is thus translated here.

7. Marpeck coins the word "Ahabic" here. Its meaning is clear from the context. The true prophets give God's message even to the king and even when it is unpleasant.

8. The reference is obscure.

9. Only a fragment of this sentence is taken from the *Bekentnisse*. For the most part the preface of the *Bekentnisse* is ignored and a much longer one is written.

10. A reference to the controversies in 1530, when the Marpeck group first rejected the Spiritualism of Bünderlin and Schwenckfeld, as well as the magisterial Reformation. See Klassen, *Covenant*, pp. 25-32.

11. For *nicht uneven*, the *Vermanung* reads *nicht ungleich oder uneben*, but the addition is merely for clarification.

12. Rothmann has *sacramentum*. The Vulgate uses *sacramentum* to translate the Greek word *mysterion*. Only with Augustine is the term occasionally used to designate means of grace which Christ has provided the church for the sanctification of men. See the article, "Sacrament," in *ME*, IV, pp. 397, 398.

13. The text reads *auss freier herligkeyt*.

14. The Rothmann text reads: *Sacramentum heth eygentlicke geyn wesentlick dinck . . .* A footnote states that the *Vorlage* has *eygentlick egeyn*. The Marpeck text reads *heyst eygentlick, ein weslich ding*, and this is also supported by the British Museum text. Does Marpeck intend to change Rothmann's denial into an affirmation? The context seems to indicate, rather, that it is merely an error of translation. Nevertheless, Marpeck's view of the reality of the sacrament differs from that of Rothmann, and Marpeck's total position can accommodate the statement that a sacrament is part of an essential

thing, like body, bread, wine, and water. See R. Armour, *Anabaptist Baptism* (Scottdale, 1966), pp. 113-134.

15. This is one of the few places where Marpeck does not add *oder begiessen.*

16. Rothmann has *dan nummermeir Chrystiane,* and Marpeck writes *oder nimmer mer, catholice.*

17. The words are freely translated here by Marpeck.

18. Rothmann has *thobrokenen* ("broken"), for which Marpeck places *bekennern.*

19. For no apparent reason, Marpeck here omits the words *versoenet unde van sunden gereynigeth voertan in Godt durch Christum.* It looks like an error of homoeoteleuton.

20. Marpeck omits here the words *dan yeder mennichlick weet wael, dat doepen heth underducken oft int water steken* ("For every one knows well that baptizing means to immerse or to thrust into water").

21. Rothmann has "papal sophists," while Marpeck reads "papists and sophists." Cf. below, note 23.

22. Marpeck omits the words *se syn alle in Mosen gedoept* and, after *versappen,* adds *od'erdrunken.* 1 Corinthians 10:2 is cited in *TE,* p. 285 without explanation, and dealt with in *TE,* pp. 274-283 and in V., pp. 348-350.

23. As above, p. 183. Marpeck changes "papal sophists" into "papists and sophists."

24. At this rather critical point, we have a textual problem. The BM copy reads "*und vermeynt Petrus, das die seligkeyt nicht daran belegen sei,*" while Hege's text does not have the crucial word *nicht.* Rothmann reads "*und verneynet Petrus, dat dar salicheit anne gelegen sy*" (p. 19). Our translation follows the Hege text. A few lines later, he asserts: "Such a covenant or sign of the grace of God . . . is not tied at all to baptism or any element of work, but is received alone by the believers through faith."

25. Marpeck drops the words *welcher beteckent wort* here.

26. Origen, *Comment. in Epist. ad Romanos,* lib. 5, cap. 8.

27. Tertullian, *Liber de Poenitentia,* cap. 6.

28. Marpeck uses his common term *mitzeüge* to translate Rothmann's *teken.*

29. *Missale Romanum,* the Collect in the Mass of *feria quinta post Pascha.*

30. These words are substituted for Rothmann's *mit sack unde pack.*

31. Marpeck omits *also dat se syn eyn hillige gemeynte, de willich unde bereit sy, alleyne den willen Gades voertan tho vullenbrengen.*

32. Marpeck says *ein jeder bringe sein pfund mit zum wucher,* for Rothmann's *eyn yder brenge syn pundt by.* Cf. 252/56.

33. Rothmann *werkstünd,* Marpeck *würckliche stünd.*

34. The original is *Widerchristen,* whose original source is 1 John 2:18.

35. *Erkandtnus Christi* and *bekandtnüs Christi.*

36. *Widertauff.*

37. The words "*also oick, dat schyr geyne erkentnusse Gades mer is averbleven up erden*" are omitted. It is an instance where Marpeck omits a pessimistic note. His own indictment about the condition of faith on page 209 is related to the use of the sword by Christians.

38. For Rothmann's *nicht bekennen,* Marpeck reads *nit kandten.*

39. *das sy da mit Christo recht schaffen vertrowet.*

40. In Rothmann, this is phrased as a question.

41. *Die pürgen soll man würgen.* See Proverbs 27:13 and Sebastian Franck's *Sprichwörtersammlung* of 1532, edited by F. Latendorf (Poesneck, 1876), p. 71.

42. *bopperei.*

43. Rothmann has *vernunftige.* Marpeck's predilection for the word "sophistic" is evident here. Cf. *TB,* 179.

44. Note that Marpeck slips in a negative, thus denying what Rothmann affirms.

45. Rothmann continues: "Who had been born of Abraham, according to the flesh, were Abraham's children, even if they did not believe, for the promise demanded faith of no one but Abraham. For the others it was enough that they were related to Abraham. Then, they were all reckoned under the covenant or under the promise." For Marpeck the word "external" becomes central here. Marpeck was undoubtedly aware of the rejection of Rothmann's position by the Strasbourg ministers, but he also had his own reasons for viewing the covenant relationship of Abraham more dynamically. See Krumbholtz, *op. cit.,* p. 42, footnote 3.

46. Marpeck deletes *Abraham is eyn vorbelde up Godt dem vader, ghelyck als Isaac up Christum.* He omits one further line, and makes the longest insertion of material into the text, extending from 226:32-238:22. In these twelve pages, the position of the Marpeck group on the relation of the old and new covenants is treated in detail. Cf. Klassen, *Covenant,* pp. 101-147; especially pp. 136-145. On this omission see pp. 141-145.

47. From here to p. 240, there is no use of Rothmann material.

48. It would appear that he meant to say *unverstendiger.*

49. A position which Marpeck rejects here, although he accepted it in his books of 1531.

50. *So gar ein ding.* Cf. Klassen, *Covenant,* p. 158.

51. For *gerewet,* we read *gefrewet.*

52. The reference is to the covenant community prior to Christ, although for Marpeck to use the term "church" for the Old Testament believers is exceptional.

53. The question of intrauterine baptism was a point of some contention in the sixteenth century. See the anonymous pamphlet, *Eyn vnterricht für die Hebammen, wie sie in der not Tauffen sollen* (no date, no place), BM copy about 1530. On the topic in general, see Walter J. Conway, *The Time and Place of Baptism* (Washington, D.C.: Catholic U. of America Press, 1954), esp. pp. 94-97, 101, 102, and 144.

54. The words *Dan hyrvan ghenoich* are deleted.

55. *up erden* is deleted.

56. The reference is most likely to Luke 18:1-8. In Rothmann, the reference is clearly to Matthew 19 and 18, but here it is not clear.

57. For Rothmann's *gedreide rede,* Marpeck has *gegenred.*

58. Here follows an insertion which continues on to the bottom of p. 253.

59. There is no passage in Luther's works where he rejects original sin in

children "with the use of many arguments." Luther deals with the concept repeatedly, but always assuming the reality of original sin. It is, therefore, clear that Marpeck is in error here. See Armour, *op. cit.*, p. 184, n. 106.

60. It has been impossible to locate precise references on this matter.

61. BM copy has on the margin: "Johannes hat den h. geist schon im Mutterleib, Ergo auch den Glauben eine gabe der Krafft Gottes ist."

62. On the topic of the "creatures," see G. Rupp, "Thomas Müntzer, Hans Huth, and the Gospel of All Creatures," *Bulletin of John Rylands Library*, 43(1960/61), pp. 492-519.

63. A line or two are omitted here from Rothmann.

64. While Rothmann has a reference to the mass, *De missen*, for Marpeck the word becomes *Dermassen*.

65. What is meant is the *Decretum Gratiani*, par. 3: *de consecratione, distinctio* 4; see Armour, *op. cit.*, p. 84, n. 112.

66. Apparently, *Tertulliani Opera*, ed. Beatus Rhenanus (Basel, 1528), p. 451, is meant here, but the reference comes most likely from Hubmaier. See Armour, *op. cit.*, p. 157, n. 206, 211. See Detmer and Krumbholtz, p. 51.

67. The reference could be Luther's *Grund und Ursache*, WA, VII, pp. 424, 425; see Armour, *op. cit.*, pp. 184, 185.

68. Eugenius II (824-827) and the Synod of 826 is most likely meant.

69. There is some shifting of material here.

70. Marpeck omits a paragraph here dealing with Mk. 16:9.

71. Rothmann has *ordel Gottes;* Marpeck reads *ordenlichen willen Gottes.*

72. Marpeck does not translate here at all. The cry *Rake* ("Hit the mark") becomes a reference to *Rache* or "vengeance."

73. Rothmann has *van munde,* for which Krumbholtz speculates that we should read *stunde.* Marpeck sees an idiom here: "van mund uff, wie man sagt."

74. Rothmann has *heiden underfrupen.*

75. Marpeck drops out the word "*ghereynigeth.*"

76. *leiblich und lieblich.*

77. The source here is *The Didache*, chap. IX. Cf. also Luther's sermon "Von dem hochwürdigen Sakrament." Lydia Müller, *Der Kommunismus der mährischen Wiedertäuffer* (1927), pp. 40, 41.

78. Rothmann has *verloeser unde exempel.* Marpeck deletes the word "redeemer."

79. Some five lines are omitted here, but the reason for the omission is not clear. For Rothmann, forgiveness of sins seems central; for Marpeck, the central point here is the full humanity of Christ.

80. See H. Bullinger, *Von dem unverschamten Fräfel ... der Widertöufern* (Zürich, 1531), fols. K iiff; K viff; X iff. for a discussion of community of goods. A parallel statement is found in Bullinger's *Of the Holy Catholic Church*, in *Zwingli and Bullinger*, G. W. Bromiley, ed. (Philadelphia, 1953), p. 300. Heinrich Bullinger was Zwingli's successor in Zürich from 1532 to 1575.

81. The debt here is to Franck's *Chronica* (Strassburg, 1531), fol. 495. Sebastian Franck was an unattached dissenter who rejected all churches, including Anabaptism.

82. Franck quotes directly from Bullinger's work, *De origine erroris in negotio eucharistiae ac missae* (Basel, 1528). (See R. Stupperich, *ad loc.*)

83. He follows Franck, *Chronica*, fol. 438a verbatim. See Krumbholtz, p. 71.

84. Rothmann here quotes from Franck, *Chronica*, fol. 495a Cf. Krumbholtz, p. 71.

85. Rothmann: "koke unde broit weren." Marpeck: "kocht kuchen und brot weren."

86. *Opp.* ed. Clericus, Tom. 6 (1705), Folio 446. Note. (See Stupperich, *ad loc.*)

87. Marpeck omits a reference from Rothmann to John. Sichardus, *Divi Clementis recognitionum libri X ad Jacobum, fratrem Domini, Rufino Torano Aquileiensi interprete. Cui accesit non poenitenda epistolarum pars vetustissimorum episcoporum, hactenus non visa* ... (Basel, 1526). His reference to *Paraphrasibus* could be to any of the twelve editions published between 1524 and 1542. Likewise, the *Annotationes* went through many editions. See, *Bibliotheca Erasmiana* (Nieuwkoop, 1966, first printed in 1893).

88. This sentence is taken from Franck, *op. cit.*, fol. 495b. Arcadius and Honorius were brothers who were both emperors about 397.

89. "dan eyn pandt, teken unde losunge ..." becomes "dann ein bundzeychen und losung."

90. Marpeck substitutes *unnöttiges* for Rothmann's *morderyssches*.

91. Rothmann has *änfencklick*, for which Marpeck places *einfältigklich*.

92. Matthew 26:26-28; Luke 22:19, 20; Mark 14:22-24; 1 Corinthians 11:23-25.

93. Rothmann's text is: "und is tusschen Luther unde dusse oerer menunge halven eyn heftich. ..." But Marpeck deletes the reference to Luther, and reads: "und ist hin und wider under dem volck (von wegen diser jrer meynung halben) ein hefftig. ..."

94. Rothmann and BM text have *reynen*, while Neff has *seynen*.

95. The imagery of the fishnet is developed especially by Peter Chelciki (1420-1460), the Czech precursor of the Reformation, in his *Das Netz des Glaubens* (Dachau, 1923). It is possible that Marpeck-Rothmann took it directly from the gospel parables.

96. Omitting "thom derden dat hoichwerdige nochtmal hyrmedde sol die hillige kerke in eynicheit bewareth werden."

97. Marpeck has "dann der rechten gebrauch wirt eines jeden verstand, durch die geheymnus der gnaden Gottes wol erfaren dann leyder nach dem die ordnung zerstört worden, da ist auch Gottes wort in lügenhafftigen verfallen. ..." Rothmann has "want de rechte gebruck wörde eys yderen verstandt unde geheimnisse wal entöppenen. Dan leyder, nadem `de ordenunge Gades versturth is, Gades wort in loegenhaftigen fabulen. ..."

98. Marpeck is not following Rothmann literally here, although the sense is not much different.

V. The Letters of Pilgram Marpeck—Introduction

1. Delbert Grätz (*MQR*, XXXI, 1957, p. 297) assumes that the *Kunstbuch*

"is quite well known," but he is in error. Microfilming a manuscript is not the same as discovering it. The credit for its discovery belongs to Goeters and Fast.

2. T. W. Röhrich, "Zur Geschichte der strassburgischen Wiedertäufer . . ." in *Zeitschrift für historische Theologie* (1860), pp. 57 ff., by Ludwig Keller in *Monatsheft der Comenius Gesellschaft*, V (1896), pp. 311-313, and by Krebs-Rott, pp. 529-530. Our translation follows the Krebs-Rott text.

3. Scharnschlager's "Appeal for Tolerance to the Strasbourg Council" is published by Krebs-Rott, II, pp. 346-353, and by Fast, *Der Linke Flügel*, pp. 119-130.

4. J. Loserth, *Quellen und Forschungen zur Geschichte der oberdeutschen Taufgesinnten* (Leipzig: Carl Fromme, 1929). The letter to Schwenckfeld appears on pp. 55-59; the letter to Helene von Streicher appears on pp. 179-188. The letter to Schwenckfeld was also published by Christian Neff in his text of the *Admonition* (*Gedenkschrift*, pp. 174-178). The text followed here for both letters is that of Loserth.

5. The definitive work on the *Kunstbuch* has been done by Heinold Fast, "Pilgram Marbeck und das oberdeutsche Täufertum. Ein neuer Handschriftenfund," *ARG*, 47 (1956), pp. 212-242. See also *"Kunstbuch," ME*, III, p. 259. William Klassen, in *Covenant*, pp. 53-56, also uses it extensively to arrive at Marpeck's position.

6. On Rothenfelder, see *ME*, IV, pp. 365-367, and also the article on "Scharnschlager, Leupold," *ME*, IV, pp. 443-446. See Fast, *ARG*, p. 241.

7. Heinold Fast, "Epistle on Five Fruits of Repentance," Augsburg, 1550, *Der Linke Flügel der Reformation: Glaubenszeugnisse der Täufer, Spiritualisten, Schwärmer und Antitrinitarier* (Bremen: Carl Schünemann, 1962), pp. 105-117. The two which have been translated into English use Torsten Bergsten's transcription of the text of numbers 15 and 37 from the *Kunstbuch*. They were published by Bergsten, and translated by W. Klassen in the *Mennonite Quarterly Review*, XXXII (1958), pp. 192-210. At many points, improvements have been made on that translation.

1. To the Strasbourg Council

1. See also Krebs-Rott, I, p. 360.

2. *Ibid.*, p. 350.

3. See introduction to Confession, p. 107f.

4. Text according to Krebs-Rott, pp. 529-530. According to them it was first inexactly printed by Röhrich, *op. cit.*, pp. 57 f. and later by Ludwig Keller, "Zur Haltung Strasbourgs in den Religionshandeln des 16. Jahrhunderts," in *Monatshefte der Comenius-Gesellschaft*, 5 (1896), pp. 311 f. Keller's version was reprinted by W. Wiswedel, *Bilder und Führergestalten aus dem Täufertum*, 3 (Kassel, 1952), pp. 73, 74.

2. Judgment and Decision

1. The date is likely wrong, particularly since, as H. Fast points out (*ARG*, XLVII, 1956, p. 227, n. 63), the letter clearly is intimately related to the one to the Swiss Brethren, dated 1543. This one evidently preceded it, in which case it

must be dated about 1542. Perhaps the correct date is 1541, in which case the scribe wrote a "3" instead of a "4."

2. Original: *von dann wir warten seind, ouch unser uffersteen.*

3. Original: *trounusz = dräunis* = "threat."

4. Original: *gleich der son (on manssomen und sundt).*

5. Original: *wie reisst sich der schlangen güjft vast in allen menschen durch eigens annemen.*

6. Original: *jnn seinem eigenthum gefangen ist.* What Marpeck appears to mean here is the natural state or condition of man after the Fall.

7. Original: *Die recht ware freyheit jmm Sun gotes vnd den seinigen ist vnnd send zu herren gesetzt alles gsatz gebot vnd verboth.*

8. Original: *leuchteren werd—leichteren wert.*

9. Original: *nachlast.*

10. Marpeck is referring here to the baptized masses in the Protestant and Catholic churches.

11. Original: *pflichtig zusein dem gantzen leben der sundt zu der maledetjung.*

12. Original: *zwang.*

13. Original: *ich streckh die freiheit Christi zuweith.*

14. Original: *pluee = pluet = Blüten.*

15. These two sentences are an accurate summary of a rather grammatically confused and repetitive passage.

16. Original: *fals.*

17. Original: *inn theil und stuckhweis.*

18. Original: *was hÿnnen ist.*

19. Fingersign in the margin.

20. Original: *sitlich.*

21. *spreissen.*

22. Original: *begibt.* In the above, Marpeck is in error; the point of the passages he cites is that Paul's freedom is subjected to the brother for whom Christ died.

23. Original: *dann die recht art der lieb furcht sich jnn aller grechtigkheit sÿ thuee jm zeuil oderr zu wenig vnd ist doch des wolgefallen gotes.*

24. *Denn wes des gsatz ist, der ist nit ein got des gsatz.*

25. Fingersign in the margin.

26. This is the third reference Marpeck makes to his own baptism. Compare Krebs-Rott, I, p. 352 and *KU* C v recto.

27. For example, patience with deliberate and open sin.

28. This gloss, like the previous two, appears to be by the copyist, J. Maler.

29. Original: *Einzenemen vnd auszuschliessen.*

30. Falling away, because of worry about the family and physical death, was a common experience among Anabaptists. The answer to this problem is given in point 4.

31. Original: *sorgklich.*

32. This marginal gloss is unintelligible at this point. It should, perhaps, be placed opposite the previous sentence. Then the world's proverb could be something like, "As long as I say, 'I'm sorry,' God will forgive." This was a standard Anabaptist criticism of what they considered to be Catholic and Protestant

teaching about repentance and forgiveness.

33. *ungnad.*

34. Original: *sonder es ist vnd pleibt lauter gnad vnd guet vor got.*

35. This point could be a reference to legal provisions for Sabbath observance as was the case, for example, in Zürich in 1541.

36. This is a reference to saints' days, of which there were a great many. In Cologne in the latter Middle Ages, approximately one hundred saints' days a year were observed.

37. Cf. R. H. Bainton, *Erasmus of Christendom* (New York, 1969), p. 204.

38. There were Anabaptists, especially those under the leadership of Oswald Glaid, who observed the Sabbath because they believed that the Ten Commandments continued in force. This group existed at Jamnitz, Moravia, which was Glaid's hometown. See "Sabbatarian Anabaptists" in *ME*, IV, and also G. Hasel, *op. cit.*

39. Original: *souil man brauchen mag vsserhalben des menschen hertzen.*

40. Original: *sittlichen,* meaning those laws which apply to all men, and which give order to man's life outside of Christ.

41. That is, belonging to the natural order outside of Christ.

42. Original: *walbrediger,* i.e., those who preach about God's election.

43. Original: *got vermöges.*

44. Original: *vff alle Ziechen.*

45. Although there is no antecedent, the reference is presumably to Jesus.

46. Here, the reference to Luther, but not to Calvin or Bucer, may be an argument for an early dating of this letter.

47. Marpeck clearly means God's revealed Word, that Word about which we know. To go beyond that is to deal with things we know nothing about. To do so is presumption and rebellion, for it implies that we are not satisfied with what God has revealed.

48. Original: *aus der arth gotes.*

49. Original: *die menschen sein götlicher art.* The translation here is somewhat unusual, but it conveys Marpeck's idea better than a more literal rendering.

50. Original: *gsait = gesicht.*

51. Original: *so man ansicht des leibs ersetigung.*

52. The original here is confused: "*ouch unsers rechtens verzeihen gegen dem nechsten zu ersuchen lassen und vil lieber onrecht thun.*" This last phrase should surely read: "*lieber onrecht leiden.*"

53. Original: *schampere* = perhaps *schandbare.*

54. Original: *deren die sch. . . . . .igen send.* Text smudged, but the scriptural reference indicates what it is (Jn. 10:12).

55. Perhaps a reference to Luther's insistence that faith is the one and only work required for salvation.

56. Evidently, there was also criticism of the clothes, and perhaps of the house furnishings, of some people.

57. The negative is omitted.

58. Likely a reference is 2 Thessalonians 2:4.

59. This paragraph is a reversion of the charges against Anabaptists that they were wolves in sheep's clothing.

60. Antiochus Epiphanes, 176-164 BC.

61. Maler evidently regarded Marpeck's behaviour as impatience.

62. Original: *wölchen der tod zum tod vorgeet.*

63. The original, which is not clear, reads as follows: " . . . *darnach erst, so vor der gmein bezeugt ist wo er auch die nit hören will so geet erst das urtl mit truebsal angst und trauren und mit grossem schmertzen und laid (dann es gilt ein glid am leib Christi des herren) send die andern glider am leib Christi so sy ein glid verlieren muessen uff das di andern gsundt glider nit schadhaft werden und der ganntz leib verdürb. . . ."*

64. Literally, Second Law.

65. Original: *nit wol lassen mögen.*

3. Another Letter to the Swiss Brethren

1. According to H. Fast, *ARG*, XLVII (1956), p. 26, footnote 66, this man is identical with Ulrich Yler of Strasbourg who was expelled from Basel in 1530. See Krebs-Rott, I, p. 266, No. 218.

2. Original: *und zubesorgen noch beschechen möcht gar zum verderben.*

3. Original: *bann.*

4. Original: *leipliche,* referring to the state of man outside of Christ.

5. There is a discrepancy in the numeration here, the number given being 68v.

6. The rest of the letter was cut out of the original codex and is therefore lost. Or did Maler prefer to use it in his own discussion of the oath in fol. 157 ff. in the *Kunstbuch?* It is also possible that he rejected Marpeck's position and did not wish to present both positions in the *Kunstbuch.* On the oath see "Oath" in *ME.*

4. To Caspar Schwenckfeld

1. The *Admonition* of 1542, found on pp. 159-302.

2. *CS*, VIII, p. 162.

3. *CS*, VIII, p. 222.

4. *CS*, VIII, Doc. CCCLXXX.

5. This work was the *Verantwortung;* see above pages 9-10.

6. S. G. Schulz, *Caspar Schwenckfeld von Ossig* (Norristown, Pa.: The Board of Publication of the Schwenckfeld Church, 1962), p. 285.

7. The text is taken from J. Loserth, *Quellen und Forschungen*, pp. 55-59.

8. The writing has not been located. Likewise, the thirty-eight articles referred to, which seem to have been a summation of Marpeck's *Admonition* of 1542, have not been located.

9. On Valentin Ickelsamer, see *ME*, III, pp. 2, 3. The unnamed person is undoubtedly Magdalena von Pappenheim, who had contacts with both Schwenckfeld and Ickelsamer. See *ME*, IV, p. 115.

10. There has been considerable research on the dating of this letter. It hinges on the interpretation of "Neuenjahrsabend." The three possibilities are December 31, 1544; January 1, 1544; or December 31, 1543. This latter possibility is considered most probable by W. Klassen, *Covenant*, pp. 48, 49.

5. To Helena von Streicher

1. Although no date is assigned to the letter, it must be after 1542. The tone and the language suggest that relations between Marpeck and Schwenckfeld had deteriorated. There are clear affinities between this letter and the one to Schwenckfeld which is dated 1544.

2. The text is taken from J. Loserth, *Quellen und Forschungen*, pp. 179-188.

3. The two preceding paragraphs are scribal notes written by the circle of Marpeck's friends. They occur in both of the extant manuscripts.

4. The reference is vague. The text reads: *Caim, das ist Hautzer,* but that does not clarify the matter. It is possible, however, that the word "Hautzer" is related to the word "hauszer," whose figurative meaning is "despicable."

6. The Churches of Christ and of Hagar

1. The following is Marpeck's version of the Song of Solomon, 1:1-4.

2. This is an accurate translation. This particular formulation depends upon the version of the Bible Marpeck used. See W. Klassen, *Covenant*, pp. 146, 147.

3. The antecedent is not clear. Likely, "it" refers to the washing of the water of the Word.

4. Original: "*Inn di gspons und prauth, ja eegmahl als zwey ein leib fleusst von wölcher leib lebenndige wasserr fliessen. . . .*"

5. *gesignen = versiegten* = dried up, withered, shrunken.

6. *eingefasste speiss.*

7. This is likely an allusion to Bucer's covenant theology, in which Christians are referred to as children of Abraham because God's covenant with Abraham is an eternal covenant and did not end with Christ. See Marpeck's Strasbourg *Confession* of 1531/32, and Bucer's reply.

On Bucer, see the excellent study by Johannes Müller, *Martin Bucers Hermeneutik* (Gütersloh: Gerd Mohn, 1965), especially 202 ff.

7. Concerning the Libertarians

1. The original is unintelligible here: *sonnderr allein in dem geschennkt zur pesserung.* The context suggests the translation.

2. Original: *und wellen doch mit Christo und dem h [eilige] n Paulo niemants geschennkt sein.*

3. Cornelius Veh, overseer of an Anabaptist congregation at Austerlitz in Moravia. He was a convert and co-worker of Marpeck. Further information in A.J.F. Zieglschmid, *Die älteste Chronik der Hutterischen Brüder* (Carl Schurz Foundation, 1943), p. 224; Heinold Fast, *ARG*, XLVII (1956), pp. 231, 232; W. Klassen, "Veh, Cornelius," *ME*, IV, p. 803.

4. The leader of the Austerlitz congregation after Cornelius Veh. A DeWind, "A Sixteenth-Century Description of Religious Sects in Austerlitz, Moravia," *MQR*, XXIX (1955), p. 45.

8. Those Dead in Sin

1. See also *ME*, IV, pp. 115, 116.
2. Original: *dann das tod mit laid zu fergraben.*

9. An Epistle Concerning the Heritage and Service of Sin

1. *plutflusz:* literally, "menstrual flow."
2. On Scharnschlager, see *ME*, IV, pp. 443-446.
3. Martin Blaichner; see *ME*, I, p. 351, and also Heinold Fast, "Pilgram Marpeck . . .", pp. 103-117.
4. Original: *vertraut.*
5. Original: *blödigkheit.*
6. Apparently an Anabaptist of whom nothing further is known.

10. On the Inner Church

1. Text according to Torsten Bergsten, "Two Letters of Pilgram Marpeck," *MQR*, 32, (1958), pp. 201-205.
2. "Mitzeugnis" or "mitzeugen," a term which Marpeck uses very frequently, especially in his later writings. See Klassen, *Covenant and Community,* pp. 80, 82; and Rollin Armour, *Anabaptist Baptism* (Scottdale, Pa.: Herald Press, 1966), pp. 121-127, 134, 137, 140.
3. *Funckhli der gnaden.*
4. Leopold Scharnschlager, Marpeck's closest co-worker. Apparently, he was with Marpeck in Augsburg at this time. Fast dates this letter about 1545.
5. Nothing further is known of him.
6. This unusual reference to a wife as "eine eheliche Schwester" would seem to support the idea that, for the Anabaptists, marriage was seen as a partnership for the purpose of more effective service in the kingdom. Roland Bainton writes: "This third Christian attitude to marriage, which considers companionability as the prime ingredient, came into its own most fully with the more radical varieties of the Reformation such as the Anabaptists, later the Quakers . . ." *What Christianity Says About Sex, Love and Marriage* (New York: Association Press, 1957), p. 91.

11. Concerning the Lowliness of Christ

1. *Leipliche:* literally, "bodily" or "physical."
2. *Tueffe:* literally, "depth," here translated as "Pit" or "Abyss."
3. That is, all the believers of the Old Testament who were saved by their hope and expectation of God's salvation.
4. At the death of Christ.
5. Original: *Art.*
6. *verbracht:* likely, *vollbracht.*
7. Original: *Art;* the context suggests subtlety in a pejorative sense.

8. Marpeck is here directing himself against the Roman teaching, which propounds the presence of God in the Eucharist. Marpeck also directs criticism against the popular assumption that He is to be found in man-made temples, that is, in church buildings.

9. Preposition probably is a locational parallel to the altar. In light of the verbs, it could also be a parallel to the holy mountain of Exodus 19 and 20.

10. The original adds: *ja wz gsagt ist und wirt.*

11. *Reichtungen,* read *Reichtümer.*

12. This is a reference to the order of society outside of the church, for example, the state.

13. *Geoberuert oder guewürckt fleisch.*

14. Here, Marpeck clearly has in mind the contemporary practice of reserving some of the consecrated bread of the mass for emergencies. It was kept in a special vessel, and locked tightly to protect it from sacrilege. During the feast of Corpus Christi, this special vessel was carried in the procession. By the time of the Reformation, this kind of public manifestation had become the major festival of the church. Most likely, he also had in mind the "golden urn containing the manna" or, as Luther renders it, "der goldene Krug mit dem Himmelsbrot" which is mentioned in Hebrews 9:4. Froschauer has "der guldin eimer, der das himmelbrot hatt."

15. *vnd einander wurden vnd schon worden send.*

16. That is, not good by contrast to the blameless Jesus.

17. Catholic and Protestant.

18. *Kunst,* with a negative meaning.

19. *denen got sein gnad entgegen hat.*

20. "Breaking" here means the initial plowing of virgin soil.

21. For "*der*" read denn.

22. In other words, there is a church in Strasbourg only so long as the faithful actually live in Strasbourg. The presence of the cathedral does not say anything about the presence of God, nor does the meticulous performance of preaching and the sacrament.

23. *Kunst.*

24. That is, the plan of the tabernacle and its furnishings which Moses saw on the mountain with God (Ex. 25:9).

25. *Aeferbuch:* literally, "book of mimicry," from *äffen,* "to mimic."

12. Men in Judgment and the Peasant Aristocracy

1. *Das heist den mund inn himel aufgeton.*

2. Section headings added by editors.

3. House, here in the sense of, e.g., house of Hapsburg.

4. *Die tugennth ans wappen schreiben.*

5. Cf: an interesting passage in the *Reformation Sigismundi,* in which the author, writing in 1439, states that a man is a noble only when he is also virtuous. H. Koller, "Reformation Kaiser Siegsmunds," *Monumenta Germaniae Historica,* VI (Stuttgart, 1964), p. 252.

6. See the adage originating in the English Peasant's Revolt of 1388 and well known among the sixteenth-century German peasants cited in the preface

to this letter. It is quite probable that Marpeck had this in mind.

   7. *Bolozeyische=polozeyische=*"police?"

   8. Nothing further is known of "Brother Veit."

13. Five Fruits of Repentance

   1. The text is taken from Heinold Fast, *Der Linke Flügel*, pp. 105-117.

   2. Fast, *Der Linke Flügel, pp. 104, 105.*

14. To the Church in St. Gall and Appenzell

   1. *entninkt = einninken =* "To take a nap."

   2. *"Als dann mitl im feur des zorn gotes, so es zum höchstenn prjnnt an allen orten."*

   3. *verweisstt* could also mean "approve."

   4. This sentence and the following one appear incomplete: *"Dann schwär ist die gaben des heiligen geistes, die er geistet, etc."* There is no main verb.

   5. *wurmle.* Possible copyist's error for *murmle* ="murmur"="complain."

15. Concerning the Humanity of Christ.

   1. The text is taken from "Two Letters by Pilgram Marpeck," by Torsten Bergsten, (*MQR*, 32, 1958, 196-200). The translation found there by W. Klassen is somewhat revised. The page numbers in the text refer to the *MQR*.

   2. Cf. *Admonition* p. 234.

   3. At this stage in his life Marpeck urges caution in provoking the government to take measures against the Anabaptists.

   4. Kabaskraut.

   5. A similar prescription clearly attributed to Pilgram Marpeck found its way into a medical codex (#11,182) in the Vienna Royal Library. There it is No. 36 and discusses how to make blackthorn juice to cure syncoma. It is dated 1555, and for those interested in pursuing this facet of Marpeck's personality mention should be made of Loserth's article, "Zwei biographische Skizzen . . ." in *Zeitschrift des Ferdinandeums für Tirol* . . . XI (1895) 288. Robert Friedmann also had a transcript of this prescription, which he kindly supplied to the present writer. Did Marpeck derive his interest in medicine from Otto Brunfels in Strassburg? For Brunfels's interest in gynecology and his publications in the area of medicine and botany, see F. W. E. Roth, "Die Schriften des Otto Brunfels 1519-1536," *Jahrbuch für Geschichte . . . Elsass-Lothringens* XVI (1900) 257-288.

16. Concerning Love

   1. Original: *gar uber eigen.*

   2. Original: *Glänntz.* The conjecture is that this should be *länntz = Lentz.* This is confirmed by Luther's rendering of Cant. 2:12. But compare 13r in the next letter.

   3. Original: *Augen* = eyes.

17. The Unity of the Bride of Christ

1. On the history of the interpretation of the Song of Songs see G. Gerlemann, *Ruth-Das Hohelied* (Biblischer Kommentar, Altes Testament XVIII), Neukirchen-Vluyn, 1965) 43-51. For Marpeck's use of it and further literature, Klassen, *Covenant and Community* 120 f.
2. Two river valleys, in the Black Forest and Alsace respectively, both near Strassburg.
3. About the identity of this man nothing further is known.
4. December 21, new reckoning.
5. Heinold Fast in *ARG* XLVII (1956), 223, Footnote 44, identifies Probin as a local place-name near Ilanz.

18. Concerning the Love of God in Christ

1. By a later hand identified as Jacob.
2. This is a reference to the mystic spiritualizers like Bünderlin and Schwenckfeld, who in the neoplatonic manner held to the idea of absorption in the divine.
3. Original: *verclärung*.
4. The original text reads: *Dz die vmb des vermenshten worts als umb anfanng mitl vnd endt allen creaturen willen seÿ*.
5. A marginal gloss from another hand reads: *Hie geht (vacht) er an sagen von bin der verdampten(r) in der hellen*. (Here he begins to speak about the torment of the damned in hell.)
6. It is to be noted that Luther also referred to the princes as gods on the basis of Psalm 82.
7. At this point a marginal gloss in the hand of the copyist: The reason for governmental authority in this time.
8. The negative prefix does not appear in the original, but the context demands it.
9. Marginal comment "Take note" in the hand of a later owner (Jacob) together with a pointing finger.
10. Marginal gloss by copyist at this point: The difference between physical (bodily) authority and the authority of Christ.
11. The Turks at this time treated the Jews with much more favor and respect than the Christians. Jews held high and influential political, social, and economic positions in the Ottoman Empire.
12. The free cities of the empire, which, in many ways were a law unto themselves.
13. This is quite possibly a reference to the Münsterites or some remnants of Müntzer followers. The latter especially continued for a long time in sections of Thuringia.
14. This last clause is a sarcastic reflection on the fact that they will die and thus achieve the rest of the body.
15. *gsponschaft. vermenschtes wort* = humanized word.
16. *"feintschaft der"* in the margin.
17. *"vn durch"* in the margin.

19. The Servants and Service of the Church

1. A small center about 100 miles northeast or Vienna in Moravia. A small group of Marpeck followers lived there.

2. A city in Moravia whose lords granted religious freedom to all. In addition to a Hutterite gathering there was also a circle of Marpeck followers.

3. A shoemaker, about whom nothing is otherwise known.

4. A reference to Revelation 14:6. This phrase was given new significance by writings attributed to Joachim of Fiore who in a mystic experience had a vision of the "everlasting gospel." This was identified with the true gospel as contrasted to the watered-down gospel of the church's teaching and not tied to the earthly institutions of church and empire which were temporal in nature. In this sense the idea was picked up by the Spiritual Franciscans and came to have currency in mystic circles and so ultimately found its way into Anabaptist writings. The Pietists of the seventeenth century were also fond of it.

5. Original obscure: *Darum ist es unns alles geben damit zudienen das wir weder gegen der unaussprechlichen guet und begnadung gotes on einig alefanntz roub name alles wider verschätzt und bey uns nicht geacht werden soll* . . .

6. Literally, testimonies of the covenant or union. It may be a reference to a common confession of twenty articles, but more frequently taken to refer to copies of the 1542 *Admonition* which was also called *"das buch der bundesbezeugung."* See Fast, *ARG* 47 (1956) 232 and Klassen, *Covenant* 47.

7. *Gelassenheit.*

8. An otherwise unknown Anabaptist from Silesia, which in the 1520s and 1530s had numerous Anabaptist congregations.

9. Original: *jnnder schuldigen dienstbarkeit.*

Preface to the "Explanation of the Testaments"

1. The text is published by J. Loserth in *Quellen und Forchungen*, pp. 579-584. The work exists in only two extant copies, one in the Stadtbibliothek in Zürich and the other formerly at the Prussian State Library in Berlin. A microfilm of the former is at the MHL in Goshen.

2. The *Testamentserleutterung* is cited in the second part of the *Verantwortung* no fewer than 76 times. The authors of the *Verantwortung* point to *their* work in the *Testamentserleutterung* for further evidence and explication. Thus it is clear that the authors of the *Verantwortung* are also the authors of the *Testamentserleutterung.*

3. See Klassen, *Covenant*, 51-53 and *ME, sub vocem.*

4. This is clearly Schwenckfeld's position.

5. *wesenliche*

6. By "today" the authors mean the present age of God's grace in Christ.

7. *figürlich.* The authors often use this word also to describe the actuality of events yesterday, *i.e.*, in the Old Testament.

8. This is clearly the position of the authors.

9. By yesterday the authors mean the Old Testament period which was under the law.

10. *Haidnischen,* meaning non-Christian.
11. *unerkanntnus*
12. The Froschauer translation. Editions in 1524, 1531, 1534, and 1536. The latter has been photomechanically reproduced in 1975.
13. The translation of the Old Testament prophets by Ludwig Hätzer and Hans Denck.
14. The rest of the sentence is unintelligible. *". . . der ain thail oder also anzogen (hie sagt der ain thail)"*
15. This translation is a conjecture. The text says: *"Obs aber etwa nit so gar nach seiner haltung wer anzaigt und durch in etwa in aim oder mer puncten gewandlet würd, wils doch der arbaiter auch gewandlet haben und die übrigen artickel drauff kein red sein des ein theils, ist gesetzt, ainem andern trewen gerügten arbaiter befalhen, im ist derarbeit jetz genug gewesst."*
16. Hebrews 10:1
17. Schwenckfeld belonged to the nobility.
18. Anabaptists were generally of socially lowly origin.
19. An allusion to Schwenckfeld as pretending to be scholarly and to the Anabaptists who prided themselves on their simplicity.
20. The text for this statement is taken from the microfilm copy at Goshen. It follows immediately upon the longer preface.
21. Marpeck's text reads: *"verheb nit mit gwalt den stramen des flusses"* (Froschauer). The RSV translation, "do not try to stop the current of a river" is closer to his version than the NEB: "Never be ashamed to admit your mistakes, nor try to swim against the current."

Bibliography

A. PRIMARY SOURCES PERTAINING TO PILGRAM MARPECK
(listed chronologically)

(Pilgram Marpeck) *Ain klarer vast nützlicher vnterricht/wider ettliche Trück/vnd schleichendt Geyster/so jetz in verborgener weiss aussgeen/* ..., 1531 (photostatic copy of title page in MQR, XXXIII [1959], 20). Photostatic reproduction of British Museum copy, Associated Mennonite Biblical Seminaries (AMBS) Library.

(Pilgram Marpeck) *Clare verantwurtung ettlicher Artickel/so jetz durch jrrige geyster schrifftlich vnnd mündtlich ausschweben/von wegen der ceremonien dess Newen Testaments* ..., 1531. Photostatic reproduction of Stuttgart Library copy, AMBS Library.

Krebs, Manfred, and Hans Georg Rott, *Quellen zur Geschichte der Taüfer,* VII. Band, Elsass, I Teil Stadt Strassburg, 1522-1532 (Mit Benutzung der von Joh. Adam hinterlassenen Materialsammlung), Gütersloh, 1959 (Marpeck's *Confession* of 1532).

Wenger, John C., ed., "Pilgram Marpeck's Confession of Faith, 1531 (!), A Hitherto Unpublished Document Transcribed and Edited from the Original," MQR, XII (1938), 167-202.

Das Kunstbuch, ed. Jörg Propst Rothenfelder, auch genant Maler, 1561 (Manuscript) containing sixteen letters by Marpeck.

(Pilgram Marpeck) *Vermanung auch gantz klarer gründtlicher un(d) unwidersprechlicher bericht zu warer Christlicher ewigbestendiger pundtsvereynigung allen waren glaubigen frummen und gutthertzigen menshen zu hilff* ... (1542?). Hege's edition in the *Gedenkschrift* was checked with a photostatic reproduction of the British Museum copy.

(Pilgram Marpeck) *Verantwurtung über Casparn Schwenckfelds Judicium* ..., Johann Loserth, ed., *Quellen und Forschungen zur Geschichte der oberdeutschen Taufgesinnten im 16. Jahrhundert. Pilgram Marbecks Antwort auf Kaspar Schwenckfelds Beurteilung des Buches der Bundesbezeugung von 1542,* Vienna and Leipzig, 1929.

Bergsten, Torsten, "Two Letters by Pilgram Marpeck," MQR, XXXII (1958), 192-210.

(Pilgram Marpeck) *Testamenterleütterung, Erleutterung durch auss-
zug auss Heiliger Biblischer schrifft/tail vnd gegentail/sampt ains-
tails angehangen beireden* . . . (no date, no place), microfilm in
AMBS Library.
Röhrich, T. W., "Zur Geschichte der strassburgischen Wiedertäufer
. . .," *Zeitschrift für die historische Theologie*, 1860, pp. 3-121.
Fast, Heinold, ed., *Der linke Flügel der Reformation*. Bremen: Carl
Schünemann Verlag, 1962, pp. 105-137.

B. SECONDARY SOURCES PERTAINING TO PILGRAM MAR-
PECK

Bender, H. S., "Pilgram Marpeck, Anabaptist Theologian and Civil
Engineer," MQR, 38 (1964), 231-265.
Bergsten, Torsten, "Pilgram Marbeck und seine Auseinandersetzung
mit Caspar Schwenckfeld," *Kyrkohistorisk Arsskrift*, 1957 and
1958, pp. 39-135 (offprint).
Fast, Heinold, "Pilgram Marbeck und das oberdeutsche Täufertum.
Ein neuer Handschriftenfund," ARG, 47 (1956), 212-242.
Kiwiet, Jan J., *Pilgram Marbeck, ein Führer der Täuferbewegung der
Reformationszeit*, Kassel, 1957.
Klassen, William, *Covenant and Community*, Grand Rapids, 1968.
Loserth, Johann, "Zwei biographische Skizzen aus der Zeit der Wie-
dertäufer in Tirol," *Zeitschrift des Fernandeums für Tirol und
Vorarlberg*, III, Folge, Heft 39, Innsbruck (1895), pp. 279-288.
Quiring, Horst, "Die Anthropologie Pilgram Marbecks," *Menn.
Geschbl.*, 1937, pp. 10-17.
Wenger, John C., "The Life and Work of Pilgram Marpeck," MQR,
XII (1938), 137-166.
————, "The Theology of Pilgram Marpeck," MQR, XII (1938), 205-
256.
————, "Additional Note on the Life and Work of Pilgram Marpeck,"
MQR, XII (1938), 269-270.
Wiswedel, Wilhelm, "Die Testamentserläuterung. Ein Beitrag zur
Täufergeschichte," *Blätter für württembergische Kirchenges-
chichte*, 41 (1937), 64-76.
Wray, Frank J., "The 'Vermanung' of 1542 and Rothmann's
'Bekentnisse,' " ARG, 47 (1956), 243-251.

C. PRIMARY SOURCES PERTAINING TO THE REFORMATION
AND ANABAPTISM

Bergsten, Torsten, and Gunnar Westin, *Balthasar Hübmaier: Schriften*,
Gütersloh, 1962.

Denck, Hans, *Schriften 2. Teil, Religiöse Schriften,* Walter Fellmann, ed., Gütersloh, 1956.

Kessler, Johannes, *Sabbata,* Emil Egli and Rudolf Schoch, eds., St. Gallen, 1902.

Rothmann, Bernhard, *Zwei Schriften des Münsterschen Wiedertäufers Bernhard Rothmann,* Heinrich Detmer and Robert Krumbholtz, eds., Dortmund, 1904.

Stupperich, Robert, *Die Schriften Bernhard Rothmanns,* Münster, 1970.

Williams, George Huntston, and Angel M. Mergal, *Spiritual and Anabaptist Writers,* Philadelphia, 1957.

D. SECONDARY SOURCES PERTAINING TO THE REFORMATION AND ANABAPTISM

Armour, Rollin, *Anabaptist Baptism,* Scottdale, Pennsylvania, 1966.

Bauman, Clarence, *Gewaltlosigkeit im Täufertum,* Leiden, 1968.

Bender, Harold S., *Conrad Grebel,* Goshen, Indiana, 1950.

Blanke, Fritz, *Bruder in Christo,* Zürich, 1955.

Bornkamm, Heinrich, *Martin Bucers Bedeutung für die europäische Reformationsgeschichte,* Gütersloh, 1952.

Chrisman, Miriam U., *Strasbourg and the Reform,* New Haven, 1967.

Clasen, Claus-Peter, *Anabaptism: A Social History,* 1525-1618; Ithaca, 1972.

Davis, K. R., *Anabaptism and Asceticism,* Scottdale, Pennsylvania, 1974.

Estep, W. R., *The Anabaptist Story,* Nashville, Tennessee, 1964.

Fast, Heinold, *Heinrich Bullinger und die Täufer,* Heidelberg, 1961.

Friedmann, R., *The Theology of Anabaptism,* Scottdale, Pennsylvania, 1973.

Hershberger, Guy F., ed., *The Recovery of the Anabaptist Vision,* Scottdale, Pennsylvania, 1957.

Hillerbrand, Hans, *Die politische Ethik des oberdeutschen Täufertums,* Leiden, 1960.

Kiwiet, Jan J., "The Life of Hans Denck," MQR, XXXI (1957), 227-259.

Klassen, Herbert C., "The Life and Teachings of Hans Hut," MQR, XXXIII (1959), 171-205; 267-304.

Littell, Franklin H., *The Anabaptist View of the Church,* American Society of Church History, 1952.

McClelland, Joseph C., *The Visible Words of God,* Grand Rapids, 1957.

Müller, Johannes, *Martin Bucers Hermeneutik,* Gütersloh, 1965.

Müller, Lydia, *Der Kommunismus der mährischen Wiedertäufer,* Leipzig, 1927.

Oyer, John, *Luther and the Anabaptists*, Nijhof, 1964.

Plümper, Hans-Dieter, *Die Gütergemeinschaft bei den Täufern des 16. Jahrhunderts*, Göppingen, 1972.

Roth, Friedrich, *Augsburg Reformationsgeschichte*, I-IV (1901-1911), München.

Schäufele, Wolfgang, *Das missionarische Bewusstsein und Wirken der Täufer*, Neukirchen-Vluyn, 1966.

Schrenk, Gottlob, *Gottesreich und Bund im älteren Protestantismus vornehmlich bei Johannes Coccejus*, Gutersloh, 1925.

Stayer, James M., *Anabaptists and the Sword*, Lawrence, Kansas, 1972.

Stupperich, Robert, "Melanchthon und die Täufer," *Kerygma und Dogma*, III (1957), 150-170.

Verduin, Leonard, *The Reformers and Their Stepchildren*, Grand Rapids, 1965.

Williams, George H. *The Radical Reformation.* Westminster Press, Philadelphia, 1962.

Windhorst, C., *Täuferisches Taufverständnis*, Leiden, 1976.

Yoder, John Howard, *Die Gespräche zwischen Täufern und Reformatoren in der Schweiz, 1523-1538*, Basel Diss., 1957.

Yoder, John Howard, *The Legacy of Michael Sattler*, Scottdale, Pennsylvania, 1973.

Inòíces

Index of Subjects and Titles

281, 300, 456, 470-471; of goods, 279-281, 485

Confession of Faith, 107-157

Corinthians, 104, 265, 271, 276, 279, 382-383, 543

Covenant, 109, 112, *116-118,* 124-125, 129, 133, 140, *142-143,* 160-161, *163-167,* 169, 172, 184, 189-190, 215, 219, 222-224, 230, 431, *446-447,* 556, 559, 564; new covenant, 61, 446-447, 461; old covenant, 49, 65, 119, 132, 225; of baptism, 189-190, 239; of circumcision, 226; of good conscience, 112, 117, 142, 167, *187,* 189-190, 196-197, 207, 216, 240, 301, 394; of love, 198; of promise, 119, 133, 222, 225, 235; separation of old and new covenants, 36, 555-566; theology of, *116-119,* 555-566

De Corona Militis, 251

Der Linkel Flügel, 485

Discipline, 149

Discipleship, 364

Dress customs, 309

Elect, 59, 62, 72, 76, 86, 97, 326, 352, 390, 406, 419, 435, 437, 466, 531, 535, 549

Election, 129, 234-235

Faith, 71-83, *87-94, 128-134, 142-157,* 165-167 passim, 186-188 passim, 190-193 passim, 196-199 passim, 204-207 passim, 209-211 passim, 218-220 passim, 233-243 passim, 247-260 passim, *296,* 316-318 passim, 364-367 passim, 370-373 passim, 387-388, 397-399 passim, *408-411* passim, *445,* 449-450, 453-456 passim, *470,* 479-481, 500, 509-510, *517,* 519, *529,* 534, 538, 543-544, 563-565 passim

False prophets, *71-82* passim, 84-85, 87, 90-94 passim, 97-98, 100-106 passim, 150, 157, 161, 284, 296, 364, 482

Flesh, 56, 60, 66, 73, 76-83 passim, 89-91 passim, 98-103 passim, 108-109, 117-118, 121, 128-129, 131-133 passim, 138-139, 143, 149, 155, 164-165, 175, 178, 185,

187, 189-190, 198, 206, 209, 211-212, 214, 220, 222, 228, 231, 238-240 passim, 248, 256, 294, 299, 314, 318-321, 323, 330, 335, 337, 343, 353, 361, 364, 371, 388, 394, 403, 410, 415, 439, 441, 445, 447, 457, 463, 475, 492, 509, 515, 527, 533, 542, 546; freedom from, 322-323

Foot washing, 51, 79, 98, 265, 318, 340, 453

Free will, 79, 256-257

Gelassenheit, 549

Gentiles, 49, 56, 101, 103, 118, 129, 132, 140, 155, 213, 231, 341, 348, 353, 371, 386, 431, 468, 512, 539

God, children of, 43-44, 102, 109, 112, 133, 137, 182, 201, 211-212, 293, 345, 351, 399, 404, 452, 540; kingdom of, 111, 128, 138, 140, 145, 174, 199, 202, 211-212, 225, 240, 321, 353, 355, 388

Godfathers, *217-218*

Gospel, and law, 132, 136; function of, 152-153; in Christ, 136; of the creatures, 310-311, 352-359; to all creatures, 56, 181, 211, *250-251*

Government, authority of, 150

Grace, 58, 72-73, *120-123,* 163-166 passim, 188-190 passim, 236-237, 297-299 passim, 307-308, 319-329 passim, 334-336 passim, 340, 347, 365-368 passim, 371-374 passim, 397-398, 400, 402, 408, 415-417, 424-426, 445-446, *468-472, 482-486* passim, 488-490 passim, 495-499 passim, 510-511, 529-532 passim, 543-545 passim, 552-559 passim, 562-565 passim, 572

Holy Spirit, 50, 52, 59-60, 77, 88-90 passim, 95, 97, 100-102, 112, 119, 121, 127, 132, 136, 142, 145, 148, 150, 163-167 passim, 174-175, 178, 180, 182-184, 187-188, 190, 193, 195-196, 198, 203, 224-228 passim, 231-232, 237, 240, 274, 300, 313-318 passim, 320-329 passim, 331-332, 334-336, 360-361, 366-368 passim, 377-381 passim, 391-400 passim, 403-404,

410, 422-425 passim, 435-436, 440-441, 443-446 passim, *451-460* passim, 472-475 passim, 485-486, 495-496, 498-500 passim, 505-506, 508-513 passim, 522-526 passim, 532-533, 540, 542, 545, 554, 562; gifts of, see Spirit
Hutterites, 303, 412, 586
Hutterian Chronicle, 38

Idolatry, 44, 47, 57, 96, 130, 152, 168, 210, 245, 258-259, 281, 296, 298, 338, 344, 387, 450; of infant baptism, 213-214, 243, 245, 247, 258-259
Images, 130
Israelites, 46, 58, 148, 239

Jerusalemites, 46
Jewish commentaries, 94
Jews, 46, 50, 58, 74-75, 80, 82, 84, 89, 91-92, 96, 99, 109, 119, 132, 134, 136, 140, 155, 198, 209, 213, 231, 237-238, 259, 326, 334, 341, 348-350, 384, 386, 449, 468, 528, 539-541 passim
Judgment, true and false, 333-338 passim; types of men under judgment, 464-483
Judgment and Decision, 309-375 passim
Judicium, 369, 374-375, 377
Justification, 58, 89, 118-119, 128, 156, 233, 236, 327, 366-367, 374, 430, 445, 453, 469, 471, 474, 480-481, 553, 556, 559; by faith, 86, 471

Knowledge of good and evil, 108, 111, *114,* 129, *131,* 139, *204-207,* 210, 214, 246, 251-252, 257, 316, 325, 336-338 passim
Kunstbuch, 18, 303-305, 549

Last days, 43, *47-49* passim, 51, 58, *60,* 63, 74, 104, 164, *371*
Law, 46-47, 49, 53, 58-60, 63, 75, 80-81, 96, 102, 105, 109-110, 116, *119-127* passim, 129, 132, 134-136 passim, 205, 235, 237, 241, 260, 262, 309-310, 312, *315-322* passim, *327-331* passim, 334, 337-338, *342-343,* 345, 348, 350, 353, 364, 385-386, 403, 410, 439,

441, 458-459, 472, 478, 480, 486, 525, 551, 556, 559-561 passim; ceremonial, 338; freedom from, 309-310, 312, 315; natural, 102, 478-479; spiritual, 316, 350, 479-480
Laying on of hands, 71-72, 81, 242, 253, 340
Legalism, 303, 309, 478
Libertarians, 402-406
Lord's Supper, 26, 43-44, 47-49 passim, 51-52, 54, 64-65, 71-72, 81-82, 93, 96, 104-105, 112-113, *147-149,* 159-163 passim, 168, *170-172,* 194-195, 220, 248-250, 254-255, *261-292,* 295-297 passim, 318, 337, 340, 364, 380-381, 383-384, 386-387, 389, 422-423, 425, 453-454, *486,* 488, 522, 549, 554; agape meal, 280-281; as an assembly of love, 264-268 passim, 271, 275-277 passim, 279-280, 282, 285, 294-296 passim, 299; as a covenant sign, 281; Bullinger's view, 278-279; description of, 263-268; interpretations of, 162-163, *284-292;* in the Apostolic Church, *278-282,* 284; Luther's view, 148, 287; Decolampadius' view, 288; purpose of, 162-163, *269-278 282-284, 292-300*
Love, 53-54, 63, 65-66, 73, 109-110, 119, 124, 145, 166, 169-170, 190, 196, 209, 220, 224, 250, 260, 271, 274-283 passim, 293-299 passim, 304, 315, 317, 319-320, 324-326 passim, 338-340 passim, 350, 357, 359-360, 364-365, 384, 395-396, 399, 413, 423, 426-427, 438, 441, 445, 450-451, 454, 458, 460, 463, 467, 472, 501, 513, 515, 538, 546-547, 553-554, 556, 558-559; nature of, 53-54, 148, 156-157, 248-249, *264-267* passim, 310-312, *327-330* passim, 343, *347-349* passim, 391-392, 402-405 passim, 420, 422, 437, *516-524* passim, *528-536* passim
Lutheranism, 21-22, 38
Lutherans, 26, 249, 287, 351

Magistrate, Christian, 150; worldly, 557-558

Index of Persons and Places

600

601

Index of Modern Authors

Armour, R. S., 573, 575, 582

Bainton, R. H., 579, 582
Bauman, C., 570
Baxter, N., 108
Bender, H. S., 20-21, 27, 567-569
Bergsten, Torsten, 568-569, 577, 582, 584
Bromiley, G. W., 575

Clasen, C. P., 24, 567-568
Conway, W. J., 574
Crous, Ernst, 569

Detmer, H., 572, 575
DeWind, A., 581

Fast, H., 304, 310, 484, 576-577, 580-582, 584, 586
Friedmann, Robert, 40, 159, 584

Gerbert, Camill, 569
Gerlemann, G., 585
Gothein, Eberhard, 567
Grätz, Delbert, 576

Hasel, G. F., 311, 579
Hege, Christian, 572-573
Hillerbrand, Hans, 43, 569

Keller, Ludwig, 577
Klassen, William, 69, 305, 310, 567-572, 574, 577, 580-582, 584, 586

Klassen, H. C., 571
Klaassen, Walter, 108, 305
Koller, H., 583
Krebs, M. and Rott, H. G., 108, 568, 570-571, 577-578, 580
Krumbholtz, R., 572, 574-576

Latendorf, F., 574
Littell, F. H., 569
Loserth, J., 304, 567, 577, 580-581, 584, 586

Mecenseffy, G., 567-568
Müller, Johannes, 581

Neff, Christian, 577
Nicoladoni, A., 569

Röhrich, T. W., 577
Roth, F., 584
Rupp, G., 311, 570, 575

Schäufele, Wolfgang, 569
Schultz, Selina Gerhard, 580
Stauffer, E., 570
Stolz, Otto, 567-568
Stupperich, R., 572, 576

Wenger, J. C., 40, 108, 567, 569, 571
Williams, G. H., 569
Wiswedel, W., 577
Wray, F. J., 159, 572

Zieglschmid, A. J. F., 581

Index of Biblical References

605

606

The Authors

Walter Klaassen is the son of Heinrich T. Klaassen of Rosthern, Saskatchewan, husband of Ruth Strange Klaassen, and father of sons Frank, Michael, and Philip. He is presently professor of history at Conrad Grebel College, specializing in Anabaptism and other radical social and religious movements. He is active in the Kitchener-Waterloo House Churches where he functions primarily as a teacher.

He has written numerous articles which have appeared in various journals as well as several monographs. He has been editor of the *Mennonite Quarterly Review* and book editor of *The Mennonite Reporter*. His academic degrees were earned at McMaster and Oxford Universities.

William Klassen

Walter Klaassen

William Klassen is professor of religion and head of the department at the University of Manitoba, Winnipeg, Canada. He has studied at Goshen College and Seminary, obtained his doctorate at Princeton Seminary, and done postdoctoral work at the Menninger Foundation, Topeka, Kansas. Before coming to the University of Manitoba he taught at Goshen College, The Associated Mennonite Seminaries, New York Theological Seminary, Indiana University (South Bend), and Notre Dame University. He was awarded a Canada Council

611

Leave fellowship for a year of research at the Ecumenical Institute in Jerusalem.

Among the books he has published are: *Current Issues in New Testament Interpretation* (ed. with G. F. Snyder, Harper, and Row, 1962), *The Forgiving Community* (Westminster, 1966), *Covenant and Community, A Study of the Hermeneutics of Pilgram Marpeck* (Eerdmans, 1968). He has contributed articles to the *Mennonite Quarterly Review, New Testament Studies, Catholic Biblical Quarterly, Expository Times, Canadian Journal of Theology, Studies in Religion,* and three articles to the recently published supplement to the *Interpreter's Dictionary of the Bible.*

He has served on the executive committee of the Canadian Society for the Study of Religion, serves now on the executive board of the International Association for the History of Religions, and is cochairman of the National Planning Committee for the XIV Congress of the IAHR to be held in Winnipeg in 1980. He served on the Mennonite Mental Health Services Board and also as executive director of that Board. He is a member of the Studiorum Novi Testamenti Societas as well as other scholarly societies.

127834